UFOs In The Headlines

Real Reporting on a Real Phenomenon

By
Rob Simone

www.RobSimone.com

D1293439

UFOs IN THE HEADLINES
Real Reporting on a Real Phenomenon
by **Rob Simone**

www.**RobSimone**.com

Headroom Publishing

First Edition 2008
© Copyright Rob Simone

ISBN 978-0-6151-7177-7

UFOs
In The
Headlines

Real Reporting
on a Real Phenomenon

By
Rob Simone

Headroom Publishing

Box 9 Lafayette Hill, PA 19444

(614) 748-9471

Table of Contents

Introduction by Rob Simone

The abundance of ancient references to "Star people," gods in "flying chariots" and advanced technology written into hundreds of historical accounts, woven into oral traditions and depicted in folk art dating back as far as 30,000 years, lays the foundation of the UFO/E.T. contact in many past civilizations.

The explosion of reports, video evidence, eyewitness accounts, and official sourced testimony over the last 60 years demonstrates a clear and continual rise in the frequency of contact cases and sightings now being documented.

With this, comes an unprecedented level of "official" disclosure events like the release of the Mexican Air Force footage, the testimony of the Russian Air Force generals, and the Brazilian government's formal recognition of the field of Ufology. The latest opinion polls reflect the public's growing interest and belief that some UFOs represent intelligent contact from beyond our world.

All of these factors clearly point to an expansion of the field of Ufology and the inevitable impact it will have on politics, religion, technology and society.

Ufology, in my opinion, should be seen as an "emerging science" to reflect the deeply held belief of humanity's place in a larger universe.

No longer isolated by time and space, no longer kept hidden by secretive governments, the truth of the on-going human interaction with other races from beyond the stars will expand and unite the awareness of our collective consciousness and diminish the destructive and limiting characteristics of earthly belief systems.

You get to reach these conclusions, in my case, by poring over the thousands of eyewitness reports and examining the thousands of declassified government documents that prove beyond a shadow of a doubt that this phenomenon is taking place, not only in the skies above, but directly to us.

There are vast amounts of theories to try to explain the constant involvement of extra-terrestrial contacts that have been reported by people from every walk of life, and from every quarter of the globe.

There is an abundance of evidence that suggests some sort of off world or extra-dimensional intelligence was in touch with the great civilizations of Sumer, Egypt and other ancient cultures. There are many examples in cave paintings dating back 20,000 years and medieval and renaissance artwork that show clear UFO type objects and humanoids that don't conform to the natural environment or experience of the artists of that time.

Recently, in our modern militarized world, ufologists have drawn many conclusions about the frequency of UFO reports in relation to nuclear missiles and advanced military activity.

I have traveled around the world, through 27 different countries researching the E.T. phenomenon from the Asian, Middle Eastern, Aboriginal, and European perspectives, only to find it is just as prevalent in their societies as it is in the West.

From as far back as man was able to scratch out an image on a cave wall, to today, with newspapers and global news agencies, UFOs have been recorded, researched and reported on as part of the yet un-disclosed component of human history.

What follows is a series of articles from major newspapers from around the world that reflects this ongoing E.T. reality through a journalistic perspective.

Headlines From The U.K.
1950-1954

The following articles span from 1950 to 1954 and tell a fascinating story of the UFO phenomenon from the perspective of the British press.

Special thanks to the late Graham Birdsall for his tireless efforts in the field of Ufology and Russel Callaghan from the new UFO DATA Magazine, U.K.

Compiled by L. B. Cooper from the U.K., they are a time capsule to the "golden age" of Ufology. This series of "scrapbook" articles are presented in chronological order, exactly as they were discovered in a forgotten locker box in England several years ago; they appear just as they were printed that day, bringing you into the moment with the readers of the time, experiencing the drama of these amazing news stories first hand.

Contained in these news stories are:

and much more...

FLYING SAUCERS "EXPLAINED"

U.S. MOTOR-PROPELLED ROCKET TESTS

FROM OUR OWN CORRESPONDENT
NEW YORK, Friday.

The United States Army's decision to make public certain details of the rocket motor research programme being conducted for it by the General Electric Company is "a long step" towards providing an official explanation of the "flying saucers," it was stated to-day.

Writing in the New York Herald Tribune, Mr. David Lawrence, editor of the United States News, which recently published an article on the "flying saucers" that attracted widespread attention, says:

"This particular rocket, propelled by a motor, has been tested at the White Sands proving ground, in New Mexico, but it is only one of a number of objects which observers could have seen flying in the air in that area.

"The Defence Department says that the public has been misinterpreting 'conventional aircraft,' but what is 'conventional' to experts and scientists is not conventional to the observing public. Thus pilotless planes are now flying around which are capable of great speeds.

DIFFERENT TYPES

"Propelled objects being seen in the air are of different types," he went on. "The research being done is extensive.

"If you ask officials whether they know of any 'flying saucers' they will say 'No.' If you ask whether objects of various kinds unfamiliar to the public are being flown as part of numerous experiments by private companies doing Government work they will concede that this is what the public may be seeing—that is misinterpreting 'conventional' aircraft.

"For officials to explain all the different experiments would be to disclose military secrets. That is the principal reason why the Defence Department has called a halt on investigating the different reports.

"One thing that Government officials are ready to say positively is that the flying objects being seen by the public are not from another planet or foreign country." Mr. Lawrence concluded. "They are what experts call 'conventional' aircraft and in due time the public will learn what they mean to future warfare."

THINGS THEY SEE

That monster again

THE Loch Ness monster is back.

A small girl with a motoring party called attention to a dark object out in the Loch opposite Glen Urquhart Castle.

She asked if it was a rock.

While the party watched the object began racing through the water, leaving a foaming wake.

ONCE MORE, A SAUCER

April 29-1950. N.C.

ALSO back, the Flying Saucer. One was seen on Thursday night by the pilot, crew and 19 passengers in a plane flying from Washington to Kansas City, the News Chronicle Washington Correspondent reports.

The pilot, Capt. Robert Dickes, said a disc glowing red, flew parallel with his machine for five minutes at an altitude of 2,000 feet.

Then it "whizzed off" at 400 miles an hour.

Capt. Dickes was angry. "It was no Martian invader," he said, "but, in my view, a jet flying machine with gyroscopic control.

"If one of those things got out of control, it would be very dangerous flying about the airways."

And here both together

April 29-1950. N.C.

IN Sydney (British Columbia), residents on the beach said that while a flying saucer was whizzing overhead yesterday, a 50ft. three-humped sea-serpent broke surface 100 yards off shore.

FUNDADO EN MADRID EN 1922

NUM. 7.895 — **LUNES 3 DE ABRIL DE 1950** — **PRECIO DEL**

UNA FOTOGRAFIA SENSACIONAL

MISTERIO EN LAS NUBES PLATILLOS VOLANTES

INFORMACIONES, siempre al servicio de sus lectores, les ofrece hoy una fotografía sensacional para documento en la apasionante polémica acerca de los platillos volantes.

The picture that Spanish newspaper readers saw.

Daily Graphic, April 20th. 1950.

↓ FLYING SAUCER—AS SPAIN SEES IT

First picture of a flying saucer comes from the Spanish newspaper *Informaciones*.

DAILY GRAPHIC correspondent in Madrid explains:

The caption stated that this picture was obtained at 3 a.m. in the Balearic Islands by Enrique Hausmann Müller, a newsreel cameraman.

It added that he and his assistants heard a loud noise and saw a luminous trail crossing the sky. He pulled out his camera and obtained a picture—but expresses no opinion about flying saucers.

FOOTNOTE from Texas: Ira Maxey, wartime member of a U.S. bomber crew, photographed two groups of "flying saucers" near Fort Worth. "But," he said, "they were more like flying bananas than flying saucers."

BACKGROUND TO THE NEWS

Flying Saucers: The Facts

THE British destroyer *Broadsword* will shortly sail from Portsmouth for a series of special gunnery trials with the U.S. Navy. The targets will be Flying Saucers.

So far, U.S. gunners have not succeeded in hitting the Saucers, which are designed and built as targets for America's newest anti-rocket weapons.

Flying Saucers are launched from 45-degree ramps, where they reach a momentum of over 500 m.p.h. before automatically taking off. In flight they reach a height of 40,000 ft. and a speed of more than 1000 m.p.h.

Backroom scientists who will sail across the Atlantic in *Broadsword* are confident that the Royal Navy's latest weapons will succeed where the U.S. Navy's have failed.

Their confidence results from recent Mediterranean trials, which proved conclusively that *Broadsword's* radar-controlled twin four-inch guns can shoot down very fast targets at extremely long ranges.

Radio - controlled "Queen Bee" planes were used at first, but after six had been destroyed the Admiralty used miniature rockets.

Broadsword's first American port of call will be Norfolk, Virginia, but target practice will probably take place near the Californian islands of St. Nicholas and Santa Rosa, where Flying Saucer experiments are carried out.

☆ ☆

All in Count

A FLYING SAUCER ?

Over Isle of Wight

Evening Standard Reporter

SOUTHAMPTON, Thursday.
—A flying "object" was reported at 20,000ft. to-day over Cowes, Isle of Wight.

It was reported by the chief engineer of Cowes Airport, Mr. George Wilkes, and a pilot, Captain J. Jessop.

Mr. Wilkes described the "shining object" as round and travelling four times as fast as a jet aircraft.

"The speed must have been 2000 m.p.h.," he said. "It had a hard white light and the speed was incredible. It disappeared south of the island.

"It seemed to be descending in a gentle arc towards the sea."

"ROUND OBJECT" OVER AIRPORT

BRILLIANT LIGHT

An unidentified round object with a brilliant white light was reported to have been seen at a height of nearly 20,000ft over Cowes Airport, Isle of Wight, yesterday. It was thought to have been travelling at about 2,000 m.p.h.

Capt. J. Jessop, a former R.A.F. pilot, of Coastguard Cottages, Gurnard, saw a white object in the sky while taxi-ing a plane with Mr. G. W. Wilkes, of Mill Hill, Cowes, chief engineer at the airport. They got out of the plane, and noticed a Meteor jet plane disappearing south at 500 m.p.h.

Capt. Jessop thought it was a rocket fired from the Meteor. R.A.F. authorities say that no firing was carried out in the area yesterday morning. The Air Ministry can only attribute what was seen to a "meteorological phenomenon."

E. News, April 26, 1950

'SAUCER' FILM

Denver, Colorado, Wednesday.—Grant Edwards says he has made a colour film of what he believes are two "Flying Saucers" seen near Fort Garland, Colorado.—B.U.P.

IT is seen again

An engineer driving to work at Cwmbran (Mon.) saw IT yesterday. IT was flying at 600ft. IT was dove-grey in colour. IT looked like the planet Saturn. IT made no sound. IT was "definitely a manufactured object."

IT, he says, was a flying saucer.

BALLS OF FIRE OVER FINLAND

HELSINKI, Friday.
"FLYING balls of fire," moving in the direction of the Soviet frontier, were today reported to military authorities by people in different parts of Eastern Finland.

Flying objects have been reported in Northern Sweden and Finland during the last two years, but investigation showed them to be natural phenomena.—Reuter.

[Russian astronomers claim to have discovered a new kind of star system, the "star association," whose study has led to a new theory of the evolution of the stars.]

'Strange Object':
THE STORY BEHIND
THE PICTURES

July 2nd. 1950.

THE Sunday Dispatch presents to British readers today two of the most remarkable photographs ever printed. Here is the story behind them:

Near the small town of McMinnville, Oregon, U.S., lives a farmer named Paul Trent, an honest and highly respected member of the community.

He has a small camera and occasionally takes pictures of his family or friends. Last winter he put in a new roll of film and took a couple of photographs. He left the unfinished roll in his camera in readiness to take anything else interesting.

Noiseless, Shone Like Silver

On May 11 he and his wife saw a strange object flying over his farm and he took two pictures of it. Farmer Trent was not particularly excited by what he saw. He described it as looking like a saucer and added that it shone like silver, made no noise, showed no smoke, and after a few minutes went over the horizon to the north-west.

Farmer Trent still kept the roll of film in his camera until he had completed it with snapshots of a family picnic on Mothers' Day. Then he had the film developed and printed.

That was when the world got to know about the "Flying Saucer" over Paul Trent's farm and saw the photographs he had taken.

No Signs Of Tampering

The local newspaper, the McMinnville *Telephone Register*, broke the news by printing the pictures and story.

Then they appeared in *Life*, the biggest illustrated magazine in the world, whose photographic experts declared that "the negatives showed no signs of having been tampered with."

Now copies of Farmer Trent's pictures have come into the possession of the *Sunday Dispatch*, and this newspaper has shown them to leading air and scientific experts in this country.

(Trent's story, Expert opinions on the pictures: Page Five.)

Sunday Dispatch

149th Year. No. 7,756.　　2d.　　JULY 2, 1950.　　Radio Page 6.　　7

Experts' Views On Remarkable Pictures

FLYING SAUCER ASTONISHING PHOTOGRAPHS

Sunday Dispatch Exclusive

Paul Trent, of McMinnville, Oregon, U.S.A., photographed the saucer-shaped object (left) which, he said, appeared over his farm in 1948, cruising silently and leaving no vapour trail

The Flying Saucer

(Continued From Page 1)

S.Dispatch, July 2nd,1950

The Flying Saucer—enlarged from the Page One pictures.

How I Took The Photos, By Trent

From Our NEW YORK Reporter

"IT was late in the evening when we saw the object in the sky," Mrs. Evelyn May Trent, 28, told the McMinnville *Telephone Register.*

"The camera! Paul raced for it and took the first picture. The object was coming in towards us and seemed to be tipped up a bit."

Paul Trent, her husband, told the *Oregon Journal*: "It was about 20ft. or 30ft. in diameter and was moving fairly slowly. After I had snapped the first picture it moved a little to the left and I prepared to take another picture.

Picked Up Speed

"Then it seemed to pick up speed suddenly and in no time at all it vanished."

Trent said he did not tell anyone about the pictures immediately after taking them because "I was kinda scared. You know you hear so much about those things—and the Government . . . I didn't believe all that talk about Flying Saucers before, but now I have an idea the Army knows what they are."

He scoffed at the idea that the object might have been a clay pigeon used in target practice.

Mrs. Trent said in a radio interview that the object looked "like a good - sized parachute canopy without the strings, only silvery bright mixed with bronze." It was not rotating.

What The Experts Have To Say

THE pictures taken by Farmer Trent were shown by the *Sunday Dispatch* to British military, scientific and aeronautical experts.

Here are their reactions:

NOT A METEORITE, SAYS AIR CHIEF

Air Chief Marshal Sir Philip Joubert: The object pictured is very odd, and it is impossible even to guess what it is.

It is clearly not a meteorite. Therefore it is either a machined or cast structure.

It shows no signs of any method of propulsion. It looks like a "skimming dish"—except for that little stump at the top, which in both pictures is at the same angle.

What is the idea of that little projection at the top? And what is the object's propulsive force? What keeps it in the air?

We have had at least 30 instances of this sort of object being seen, but not one has been picked up. It seems as if they have all been absolutely successful in leaving their point of departure and returning somewhere out of the sight of man.

WEATHER DISCS, SAYS ADMIRAL

Rear Admiral G. P. Thomson, war-time Chief Press Censor: I have always believed that no military importance attaches to so-called Flying Saucers observed outside the United States. They have all been some sort of vortex in the atmosphere.

In this connection I recall the experience of a BOAC pilot, a very reliable witness. He saw a Flying Saucer over the Bay of Biscay, and thought that it was some sort of meteorological phenomenon.

But Flying Saucers seen in the States cannot be so easily dismissed.

I have no doubt that they are discs, with no one on board, forming part of scientific experiments by U.S. authorities—probably to obtain precise data about the atmosphere.

I COULD MAKE ONE, SAYS MILES

Mr. F. G. Miles, builder of many successful aircraft: If you would like me to make something of that shape, which could fly, I could do it in two years with material and power plants existing today. I would make one, or perhaps two, external rotating rings, with vanes which could change their incidence (angle) according to the position required of the craft.

Any competent designer could make such a machine.

VISITOR FROM ANOTHER WORLD?

Mr. A. C. Clarke, B.Sc., member of the Council of the British Astronomical Association, assistant secretary of the British Interplanetary Society :

There is nothing in the whole aeronautical field which gives a clue about this pictured object. It makes one wonder if there are extra-territorial visitors. We can neither prove nor disprove such a theory till one lands.

They *may* be revolutionary types of craft, or they *may* be extra-territorial. We shall certainly achieve space flight in 50 years or so. Others may have done so before us.

SOMETHING FROM A ROCKET?

Professor A. M. Low, well-known inventor and scientist : I wonder if it is something discarded from a rocket plane, say, the end of a canister container?

Yet against the theory that it has been discarded is the fact that it is moving over the horizon. Perhaps some mechanical device was being tested in the neighbourhood.

If the money can be spent, we shall be visiting the moon within a century. But many centuries may pass before we can visit other planets.

Suppose we achieve this in 500 years. It is reasonable to ask: If beings on another planet are 500 years ahead of us, why should they not visit us now?

Not to consider the possibility of interplanetary flight is a little more silly than considering it !

STUMP MIGHT BE RADIO MAST

Charles Gardner, ex - R.A.F. pilot, whose work as B.B.C. commentator has taken him to most aeronautical establishments in Britain and America :

If the object in the picture was fired from a gun, there must have been a terrific charge, and it would have to crash somewhere unless guided home by radio. Could the projection on top be a radio mast, remaining upright by gyro-control in the central part of the body while the rest tilts?

If it is a guided missile, I cannot see where the "urge" comes from.

Girl Found Dead In Tunnel

FLYING SAUCER RIDDLE

S. Dispatch, July 9, 1950.

'I believe they are disc-type aircraft,' says—

G. TILGHMAN RICHARDS, senior Research assistant and official lecturer at the South Kensington Science Museum, London, who has studied all the evidence.

SO far flying saucers have been treated by the majority of British people with incredulity and polite ridicule. But why?

I have studied all the reports available. I have seen photographs—those in the *Sunday Dispatch* last week were particularly clear—and I believe they are photographs of disc-type aircraft.

Earlier pictures published in the Spanish Press last April, and alleged to have been taken in the Balearic Islands, might have been anything and could have been a leg-pull. It is not always easy to sort the wheat from the chaff.

SECRET TRIALS

IN all the reports the objects fall into three groups. The most substantial of them come from America.

First group are those saucers which are capable of being explained away as glimpses of experimental trials of various devices.

Under this heading fall many of the objects seen in Southern U.S. and other areas where secret experiments are in progress. For this group I am prepared to accept the explanation given by the United States Army Air Force as "misinterpretations of conventional objects."

These conventional objects are giant experimental · cosmic ray balloons which fill out to 100ft. long and 70ft. in diameter as they rise, radar target balloons capable of rising to 70,000ft. and trailing glittering aluminium foil strip, guided missiles, and stratospheric experiments from Los Alamos, whence rockets are stated to have reached 250 miles above the earth's surface.

Group Two consists of those apparently mysterious visitants which have led to wild surmises about space ships, missiles from other planets and inter-planetary snooping.

The descriptions are remarkably consistent and generally the object is either white or silver, darting about without directional

control or travelling at prodigious speeds, vanishing suddenly, and associated with brilliant light, fringes of fire or flames of peculiar colour and generally rotating or whirling.

From many parts of the world come these reports. The very fact that their descriptions are so consistent has led to their being dismissed as hallucinations, defective vision, or mild hysteria.

It might be that the solution of this riddle could lie in a very unorthodox approach, and I have wondered if there could possibly be turbulences set up in our atmosphere which could cause whirling "dust devils" of luminous gases caused by jet or other high speed experiments which might be responsible for the generation of small atomic whirlpools in the atmosphere.

Group Three reports suggest that the saucers are high speed aircraft of circular or disc shape travelling at speeds much higher than those attained by normal planes.

SAFETY SEARCH

THERE is no reason at all why annular and circular disc-like aircraft should not have been common objects at any time during the past 30 years.

The early history of these very unorthodox-looking aircraft was, ironically, based on a search for safety.

Before 1910 it had been shown that square and circular surfaces had very good non-stalling characteristics up to large angles. But when powered aircraft arrived it was found that the easiest way to minimise the losses due to the end slip of the air from the wing tips was to increase the span of wings while keeping them narrow.

This compromise brought other trouble. Early planes reached their stalling angle at some 15 degrees, and stalling must result in a dive since the only correction of a stall is a flight at some speed greater than the stalling speed.

Very early in the 1905 - 14 period there were people who would not accept that aircraft

Enlargements from flying saucer pictures—front-paged last week—which set everyone talking. They were taken by Farmer Trent, McMinnville, Oregon, U.S.

must, of necessity, be subject to these dangers. They turned aside to investigate possible wing forms which should be safe from stalling and spinning.

Among these "rebels" a few names have become air history. Jose Weiss and Arthur Keith with their completely stable swallow-like monoplane in 1909. Etrich and Wels in Austria in 1911, evolving a stable wingform based on the Zannonia leaf from which Rumpler and the majority of German builders developed the Taube monoplane. Dunne, with his too stable, tailless, back-swept wing biplane in 1912, and the Lee-Richards annular monoplane of 1910-14, with which I was associated.

NOT PERFECT

WITH the outbreak of the 1914 war research of this type was abandoned, and study concentrated on performance rather than safety.

By 1918 the modern plane was established, and earlier research was forgotten.

Civil airlines naturally used adapted war planes, and then came World War II. Once more limitations were imposed.

In spite of the orthodoxy of design there was throughout the inter-war years, and even today

there is still, a considerable bo of technical opinion not satisf that perfection has been reach And here, I think, lies the r answer.

This body of opinion has be continually searching for t "safe" design. Designers of ma nationalities have been strivi since the early 1920's with gr success toward a foolproof pla of disc type.

In 1934-35 Charles H. Zimm mann, in the United States, bu a disc wing airplane combin with a helicopter capable vertical ascent and descent a a high forward speed.

NAVY STEPS IN

IN 1937 he granted licenc for his patents to Chance Vought Aircraft Divis of the United Aircraft Corpo tion in the U.S.

But at that point the U.S. N stepped in, and all further de opment has been of a sec nature, though it has been sta that this combination is capa of speeds from 0 to 500 miles hour.

This performance is in acc with reports that flying sauc travel at great speeds, ho ascend and descend with lit forward motion.

It is, perhaps, a little hard believe that there can, as yet, ist enough of these types to m the many reports, but there is reason at all why such aircr should not have been seen prov ing that full scale work follow the experimental period. And secrecy would suggest that t is so.

And *there* could lie the m solid proof that flying saucers exist. ·

Flying saucer bursts in mid-air

No sign of wreckage

Sunday Express
Sept. 3rd. 1950.

INTRIGUING reports of a "flying saucer" coming to grief — the first ever received — are being investigated by the Canadian Air Force.

Hundreds of people living along the Miramichi River, in New Brunswick, say they saw "a flying saucer or some strange object" disintegrate in the air at about 8.30 on the evening of August 16.

They say that there was a series of explosions. But no wreckage has been found.

Shattering

The object in the sky is described as "gleaming with a phosphorescent blue light." A similar intense blue light has been reported as a feature of several of the mysterious sky objects—usually called "flying saucers" though they take a variety of shapes—seen over various parts of the world in recent years.

The New Brunswick "flying saucer" was seen by many eye-witnesses to climb, dip, and move at varying speeds. There was a shattering blast which blew it into several sections. Then each smaller section exploded.

Many saw it

Wing-Commander E. B. Hale, the officer commanding the R.C.A.F. jet-plane base at nearby Chatham, said : "A lot of people saw it, and we are gathering information from them."

Before it exploded the object was seen over a number of villages in the area.

The places and times of the reports suggest that there may have been other similar objects over the area at the same time.

Excitement ran high through the district. Telephone switchboards were jammed with calls from people seeking an explanation.

Wilfred McMahon, who lives six miles from Newcastle and saw the explosion, says the object was "a fluorescent blue object."

He reports seeing pieces breaking away "like four or five stars." Then, he says, after the explosions a cloud of smoke lingered in the air.

Estimates of the height at which the object was moving vary from as low as 150 feet to almost 1,000 feet.

D.T. Sept. 20. 1950.

"FLYING TUB" IS SEEN OVER U.S.

From Our Own Correspondent

NEW YORK, Tuesday.

Excitement has been caused in a wide area of the south-eastern part of the United States by the appearance high in the skies yesterday of a spherical object described by some observers as a "flying tub."

Two Missouri airmen said it was "something like two big white balloons tied together, one underneath the other."

A lieutenant of the Air National Guard at Memphis, Tennessee, who took his jet plane to a height of about 35,000ft in an attempt to solve the mystery said he was sure it was "some kind of weather balloon."

Pilots of civilian aircraft who also observed the object reported it was moving erratically, spurting at high speed and then appearing to hover.

Was it a Flying 1/10/50 Saucer?

Sunday Express Correspondent

NEW YORK, Saturday.

FLYING saucers dissolve into thin air, according to four Philadelphia policemen.

Patrolmen John Collins and Joseph Keenan say they saw a mysterious object about 6ft. in diameter floating to earth in an open field.

They called in Sergeant Joseph Cook and Patrolman James Casper, and all approached with flashlights.

Collins tried to pick up "the thing." He says : "I touched part of it and it just dissolved leaving my finger sticky."

FOOTNOTE.—This is the first recorded report of any of the mysterious sky objects commonly called Flying Saucers ever touching earth

---

'SAUCERS ARE OURS'
C.J.M. Oct 3/50

CHILDREN CALMED

Colombus, Ohio, Monday.— American schoolchildren have been told that some "flying saucers" are real and that they belong to the United States Air Force. The statement was made in a weekly newspaper for students published here by an educational publishing firm.

Miss Eleanor M. Johnson, managing editor of the firm's elementary school publications, said the article was aimed at calming "any hysterical fears some children might have built up from hearing too much talk about mysterious visitors from other planets."

She added : "We have had letters from youngsters indicating a widespread hysteria about tiny, big-headed men from Venus riding to earth in outlandish contraptions. We wanted to reassure them by telling them the saucers are our own."—Reuter.

'Flying wing' was
D.E. all lit up 1/10/50

SAN FRANCISCO, Friday.—Two airline pilots today reported that "a mysterious aircraft" dived on their plane over Burbank, California. It looked like "a flying wing showing six to eight brilliant lights."—B.U.P.

E. News. 21/10/50.

SAW FLYING SAUCERS'

Limoges, Central France, Saturday.—Villagers of Nexon (Haute-Vienne) have reported seeing what they described as "flying saucers" passing over from east to west. The objects made a loud noise, they said.—Reuter

---

Now—'Flying Saucers' over Britain
October 21, 1950.

By Daily Mail Reporter

SIX men saw what they claim was a Flying Saucer over Ramsey, Isle of Man, at 10.5 a.m. yesterday.

As far as is known no R.A.F. or civil planes were over Ramsey at the time.

The six, engineering workers, were having their mid-morning break by an open factory door when they saw the object.

Mr. Bob Marshall, 25, of Sulby, Isle of Man, said : "It first appeared in a break in the clouds. It was a long, narrow oblong, with rounded corners.

"It had a clear-cut outline. Each end of the oblong was dark and solid-looking, but the centre seemed to be almost transparent."

His workmates—Messrs. Brian Cottier, William Kelly, Michael Ball, Rex Bishop, and Clifford Skillithorne—confirmed his story.

Flying saucers 11/10/50
skim over France
S. Express

LIMOGES, Saturday. — Flying saucers were seen yesterday crossing the sky from east to west over a small town in Central France. People who saw them said they made a great noise.—A.P.

Six saw saucers

Six people having tea in a café on the sea front at Bridlington, Yorks, yesterday claim they saw three "flying saucers" over Bridlington Bay.

D.G. Oct 30-1950.

MOUNTIES HUNT FOR A SUBMARINE

Oct. 23, 1950.

From Daily Mail Reporter   MONTREAL, Sunday.

CANADIAN Mounties are investigating a series of strange happenings reported by whites and Indians living in parts of Quebec and Ontario around James Bay. Stories of mystery lights in the sky, explosions, and the sighting of a submarine in shallow waters are puzzling people over an area of several hundred miles.

Two Indians, 30-year-old Sydney Lowtit, and 50-year-old Erland Vincent, transporting lumber by barge from Moose Factory to Rupert House, say they spotted a strange vessel.

They watched it from distances of two to six miles as it moved across Moose River mouth.

A third Indian, 36-year-old ex-Army man Oliver Rickard, saw the vessel later. All three examined it through binoculars. They say it had a centre projection like a house.

The Indians—all did coastguard duty during the war—are certain it was a submarine. But the authorities say no Canadian or U.S. submarine would venture so far south because of the shallow waters.

The Indians say that there is about 21ft. of water where the vessel surfaced. Before it disappeared there was a kind of explosion. Black smoke spouted from the vessel.

At the Hudson's Bay Company post at Nemaska, 80 miles inland from James Bay, William McKee, the factor, and his assistant saw a red light almost stationary in the sky.

Three blasts

They said: "It was like a traffic 'stop' light. It travelled slowly round the post, then moved south."

Later excited Indians raced 50 miles to Nemaska to say they had seen a large aircraft, together with a smaller one, standing still in the sky.

The objects are thought to have been a helicopter and large aircraft, but no Canadian or American plane is known to have been there.

Further north, in the wild territory inland from the bay's east coast, three big explosions like earthquakes shook every building at Old Factory River post some time ago.

Dr. B. H. Harper, an Indian, said: "The shocks lasted two or three minutes. We thought it was a severe earthquake."

More than 100 miles north, near Fort George, Indians spotted a strange white man. They tried to speak to him, but as they approached he vanished. All the reports are being investigated.

What Did The People Of Devon See Last Week?

WAS IT A FLYING SAUCER?

Nov. 5/1950.

By Sunday Dispatch Reporter

WEST OF ENGLAND newspapers gave much publicity last week to reports of "flying saucers" over Devon.

The saucers were reported by a number of independent witnesses from places as far apart as Woolacombe (near Ilfracombe), Exeter, Cullompton, Sidmouth Junction, and Paignton (60 miles south of Woolacombe).

Eye witnesses' descriptions of what they saw are substantially in agreement—there was no noise and a trail of fire streamed from the back. The observations were at about 11 p.m. in all instances.

Mr. J. Stewart, 70-year-old Woolacombe pensioner, who has worked in aircraft factories in two wars, was one of the five people who told the Exeter *Express and Echo* what they had seen.

At 10.50 on Monday evening, he noticed an object come inshore from the direction of the north end of Lundy at a "terrific speed."

Mr. H. A. Franklin, of Beacon-lane, Whipton, near Exeter, wrote to the paper that while at Countess Wear (two miles south-east of Exeter) on Monday night, he saw two circular objects.

"They were of a brilliant silvery blue, travelling south, one behind the other in close formation," he said.

"After passing overhead, the rear object appeared to catch up with the front one, and collide, whereon they disintegrated."

Bright Disc

The object was described by Miss J. Spurway, of Exeter-hill, Cullompton (12 miles north-east of Exeter), as "a bright disc travelling with a circular movement at great speed."

Two and a half miles north of Exmouth, the object was seen at 11 p.m. by Mr. and Mrs. L. Mussell, of Hill-crest, Lympstone, who described it as having been in two parts "apparently attached in some way with a lighted tail."

The sixth witness quoted in the *Express and Echo* is Mr. A. J. Powell, of Sidmouth Junction, who, while between Patterson's Cross, Ottery St. Mary and Sidmouth Junction at 11 p.m. on Monday, saw "two brilliant white lights come into view to the north-west, from behind a bank of mist."

'Long Red Trail'

"They passed swiftly," he said, "in a southerly direction and appeared to be 'in line astern' with a long red trail to the rear . . . both lights seemed to fizzle out as I watched them—they were in a clear patch of sky when this happened . . . I heard no sound."

"Two large circular objects travelling south in a horizontal position looking something like large white flames" is the description given in the *Western Morning News* of what Mr. Arthur N. Bearns, 55-year-old estate agent, of Southfield-avenue, Preston, Devon, saw at Paignton at 11 p.m on Monday.

Members of the crew of a liberty boat plying between Flagstaff Steps, Devonport Dockyard, and H.M.S. Defiance are also reported in the *Western Morning News* as having seen "circular objects travelling at an incalculable speed and emitting a trail of fire" late on Monday night.

The Torquay *Herald Express* quotes four other people who saw similar objects.

Bluish Light

Frederick Bray, fisherman, aged 39, was lying in the bunk of his boat in Torquay outer harbour, when he saw a "bluish-white light" appear over Princess Pier at about 11 p.m. "I watched the flames for about ten seconds. They seemed to surround a roundish object which was travelling towards Thatcher Rock." (to the East).

While walking along the sea front to Torquay Station, Mr. D. Jeffery, of Winner-street, Paignton, saw something in the sky. "I thought at first it was a rocket firework," he told the *Herald Express.* "Then I noticed it was maintaining a constant speed at a constant height . . . It was absolutely silent. It seemed to disintegrate suddenly and disappear."

A "ball of bluish-white light" was seen at about 11 p.m. in the sky above Paignton travelling south towards Brixham. Mr. Harry Cove-Clark, of Marine-drive, Paignton, said: "The ball of light was preceded by a thin blue blur which was overtaken by the main body.

'Like Feeble Rocket'

"Then another bluish-white light appeared and a broken stream of lights seemed to fall from it. They all seemed to be following each other straight across the sky, then there was a spurt of flame from the end of the broken pieces—just like a feeble rocket."

The last of the witnesses, Mr. H. Warren, of East-street, Torre, Torquay, saw from his bedroom window an object "going towards Brixham, due south of Torquay." Describing it in a letter to the paper, he said: "I thought it was like three stars with a long tail of light trailing behind them."

THE MOST FANTASTIC FLYING SAUCER STORY—PAGE FOUR.

14lb PIECES OF ICE FOUND ON EXMOOR FARMS

Nov. 10th. 1950.

WEATHER EXPERTS MYSTIFIED

DAILY TELEGRAPH REPORTER

Exmoor farmers are mystified by the sudden appearance on their farms of large lumps of ice weighing 12lb to 14lb. The ice has the appearance of being dropped from the air, and pieces have been found over an area of several square miles in the middle of Exmoor.

The first report came from Popham Farm, near North Molton, a lonely hill farm, where Mr. Edward Latham found one of his sheep dead in a field. It had a deep wound in the neck, and a few yards away lay a piece of ice, about 14lb in weight.

The ice obviously had fallen from a height. It had dug itself into the ground to a depth of several inches.

"LARGE AS DINNER PLATES"

Mr. Latham said yesterday: "The sheep had been killed as though struck by lightning. Round the field and along the roadway were lumps of ice as large as dinner plates."

Other farmers reported ice among their cattle in the fields. It was also found on the roadway by a tractor driver at Sandyway, four miles from North Molton.

The Air Ministry's meteorological office could not offer any explanation for the appearance of the ice. It was not considered likely that it was due to natural causes. The possibility of its having been dropped by aircraft has been ruled out by the R.A.F. It was stated that all planes carried de-icing equipment.

A meteorological expert's theory was that the lumps were large hailstones which could have fallen from thick cloud extending to 20,000ft. He said that the mild weather would have made no difference as the cloud must have extended into regions well below freezing point, at which hailstones were formed.

"SUSPENDED HAILSTONES"

"For a time the hailstones are kept suspended in the cloud, but when heavy enough they fall so rapidly that they reach the ground before melting." Those of the size reported were rare, but it had been known for some as big as tennis balls to kill small animals.

The density of the ice, and consequently the weight of the stone, varied frequently. Sometimes a number of large hailstones would freeze together when lying on the ground, thus accounting for irregular shapes and greater weight.

About 40 years ago three sheep were found dead in a field not far from North Molton, on Exmoor. Ice was scattered round them.

A special note included in the 9 p.m. weather forecast issued by the Meteorological Office in London last night stated: "Reports of large blocks of ice weighing up to 14lb falling at North Molton were received from various sources, but the conditions there do not suggest that this was any normal meteorological phenomenon."

STRIPE PRIST

Flying ice 'bombs' moorland farms

PIECES of thick ice as big as dinner plates—one weighed 14lbs—are puzzling farmers and weather men.

They have been found scattered over farms in a wide area round North Molton and Simonsbath on Exmoor.

The 14lb. piece killed a sheep on Mr. Edward Latham's farm near North Molton.

The animal had a deep wound in the back of its neck and the ice was found dug into the ground about 10 yards away as if it had fallen from a height.

Round the field and along a roadway were other large pieces.

The weather has been exceptionally mild in the area for several days.

R A F officials at Chivenor Aerodrome, 15 miles away, discounted a theory that the ice might have fallen off one of their planes. All aircraft operating from the field have de-icing equipment.

Dr. H. T. S. Britton, of University College, Exeter, took the view last night that it was unlikely that such lumps of ice could have been formed naturally.

And an official of the Meteorological Office said: "There is no natural cause that I know of to account for such a business.

"In the tornado in the Home Counties last May we got hailstones two inches in diameter. I've never heard of anything bigger than that in Britain."

Strange light

Lacking any other explanation, farmers were wondering yesterday whether the ice had any connection with a strange light which passed over Exmoor some days ago.

It was seen in several parts of the West Country, where it was dubbed a "flying saucer."

In the 9 p.m. radio weather forecast last night there was a special note about the flying ice, which added: "The conditions do not suggest that this was any normal meteorological phenomenon."

Report of 12 Cities

17 APR 1954

Many Pitted Windshields Baffle State of Washington

By the United Press

SEATTLE, April 16.—An epidemic of pitted automobile windshields has hit at least 12 northwest Washington cities and police today said they were at a loss to explain the attacks.

Seattle officers said they believed the mysterious pits were caused by chemical reaction rather than vandals. Police Chief H. J. Lawrence said it would take a small army of vandals to inflict the amount of damage reported.

Meanwhile, with the windshield phenomenon spreading from Bellingham south to Tacoma, law-enforcement officers decided to meet later today to compare notes.

Seattle officials said they could find no solid residue of any type of pellets which might have struck the windshields. However, they reported finding tiny globules of an oily tar-like substance which led to the theory that a rain of some chemical was eating into the windshields, which police said were made of a different kind of glass from other windows.

In some cases, officers said, windshield damage reports were believed to be the psychological result of publicity, which caused motorists to notice old pits not previously observed.

The Seattle Police Department was forced to put four extra officers on the complaint desk to handle windshield damage reports, sometimes coming in at the rate of 10 a minute.

Two King County sheriff's deputies reported they actually watched two pitmarks appear in the windshield of a truck.

At Tacoma, two reporters got out of their car for about five minutes to talk to a policeman and said that when they returned to the car it had four fair-sized pits that were not there before.

Gilbert Albrecht, a warehouse worker at Tacoma, said 34 pitmarks appeared on his windshield this afternoon.

DO "FLYING SAUCERS" COME THE ETHERIC WORLD?

THE latest and most extraordinary theory to account for "flying saucers" is that they originate in the etheric world. The theory comes from America and is outlined in a publication, "Flying Discs," by Meade Layne, M.A.

Layne is Director of the Borderland Sciences Research Associates, who investigate data which orthodox science "cannot or will not recognise."

A well-known American trance medium, Mark Probert, has assisted the B.S.R. associates. Through his mediumship messages have been received, it is said, from "highly intelligent entities" which have been of value to the investigators in developing their "etheric" theory.

Here is an extract from statements made by the chief communicator, an Oriental, with surprising technical knowledge:

"There is a heat wave which passes over the entire exterior of the disc. Have you noticed the glow around some of these objects? Some of them reach what you call white heat. This is heated and cooled at an extremely high rate of speed.

"The heat wave does not affect the interior of the disc or the people in it. You can call it a pick-up and lay-down motion, with the expansion and contraction at quantum rates."

The next point of interest is that the etheric world, from which the discs are supposed to come, is not inhabited by those who lived on this earth—it is not the spirit world.

"Etheria is *here*," we are told, "alongside, inside, outside our world."

In this etheric region, it is claimed, there flourish civilisations, cultures and a race of beings which are born into that world and die there. They are not discarnate humans. They have knowledge of our world and can and do penetrate it.

"Why," we may ask, "have we no knowledge of this other world? Why have those in the spirit world not told us of its existence?"

Layne answers: "Many dwellers on the astral plane are aware of the etheric worlds also, and have the power of visiting them.

GREAT PSYCHICS

"This ability, however, does not seem to be a common and natural endowment, but belongs to persons of a certain degree of development, corresponding to those whom we here call adepts, or possessed of exceptional psychic powers of projection or clairvoyance."

The discs are "built in matter of the etheric plane," we read, and are imperceptible to us, since they exist in what we call "empty space." They enter our level of perception by a process of materialisation.

A better analogy would be that of apports. As apports are brought through space and walls to be made visible in our seance rooms by a system of increasing and decreasing the vibratory rate of the object, so these aerial phenomena are made visible to us.

ONE ODD FEATURE

This ties up with eyewitnesses' accounts of the mysterious suddenness of the appearance and disappearance of the craft, although their strange noiselessness might also account for this.

Both the "Sunday Dispatch" and the "Sunday Express" are featuring weekly articles on the discs. In the first article in the "Express" appears the statement: "The suddenness of the appearances is one of the odd but consistent features of these visits."

Another important feature of the discs is their manoeuvrability. The speed which they sometimes attain is obviously far above that which a human being could withstand. Yet in the "Express" the following incident is related:

Captain C. S. Chiles, with his first officer, J. B. Whitted, was flying a passenger aeroplane from Houston, Texas, on July 23, 1948.

At 2.45 a.m. there was a good moon visible through some broken cloud. On this well-lit, quiet scene suddenly "a brilliant super-giant torpedo" dashed towards the aeroplane.

Both officers saw it. It was coming straight down the air traffic lane they were on, but slightly above them.

"GUIDING INTELLIGENCE"

It suddenly swooped down. Chiles swung his machine violently to the left. Fortunately the "torpedo" veered as sharply, too, to the right, and they rushed past each other.

The writer of the article declared, "*Clearly some guiding intelligence, and one wishful to avoid disaster, was in control of this great shaft of speeding force.*"

It is also apparent from this extract that these enigmatic craft are not only in the shape of saucers and discs. Layne mentions long, cigar-shaped objects, such as the one Chiles saw, and others shaped like balloons or dirigibles, and some which have wings or wing-like attachments.

Many appear to change shape while in the air. Some resemble "fire-balls," others being accompanied or followed by smoke, vapour and luminous appearances.

That these objects do exist there can be no doubt. Sufficient evidence for their existence has been collated so as to satisfy all except those who will not believe what they themselves have not seen.

FROM ANOTHER PLANET?

The accounts in the two Sunday papers are authentic, names, times and places being supplied. A photograph appears in the "Sunday Express" of a flying disc, taken by William Rhodes of Phoenix, Arizona, on July 9, 1947. He describes the disc as "like a rubber heel with a small hole in the middle."

In spite of a much-publicised article by Henry J. Taylor, internationally known journalist and radio commentator, in which he declared the discs to be part of "a big and expanding experimental project which has been progressing in the United States for nearly three years," the most favoured contemporary theory is that they come from another planet. Certainly Taylor has received no official corroboration of his claims.

An article in "Everybody's" mentions that at least three unknown types of aircraft have been reported as flying in our atmosphere and far above it for something like 200 years, but in increasing numbers during the last three. The "Sunday Dispatch" asks, "How can we explain reports of them dating back into the last century?" How indeed?

WAR REPERCUSSIONS?

Only, it seems, by also considering the "planetary" and "etheric" theories. With regard to these, Layne suggests that the increasing frequency with which the discs are appearing may have something to do with the new trends of warfare on earth.

He declares that atomic explosions, such as at Hiroshima and Nagasaki, and subsequent experimentation, may have had repercussions in the etheric world.

The "Etherians" who, we are informed, have had this planet under observation for centuries, are becoming disturbed at our atom-splitting ventures, and are making more frequent observations of our progress (?) in such matters. It is thought that they may want to take a hand before we go too far.

According to statements made by those who have seen them some of the craft are too small, others too fast to be occupied by human beings. Yet occupied they appear to be, for they manoeuvre with great skill. Remember, too, that the discs emit no sound. How, then, do they fly?

Donald Keyhoe, former Information Chief of the Aeronautics Branch of the U.S. Commerce Department, who is a leading American aviation writer, has writ-

FROM

ten the book which the "Sunday Dispatch" is serialising. He believes, "This earth has been under periodic observation from another planet, or other planets, for at least two centuries."

Layne postulates an etheric world; and from this unknown realm, he says, come occupied "Etherian" space-ships which can materialise and dematerialise in and out of the earth's atmosphere most conveniently.

Gerald Heard, who is writing the "Sunday Express" series, has a world reputation as a science investigator. He states: "It is clear now, beyond any reasonable doubt, that something has been continually haunting the upper skies." His opinion of what that something is, he has not yet disclosed. Yet whatever theory we choose to uphold, one thing, at least, is clear: "flying saucers" are one of the most outstanding and amazing phenomena of the 20th century.

W.F.N.

ICE BLOCK FALLS AT HIS FEET

Nov. 28th 1950.

Two Ministries start probe

By Daily Mail Reporter

ANOTHER block of ice fell from the sky yesterday—at Braughing, Hertfordshire.

It was a foot long and four inches thick, and landed unbroken on a grass verge almost at the feet of R.A.C. Scout D. Tunmore.

Mr. Tunmore, who was on patrol, said: "When I first saw the ice I thought it was a piece of paper floating in the slight breeze.

"Then it fell almost at my feet."

He thought people would say he had made up the story, so he stopped motorists, showed them the ice and told what he had seen.

Air Ministry experts were puzzled. "Blocks of ice of this description would not fall from R.A.F aircraft," said a spokesman.

Ministry experts are collecting evidence of falling ice.

A Ministry of Civil Aviation official said their safety experts are working in close collaboration with the Air Ministry, trying to find why the ice falls.

Air line officials said it is possible but highly improbable for large ice formations to fall from civil planes. Aircraft are not permitted to discharge water or fluid when in flight.

All airliners are either fitted with a de-icing fluid system or use inflated rubber layers at the leading edges which "breathe" to prevent ice from forming.

A 5lb. block of ice from a plane fell through a garage roof at Wandsworth, S.W., last Friday. Blocks of ice fell on Exmoor on November 9.

Theory on Ice

E.N. Nov. 28. 1950

Science is Keeping Eye on Saturn

The universe, showing the position of the planets. Saturn is at the top, then Jupiter and Mars with the Earth at the bottom.

By CYRIL BIRKS

IS the earth being bombarded by ice meteorites from Saturn, the planet that is 885,900,000 miles from the sun?

Scientists at British universities and "met." experts are studying this theory as a probable explanation for the blocks of ice that have been falling in this country.

To enable these investigations to be taken further reports have been requested from the Air Ministry by Professor F. A. Paneth, Professor of Chemistry at Durham University and a leading expert on meteorites, and by the authorities of Sedgwick Museum of Geology at Cambridge University.

Other scientific bodies in the country are also offering help to the Air Ministry's "met." experts to solve the origin of the ice blocks—a source which is one of the biggest mysteries of the century.

HARD, COLD CORE

Why is Saturn suspected as a probable source?

A "met." expert told me to-day: "It is now known that the planets have got shells of ice around them. It is also believed that Saturn's inner satellites consist virtually of large balls of ice and snow and the planet's rings of smaller particles of ice. One theory, therefore, is that the ice blocks that have fallen have been ice meteorites."

Western Mail & South Wales News.
November 2nd. 1950.

More say they saw flying saucer

FURTHER claims to have seen flying saucers over Wales on Monday night were made by a number of people yesterday at Swansea and neighbouring towns and at Hirwaun, near Aberdare.

Mrs. Mary J. Stephens, Brecon-road, Hirwaun, a miner's wife, was with her sister-in-law, Miss Doris Stephens, when she claims she saw two objects "like big stars with long pointed tails" moving slowly in the direction of Aberdare.

"They were glittering and appeared to be quite low," she said.

Mr. James Hardwick, Brecon-road, Hirwaun, also said he saw the objects.

Several people in the Swansea, Penclawdd and Gowerton districts claim to have seen an object resembling two large stars with a golden tail gliding across the sky.

Glided in sky

One Swansea woman said she watched the "stars" for several minutes gliding across the sky over Swansea. They disappeared over the Bristol Channel.

The reports agree that the star-like objects travelled together and were either attached or very close to one another.

Mr. B. E. Featherstone, honorary observation director of Swansea Astronomical Society, told a Western Mail reporter yesterday that he had received a number of letters from people reporting they had seen the objects, but he had not sufficient detailed information to form an opinion.

The general trend of information seemed to show that the objects approached from the west and proceeded eastwards. Some spoke of them dividing and continuing on parallel paths, and others said that they later saw the objects returning.

Detective's version

Detective - sergeant Ambrose Davies, Gowerton, said that he saw a white ball of flame about 10 times larger than a star travelling at a terrific speed. It broke into two stars and a shower of reddish sparks flew out of the rear.

It was not an aircraft or a meteor, he asserted. A bar of light joined the two parts.

Nov. 1. 1950. D.M.

FAR AND NEAR

Star dust in his eyes

MR. A. SCHENAGI, of Esmond-road, Chiswick, W., told the police yesterday he had seen "a long, cigar-shaped object flashing across the sky."

He said a trail of sparks—"like hot ashes" — disappeared towards Kew. Official explanation: It was a shooting star.

3, 1950 Western Mail & South Wales News.

"Flying Saucers" in Wales?

November 3rd. 1950.

ALTHOUGH unexplained brilliant objects travelling at unimaginable speeds across the heavens are reported to have been seen in many parts of Europe and the United States, Wales's interest in the "flying saucer" controversy has until this week been more or less academic.

On Wednesday the Western Mail reported that eye-witnesses in Penclawdd, near Swansea, had seen two huge "stars" travelling across the sky at about 11 p.m. on the previous Monday. At the same time approximately a man in Paignton, Devon, saw a similar sight.

Since the report was published observations of the same nature have been described in letters and telephone calls to the Western Mail office from all parts of South and West Wales and the West Country.

Distances of more than 80 miles separated the observation points, which lie mainly on a line between Haverfordwest and Cardiff, and Cardiff and Paignton. Despite the distances between them, the watchers agree in the main on two important particulars — the time and the appearance. They differ only about the course of the strange body, or bodies.

Golden stars

The time was 11 p.m., within minutes either side. The appearance has been most generally described as like that of two large golden stars with a kind of flaming tail stretching across the heavens. They were travelling at terrific speeds and were quite soundless.

The courses reported present the strangest puzzle. Observers in the west say unanimously that the objects were heading roughly from west to east with a tendency towards south. Those in the east, the Cardiff and Rhondda area, are equally sure that the course was in the main south to south-east.

These general directions, which are approximate at the best, were constructed from readers' information, of which the following are samples.

"Between 10.45 and 11.30 I saw two huge lights, like car lights approximately 20ft. apart, extremely bright and followed by a large flame jet tapering off into a series of sparks travelling from the Cowbridge area over Wenvoe" (R. W. Kemp, Dinas Powis).

"I saw this phenomenon in the sky at 11.0 p.m. on Monday night appearing from the west and disappearing due south" (Howard C. James, Rhiwbina).

Object vanished

"I saw two lights at 11.5 p.m. moving in a southerly direction" (Mr. C. W. V. Davies, Radyr).

"There was a bright light towards the tail and the object seemed to vanish into thin air. It travelled at a terrific speed" (Mrs. H. R. Kelly, Pontyclun).

"I observed a bright flash in the sky roughly south-west of Penrhiwfer at 11.02 p.m. It remained stationary then moved across the sky at a terrific speed in the shape of a small sun. travelling towards the south, approaching the earth at an angle of roughly 10 degrees. It appeared to have a kind of tail which broke off." (Frederick Walsh, Penygraig).

"I saw an object passing over Carmarthen in an easterly direction about 11.10 p.m. It looked like two golden stars with a tail, the second star being smaller than the first" (Miss V. L. Tew, Carmarthen).

No noise

"I also saw the peculiar object about 11 p.m. It appeared to be about three or four times the size of ordinary falling stars travelling east" (Lem Emmanuel, Penclawdd).

"My friend and I saw two highly illuminated objects travelling from west to east about 70 to 80 miles south from here, close together at a terrific speed, but no great height." (W. F. Edwards, Haverfordwest.)

"I noticed a peculiar object about 11 p.m. gliding east, bigger and brighter than a shooting star." (Miss M. E. Davies, Cilycwm, Llandovery.)

"I saw the object about 11 p.m. It was brilliant and there was no engine noise as it went over the Channel. The tail did not seem to be connected. It looked like a shadow of something burning, with a red tint running through the shadow." (J. S. James, Splott.)

Local astronomers have been puzzled by the reports, and the "flying saucer" theory has been discredited by Mr. Llewellyn Lloyd, hon. secretary of the Cardiff and District Astronomical Society. He has suggested that what was seen might have been a fire-ball or bolide, which have in the past been observed to break into two or more pieces.

However, Mr. Lloyd, who lives at 164, Whitchurch-road, Whitchurch, and the vice-president (Mr. G. H. Corbett) are anxious to acquire as much data as possible on the sightings from correspondents.

D. Mail, Nov. 6/50.

Blue riddle over London

Men working on airliners at London Airport last night stated that they saw something flash across the sky with a "high-pitched hissing noise."

Mr. Alastair Wilkinson, of Pan American Airways, said: "It was a white light with a blue flame flashing out behind. It went from north-east to south-east."

D. Mail, Nov. 8/50.

Flying Sausage is the latest

A flying "sausage" with disc-like ends, 150ft. to 200ft. long, was yesterday reported flying north over Barrow-in-Furness by two residents, Mr. A. Docker and Mr. A. Norman.

"It was something of a cross between a submarine and a barrage balloon," said Mr. Docker, "and was travelling at a fair speed."

4/11/50.

More about the flying saucers

LETTERS continued to reach the *Western Mail* offices yesterday from people who either claim to have seen Wales's now famous "flying saucers" on Monday night or from people who saw them but say they were perfectly natural phenomena.

Their appearance was first reported in the *Western Mail* on Wednesday as having been seen by people at Penclawdd at about 11 p.m. Since then they have been reported as having been observed that night in all parts of South Wales and in the south-west of England.

Correspondents from Llanelly, Llandilo, Pengam (Mon.), and New Tredegar all claim to have seen the mysterious lights at "approximately 11 p.m." Another reader saw it flying over Cardiff at 10.50 p.m.

Grand sight

All are agreed on the description.

Mr. Meyrick Williams, of Aberbargoed, writes:

"It was coming in the direction of Swansea to Newport and travelling at a great speed. There were two distinct lights and a long trail behind. . . . At first glance I thought it was an aeroplane, but the speed was too great for any aeroplane and it was flying level and not at a very great height. It was a grand sight."

Mr. E. R. Evans, Golden Grove, Carmarthenshire, who saw it approaching from the direction of Carmarthen, describes it as "like the headlamps of a car which were overlapping one another." It was travelling very fast and vanished in the direction of Bristol, with no sound.

Another appearance is reported by Mr. David Morgan, of Lampeter. He writes.

"On Wednesday night, October 25, about eight o'clock, I was standing in the village of Bwlchyllan, overlooking the vale of Aeron. I saw what I thought were five or six stars in formation flying towards Cardigan Bay in a north-westerly direction. The lights were bright and distinct."

Disbeliever's view

Among the disbelievers in this "flying saucery" is a gentleman from Lampeter who signs himself "South Walian." He suggests the lights were caused by beams thrown upon the clouds by searchlights or similar light projectors.

A practical explanation is given by Mr. Trevor T. Edwards, of Swansea, who writes.

"I, too, saw it. It was flying up-Channel in an easterly direction, bearing 12 to 15 degrees above the horizon . . . The wind was north-easterly (which accounted for lack of sound). The speed, the lights and the exhaust told me it was a jet aeroplane—probably a night fighter out on practice switching on his recognition lights . . . As we used to say during the war, 'She's all right, boys, that's one of ours!'."

The only observer who heard a noise from the phenomenon is Mr. C. J. Mitchell, a commercial traveller, who was staying in Cardiff that night.

He told the *Western Mail* yesterday that he and a male friend were near Cogan railway station at 11 p.m. when his friend saw for a few seconds what he thought was a shooting star. A minute later they both heard a loud noise like the exhaust of a jet aeroplane.

He Saw A Flying Saucer Over Britain

Nov. 19th.1950.S.D.

Says Wing-Commander

By Sunday Dispatch Reporter

DID a "flying saucer" hurtle across the night sky of Kent last week?

Wing - Commander Denis H. Carey, aged 51, ex-R.A.F. pilot and bombing expert, believes he saw one racing towards the Strait of Dover as he was driving near his home at Benenden, Kent, on Tuesday.

Here is his story:

"I was driving my small van towards Sandhurst at 6.24 p.m. The sky was clear except for a small cloud bank to the south. There were plenty of stars. I was in open country with the nearest house three-quarters of a mile away.

"I was about midway between Link Hill and Hopehouse Farm, Benenden.

"Through the windscreen I saw a ball of light streak across the sky about 1¼ miles ahead of me, moving from west to east.

Television Blue

"It was either circular or spherical, I cannot be sure, and there was no 'tail.' The colour was unmistakably blue . . . the shade you see on the television screen.

"I watched it for a few seconds and then it disappeared in the East. I estimate that it was travelling at an altitude of roughly 2,000ft., and I probably saw it cover a distance of two miles on a line between Hurst Green and Northiam. It was moving absolutely horizontally and ought to have crossed the coast in the region of the Romney Marshes.

"It was certainly not an aircraft of any type that flies over Britain. It was travelling several times as fast as the fastest jet planes. It was not a comet and its colour and speed rule out the possibility that it could have been a spark of any sort."

Wing - Commander Carey's testimony is backed by good scientific qualifications and an airman's ability to interpret accurately and quickly what he sees in the sky. He was a fighter pilot in World War I, a test pilot during the inter-war years, and concerned with the production of guns and aircraft armament during World War II.

We Shall Fly To Other Worlds, by Prof. A. M. Low: Page FOUR.

American column

No attack by Mars —official

From NEWELL ROGERS

NEW YORK, Tuesday. — Little men from Mars are not invading America. Britain is not bombarding the U.S. with flying saucers. The U.S. Navy said so tonight.

And that put a stop to an outbreak of new flying-saucer rumours in the mountains of New Mexico.

Deer-hunters thought they had a flying saucer at last when they picked up an 18in. metallic sphere, apparently of duralumin. In the sphere was an object resembling a plastic flower pot with nylon shreds, a cheap alarm clock, and three packages of the kind of film used in atomic research.

A theory that it was from another world blew up when they found this note on the film packages: "November 14, 1949; Ilford Limited, London, England."

The navy said it is probably one of the things they had been sending into the stratosphere by a balloon to carry on cosmic ray research. The alarm clock trips a switch which exposes the London-made film to the impact of the rays.

Added the navy: "It has nothing to do with little men, strangers from heaven, or the atom bomb, It is part of our project Skyhook."

THE AIR FORCE is calling out five Air National Guard (Territorials) groups. Most groups are fighter units. There are about 75 planes to a group.

SIX HUNDRED GUESTS are invited to the official opening tomorrow night of the smart Park-avenue Theatre's atom bombproof shelter, 50ft. below street level. If the sirens go off, cinema patrons can retire behind its 36in. walls to beds, furnished rooms, kitchens, and first aid stations—all air-conditioned.

DOLLAR HARVESTS are being gathered, the Attorney - General suspects, by swindlers who do not move from the safety of the Canadian side of the border. To victims who respond to get-rich-quick lures, smooth-talking salesmen put in trunk telephone calls. They sell stock in non-existent uranium mines for two shillings a share.

MRS. AL JOLSON will be assured of an income of at least £1,190 a month under the will of her late singer husband.

SHOW BUSINESS: Every newspaper in New York except one gives four-star approval to Britain's atom-bomb picture "Seven Days to Noon." Says one of the majority: "Best melodrama of the year." Says the minority of one: "Preposterous and stupid."

WHAT FLEW ACROSS ENGLAND YESTERDAY?

Football Crowds See 'Flying Saucer'

Dec. 3/50 By Sunday Dispatch Reporter

THOUSANDS of people in many parts of Britain, including spectators at football matches, saw what many of them believed to be a flying saucer yesterday.

In each case the phenomenon—a strange white flash which darted across the sky at terrific speed—was seen about 4 p.m.

These reports of the passage of this object through the sky were received by the *Sunday Dispatch* last night:

More than 500 spectators at a Soccer cup match at **Chard**, Somerset, saw a strange white phenomenon dart across the clear sky high above the grandstand at about 3.45. Within a split second of passing it seemed to disperse on the horizon.

Spectators Cried 'Oh'

Spectators in the stand cried "Oh!" as the white, liquid form sped inland from the direction of the English Channel.

Spectators at a Rugby match two fields away saw it.

One, Mr. Arthur H. Jenkins, postmaster of Chard, said: "It was like a diamond flash; its shape was like a big peardrop, with the thin end tapering behind. Suddenly it 'melted' into nothingness."

Other people described it as a "blob of brilliant whiteness" and a "sheet of white hot metal."

Chairman of Chard F.C., Mr. William Taunton, sitting in the stand, said: "It came right over the top of us like a brilliant streak and then seemed to dissolve before our eyes."

Snake-Shape

Miss Myra Scott, who was watching a football match at **Perry Street**, three miles south of Chard, said she saw a "low-flying, silvery star with a tail" shortly before four o'clock.

At **North Petherton**, near Bridgwater, spectators at another match saw an object in the north-west sky shortly before four o'clock.

It was described as "a long snake-shape thing which streaked through the sky at a terrific rate."

Mr. T. Hollinghurst, of North Petherton, said: "It appeared suddenly and went away suddenly, leaving a creamy smoke. There was no noise and there were no planes about."

Channel Explosion

A few minutes later a flash, as though from an explosion, was seen at a great height over the Bristol Channel, 50 miles to the north of Chard.

Reports from places as much as 130 miles apart were received at the Air Ministry.

Portishead (near Bristol) police reported that a white flash was seen between 4.5 and 4.10 p.m. which appeared to be an explosion. It turned pink and disintegrated. The estimated height was 20,000ft.

Weston-super-Mare police reported to the Air Ministry that they saw a similar flash in the Portishead direction at the same time.

Another sighting was reported from as far away as **Durham.**

Airmen Saw It

Pilots of four jet aircraft of the Royal Auxiliary Air Force coming in to land at **Llandaw**, near Cardiff, reported a flash of light at 15,000ft. to the north-east of the airfield.

At a football match at **Easton-in-Gordano**, near Bristol, spectators saw a flash. Mr. M. V. Perrett, of Ham Green, said: "It looked like a rocket coming down from 2,000ft. There was an intense white flash which left a trail of vapour."

Spectators at the match between Shaftesbury and Longfleet St. Mary reported what appeared like a giant rocket. It seemed to fall from the sky.

Bovingdon airport in Hertfordshire, 150 miles east of Llandaw, also reported to the Air Ministry that a brilliant white light was seen a long way to the west at 4.5 p.m. Observers estimated that it was at about 20,000ft. and say that it vanished in a trail of smoke.

Air Ministry said last night: "A thorough check has been made and no aircraft is missing or believed to have blown up in the air.

"It is most unlikely that an unscheduled private flight could have taken place at such a height. We cannot explain the phenomenon.

"No aircraft was flying in the Portishead area."

Game Stopped

At **Towyn**, near Rhyl, North Wales, Rugby players dropped the ball and, with spectators, stared into the sky as a yellow object trailing sparks flashed across it.

It vanished over Tower Hill, Abergele, within ten seconds.

At about 4 o'clock spectators at **Amersham**, Buckinghamshire, football ground saw a brilliant object "like a huge star" flash across the sky, leaving a volume of smoke in its wake.

Among people who saw the object at **Launceston**, Cornwall, were two ex-R.A.F. officers who were watching a Rugby match.

The object, which was circular, gave off a bright bluish-white light.

Footnote: One theory advanced last night by Professor F. A. Paneth (Professor of Chemistry at Durham University and a leading expert on meteorites) was that the object was a meteor. "If pieces of meteorite are found," he said, "it will be only the tenth to have fallen in this country.

"I would like to appeal to anyone in the areas from which it was reported to report at once if they notice a hole in the ground or a damaged tree that was not there yesterday."

Flying Saucers

THE BEST EXPLANATION SO FAR

WHEN the "Sunday Dispatch" published a series of articles about the mystery of the Flying Saucers recently, all the known facts and theories—intelligent and fantastic—were set out for consideration.

The only answer that the *Sunday Dispatch* rejected out of hand was one put forward by some newspapers — that Flying Saucers did not exist at all and that people who said they had seen them were the victims of mass hysteria and delusions.

Today, knowing that many thousands of readers followed the series on Flying Saucers with the keenest interest, the *Sunday Dispatch* publishes in detail a report that throws the clearest light on the mystery so far and provides the most reasonable and intelligent explanation of many Flying Saucers.

It is written by a leading American journalist. His report is based on the researches of Dr. Urner Liddel, chief of the U.S. Navy's nuclear physics branch.

The 'Saucers' Are Balloons—U.S. Research Chief

By RICHARD WILSON

A FLYING SAUCER is the base of a huge plastic balloon, 100 feet in diameter, called a "Skyhook." It is seen travelling at speeds up to 200 miles per hour at heights up to 19 miles.

These balloons are carrying delicate instruments to plumb the secrets of the cosmos, 100,000ft. up, where the atmosphere reaches the vanishing point.

The instruments on the balloons observe and measure the countless explosions of atoms in the atmosphere as they are smashed by cosmic particles hurtling in by the billions from the cold reaches of outer space.

The balloons seek to break the secret of how matter is put together by recording how it is blown apar'

---

completed at Wallsend.
S. Express Jan 23-1951.

The 'flying cigar' puzzles pilot

NEW YORK, Monday.—A "flying cigar" was seen over Sioux City, Iowa, by an airline pilot. He said it was larger than a Superfort with long, straight wings, no engine mountings, no lights, no windows.—Express News Service.

Dr. Urner Liddel, chief of the nuclear physics branch of the Office of Naval Research, is in charge of the Skyhook project.

"When this project first began," he said, "it was kept secret. Now there is no longer any need for secrecy."

Sifted Reports

One of the most convincing factors supporting Dr. Liddel's findings is that Flying Saucers or flying discs were unheard of until the Office of Naval Research experiments in the stratosphere began.

There were some flights in 1947, the first year that strange objects were seen in the skies. Reports of strange objects multiplied in 1948, when Skyhooks were put in the air in large numbers, and continued through 1949.

Reports diminished in 1950 when the number of Skyhook balloon flights was reduced.

Dr. Liddel and his associates arrived at their findings by studying about 2,000 reports of Flying-Saucer observations of every kind and description.

One report of "little men" found in the wreckage of a Flying Saucer near Mexico City turned out to be the unsubstantiated story of a traveller.

There was a solid base of reports from aeroplane pilots, scientific observers, and reliable laymen which could not be brushed aside.

After a thorough investigation, Dr. Liddel said: "There is not a single reliable report of an observation which is not attributable to the cosmic balloons."

No Oxygen

The most tragic report the nuclear physicists had to consider was that of Captain Thomas Mantell.

A circular object, metallic in appearance, was seen over a U.S. Air Force base on January 7, 1948. Three fighter planes, one piloted by Captain Mantell, flew in pursuit.

From their relatively low altitudes, the balloon seemed to be travelling at the rate of 360 miles an hour. Two of the planes turned back at 18,000ft. Captain Mantell kept going.

None of the planes was equipped with reserve oxygen supplies, and thus could not fly long at high altitudes.

Mantell was not heard from again. His plane crashed, and the instruments found in the wreckage indicated it might have risen to 30,000ft.

"Our studies show," said Dr. Liddel, "that Captain Mantell and the other pilots were pursuing a balloon of the Skyhook type."

Little Discs

Several reports have been received of "squadrons" of Flying Saucers. People have seen little discs apparently flying together in the sky.

This is explained by Dr. Liddel as clusters of 20 to 30 balloons, 10 to 15 feet in diameter, which are sometimes used in place of the huge Skyhook.

Under certain conditions, they might be more visible than the single plastic bag, and would certainly be unexplainable by anyone who didn't know their purpose.

After Dr. Liddel had sifted all the reports which appeared to have

Turn to Page FIVE.

'SAUCERS': NEW FACTS

(Continued from Page One.)

some foundation, he used his entree as a Government nuclear physicist to check other Government agencies.

He is satisfied that no other

SKYHOOK AT 77,000ft
pictured through telescope.

research or experimental project has utilised anything even roughly resembling a flying saucer.

"And secondly," he said, "interplanetary travel is not possible at the present time."

The Skyhook's distinct visual similarity to a flying-saucer description was noted. Telescopic photographs brought out the similarity so clearly that Dr. Liddel could offer visual proof of his findings.

Most of the total of 270 flights so far made have been launched at Camp Ripley, near Little Falls, Minnesota, at University Airport, Minneapolis, Minnesota.

Balloons have ascended from Chicago, from Holloman Air Force Base and White Sands, New Mexico, and from aircraft-carriers in both the Caribbean Sea and the Pacific.

Workers at the aeronautical

laboratories advised Dr. Liddel that they were able to trace lost balloons by published reports of flying saucers.

The big bags are engineered to stay up eight hours, but some have actually stayed up more than 30 hours.

Elaborate arrangements are made to trace the balloons, for the data the cosmic physicists want

ON THE GROUND
Skyhook being prepared for research flight.

are recorded on the instruments dangling from them. The instruments are released electronically by parachute at the end of the flight.

SAUCER SEEN IN AFRICA
FILMED FROM AIR

Mombasa, Monday.—Seven passengers and two of the crew in an East African Airways plane flying from Nairobi to Mombasa this morning have signed an affidavit swearing that they saw a flying saucer hovering over Mount Kilimanjaro, the highest mountain in Africa.

Two American passengers took cinecamera pictures of it with a telescopic lens and another photographed it with a miniature camera.

One of the passengers, Captain H. B. Fussell, who studied it through powerful marine binoculars, said that it sausage-shaped, like an airship. It hovered a short while, rose to 40,000 feet, and then moved off at a "terrific speed."
—A.P.

Continental D. Mail Feb. 13th. 1951.

Flying 'saucers' do exist, says scientist
THEY ARE 200 M.P.H. BALLOONS

New York, Monday.—Flying saucers are real—but they are only huge plastic balloons used in cosmic rays studies, according to Dr. Urner Liddel, chief of the Nuclear Physics Branch of the U.S. Office of Naval Research.

Dr. Liddel declares in the American magazine *Look* that, at dusk, the slanting rays of the sun light up the under-side of the balloons, giving them a saucer-like appearance.

The balloons, which carry instruments to record what happens when cosmic rays hit atoms in the earth's atmosphere, can rise to a height of 100,000 feet, and winds sometimes sweep them along at 200 miles an hour.

The balloons, called "skyhooks," were first used in 1947, for gathering information about atoms, and it was then that flying saucer reports began. There were more balloons in the next two years and more saucers were seen. Fewer balloons were sent up in 1950, and fewer saucer reports were made.

'Little men'

Dr. Liddel and his associates studied 2,000 reports of flying saucers, eliminating those "seeming to be the visions of crackpots or psychopaths, or clearly the result of inaccurate vision."

One report of "little men" found inside the wreckage of a saucer near Mexico City turned out to be the unsubstantiated story of a traveller.

"This left a solid base of reports from aeroplane pilots, scientific observers and reliable laymen, which could not be pushed aside."

After a thorough investigation, Dr. Liddel concluded there was not a single reliable report which could not be attributed to the cosmic balloons.

He declares that no other Government research or experimental project has utilised anything roughly resembling a flying saucer.
—Reuter.

"FLYING SAUCERS" ONLY BIG BALLOONS

Times, February 13, 1951

PHYSICIST'S EXPLANATION

NEW YORK, Feb. 12.—Dr. Liddell, chief of the nuclear physics branch of the United States Office of Naval Research, writing in the current issue of the American magazine *Look*, states that "flying saucers" are real, but are only huge plastic balloons used in cosmic ray studies.

He explains that the balloons, which carry instruments to record what happens when cosmic rays hit atoms in the earth's atmosphere, can rise to a height of 100,000ft.—about 19 miles. Winds sometimes sweep them along at 200 miles an hour. At dusk the slanting rays of the sun light up the under side of the balloons, giving them a saucer-like appearance.

The balloons, called "skyhooks," were first used in 1947, and it was then that flying saucer reports began. Dr. Liddell, whose department is said to have examined 2,000 of these reports, adds: "Even seasoned airmen have no way of estimating the size and speed of the object they see. To peg size and speed, the mind must know the nature of the object." The explanation could not be given until now because at first the project was secret.—*Reuter.*

D.E. Feb. 20. 1951.

'Sign please about this saucer

DAR-ES-SALAAM, Monday.—Captain Jack Bicknell and passengers in his East African Airways plane saw a flying saucer five miles up over Mount Kilimanjaro, Tanganyika, today. Bicknell asked the passengers to write a description and sign it.

They said the saucer was silver bullet-shaped, and marked with three vertical black bands. It hovered for more than ten minutes and then climbed out of sight.—Express News Service.

The Most Authentic Flying Saucer Story Of Them All

2/3/51

NINE men and two women who saw a mystery object flying near Mount Kilimanjaro, Tanganyika, last week have signed an affidavit giving the most authentic Flying Saucer report so far. They saw the mystery object clearly for 17 minutes from their plane, and describe it as bullet-shaped and metallic.

They refuse to accept the explanation of Dr. U. Liddel, U.S. research chief, who says Flying Saucers are "Sky-hook" experimental balloons. Here is a detailed account of what they saw.

By Our MOMBASA Reporter

THE object was first seen by Radio Operator Dennis W. Merrifield, 34, in the East African Airways plane Lodestar, en route to Mombasa from Nairobi.

"Have a look at a Flying Saucer," he said to Captain J. Bicknell, 30, an ex-B.O.A.C. pilot.

The object was absolutely motionless 10,000ft. above Kilimanjaro. Merrifield, ex-R.A.F., radioed Nairobi that the object was a "bright gleaming spot."

Nairobi reported that there were no other planes in a wide area and said: "Take more water with it."

Terrific Speed

Captain Bicknell told me: "The morning was clear and cloudless, visibility was good and the weather perfect. I timed the Saucer for 17 minutes while the Lodestar kept to its course. Twice it rose vertically to a final height of 40,000ft., then it moved east towards the coast at a terrific speed.

"There was a large fin-like object attached to the rear, although it wasn't clearly defined. There was no apparent propelling power when the Saucer moved. There were definitely no vapour trails."

Captain Bicknell immediately after landing at Mombasa prepared an affidavit, which Merrifield and his seven men and two women passengers signed.

One passenger, Captain H. B. Fussell, a Newport, Monmouthshire, sports dealer, who had a pair of powerful binoculars, said: "Through the glasses the object appeared bullet-shaped. Its colour was whitish-silver with three vertical black bands down the side.

"For ten minutes it remained stationary, then it suddenly rose vertically by 5,000ft.

Merrifield.

"Again it became stationary, and then a minute later it rose again and moved laterally away at a great speed, probably 400 m.p.h."

Captain Fussell said that Dr. Urner Liddel's balloon theory did not fit what he saw.

"Suppose it was a balloon—how could a balloon both hover motionless and move at 400 m.p.h. in the same weather conditions?" he asked.

"I emphatically reject the theory. The object was definitely metallic."

Immense Size

A radio officer named Overstreet, from the American freighter Robin Mowbray, who was another passenger, said: "I wouldn't swear, but through the binoculars I thought I could identify a row of circular windows."

Charles J. Vernon, also American, and purser on the Robin Mowbray, said: "The object must have been immense, two or three times the size of the largest passenger plane."

Three separate attempts to photograph the object were made from the plane. Captain Fussell snapped it with his miniature camera. Mr. Overstreet shot 30ft. of colour film with a telescopic lens on his cinecamera, and Mr. Vernon also tried to snap it.

Two Flashes

After landing, Captain Fussell developed his film in the presence of a newspaper reporter and a commercial photographer, who certify that the film was not faked or retouched.

Three exposures were blank, but the fourth showed a small black object.

Mr. Vernon's film showed nothing, and Mr. Overstreet's colour-film has not been developed.

During the night after the Saucer was reported, two unexplained flashes lit Mombasa.

Captain Bicknell was born in Exeter and lived in London before joining East African Airways in 1948.

Radio Operator Merrifield's parents live at Ellison-gardens, Southall, Middlesex.

Pilot Made Sketch Of 'Flying Saucer'

FLYING in a cloudless sky over Mount Kilimanjaro, in Tanganyika, Captain Jack Bicknell, pilot of a passenger plane bound for Mombasa, saw through binoculars "a metallic, bullet-shaped object which must have been more than 200ft. long." The "Sunday Dispatch" last week gave a detailed report of this "Flying Saucer" sighting, the most authentic so far recorded.

When he brought the plane down Captain Bicknell drew a sketch of what he had seen.

The diagram above was prepared from Captain Bicknell's sketch and shows the "large object attached to the rear."

One passenger, Captain H. B. Fussell, of Newport, Monmouthshire, also told of the "three vertical black bands down the side."

Captain Bicknell, an ex-BOAC pilot, giving additional details, said the mystery object was stationary when first seen, and remained so for 17 minutes.

"Then it began to move eastwards, rising as it did so. It disappeared at about 40,000ft.," he said.

"We've calculated that in the three minutes of visible movement it covered about 60 miles. That gives a speed of well over 1,600 m.p.h."

Sunday Dispatch, March 4th. 1951

31

FIREBALLS IN SKY PUZZLE U.S. EXPERTS

D.M. 10 NOV 1951

Unusual Meteorites, Says Scientist

From Daily Mail Reporter

NEW YORK, Friday.

SCIENTISTS are puzzled by the unusually large number of meteorites flashing through the night skies over the south-west of the United States in the past few weeks.

Nine fireballs of exceptional size have been seen in the past 11 days, the most remarkable concentration of meteor-like objects in history, according to Dr. Lincoln La Paz, head of the Institute of Meteorics, New Mexico University.

"If this rate continues I shall suspect that it is not natural," he said today.

There are other unusual aspects of these meteorites, according to the doctor. They travel in straight lines when they should follow a curved course.

Frequently they are silent, when meteorites of that size should make a noise. They have a blindingly bright greenish colour, not the usual red. Some have crashed, one near Oklahoma City, where the particles are being collected for study.

Officials at the Nevada atomic testing station state that they have made no experiments other than with the bomb. The Defence Department say they know nothing that could connect the meteorites with rocket experiments.

BALLS OF FIRE

Times, Nov. 10th 1951.

STRANGE APPEARANCES IN SOUTH-WEST U.S.

FROM OUR OWN CORRESPONDENT

NEW YORK, Nov. 9

Balls of fire which might be meteorites but behave differently from the general run of them have given rise to excited speculation in several of the south-western states. Seven of these balls in 11 days have been seen by persons in Arizona, New Mexico, Oklahoma, Texas, Colorado, Utah, and Nevada, flashing through the skies, some of them silent when they should have been making a noise, and all travelling in straight lines instead of in arcs.

Dr. Lincoln La Paz, director of the Institute of Meteoritics at New Mexico University, said that the frequency of their falls was unprecedented: never in history had there been a fall of meteorites one-fifth as great as the present fall. "If the rate should continue," he said, "I would suspect that the phenomenon is not natural."

He said that a fall yesterday was perhaps the oddest of the whole series. Two objects, flying parallel, crashed near Cloverdale, New Mexico, sending up a double mushroom of smoke but making no noise. "Such a case of two meteorites falling together without noise would be hard to duplicate in history," he said.

---

10 NOV. 1951 10 NOV 1951

Flying fireballs

On Mexican border

ALBUQUERQUE, New Mexico, Saturday. — Scientists were to-day trying to track down mysterious "fire-balls" seen flashing across the sky near the Mexican border. Observers said they were momentarily blinded by two "meteors."

The mystery objects have kept up an 11-day "meteor bombardment" of the south-west United States. A Defence Department spokesman in Washington said he knew nothing of any tests in the south-west.—Reuter.

Fireballs Oust Flying Saucers

E.N. 10 NOV 1951

From TOM DOWNES

NEW YORK, Saturday.

FLYING fireballs have ousted flying saucers from the skies and news of the United States. Apart from seven green ones seen over the South West, a pink one has now been observed over New York and Pennsylvania. All apparently have been travelling from the north-east.

Some who have seen them suspected that they were connected with atom bomb tests in Nevada. But experts believe they are meteors, although they have been behaving in a very unmeteoric manner.

Soon after the pink fireball was seen at Scranton, Pennsylvania, a hunter and his son in another part of the same State said they had seen two silvery objects, larger than footballs, drop from an aeroplane and, leaving smoke trails, move off in different directions.

New News About FLYING SAUCERS

WHAT has happened to the Flying Saucers? That is a question many people have asked during the past few months.

It is just over a year since the *Sunday Dispatch* published a series of articles about Flying Saucers and aroused world-wide interest in this riddle which has baffled scientists and observers everywhere.

Because there has not been much in the papers since then about this greatest of all mysteries of the skies some people suppose that no more has been seen or heard of these strange "visitors." But that is not so

The *Sunday Dispatch* has continued to keep a careful record of sightings and today we report—

FLYING SAUCERS ARE STILL BEING SEEN

Reports come from :

Korea.—A Spinning Disc seen by U.S airmen.

India.—Flaming Cigar seen by flying club instructor

New Mexico. — Bright green objects reported by meteorologists.

South Africa. — Hovering light and silvery noiseless object seen in the night sky.

● BECAUSE of these and many other new sightings, United States Air Force experts, once inclined to be sceptical, are now having second thoughts about the whole mystery.

And experts in civil aviation have formed a new organisation called the CIVILIAN SAUCER INVESTIGATION to make their own independent probe.

Flying Saucers are attracting the attention of more and more serious scientists. The *Sunday Dispatch*, which gave you the first authoritative reports now brings you :

THE LATEST FACTS ABOUT THE FLYING SAUCERS

in a remarkable series of articles starting next Sunday

The sales of the *Sunday Dis-*

U.S. THINKS AGAIN ABOUT 'SAUCERS'

Air Force alerted to report on 'unconventional aerial objects'

D.M. 5 APR 1952

Daily Mail Special Correspondent

Washington, Friday.—An admission that some " flying saucer " reports cannot be explained as natural phenomena was made for the first time today by the U.S. Air Force.

Field commands have been alerted to report on " unconventional aerial objects."

A spokesman in Washington read this statement : " Every attempt is being made to investigate sightings reported to the Air Force. In most cases the sightings have proved to be weather balloons and natural phenomena.

" There remain a number of reported sightings that cannot be thus explained, and as long as this is true the Air Force will continue to study the problem.

" The U.S. field commands have been alerted to report unconventional aerial objects in an effort to obtain additional information.

" The public should not interpret these continued efforts to mean that new revelations or that new conclusions have been reached.

Photos wanted

" Detailed reports, and particularly photographs from people who have sighted unusual aerial manifestations, will be welcomed.

The statement followed an article in *Life* magazine saying that the Air Force maintains a constant intelligence investigation into unidentified aerial objects and that " military aircraft are alerted to attempt interception."

As *Life* pointed out, this is a sharp change-over from the former Air Force policy of " official calm " tempered with a good deal of scepticism about reports of strange objects in the sky.

Its own investigations *Life* claims, indicate that solid objects have existed, and may still exist, in the earth's atmosphere that are not made by man at all.

The magazine states that it is " plausible " therefore that they originated beyond the earth, possibly on other planets. It publishes pictures taken over Lubbock, Texas, last August of a series of lights apparently flying in V-shape formation like a flight of geese.

Discs and cylinders

It has been known for some time that these pictures are considered by the Air Force as the most unexplainable phenomena yet observed.

The magazine said out of its " exhaustive inquiries the following propositions seem firmly backed up by the evidence : —

" 1. Discs, cylinders, and similar objects of geometrical form, luminous quality, and solid structure, for several years have been, and may now be, actually present in the atmosphere of the earth.

" 2. Globes of green fire, also of a brightness more intense than the full moon, have frequently passed through the skies.

" 3. These objects cannot be explained by present science as natural phenomena—but solely as artificial devices created and operated by a high intelligence."

Pictures That Have Baffled U.S. Scientists And Air Force

S.D.   6 APR 1952

One of the most baffling of Flying Saucer incidents is that of the "Lubbock Lights." The lights were seen moving in V-formation at Lubbock, Texas, on August 30, 1951, and these photographs were taken by 18-year-old Carl Hart. Despite exhaustive inquiries experts cannot find an explanation for them. The photographs have not previously been published in this country. They were secured yesterday by the *Sunday Dispatch* so that readers can consider them with the new series of articles beginning today in Page 4.

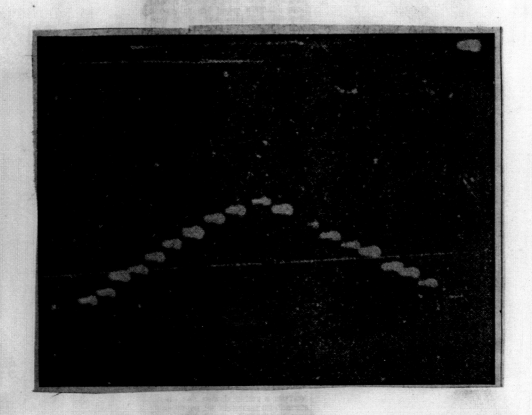

Flying Sauc
Still Fly

Flying Saucers are still being seen in various parts of the world, and experts have started a new probe into this most baffling of all mysteries. This is the first of a series of articles giving the latest facts on these strange "visitors."

S.D.   6 APR 1952

THE crew of an American Superfortress bomber which had been out on a night mission over the North Korean battlefront climbed wearily out of their plane at their home airstrip with a very strange tale on their lips.

This night mission had taken them over Wonsan, important war-scarred harbour on the north-east coast. And it was while the bomber was in the air above this port that a queer thing had been spotted against the background of the dark night sky.

It was a spinning disc-shaped object that suddenly loomed into view, an object orange in colour and with small, bluish flames playing about its revolving rim.

The bomber was travelling at some 200 miles per hour. For five minutes the disc, flying above the bomber, kept pace with it on a parallel course. Then, suddenly, it was gone, vanishing abruptly into the blackness of the night.

Their Report

TWO pairs of eyes had watched it, with fascinated interest, from the bomber. They were the eyes of the central firing controller, alert in his high-up post, and of the equally alert tail-gunner.

They told of what they had seen to incredulous comrades. They told the story in greater detail to Intelligence officers when they landed. The latter, knowing the two men for experienced flyers of

A "BULLET-NOSED, CIGAR-SHAPED OBJECT ABOUT 100FT. LONG WITH A RING OF FLAMES AT THE END" WAS SEEN FOR 20 MINUTES OVER NEW DELHI, INDIA. IT WAS FLYING AT A HEIGHT OF SOME 5,000FT., TRAVELLING SOUNDLESSLY, AND HAD A MAXIMUM SPEED OF ABOUT 2,000 MILES AN HOUR. TWO JET FIGHTERS SOARED INTO THE AIR TO FIND OUT ABOUT THE STRANGE OBJECT. ONE SECOND IT WAS THERE—THE NEXT SECOND IT HAD VANISHED. . . WHERE?

the world-war days, were not incredulous but puzzled. They realised that, with these two men, imagination was not the answer.

They had seen what they had seen from different parts of the plane, and their stories tallied. Both fixed the size of the spinning disc as about 3ft. across, as seen by them. Its actual size, of course, was anybody's guess.

While the Intelligence officers were wrinkling their brows over this queer report, a somewhat similar story was being listened to at the headquarters of another squadron of Superforts some miles away.

This squadron had also been out on a night mission. It had taken the bombers over Sunchon, some 80 miles distant from Wonsan. And it was over Sunchon that, from one of the bombers,

something that looked like a revolving globe had been spotted.

Just as in the other case, this strange globe had come into the view of the central firing controller and the tail-gunner of the plane. It was orange in colour, and had followed the bomber for about a minute. Then it had vanished.

All this happened on the night of January 29 last. Full details of what the four airmen swore they clearly saw have been sent back to the United States Air Force headquarters in Washington and are now being pored over by experts who have probed many hundreds of flying saucer

are inclined to treat these mysteries of the skies as being worthy of rather deep consideration.

In other words, flying saucer stories, however fantastic they may seem to be, have acquired a renewed significance.

The central point, which the experts have found it impossible to dismiss is that no conclusive explanation has yet been found to account for all the strange things that have been and are still being reported from various quarters of the world.

Since, nearly 18 months ago, the *Sunday Dispatch* concluded its striking investigation into the whole subject of flying saucer

They Have Been Seen In Korea, New Mexico, India, South Africa

stories over the past four years or so.

One theory, an obvious one perhaps is that the spinning objects might have been the exhausts of Red night fighters—sometimes there are luminous exhausts from jet engines that glow orange and blue.

But that is not a theory the experts are prepared to accept out of hand.

The results of their probings over the years had, until fairly recently, tended to make them extremely sceptical. Today they

happenings up to that time there have been recorded nearly 20 outstanding instances of queer and inexplicable objects having been seen hurtling across the skies.

The areas from which these reports have been charted have ranged from South Africa to India, from Bangkok to the United States, from Switzerland to British Columbia.

They combine to form a new dossier of strange happenings for which no satisfactory explanation has up to now been evolved and which, on the other hand, cannot fail to open up highly sensational avenues of speculation.

Many Seen

THE objects seen in the sky over this new period have included pale green discs over Switzerland and France last November, green saucers between Rangoon and Bangkok at the same time, a cigar-shaped object seen over New Delhi just over a year ago, and a whole series of plain "flying saucers" seen at widely separated points at different times.

The story of what has been seen over New Delhi is one of the most astonishing flying saucer stories of the past 12 months.

That story begins on the morning of March 15 last year. It was 10.20 by Indian Standard Time when thousands of dwellers in the Indian capital were startled by the sight of a strange object high in the sky which seemed to be circling the city.

Among those who found their attention riveted on this sight was Mr. George Franklin Floate, the chief engineer of the Delhi Flying Club. With several members of the club he watched the evolutions of the object with fascinated interest.

There was plenty of opportunity for steady observation, for the object was over the capital for a full 20 minutes.

Just Vanished

MR. FLOATE'S careful description of it is that it was a "bullet-nosed, cigar-shaped object about 100ft. long, with a ring of flames at the end." It was followed by a "thick white streak," and reflected the bright rays of the sun, confirming the watchers' impression that the structure of the object was made of some metal.

It was flying at a height of some 5,000ft., travelled soundlessly, and had a maximum speed of about 2,000 miles an hour.

To try to find out more about this strange object it was decided to send up two jet fighters belonging to the Indian Air Force. But the object smartly coun-

36

cers Are ying

tered this manœuvre. As the fighters soared into the air it swiftly gained altitude until it reached a height of about 20,000ft. Then it vanished. One moment it was there, the next it had gone. The fighters returned to their base, beaten.

That night the object appeared again over Allahabad, 400 miles away. It was seen by Mr. Y. R. Bhandarkar, instructor of the local flying club.

Exactly 14 days later the object made another appearance. It was sighted over Willingdon Aerodrome, the headquarters of the Delhi Flying Club. Mr. Floate was again one of those who watched it.

As before, it was travelling at a height of about 5,000ft., its speed this time being some 550 m.p.h. It was again in sight for a space of about 20 minutes. Then suddenly it climbed "at a tremendous speed and at an angle of about 80 degrees," and vanished, leaving a "whitish swirly cloud trail" that remained visible for 90 minutes.

What Was It?

MR. FLOATE'S view is that, exactly as on the previous occasion, it was the presence of some Indian Air Force planes in the sky that dictated the object's escape.

Twice more has Mr. Floate seen this unexplained sky ship, once being on a night last November, the other occasion being a night last December. Both times the craft was observed over the headquarters of the Delhi Flying Club. In the darkness of the night the object's tail appeared to be fluorescent.

In Mr. Floate's view there was every indication that the object, whatever it was, was manned. On all four occasions of his observation it came in from the north, turned eastwards, and then just vanished.

What was it? They are still discussing that riddle throughout New Delhi and wider afield. So far there is no sign of the answer. Maybe the Defence Minister holds it. Maybe not.

Now let us switch to the south-western area of the United States, where a fresh mystery of the skies has set thousands of tongues wagging and sharply revived flying-saucer speculation. And, much more to the point, is setting a riddle that is puzzling serious scientific brains.

It happened last autumn, when, over a period of 13 days, a series of eight bright-green objects which have been roughly described as "fireballs" were seen streaking across the skies of New Mexico, Texas and Oklahoma.

The first obvious explanation is that what had been seen was a shower of meteors. But the carefully gathered facts about this strange display have brought out a number of points which make the ready acceptance of this explanation difficult.

First, the number of fireballs seen is very baffling. Dr. Lincoln La Paz who is head of the Institute of Meteoritics at the University of New Mexico and who has been making a special study of the occurrences, has pointed out that meteors big enough to penetrate the lower atmosphere of the earth do not as a rule occur in showers, and that what are known as meteor showers are caused by very small particles which burn out quickly while they are still far above the earth. Then there is the colour.

Green meteors, to say the lea are not what the expert wou expect.

There is, too, the fact th these objects were complete silent as they sped through t air, whereas the passage meteors would be quite noisy they approached the earth.

Finally, though some of the objects seem to have hit t earth's surface with a flash br liant even in broad dayligl search parties sent out to recov fragments have met with cor plete lack of success.

Dr. La Paz has gathered a gre deal of information about th series of sky mysteries. After si ing it he has given the Sund Dispatch this signed conclusior

"Either the 'green fireball are an unconventional type meteor, unusual as regards colot extreme brightness, with absen of noise, frequency of occurren and other characteristics, or th

---

---

are guided missiles—our own o someone else's."

What link, if any, have thes weird fireballs with the spinnin discs observed by experienced ai men thousands of miles away i Korea? Or with the "flamin cigars" of New Delhi?

The riddle is there, real and no imaginary. And riddles are no solved by just ignoring them.

Which is why the United Statei Air Force, which has probec hundreds of flying-saucer storiei and dismissed them, has now had second thoughts and turned it: technical and scientific experts or to a fresh investigation of some thing that is baffling and in triguing the whole world.

NEXT WEEK

Do they come really from Outer Space?

Amazing theory of famous rocket scientist.

THE crew of an American Superfortress bomber which had been out on a night mission over the North Korean battlefront climbed wearily out of their plane at their home airstrip with a very strange tale on their lips.

This night mission had taken them over Wonsan, important war-scarred harbour on the north-east coast. And it was while the bomber was in the air above this port that a queer thing had been spotted against the background of the dark night sky.

It was a spinning disc-shaped object that suddenly loomed into view, an object orange in colour and with small, bluish flames playing about its revolving rim.

The bomber was travelling at some 200 miles per hour. For five minutes the disc, flying above the bomber, kept pace with it on a parallel course. Then, suddenly, it was gone, vanishing abruptly into the blackness of the night.

Two pairs of eyes had watched it, with fascinated interest, from the bomber. They were the eyes of the fire-control man, alert in his high-up post, and of the equally alert tail-gunner.

They told of what they had seen to incredulous comrades. They told the story in greater detail to Intelligence officers when they landed. The latter, knowing the two men for experienced flyers of the world-war days, were not incredulous but puzzled. They realised that, with these two men, imagination was not the answer.

They had seen what they had seen from different parts of the plane, and their stories tallied. Both fixed the size of the spinning disc as about three feet across, as seen by them. Its actual size, of course, was anybody's guess.

While the Intelligence officers were wrinkling their brows over this queer report, a somewhat similar story was being listened to at the headquarters of another squadron of Superforts some miles away.

This squadron had also been out on a night mission. It had taken the bombers over Sunchon, some 80 miles distant from Wonsan. And it was over Sunchon that, from one of the bombers, something that looked like a revolving globe had been spotted.

Just as in the other case, this strange globe had come into the view of the air control man and the tail-gunner of the plane. It was orange in colour, and had followed the bomber for about a minute. Then it had vanished.

All this happened on the night of January 29 last. Full details of what the four airmen swore they clearly saw have been sent back to the United States Air Force headquarters in Washington and are now being pored over by experts who have probed many hundreds of flying saucer stories over the past four years or so.

One theory, an obvious one perhaps, is that the spinning objects might have been the exhausts of Red night fighters—sometimes there are luminous exhausts from jet engines that glow orange and blue.

But that is not a theory the experts are prepared to accept out of hand.

The results of their probings over the years had, until fairly recently, tended to make them extremely sceptical. Today they are inclined to erat these mysteries of the skies as being worthy of rather deep consideration.

In other words flying saucer stories, however fantastic they may see into be, having acquired a renewed significance.

The central point, which the experts have found it impossible to dismiss, is that no conclusive explanation has yet been found to account for all the strange things that have been, and are still being reported from various quarters of the world.

Since, nearly 18 months ago, the *Sunday Dispatch* concluded its striking investigation into the whole subject of flying saucer happenings up to that time, there have been recorded nearly 20 outstanding instances of queer and inexplicable objects having been seen hurtling across the skies.

The areas from which these reports have been charted have ranged from South Africa to India, from Bangkok to the United States, from Switzerland to British Columbia.

They combine to form a new dossier of strange happenings for which no satisfactory explanation has up to now been evolved and which, on the other hand, cannot fail to open up highly sensational avenues of speculation.

The objects seen in the sky over this new period have included pale green discs over Switzerland and France last November, green saucers between Rangoon and Bangkok at the same time, a cigar-shaped object seen over New Delhi just over a year ago and a whole series of plain "flying saucers" seen at widely separated points at different times.

The story of what has been seen over New Delhi is one of the most astonishing flying saucer stories of the past 12 months.

That story begins on the morning of March 15 last year. It was 10.20 by Indian Standard Time when thousands of dwellers in the Indian capital were startled by the sight of a strange object high in the sky which seemed to be encircling the city.

Among those who found their attention rivetted on this sight was Mr. George Franklin Floate, the chief engineer of the Delhi Flying Club. With several members of the club he watched the evolutions of the object with fascinated interest.

There was plenty of opportunity for steady observation, for the object was over the capital for a full 20 minutes.

Mr. Floate's careful description of it was that it was a "bullet-osed cigar-shaped object about 100ft. long, with a ring of flames at the end." It was followed by a "thick white streak," and reflected the bright rays of the sun, confirming the watchers' impression that the structure of the object was made of some metal.

It was flying at a height of some 5,000ft., travelled soundlessly, and had a maximum speed of about 2,000 miles an hour.

To try and find out more about this strange object it was decided to send up two jet fighters belonging to the Indian Air Force. But the object smartly encountered this manœuvre. As the fighters soared into the air it swiftly gained altitude until it reached a height of about 20,000ft. Then it vanished. One moment it was there, the next it had gone. The fighters returned to their base, beaten.

That night the object appeared again over Allahabad, 400 miles away. It was seen by Mr. Y. R. Blandarker, instructor of the local flying club.

Two days later there were questions in the Indian Parliament about these odd happenings. Sirdar Baldev Singh, the Defence Minister, was non-committal. All he would say that there had been a flight of a "projectile. Beyond that bald statement there was no information he could or would give.

SD SAUCER TWO

"It is more than wishful thinking completely to rule out the possibility—and in saying this I speak with some knowledge gained from experience of Russian scientific and technical abilities—but I do not myself believe that the so-called 'saucers' are of Soviet origin.

"Always assuming that such unexplained aerial objects are really in existence, the logical conclusion is that they are of extra-terrestrial origin.

"In view of the extremely long distances to neighbours of our sun in galaxy, it is more logical to assume that they originate from one of the planets of our solar system.

"Mars is, according to present knowledge, the most feasible source. It offers to its intelligent inhabitants clear skies for astronomical observation, a decent climate, and favourable low gravitational force.

"With our moon as a space station such a solar system neighbour may have established astronautical flight centuries ago, appearing more frequently in our visible range only since developing a lunar-earth 'ferry system.'"

There is a top-expert view that can by no means be brushed aside. It has the weight of a life-time study of space and the technical possibilities of conquering it.

To scoff at such a theory as Dr. Riedel advances is easy—so long as one ignores both his highly specialised knowledge and the logic with which he underpins his conclusions.

And he does not stand alone in advancing the theory that the saucers are not of earthly origin. Felix W. A. Knoll, who is consulting engineer for Northrop Aircraft, also believes it, for the reasons that—

No human being could withstand the terrific acceleration which has been repeatedly reported, and the astounding manoeuvres the strange craft have performed.

The skin temperature of the craft must, in a very short time, reach heights which would cause all materials at present known to man, including heat, resistant ceramics, to melt and gasify.

The propulsion systems of the craft leave no vapour trails at high altitudes, as is the case with all internal-combustion engines and all types of jet propulsion.

Air friction at low altitude and during the high speeds reported would burn up man-made aircraft or flying missiles.

Both Riedel and Knoll are members of a civilian body known as Civilian Saucer Investigation, which, in view of the continuance of flying-saucer sightings, has lately been formed in Los Angeles.

This organisation has been brought into being by some of the aerodynamic experts who work for the great aircraft manufacturers of Southern California.

They are responsible men, and with all they know about air travel they have found the problems posed by the stream of saucer sightings from different parts of the world utterly baffling.

Purpose of the organisation, therefore, is to gather reports of authentic sightings from people throughout the United States and the rest of the world, and to attempt a scientific analysis of all the data.

The organisation has a box—No. 1971—at Los Angeles Post Office, and to this address there have in a short while poured hundreds of reports not merely from the United States but from South America and other foreign areas.

These reports have been distributed to committees set up within the group and are now being weighed up by men possessing the proper scientific attainments.

What the organisation emphasises to saucer-spotters is that speed, approximate height, and time of day are all important points to be noted and passed on to them.

What the spotter should do, it is urged, is to point a finger at the object in flight as one simple means of determining relative height from the horizon and such matters as the object's speed and rate of climb.

It will be seen, then, that from being a matter of widespread simple scepticism the world-wide riddle of the flying saucer has now become a subject for serious study by serious and highly-qualified men.

S.D. 13 APR 1952

SD — SET AND HOLD — FLYING SAUCERS — — ARTICLE TWO —

ALL types of people have, during the past five years, seen speeding across the skies the strange objects of varying kinds that are now broadly dubbed flying saucers.

They have included housewives, policemen, newsboys, business men, typists, airmen, farmers—men and women drawn from varying walks of life and of varying ages.

They have told of what their own eyes have seen. No more and no less. Most of them, ordinary people, have no specialised knowledge of aerial matters, no special interest, indeed, in aerial matters at all. To them something streaking across the sky is just that. They have seen it, marvelled about it, and naturally described in plain language what they have seen to their relatives and friends.

It is, however, a very striking fact that in addition to these ordinary men and women quite a lot of men with considerable technical background have put flying - saucer experiences on record.

Some of them are flying men who have ranged the skies in war and peace, men who are well aware that the effects of light and cloud can play strange tricks.

These technical men, whose minds are naturally precise and analytical, have been and still are utterly puzzled by what they know they have seen.

They have probed and mulled over every conceivable theory that can be dug up to give a perfectly normal and natural explanation for these uncanny sky mysteries.

Today they are as baffled as ever, having failed to find any real four-square answer.

They, equally with the laymen, cannot help feeling that there is something extremely odd going on.

One expert who makes no bones at all about expressing his considered view that the flying saucers or whatever one cares to call them might well have Mars as their starting point is German rocket scientist Dr. Walther Riedal.

He has been studying this sort of thing for years. During the last war he was the man in charge of research and development at the centre at Peenemunde where the V2 rockets that hit England were brought into being. He now works in Southern California for North American Aviation, Inc., makers of the Sabre Jet plane.

Travel between the planets is peculiarly his subject. Years ago he expressed the view that it is certain to come. And for years he has gathered and kept careful records of flying-saucer sightings from all over the world.

He has brought all his expert knowledge to a close study of these happenings. Here, in a special *Sunday Dispatch* interview, are his conclusions:

"A careful study of all available reports of unexplainable aerial objects has made it possible to weed out approximately 70 per cent. as being based on optical illusion, wrong interpretation of known objects, hysteria suggestion, wilfulness, and plain hoax.

"My interest is concentrated on the remaining 30 per cent. of reports by reliable, well-trained observers.

"That amounts to some 400 observations, out of a total of more than 1,200 evaluated sightings.

"On the assumption that these 400 are proved, the existence of a family of so far unexplainable aerial objects of high speed, extreme ease of manoeuvrability in all space conditions, very intelligent behaviour, and perfect reliability cannot be denied.

"Human pilots of such vessels would not withstand the acceleration imposed by certain manoeuvres that have been observed. Flight velocity of several thousand miles an hour in the denser lower part of the atmosphere would give the flying object a skin temperature to withstand which hitherto unknown materials, and still undeveloped refrigeration systems for both skin and cabin would be required.

"Remote control from such long distances that never a slavemaster has been sighted would also necessitate technique of a yet unknown perfection.

"And flying in close formation while performing evasive manoeuvres would require at the control panel complete knowledge of the position of the vessel in relation to its neighbours in the formation, of ground obstructions, and of piloted aircraft.

"The origin of such aerial objects is of vital interest for all of us. By far the best solution would be that they carry American insignia and that some of their components are catalogue items from American vendors. Their appearance over United States territory would then be understandable.

"But their sometimes very curious behaviour versus American aeroplanes could only then be explained by lack of discipline among the crew of such a top-secret vessel. And the absolute lack of reports of launching, landing or crash accidents would be difficult to explain. In fact neither is within the scope of probability.

"Furthermore the erratic appearance of such secretly developed flying objects over various European countries and elsewhere could not be explained at all.

"The same logic should be applied to a study of the possibility of such aerial objects originating in the laboratories of our most potent enemies.

"If Russia possessed such a perfect carrier all the odds are that Stalin and his followers would have shown a still more belligerent attitude towards the West.

The New Riddle Of The Universe

Rocket Expert Says—

FLYING SAUCERS

Could Come From Mars

S.D. 13 APR 1952

ALL types of people have, during the past five years, seen speeding across the skies the strange objects of varying kinds that are now broadly dubbed flying saucers.

They have included housewives, policemen, newsboys business men, typists airmen, farmers—men and women drawn from varying walks of life and of varying ages.

They have told of what their own eyes have seen. No more and no less. Most of them, ordinary people, have no specialised knowledge of aerial matters, no special interest, indeed, in aerial matters at all. To them something streaking across the sky is just that. They have seen it, marvelled about it, and naturally described in plain language what they have seen to their relatives and friends.

It is, however, a very striking fact that in addition to these ordinary men and women quite a lot of men with considerable technical background have put flying - saucer experiences on record.

Utterly Puzzled

SOME of them are flying men who have ranged the skies in war and peace, men who are well aware that the effects of light and cloud can play strange tricks.

These technical men, whose minds are naturally precise and analytical have been and still are utterly puzzled by what they *know* they have seen.

They have probed and mulled over every conceivable theory that can be dug up to give a perfectly normal and natural explanation for these uncanny sky mysteries.

Today they are as baffled as ever, having failed to find any real four-square answer.

They, equally with the laymen, cannot help feeling that there is something extremely odd going on.

One expert who makes no

illusion, wrong interpretation of known objects, hysteria suggestion, wilfulness and plain hoax.

"My interest is concentrated on the remaining 30 per cent. of reports by reliable, well-trained observers.

"That amounts to some 400 observations, out of a total of more than 1,200 evaluated sightings.

"On the assumption that these 400 are proved the existence of a family of so far unexplainable aerial objects of high speed, extreme ease of manœuvrability in all space conditions very intelligent behaviour, and perfect reliability cannot be denied.

Terrific Speed

"HUMAN pilots of such vessels would not withstand the acceleration imposed by certain manœuvres that have been observed. Flight velocity of several thousand miles an hour in the denser lower part of the atmosphere would give the flying object a skin temperature to withstand which hitherto unknown materials and still undeveloped refrigeration systems for both skin and cabin would be required.

"Remote control from such long distances that never a slave-master [machine that controls robots] has been sighted would also necessitate technique of a yet unknown perfection.

"And flying in close formation while performing evasive manœuvres would require at the control panel complete knowledge of the position of the vessel in relation to its neighbours in the formation of ground obstructions, and of piloted aircraft.

"The origin of such aerial objects is of vital interest for all of us. By far the best solution would be that they carry American insignia and that some of their components are catalogue items from American vendors. Their appearance over United States territory would then be understandable.

really in existence, the logical conclusion is that they are of extra-terrestrial origin.

"In view of the extremely long distances to neighbours of our sun in galaxy it is more logical to assume that they originate from one of the planets of our solar system.

'Ferry System'

"MARS is, according to present knowledge, the most feasible source. It offers to its intelligent inhabitants clear skies for astronomical observation, a decent climate, and favourable low gravitational force.

"With our moon as a space station such a solar system neighbour may have established astronautical flight centuries ago, appearing more frequently in our visible range only since developing a lunar-earth 'ferry system.'"

There is a top-expert view that can by no means be brushed aside. It has the weight of a life-time study of space and the technical possibilities of conquering it.

To scoff at such a theory as Dr. Riedal advances is easy—so long as one ignores both his highly specialised knowledge and the logic with which he underpins his conclusions.

And he does not stand alone

in advancing the theory that the saucers are not of earthly origin. Felix W. A. Knoll who is consulting engineer for Northrop Aircraft, also believes it, for the reasons that—

No human being could withstand the terrific acceleration which has been repeatedly reported, and the astounding manœuvres the strange craft have performed.

The skin temperature of the craft must, in a very short time, reach heights which would cause all materials at present known to man, including heat-resistant ceramics, to melt and gasify.

The propulsion systems of the craft leave no vapour trails at high altitudes, as is the case with all internal-combustion engines and all types of jet propulsion.

Air friction at low altitude and during the high speeds reported would burn up man-made aircraft or flying missiles.

Both Riedal and Knoll are members of a civilian body known as the Civilian Saucer Investigation, which has recently been set up by aeronautical experts to make a further probe of the mystery.

━━ NEXT WEEK ━━

Mysteries In The Skies Of Britain,

Alistair Cooke Talks Of Flying Saucers

SD 20 APR 1952

By Sunday Dispatch Reporter

FLYING SAUCERS were mentioned by Alistair Cooke in his Letter from America broadcast by the B.B.C. on Friday. Talking of the early days of New York when it was New Amsterdam, he said :

"What a time the 17th century must have been to live in. Adventurers, scoundrels, and buccaneers charted oceans and continents that had been talked about as myths, much as **we talk about Plutus and Mars and wonder if the flying saucers are really artificially controlled and come from another planet.**

"**By the way,**" added Mr. Cooke, "**the most scientific judgment today is that they most likely do.**"

More Sightings

Flying saucers were reported over Newfoundland's west coast by a resident who said he saw a strange-looking object overhead. —*Reuter.*

People on Fyan Island, off the coast of Denmark, say they have seen "flying saucers" shooting out sparks, according to the Copenhagen *Aftenbladet.*—*B.U.P.*

See "Flying Saucers," Page FOUR.

Mysteries In Skies Of Britain

S.D. 20 APR 1952

ONE of the strangest aspects of the great flying saucer riddle is the fact that sightings have not been confined to any particular country or, indeed, hemisphere. They are worldwide. And they are still going on.

A lot of records have been gathered in the United States, but sky mysteries just as baffling have been observed in, for instance South Africa and Sweden, and in this country.

Reports of what has been seen in the skies over Britain are of great interest. A great many, from responsible men and women in different parts of the country, have reached the *Sunday Dispatch*. Here is a selection from a volume of plain, straightforward accounts that has been received:

⊙ ⊙

SUFFOLK: "At lunch-time one Thursday in January 1951, I was looking out of the window of my lodgings in Cauldwell-avenue, Ipswich, where I was then living, when my attention was attracted to two silver objects in the sky.

"They looked for all the world like two silver shillings, one following the other, and they did not appear to be going exceptionally fast. I had them in full view for half a minute before they disappeared out of sight over the trees.

"They seemed to be flying very high and they were travelling in a perfectly straight line. They were completely silent and were travelling in a south-westerly direction."

—*Mrs. Irene Stubbings, 71, of Upland-road, Ipswich, well-known Suffolk botanist and ornithologist.*

⊙ ⊙

HAMPSHIRE: "Between two and three in the morning of January 28 or 29, this year, I was awakened by a bright light in my bedroom. I knew it could not be moonlight because the moon does not shine on that side of the house. So I got out of bed to see what it was.

"Hanging in the sky was an object shaped like a pear, with the big end downwards. It was glowing with a red firelight glow, and appeared to be hovering.

"I went into the next room and awakened my son, who is 14, and together we watched it for a quarter of an hour, until it gradually faded away.

"It was a very clear night and the object seemed a fairly good distance away."

—*Mrs. Gladys Keevil, 54, of Scotts Hill-lane, Purewell, Christchurch, Hants.*

⊙ ⊙

LONDON: "My parents and I were all in the garden of our home at Blackheath one bright sunny Sunday morning last September when our attention was drawn to a curious object in the sky.

"It appeared to be a solid object, flying very high, travelling slowly. It was oblong, roughly the shape of a Rugby ball, and to us, even at that height, it appeared to be two-thirds the size of a Rugby ball. It shone silvery white, and was clear and distinct.

"It was in full sight for two or three minutes, and immediately it disappeared from our view to the south another approached along the same route. In all we watched quite 20 of these mysterious objects, all following the same route. They came from the north-east, passed over Blackheath and when some distance away they swung sharply southwards and disappeared.

"They were nothing like any aeroplane or balloon I have ever seen. Their progress appeared slow to us, but that was undoubtedly due to the great height at which they were flying. They were completely silent. They looked like small oblong airships, but with nothing suspended beneath them."

—*Mrs. Monica Manders, 30, of Shooters Hill-road, Blackheath, S.E.3.*

⊙ ⊙

CAMBRIDGESHIRE: "At about 10.40 p.m. on Thursday, February 28, 1952, I was walking through the college towards my room. As I drew level with 'C' staircase, walking north I saw a bright round object in the sky travelling north-east. It was evenly bright over a perfectly round surface, which was presented to me broadside on, except that at the bottom there was a particularly bright spot of light which made the rest of it look rather like the halo round a candle flame.

"I watched it for perhaps 15 seconds until it went out of sight, and during this time it made no noise whatever. I could not tell what size or at what height it was."

—*Keith B. Wedmore, 19, undergraduate, Jesus College, Cambridge, law and history student.*

⊙ ⊙

DEVONSHIRE: "At 11 p.m. on October 30, 1950, I was walking down my garden path when suddenly I became conscious of a light almost overhead.

"I saw a funnel-shaped stream of flame chiefly white, travelling funnel-end first and descending from a great height as if debris from a falling aircraft.

"Then after being momentarily obscured by the roof of my house, it appeared to change to the horizontal, apparently at not more than 2,000 feet. The flame suddenly diminished and ahead of it I saw two large silver-blue discs, one distinctly above and slightly ahead of the other. They were climbing again, lit up by the moon or their own radiance.

"They were travelling at about the same speed, but there was no sound and they kept together so well that there must have been some guiding influence.

"These were discs not globes, and in size could not have been less than 50 feet across. They disappeared over Goodrington and Brixham. The experience lasted about 15 seconds.

"I am more inclined to think these discs came from another planet than to accept any glib explanation of secret weapons. No solution of human control so far presented has satisfied me."

—*A. W. Bearne, 57, of Southfield avenue, Preston, Paignton, well-known Devon auctioneer and estate agent.*

⊙ ⊙

KENT: "I was watching a beautiful sunset one evening in the third week of January this year—I cannot fix the exact date—when I suddenly realised that something was moving across the sky at a great height from north to south.

"It appeared to be oblong in shape and to my eyes was about 2ft. long and 6in. deep. Its colour was golden—it looked like a rod of brilliant gold—and the nose of the object appeared to have flame shooting from it as it ploughed through the sky.

"When it was over Canterbury I lost sight of it, but a couple of minutes later it reappeared, travelling this time from south to north. I watched it until it disappeared from sight behind the woods in the direction of Whitstable. All the time it maintained an even speed which, although not conveying that impression, must have been terrific to cover the distance in the time.

"As an ex-WRAF officer I am familiar with many types of plane, and aircraft are over here all day long. From my experience I can state definitely the object was not a plane. I came to the conclusion that this was something that did not belong to this world."

—*Miss Vera Matthews, of Brambles Farm, Sturry, near Canterbury.*

There, set down in their own words, are six plain statements of what people living in different parts of the country assert they have seen in the English skies. What is the answer?

Maybe one day the riddle that is baffling ordinary people everywhere will be plainly and satisfactorily answered.

FLYING SAUCERS

wear

BELFAST SEES 'FLYING SAUCERS'

GREEN objects seen in the sky giving off brilliant lights have set Belfast talking about flying saucers.

While playing tennis at Dunmurry John Sherrard, 19, saw a green object at a very great height at 8.33 p.m. last Thursday.

The objects were seen by other people in Belfast, many of whom have read about flying saucers in the *Sunday Dispatch*.

'Saucer' Over North Africa

People in the streets at Bouira, Algeria, said yesterday they saw a flying saucer.—A.P.

---

to reserve would be considered.

'SAUCER' OVER SINGAPORE

Hundreds of people claim to have seen a "flying saucer" over Singapore to-day — the first "saucer" report from the city. Some said it was cigar-shaped with a fiery tail. It was flying north at a great height.—B.U.P.

Flying Saucer Is Seen Over Sydney

A CIGAR-SHAPED flying saucer "lit up like a liner at sea" was seen moving soundlessly across the sky over Sydney, Australia, yesterday. It was also seen by people at Parkes, a town 180 miles away.

One of those who watched the "saucer," Mr. Reg Edwards, of Haberfield, a Sydney suburb, said he was with three workmates at the time. The "thing," he said, had exhausts at the back like jets. —*Reuter.*

FLYING CIGARS

SYDNEY, Sunday.—Thirteen people reported seeing cigar-shaped "flying saucers" over the New South Wales coast this week-end.— B.U.P.

"FLYING SAUCERS"

An Astronomer Explains Reports

CANBERRA, May 5.

A meteor shower was the cause of recent reports of "flying saucers" over Australia, according to Dr Richard Woolley, the Commonwealth astronomer. Reports of objects variously described as "brightly lit, cigar-shaped," "a dead white disc," and "a tremendous rocket scattering stars behind it" zooming across the sky have appeared in the Australian press during the last few days.

Dr Woolley said to-day his chief assistant, Dr A. R. Hogg, was looking through the telescope of the Australian observatory on Mount Stromlo early yesterday when he saw a bright meteor which left a persistent trail. It was one of a shower of meteors. "This type of meteor is rare and is reported usually only every few years. It was clearly visible to the naked eye as a bright light moving at high speed. Most meteors disappear in a few seconds. This one lasted ten minutes," Dr Woolley said.

Such a meteor shower could extend over several days, he added.—Reuter.

FIVE PHOTOGRAPHS OF FLYING SAUCERS Taken in Brazil

RIO DE JANEIRO, May 9.

Photographs of flying saucers which were taken here yesterday are to be sent to the General Staff of the United States Air Force in Washington for examination. Press photographers took the photographs when the objects appeared at a low altitude on the outskirts of Rio de Janeiro. Five pictures were published in the press to-day.

The photographs were also handed to the American military attaché here. He said: "I have no doubts regarding the authenticity of the photographs. They are the finest I have seen and show a neatness and richness of detail which would be difficult to surpass."—Reuter.

BLUE BUBBLE WITH 'HALO' BAFFLED THEM

By Sunday Dispatch Reporter

PEOPLE living on and around the Malvern Hills, and scientists at a Government research establishment, are wondering what strange object sped across the clear sky at about 1.30 a.m. on Friday.

It was not any known heavenly body. Nor was it anything known to British aeronautical experts.

But a bluish-green phosphorescent bubble-like sphere, roughly 20ft. in diameter and encircled with a misty green halo, swept across the night sky at tremendous speed and was lost to view behind the hills.

Two scientists saw it. So did an ex-R.A.F. officer who is now an author and playwright. All three are convinced that it was not a ground reflection, a known aircraft, or a meteor.

It Flew Past At 600 m p h

The scientists were standing on the Malvern Hills. The moon was full and what little cloud there was did not obscure more than a small area of the sky. One of them told me:

"Suddenly, about 30 degrees to our left, there appeared a circular object consisting of an inner circle about seven yards in diameter, with a halo about ten yards in diameter, both emitting a weird green phosphorescent glow.

"It was travelling in a south-easterly direction at a speed which we estimated at about 600 m.p.h. and just above cloud height—2,500 feet. It was one mile east of the Malvern Hills, moving parallel to the earth's surface, and continued in sight until it reached a point 30 degrees to our right, and vanished.

"There was no ground light of any kind, there was no aircraft, and no noise.

"Its movements suggested some controlling force. It was not a flare or distress signal, and it did not fizzle out."

At the same time Mr. Austin Stone, an ex-R.A.F. officer and now playwright and author, was returning to his home at Upper Chase-road, Malvern, after attending a performance of his play "Mystery in Pimlico" at the Birmingham B.B.C. studio.

'Very Fast'

His wife was with him.

As he neared Malvern he saw a spherical glow in the sky.

"It seemed to be like a gigantic blue bubble travelling very fast indeed," he told me. "It took only five seconds to clear my line of vision."

Other people saw the strange, unearthly object. But no one can hazard a guess what it was.

Villagers See Spinning White Flash

12 MAY 1952

PARIS, Sunday.

VILLAGERS north of Bordeaux report seeing a spinning, white sphere—similar in some ways to the object reported yesterday in the Malvern Hills area of Britain.

Watchers said the object was travelling southward at a high altitude spinning like a top. Then, they said, it turned east and climbed to a "brilliant point." Both objects then disappeared in the sky. "It was as though the 'brilliant point' was a mother-ship," said one observer.—B.U.P.

NEW YORK, Sunday.—People in S e a t t l e, Washington, were awakened early today by a giant meteor which swished over the city from the Pacific and lit up the sky like daylight.—D.M. Reporter.

SCIENTISTS NOT TO BLAME?

12 MAY 1952 SEATTLE, May 11.

A violent explosion 2,000 feet in the air awoke people in Seattle early to-day. The flash was seen for 75 miles around. It was believed that a large meteor had exploded.—Associated Press.

World news in brief
BIG BANG
12 MAY 1952
WAS A METEOR

SEATTLE, Washington State, Sunday.—People here were thrown out of bed when their houses were rocked by the terrific explosion of an object in the sky which bathed the countryside in a pale, bluish light.

It is believed to have been a meteor. The explosion broke it into about eight pieces, producing showers of sparks and balls of fire which fell to the ground.

SEOUL.—Flame-throwing tanks yesterday lined up outside the camp where General Dodd, former camp co...

METEOR EXPLOSION OVER SEATTLE

12 MAY 1952

FLASH AND A ROAR
FROM OUR OWN CORRESPONDENT
NEW YORK, MAY 11

Thousands of persons in Seattle were given a fright this morning when several hours before daylight a meteor exploded over the north-west part of the city, sending out a great flash and roar. It broke into several large pieces—some observers said four and others 10—but no fragments could be found.

The pilot of an airliner who was flying at 8,000ft. said the burst seemed to occur slightly below that altitude. A ball of fire was travelling from south-west towards north-east. A policeman said the flash had a "blue-white magnesium colour" and it "lit up the sky like chain lightning."

---

14 MAY 1952
MEN FROM MARS

'Saucers' May be Space Ships—Professor

PARIS, Tuesday.—Professor Paul Becquerel, the cosmo-biologist, said today that he believed the approach of Mars to the earth may have a definite connection with "flying saucers" and that the possibility that they were Martian space ships could not be ruled out. —B.U.P.

In Portugal crowds flocked into the streets of Alcobaca to watch strange cigar-shaped objects travelling fast at a great height.—D.M. Reporter.

American films"
19 MAY 1952
'FLYING OBLONG'

PISA, Sunday.—Airport authorities reported that "a luminous, oblong object" passed over Pisa Airfield last night.—Exchange.

Sunday Dispatch

st Year. No. 7,855.   2½d.   MAY 25, 1952.   Radio Page 8.   s

These Photographs Have Set The World Talking

EXCLUSIVE

The Flying Saucer Pictures That Have Amazed Experts

Clearest Views Ever Of The Great Sky Mystery

The Flying Saucer slows down, tilts, and gradually loses height, so that much of its top surface, with a dome-shaped centre inside an inner ring, can be seen clearly from the ground.

IT CAME IN OVER THE SEA

2 5 MAY 1952

THE *Sunday Dispatch* here presents exclusively in this country a series of pictures that may well become historic—

The most dramatic documentation yet in t h e Flying Saucer mystery.

These pictures, taken in Brazil, have already excited the interest of millions on the American continent, and amazed experts there.

This is the story behind the pictures :

Two Brazilian reporters, Ed Keffel and Joao Martins, were sent by their editor to a place called Ilha dos Amores (Isle of Lovers), in the district of Barra da Tijuca, Brazil, to do an illustrated feature for their magazine.

It was Wednesday, May 7. Keffel had a camera loaded for action at 4 p.m., when Martins suddenly drew his attention to a strange sort of plane approaching from the sea. It looked like a head-on view of an ordinary aeroplane in the distance, but was obviously not a plane, as it was moving sideways at a terrific speed.

Soundless

Keffel raised his camera and took a photograph. A few seconds later the two men realised that this flying object was a disc travelling quite soundlessly, not showing any trail of smoke or vapour, and quite unlike any flying object they had ever previously seen.

It was blue-grey in colour and it was not luminous.

It flew in a semi-circle over the Tijuca Woods, then out over the coast, where it swooped rather like a leaf falling from a tree. Then it shot forward again in a terrific burst of speed at an angle of 45 degrees and disappeared out to sea.

The whole of this lasted about a minute, and during that time Keffel took five pictures.

The film was rushed to the office of the magazine, where the two men told their story amid great excitement. The pictures were developed and printed, and showed the most remarkable photographs of a Flying Saucer ever seen anywhere in the world.

For Washington

The magazine printed a special supplement containing these pictures. Prints of the photographs, it is understood, are being supplied to Washington for inspection by the U.S. authorities, who have been investigating the whole mystery of Flying Saucers.

The *Sunday Dispatch*, when the news of this strange aerial visitor appeared in the newspapers of the world, immediately cabled an offer to the owners of the magazine to buy the exclusive rights in these pictures, and today we present them to our readers.

Prints of the photographs have been sent to all parts of the world and they have aroused the greatest possible discussion, as they are the clearest photographs of this strange mystery of the skies ever obtained

Almost perpendicular, the disc finally shot out to sea at an astounding speed—to return to its secret source.

The first sight. They thought it was a plane.

Another view of the upper surface.

J. D. S. ALAN, our Air Correspondent, writes:

Striking differences between the new sky object and several previous reports, sketches, and photographs of Flying Saucers, from various parts of the world, are that the usual, stubby central mast is replaced by a small cupola, and that there is a thickening of the disc, on upper and lower surfaces, almost halfway between the cupola and the edge of the machine.

Puzzling Silence

If the machine is driven by rotating vanes, this thickening might well house the gearing and linkages needed to alter the angle of the vanes.

The silence is puzzling, and seems to discount power by turbine jets. Many people who believe 100 per cent. in Flying Saucers argue that power may come from the crossing of lines of magnetic force. They believe that such lines exist throughout the universe, and that power may be induced from one to the other, like lightning between two clouds.

Sir Miles Thomas, chairman of BOAC, shown the pictures last night, said: "I think it is the wheel cover of a DC 3 or a DC 4. This is usually a bluish grey pressed duralumin cover which is fixed over the wheel once the undercarriage is up. As it was seen in an area normally used by aircraft, it is quite likely that one of the covers could have become detached.

This opinion conflicts, however, with the reporters' statement that the object appeared to be about twice the size of an airplane, and also a comparison of original photographs of the Brazilian pictures and DC 4 wheels does not reveal the similarity suggested by Sir Miles.

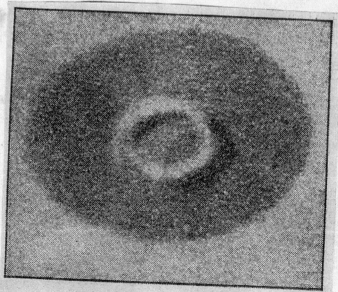

The lower side of the Flying Saucer.

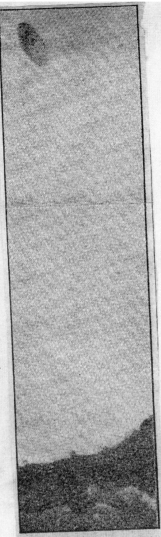

The last glimpse caught by the camera — an enlarged version of the lower picture in Columns Two and Three.

How the disc appeared as it soared over the reporters.

Joao Martins and Ed Keffel, the newspapermen who spotted and " scooped " it.

Mystery

EVENING CHRONICLE 13
Friday, June 13, 1952

light's erratic course

LEFT "HARD-BITTEN GEORDIE" PUZZLED

Mr. R. Baits, of 10, King John Street, Heaton, Newcastle, now in the Post and Telecommunications Department headquarters, Benghazi, describes himself as a " fairly hard-bitten Geordie," not given to hallucinations.

BUT a recent experience of his in Derna has left him wondering, so much so that he has written to the "Evening Chronicle" so that readers may suggest possible explanations

On the Saturday before Whit Sunday, he with Mr. and Mrs. J. Berry, of Edinburgh, and a German friend, Mr. M. Bohot, travelled to Derna by car.

Orange colour

His letter goes on:—

After a bath and a meal we drove down to the beach about 9.30 p.m. and sat chatting in the car. We had hardly settled ourselves when I noticed in the sky a soft orange yellow light which was travelling towards us from inland at a terrific speed.

It was quite soundless, and moving in a straight line.

It looked like a meteor until suddenly, as it reached a point almost overhead, it swerved violently to the left and went 'skidding' towards Derna, gaining height all the while.

CLIMBING AT FAST RATE

After a few seconds, it again started to change course to the south — and then it began moving wildly from left to right across the sky. It still appeared to be climbing at a very fast rate (faster than any jet plane I've ever seen), until in a few seconds it was difficult to pick out from the stars, except that it swerved at irregular intervals.

As can be imagined, we had a lively discussion on what it could have been and we did come to the following conclusions:—

(1) It was not an aeroplane

astronomy and I can say that it was not a meteor.

This leaves us with two possible solutions:

Solutions?

That some country has invented a machine capable of amazing manoeuvreability at immense speeds and that particular country is keeping quiet about it;

That the machines don't belong to earth at all.

Mr. R. Baits pictured with his six-year-old son in Benghazi.

Sixteen members of the New Zealand Olympic team left Wellington for Sydney by air today on the first stage of their 14,000 miles journey to Helsinki.

because no plane has yet been constructed with that amount of manoeuvreability at such a terrific speed.

(2) It was not a balloon.

(3) Speed: Mr. Bohot has watched, in Germany, experimental rockets taking off and he states emphatically it was faster than any rocket he had seen.

(4) I'm well read up in

---

for oman

...raftman, of the R.A.F. ...e West, Sunderland, who ...wcastle woman on a train

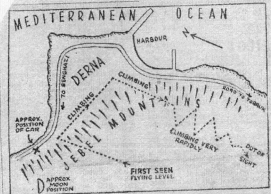

MEDITERRANEAN OCEAN

HARBOUR

TO BENGHAZI
DERNA
CLIMBING
CLIMBING
ROAD TO TOBRUK
JEBEL MOUNTAINS
CLIMBING VERY RAPIDLY
OUT OF SIGHT
APPROX. POSITION OF CAR
FIRST SEEN FLYING LEVEL
APPROX. MOON POSITION

Drove at 61
h. over
idge

KENT

Sunday Dispatch, JUNE 1, 1952   3

'Flying Saucer' Is Seen Again Over The South

By Sunday Dispatch Reporter

WHAT was the strange object seen speeding across the skies of Southern England between seven and eight o'clock on Thursday evening?

Many readers of the *Sunday Dispatch* have written reporting this latest "flying saucer" sighting.

The object was first seen passing to the north of Canterbury at about 7.30. An observer describes it as cigar-shaped.

At 7.34 something described as "a flattened ellipsoid" with a shiny surface, travelling silently and extremely fast, was seen moving south-west over Aldershot.

Reddish Glow

At 7.35 over Poole, a strange circular object glistening as though metallic and flying noiselessly and very fast, disappeared rapidly also in a south-westerly direction.

About 7.40 an object, "elongate in shape" having a faint reddish glow but leaving no trail, was seen from Portland Bill. It also disappeared towards the south-west.

About 7.40 something that looked like a "huge chicken egg" appeared over Southampton, moving in the direction of the New Forest. It was quiet, shiny, and travelling very fast.

To See 'Boy'
e Saved 50
ars Ago

Dispatch Reporter

ears. Mr. Sam
ondered what
o the 2½-year-
d out of the
tired he de-
t. So he
t in the
a local

the re-
ued."
Wil-

LES SOUCOUPES VOLANTES

by MARGARET VANE-TEMPEST-STEWART

I HAVE always had a weak spot in my heart for Flying Saucers; and I was therefore most distressed, two years ago, when they were so summarily treated by certain sections of the Press. Now I am correspondingly glad to learn that my Saucers appear to be coming into their own with a vengeance, sponsored, as they are, by *Life* magazine and also sailing under the protective cover of the Air Technical Intelligence Command of the United States Air Force.

In my gratification I can even pardon Mr Nicolas Bentley for his levity, whilst admiring his intrepidity in putting a domestic construction upon mechanisms which baffle the scientists and physicists. At the same time I would like to call his attention to a book, now almost forgotten, published in 1931 by Mr Charles Fort and entitled *Lo*. The following reports are but a few of the results of Mr Fort's researches into a subject of which little was known twenty-one years ago.

IN THE issue of the *Zoologist*, dated July 1868, it is recorded that an object was seen in the sky near Copiapo, in Chile—a construction that carried lights and was propelled by a noisy motor and which appeared to be

'a gigantic bird; eyes wide open and shining like burning coals; covered with immense scales, which clashed together with a metallic sound.'

Five years later, the writer of 'General Notes' in *The New York Times* of 6 July 1873 told of something which he considered to be 'the very worst case of delirium tremens on record'. He called attention to a story in the *Bonham Enterprise*, a Texas newspaper, in which a local resident alleged that he had seen something like an enormous serpent floating over his farm, a sight which greatly frightened him and his companions who were working in the fields. Curiously enough, there is supporting evidence for this manifestation, since in *The New York Times*, of the following day, it is noted that a similar object had been observed from Fort Scott, in Kansas:

'. . . About half way above the horizon, the form of a huge serpent, apparently perfect in form, was plainly seen!'

IT WAS in the year 1880, however, that things really started to happen and there are many allusions, in the New York newspapers of that time, to strange phenomena observed in the skies. One of them was noted by the *Louisville Courier-Journal* on 29 July, which reported that just after six o'clock on the evening of the previous day, people in Louisville saw 'an object like a man, surrounded by machines, which he seemed to be working with his hands and feet'. The object moved in various directions, ascending and descending, seemingly under control. When darkness came it disappeared.

Mr Fort comments that unless an inventor then existed on earth more self-effacing than the biographies of most inventors indicate them to be, no terrestrial inhabitant had at that time succeeded in making a dirigible airship.

In 1883 brilliant lights were seen in the sky in many parts of the world and these were thought to be comets by amateur observers and by astronomers. There is mention of them in the *New Zealand Times* of 20 September, in the *Madras Athenaeum* of 22 September, which referred to a similar light seen over Ceylon, and the *Straits Times* of 13 October, which reported that natives and Chinese at Samarung were terrified by the appearance; while in England a Captain Noble, who enjoyed a certain reputation as an astronomer, told in *Knowledge* of seeing something like 'new and glorious comet'. An amateur in Liverpool, who also wrote to *Knowledge* claimed he saw an object which looked like the planet Jupiter and which threw a beam before it. A similar phenomenon was also seen by Professor Swift, a professional astronomer, over Rochester, New York State.

THESE APPEARANCES may well have been comets. However when we come to the twentieth century the comet theory does not seem to cover the facts. According to the *Eastern Daily Press* of 28 January 1908, on a bright moonlight night a 'dark, globular object, with a structure of some kind upon the side of it, was seen travelling at great pace' in the sky by the employees of the Norwich Transportation Company, at Mousehead.

By the summer of 1910 matters became positively hectic and people started seeing Things all over the place. In July the crew of a French fishing boat, the *Jeune Frédéric*, saw, off the coast of Normandy, a large, black bird-like object which fell into the sea leaving no traces. *The London Weekly Dispatch* commented on 10 July that no terrestrial aircraft was known to have been flying on that day. Then in August *The Times* reported that labourers working in a forest in Dessau, in Germany, sighted something overhead which they thought to be a balloon. It suddenly flamed and something, believed to be its car, fell amongst the trees. A search was made by the Chief Forester but nothing was found and aeronautical societies stated that no known balloon had been sent up. At 9 p.m. on 30 August lights, as if upon an airship, were watched as they moved over New York and were reported in the *New York World* the next day. Aviators were interviewed but all aircraft were accounted for. The *New York Tribune* of 22 September tells of crowds standing in the streets of New York gaping at a procession of 'a great number of round objects' which crossed over the city from west to east.

IN FEBRUARY 1923 'intense lights', like motor-car head lamps, were seen moving across fields in Warwickshire, at times swiftly and at others almost stationary; the occurrence was mentioned in several English newspapers including the *Daily Express* and the *Daily News*. In August 1929 the *New York Herald Tribune* carried a story which has a most contemporary flavour about Thomas Stuart, third mate of the steamship *Coldwater* (owned by the South Atlantic Steamship Line), who saw a travelling light in the sky about four hundred miles off the coast of Virginia. 'There was something,' he said 'that gave the impression that it was a large, passenger aircraft' and he estimated its speed at a hundred miles an hour and its direction as that of Bermuda. An official investigation followed but it 'failed to reveal any trans-Atlantic or Bermuda flight'.

Life's remarkable article published on 7 April last is too well known to require further quotation but, perhaps, a recapitulation of a few of the salient facts which it mentioned would not be amiss: distinguished scientists and professors agreed that the silence of our new 'high flyers' could only be explained by the fact that the objects must be assumed to be flying at a minimum height of 50,000 feet and at the speed of 18,000 m.p.h.; vertical rise was between 600 and 900 m.p.h.; no known aircraft, rocket or guided missile could make such a rapid vertical ascent without leaving an exhaust vapour; no human being could have borne the tremendous 'G' load brought to bear on the craft during its abrupt vertical veer; meteors do not fly in formation; luminous objects were of a light more intense than the planet Venus; no known machine travels at 1,700 m.p.h. without making a sound or leaving an exhaust trail.

IN RECENT years it is the scientists and the experts who have taken a serious view and interest in the Saucers and not the laymen who have been apt to regard them as some sort of practical joke.

NEWS CHRONICLE, TUESDAY, JUNE 17, 1952

U.S. RADAR SEARCH

FOR FLYING

SAUCERS

Watch from atom sites

From ROBERT WAITHMAN : WASHINGTON, Monday

THE United States Air Force has suddenly and significantly changed its tune about flying saucers. It now implicitly admits there may be something New in the Air.

All the signs now are that funds have been authorised for a widespread investigation involving the use of special cameras, radar and other up-to-the-minute tracking instruments.

Painstaking analysis of hundreds of reports of sightings is under way—with special reference to phenomena observed in the vicinity of atomic energy installations and military bases.

Two statements from top officials appear today to open afresh the subject which the Air Force rather testily declared to have been closed 18 months ago.

The Secretary of the Air Force, Mr. Thomas Finletter, says: No concrete evidence has yet reached us either to prove or disprove the existence of so-called flying saucers There have been, however, a number of sightings the Air Force investigators have been unable to explain

'Not explained'

" As long as this is true, the Air Force will continue to study flying saucer reports.'

And General Hoyt Vandenberg, Air Force Chief of Staff, says: " The Air Force is interested in anything that takes place in the air.

This includes the aerial phenomena known as flying saucers. " Many of these incidents have been satisfactorily explained Others have not.

" With the present world unrest we cannot afford to be complacent."

What gives these statements uncommon interest is the sharp difference between their tone and that of the Air Force's official statement of December, 1949, announcing the closing down of " project saucer." a two-year investigation carried out by the air force base at Dayton, Ohio

No noise

General Vandenberg's statement was made after the number of reports of Flying Saucers the Air Force has received had risen to more than 800. They are still flowing in from outposts and vital atomic installation sites.

Reports up to now have mainly indicated that the phenomena observed seemed to be flying without any noise. The theory expounded recently by a number of responsible scientists here that Flying Saucers are images in the sky created by reflections of either earthly or celestial lights had begun to be fairly widely accepted.

But Air Technical Intelligence Command, which has more information on Flying Saucers than anyone else, is plainly for from being satisfied.

A FLYING SAUCER

Le Bourget Logs It— If It Exists

From our own Correspondent

19 JUN 1952 PARIS, JUNE 18.

The management of Le Bourget Aerodrome is at pains to explain to-day that although the log-book of the aerodrome now contains a reference to what might be a flying saucer, if there were such things, seen in the early hours of Friday, June 13, it has in no way committed itself to the belief that flying saucers exist. There is, however, evident satisfaction in the French capital that if you want to see flying saucers you have as good a chance here as elsewhere. The celestial phenomena of last week have not caused any local increase of international or interplanetary tension.

The log book of Le Bourget records that at one o'clock in the morning last Friday the sky was overcast. It continues :

"A ball of fire larger than a star crossed the sky to the south-west of the aerodrome after remaining immobile for a long time. The ball disappeared on the horizon after sparkling and moving with ever-increasing rapidity. This phenomenon was also observed by a regular Air France aircraft coming in from Lyons. It should be added that a telephone call was received from Montmartre at 1 45 p.m. on Friday, June 13, to darw our attention to a silvery disc to the north of Paris."

Whatever the celestial phenomenon thus recorded. it appears to have been observed even earlier than by the man who telephoned to Le Bourget at lunch-time on Thursday. On Wednesday night a woman. looking out of an attic window on the high land on the southern fringe of Paris. saw with surprise a red disc rise and fall to the northward at about 10 15 p.m., noting to herself that it was the wrong date for fireworks and then that what she was looking at did not seem to be one.

Whatever it is_ it is thrown in for nothing with your £25, but no guide with an armband offers any guarantee that he can show it to you.

---

in the last war.

E.N. 28 JUN 1952

ANOTHER "SAUCER'

Seen Over Malta

Malta, Saturday. — A flying saucer travelling at great speed, the first ever seen here, is reported by the Marine Headquarters in the north-west of the island. It was seen by six marines who were training on open ground.—*Evening News* Correspondent.

Why the—
DAILY EXPRESS

1 JUN 1952

chooses this week to take serious interest in—

DAF 1 JUL 1952

FLYING SAUCERS

by CHAPMAN PINCHER

TOMORROW the Daily Express will publish the most critical and factual analysis yet made of the mysterious objects which have become known throughout the world as "Flying Saucers."

Repeatedly during the last six years sincere observers have reported strange things in the sky ranging from six-foot discs to 100ft. "space-ships."

Most of these Flying Saucer sightings undoubtedly have straightforward explanations. They were due to optical illusions, balloons, high-flying aircraft, meteors, or imagination.

Why then does the Daily Express choose this moment to give serious attention to a subject which has become the plaything of novelists, cartoonists, and music-hall comedians?

The reason is this. After all straightforward cases have been sifted from the eyewitness accounts about 60 remain which cannot be so easily dismissed in any honest analysis.

Their possible significance increases when the points from which they were observed are marked on a map. A surprisingly high proportion of the Saucers seem to have been flying over secret U.S. defence stations.

U.S. Air Technical Intelligence Command officials, impressed by this discovery, last week ordered a full-scale scientific Saucer search. Work has already begun under the code name Project Bluebook.

Analysis

GENERAL HOYT VANDENBERG, U.S. Air Force Chief of Staff, has said: "The air force is interested in . . . the aerial phenomena commonly known as Flying Saucers. Many of these incidents have been satisfactorily explained. Others have not. With the present world unrest we cannot afford to be complacent."

Or, as an air Intelligence officer put it more crisply: "What might be dismissed as 'probably a meteor' may prove to be a global rocket."

Special instruments called camera-spectroscopes are being built to make photographic records of future Flying Saucers.

They will take motion pictures, and by analysing the jets of flame reported to issue from many Saucers they will provide information about the materials used in construction.

Alerted

SCIENTISTS at guided - missile research stations have been alerted to keep watch for Saucers and assess their speed with the cine-theodolites and other ingenious equipments they have built for trailing rockets.

There are many scientists who are now as serious as the air force Intelligence officers in their approach to Saucers.

None of them gives any support to the fanciful suggestion that Flying Saucers are machines from another planet. There is no worth-while evidence for this belief.

Professor Donald Menzel, an internationally famous astronomer of Harvard University, believes that most and perhaps all the reported objects were mirages produced in unexpected ways.

Reports by such highly trained technical observers as astronomers, radar operators and gunnery officers have been dismissed in the past without fair examination. From now on they will be investigated by the new panel of scientists.

TOMORROW'S pictorial analysis has been prepared to put the Flying Saucer mystery back into proper perspective.

IT WILL ALSO DISCLOSE that there have been incidents which at the moment seem to defy reasonable explanation.

Sunday Graphic, June 29, 1952 3

AMAZING STORY TOLD BY REFUGEE FROM RUSSIANS

I SAW FLYING SAUCER TAKE OFF

From ANTONY TERRY, Sunday Graphic Berlin Correspondent, Saturday.

A REFUGEE from the Russian-occupied zone told me here to-day that he saw a flying saucer take off from a forest clearing in Thuringia, East Germany.

The man, Herr Oskar Linke, reported that he came upon the flying saucer three miles from the U.S. zone and saw two members of its crew.

"It was uncanny," he said. "My 11-year-old daughter and I glimpsed something white through the trees.

"We crept near. And we saw a huge oval disc about 25 feet across lying on the ground.

"It looked like an enormous phosphorescent warming pan without a handle. In the centre was a sort of upper works.

'Screamed in fright'

"Then we saw two figures wearing metallic overalls. My daughter screamed in fright, and the two climbed hastily into the disc which had circular portholes round the edges.

"The upper works retracted and the saucer began to rise—slowly at first—into the air. We felt the swish of air it made. It hovered at 100ft. up then sped out of sight."

Linke is ex-mayor of an East German town who fled from Communist persecution.

In London last night Kenneth Gatland, Fellow of the British Interplanetary Society, said: "Such a contraption must come from outside this earth. Nothing like it is known here."

FLYING SAUCERS

2 JUL 1952

the fringe of doubt

TODAY the Daily Express puts the Flying Saucer mystery into perspective. This factual and critical analysis—the first of its kind ever undertaken—is based on the latest authoritative scientific data. It is in two parts: (A) Six eyewitness reports, each with a scientific explanation alongside; (B) Three significant cases on the fringe of doubt.

It is at this point that the panel of scientists—called together last week by the U.S. Air Intelligence Command—takes over.

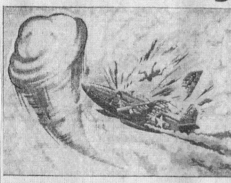

EYEWITNESS REPORT: 1.—U.S. flier Thomas Mantell and two other fighter pilots sighted, on January 7, 1948, an object "like an ice-cream cone" *(left)*. Mantell followed it up to 20,000ft., and his body and the scattered wreckage of his plane were found later. **EXPLANATION:** The object was a Skyhook *(right)*—a huge plastic balloon used by scientists for research on cosmic rays. Mantell may have collided with the balloon. A Skyhook is cone-shaped until it reaches rarefied air, when it expands to a 100ft. globe. **INQUIRY NOW CLOSED.**

EYEWITNESS REPORT: 2.—On August 25 last year, three scientists in Texas saw a formation flight of lights *(left)* move swiftly and noiselessly across the sky. Many more such flights were seen later and photographed. **EXPLANATION:** The lights were a mirage. The ground cools rapidly at night in desert areas, forming a layer of cold air overlaid by a wavy layer of warm air *(right)*. Light beams from a city could be bent along the wavy zone showing up as separate spots miles away. Winds would make the spots race across the night sky. **INQUIRY CLOSED.**

EYEWITNESS REPORT : 3.—Radar operators have detected mysterious objects flying in precise formation at night *(left)* when no aircraft were in the area and no noise could be heard from the sky. **EXPLANATION :** The spots on the radar screens were caused by wild geese migrating *(right)*. One wartime scare off the Norfolk coast is known to have been caused by geese flying to the Humber estuary. The warning spots on radar screens that night were so like the signs of enemy planes that invasion alarms were sounded. **INQUIRY CLOSED.**

 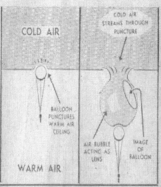

COLD AIR

WARM AIR

COLD AIR STREAMS THROUGH PUNCTURE

BALLOON PUNCTURES WARM AIR CEILING

AIR BUBBLE ACTING AS LENS

IMAGE OF BALLOON

EYEWITNESS REPORT : 4.—Many observers have reported seeing shining objects *(left)* hanging in the sky on sunny days. They describe them as shaped like saucers, tops, bananas, and crescents. Most seemed motionless ; a few moved slowly. **EXPLANATION :** All were due to chance glimpses of the planet Venus, which can sometimes be plainly seen in daylight *(right)*. The fact that Venus goes through phases like the moon explains the various shapes. Clouds travelling across the sky gave the optical illusion of movement. **INQUIRY CLOSED.**

EYEWITNESS REPORT : 5.—While watching a weather balloon released near Arrey, New Mexico, on the morning of April 24, 1949, technicians spotted "a whitish ellipse 100ft. wide moving above the balloon" *(left)*. After travelling horizontally it surged upwards and vanished. **EXPLANATION :** Another mirage. The balloon punctured the "ceiling" of a layer of warm air *(right)*. A huge bubble of cold air then streamed through the "hole" forming a "lens" of air, in which observers saw the balloon's enlarged and distorted image. As the lens changed shape the image darted about at enormous speed. **INQUIRY CLOSED.**

EYEWITNESS REPORT : 6.—At 7 p.m. on February 13 last hundreds of people in Southern England saw what they described as a "noiseless, cigar-shaped rocket, green with a red tail" *(left)* fly low over London, disappearing northwards. **EXPLANATION :** It was a meteor—a lump of stone or metal—no bigger than a walnut, and at least 30 miles high. The coloured flame and the illusion of great size were due to luminous vapour given off as the meteor shot into the atmosphere from outer space, becoming incandescent by friction with the air. The meteor was seen to burn out and disintegrate high over the Wash. **INQUIRY CLOSED.**

THREE CASES SCIENCE CANNOT YET EXPLAIN

?   ?

EYEWITNESS REPORT.—7.   EYEWITNESS REPORT.—8.   EYEWITNESS REPORT.—9.

EYEWITNESS REPORT : 7.—Officials at Sioux City Airport, U.S.A., saw a bright light in the sky on January 20, 1951. Two fliers took off and the light dived at their plane, pulling out to pass swiftly and silently overhead. Both described it as a "winged cigar." **NO EXPLANATION. INQUIRIES CONTINUE.**

EYEWITNESS REPORT : 8.—Air-liner pilots Clarence Chiles and John Whitted saw what seemed to be a 100ft. rocket ship at close range over Alabama. It had two rows of windows and moved at 800 miles an hour. **NO EXPLANATION.**

EYEWITNESS REPORT : 9.—Lieutenant George Gorman was landing his Mustang at Fargo, Dakota, on October 1, 1948, when he saw an intensely bright globe about six inches wide silently racing through the sky. He pursued it while it jinked and dived for nearly half an hour. Confirmed by control tower chief. **NO EXPLANATION. INQUIRIES CONTINUE.**

The survey prepared by **CHAPMAN PINCHER** and illustrated by **LEWIS**

OBJECTS PICKED UP
BY RADAR

23 JUL 1952

"Saucers" Again in U.S.?

WASHINGTON, JULY 21.
The United States Air Force said to-day it had received reports that from seven to ten unidentified aerial objects were sighted near the Washington National Airport at about midnight last Saturday.

The air route traffic control centre at the airport said eight unidentified objects were picked up by radar operators moving at from 100 to 130 miles an hour. The centre advised that a plane outward bound from the National Airport reported seven lights between Washington and Martinsburg, West Virginia. They were described as moving rapidly up, down, and horizontally as well as hovering in one position. "This information has been relayed to the proper Air Force authorities and the Air Force is investigating the matter," the announcement said.

Earlier to-day the Air Force said it was receiving "flying saucer" reports this summer at a rate higher than at any time since the initial flood of sightings in 1947.—Reuter

---

Jets In Air Search Over U.S. Capital

AMERICAN jet fighters searched the skies over Washington after unknown objects were spotted by radar, the U.S. Air Force reported.

The fighters made no direct contact with the objects though one pilot reported sighting four lights in front of him which disappeared before he could overtake them, Reuter cables.

The Air Force said that the Air Route Traffic Control Centre, operated by the Civil Aeronautics Administration, picked up on radar "between four and 12 unidentified objects over the vicinity of Washington."

The CAA notified the Air Force who ordered two jet fighter interceptions to make a check from the base at Delaware, 90 miles from Washington.

The planes came into the CAA radar view and were guided towards several of the unknown objects.

"One of the jet pilots reported sighting four lights approximately ten miles in front and slightly above him but he reported he had no apparent closing speed. They disappeared before he could overtake them," the Air Force state.

The same pilot reported a steady light that disappeared in about one minute.

'Saucers' Outpace Jets in Chase Over Washington

EN 28 JUL 1952

WASHINGTON, Monday.
TWO of America's fastest jet interceptors chased "between four and 12 unidentified objects" in a flying saucer hunt over Washington, the U.S. Air Force said to-day.

But the mysterious visitors left the jets standing.

The air route traffic control centre said it picked up the objects on its radar screen.

Two jet fighters took off from Newcastle airfield, Delaware, 90 miles from Washington.

Said an Air Force statement: "One jet fighter saw four lights about ten miles in front and slightly above him.

"But they disappeared before he could overtake them."

Melbourne cable: Captain J. Murray, Constellation Pilot for Qantas Airlines, to-day reported seeing a bright green object flashing across the sky south of Darwin, saying it changed colour to red and then gold as it disappeared.—A.P., Reuter.

JETS PURSUE SKY 'OBJECTS'

28 JUL 1952

WASHINGTON, Sunday.
JET fighters spent several hours chasing "unknown objects" flying over Washington last night.

Radar picked up "between four and 12" of the objects.

An Air Force statement says: "One of the jet pilots reported sighting four lights approximately ten miles away and slightly above him, but they disappeared before he could overtake them."

This is the second time in a week that unidentified objects have been observed by radar over Washington.—A.P.

Flying plate

An object like a large silver dinner plate, giving off white flashes, was seen travelling high over Liverpool yesterday, five people told the police.

A 'FLYING DINNER-PLATE'
28 JUL 1952
FLASHES BY

A FLASHING object "like a large silver dinner-plate" was seen flying high over Liverpool yesterday.

Four women and a man, an ex-R A F observer, told police they had seen it travelling east. After six minutes it disappeared behind clouds.

Said Mrs. Ann Cox Beswick: "I saw a small patch of blue in the sky . . . it increased . . . there were spasmodic white flashes. It appeared to wobble."

Mrs. Cox then told her 21-year-old daughter Wenda, her nephew Robin Williams, her neighbour, Mrs. Murray and daughter.

They, too, said they had seen the flashing object.

[*The Meteorological Office at Speke and coastguards reported that nothing had been seen.*]

In Washington jet fighters tried to intercept unknown objects spotted by radar. They failed.

Flying Saucers

"I am a believer in Flying Saucers," says a pilot who has just met one in Northern Australia. "Only a meteor," we murmur from the depths of our scepticism and armchairs. But the fact is that those who work in offices and would be too preoccupied to see a Flying Saucer if it carried them their cup of tea are forced to retreat with their horny doubts into an attitude of wait and see, which is sadly negative. "We are not complacent," says the United States Air Force with American conscientiousness. That is the trouble. Without complacency science cuts a forlorn figure. The Paris newspaper "Combat" has instinctively recognised this, and on the principle that where truth fails we must trust the intellectuals has looked to them for light. Here at least there is confidence. "If the technical services of the French Army do not believe (in Flying Saucers) that is a proof that they sorely need to brush up their knowledge of differential calculus," said a composer. A poet had more sinister intelligence: "Flying Saucers? Why not?" But it would be too good to be true" if they were unearthly visitants. (A neutralist, evidently.) An actress was confidential: friends of hers "whose scientific spirit I can not doubt" had clinched the matter. A cabaret entertainer believed in them "as alas I believe in the Thieving Saucers" that bring him his café bills. Some sceptics among the artists spoiled the record. But there is evidence here, surely, for another hypothesis—that there is some connection between Flying Saucers and the inner light. Perhaps even science has its genii.

U.S. RADAR 'PIPS' MYSTERY

3 EXPLANATIONS

From Our Own Correspondent
WASHINGTON, Tuesday.

For six hours early to-day Civil Aeronautics Administration officials watched "pips" on their radar screen for which there was no immediate explanation. It is the third time this has happened in the past 10 days.

Planes or experiments by any branch of the armed services or the Atomic Energy Commission have been ruled out. To the imaginative the pips may have been caused by "flying saucers" from another world. More sober conclusions are that they may be due to:

1.—Stray weather balloons, six feet in diameter, which carry suspended tin foil so that they can be tracked by radar to determine wind speed and direction. They often travel at more than a hundred miles per hour.
2.—Strips of tin foil dropped by B36 bombers which have been engaged in exercises in Northern United States to cause spots on radar screens and confuse the defence. The strips might have been blown south, though the prevailing winds are west to east.
3.—Some kind of electric condition in the atmosphere which bounces back radar beams as though they were hitting solid objects.

Washington has had its 15th day of hot, humid weather, with temperatures over 90 deg. This may have caused electric disturbances accounting both for the radar pips and the bright lights seen in the sky.

U.S. SKY APPARITIONS SEEN AGAIN

AIR FORCE'S OPEN MIND

FROM OUR OWN CORRESPONDENT
WASHINGTON, July 29

The unidentified aerial objects that have appeared on radar screens at the National Airport, Washington, twice in a week were again reported early to-day from about 1.30 until 6 o'clock. They were in the same area as before, moving at a speed of 100 to 120 miles an hour in a 10-mile arc around the city between Herndon, in Virginia, and the Andrews Air Force base, in Maryland.

Only a few hours earlier officials at the Pentagon had again denied that these unexplained objects were in any way connected with experiments by United States agencies. An Air Force spokesman said:—"If any Air Force activity or any project sponsored by the Air Force is conducting any experiments or tests which could even remotely account for the manifestations, we would know about it. Furthermore, if the Army, the Navy, or the Atomic Energy Commission, or any other Government agency had anything under way along this line, I am sure we would know about it, because of the necessity of advance coordination in anything affecting the air defence of the United States, which is our responsibility."

Major-General Samford, director of Air Force intelligence, with other officers, discussed the investigation of the reported phenomena for an hour and a half this afternoon and answered innumerable questions. The result was largely "an explanation of an inability to explain," but General Samford did say definitely that Air Force inquiries made since 1947 had revealed nothing constituting a danger to the United States. Of the appearances over the Washington area he expressed the opinion that material objects such as missiles were not involved. The radar reaction was probably caused by "phenomena associated with intellectual and scientific interests." Most of such phenomena would, he thought, be gradually understood in time. Earlier he had remarked that little was known, for example, about the Northern Lights.

Commenting on the appearances noted in Washington and on the renewed flood of reports of "flying saucers" and "unidentified objects" from all over the United States, the New York Times says to-day that the Air Force must produce better explanations—why, for instance, a jet fighter of Air Defence Command, capable of a speed of 600 miles an hour, failed to catch one of the "objects." Unless such questions "are answered in simple language, belief in visitors from outer space will be strengthened in those who cannot distinguish between speculation and scientific reasoning."

Several of the latest explanations take into account the extreme heat in this area recently —the thermometer was at 99deg. again yesterday. Some observers say that this may give the stars, seen through the haze that lies over the city, the appearance of glowing lights.

UNRELIABLE SAUCERS

WASHINGTON, July 29.

Radar showed that the air over Washington was full of unidentified flying objects early to-day. An airliner was sent up to investigate and found nothing.

The Civil Aeronautics Administration said that as many as twelve objects appeared on the radar screen at the same time. They seemed to be travelling at between ninety and 120 miles an hour in an area about fifteen miles long, moving from north-west to southeast, roughly at an angle of 60 degrees to the prevailing wind. The altitude was not determined.

The new development is that experienced Air Force and Commercial pilots have reported seeing "lights" at the same time as radar screens have picked up unidentified objects. The first time lights were seen both visually and on radar was on the night of July 12. The next time was last Saturday night, when a flight of jet interceptors was sent up and one of them gave chase. But the lights disappeared before it could overtake them'.—Reuter.

Sunday Dispatch, AUGUST 3, 1952

53

Coastguard Saw This V-Flight

This photograph was taken by a U.S. coastguard at Salem, Massachusetts, air station after he had seen four unknown objects in the sky. The bars of light that seem to extend in front and behind the round objects, which appear in V formation, can be seen clearly. Many Americans believe them to be flying saucers.

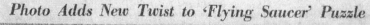

Photo Adds New Twist to 'Flying Saucer' Puzzle

U.S. Coast Guard and A.P.

This picture, showing four huge lights in the sky, was taken at the Coast Guard air station in Salem, Mass., at 9:35 a.m. July 16 and released by Coast Guard headquarters in Washington this week end. The headquarters said it was releasing the photograph only because of the widespread public interest in the subject. The picture was taken by one of the air station's photographers, who aimed his camera through a window of his laboratory as the lights appeared.

THOSE SAUCERS

432 Saw Them

Washington, Saturday.—The American Air Force said to-day that so far this year it had received 432 written reports on "sightings of unidentified aerial phenomena."—"Flying saucers" to the man in the street. These were reports by civilians and by military observers sent through regular Air Force channels.—Reuter.

E.N.   2 AUG 1952

---

5 AUG 1952

NO "FLYING SAUCERS"

Air Expert's Opinion

Six years of studying "flying saucer" reports has "reasonably well" convinced Maj.-Gen. Roger Ramey, of the United States Air Force, that there is no such thing as a "flying saucer." He said that not one of some 1,500 reports since 1947 had offered solid evidence that anything material was involved.

All the reports taken together did not establish any pattern that could be construed as menacing. Speaking of what he called "unidentified objects," Gen. Ramey said, "we know of nothing that could behave as we hear these things do. Soviet Russia has no power to produce an object that cannot be tracked as material."

About 20 per cent. of the reports in Air Force hands were unexplained. "I can say definitely the 'saucers' are not our own."

NOTE CROSS

E.N.   6 AUG 1952

MYSTERY FLASH
AT 'H' PLANT

A "shapeless incandescent flash of light" was reported over the Atomic Energy Commission's great hydrogen-bomb installation, reports Reuter from Augusta, Georgia.

The flash was first reported by an official of the E.I. Du Pont de Nemours Company—under contract to build the hydrogen-bomb installation. He said the flash "looked to me like a huge bulb in a flash camera."

An official of the commission said the security section of the project had conducted an investigation.

D.D.   10 AUG 1952

Saucers Over Austria

Flying saucers, "changing their shape from discs to balloons," were seen in Austria yesterday, Vienna radio reported last night.

Radar Picks Up a 'Fleet of Saucers'

D.M.   7 AUG 1952

PLANES SEARCH, FIND NOTHING

WASHINGTON, Wednesday.

ACROSS radar screens today moved "the heaviest concentration of unidentified objects ever seen in the sky." They looked like a fleet of flying saucers.

They were seen at Andrews air base, near here. Their speed: About 60 m.p.h.

Planes were directed by radio to intercept them, but they failed to find anything. Some planes climbed 15,000 feet before bad weather turned them back.

One experienced radar operator insisted: "We are not seeing spots before our eyes," and said the incident was "the most puzzling phenomenon we have ever observed."

The *Washington Evening Star* said today that Army engineers have produced phenomena in a laboratory at Fort Belvoir, Virginia, which might explain flying saucers.

The experimenters used a vacuum bell as a tiny working model of the stratosphere and reproduced "two forces—very low air pressure which is balanced against static electricity in a way to give off light."—Reuter.

HIS 'SAUCERS' FLY INSIDE A GLASS JAR

D.M.   7 AUG 1952

Scientist's Tests Help to Explain

WASHINGTON, Wednesday.

MR. NOEL SCOTT, a U.S. army physicist, experimenting with a glass jar, has produced fiery objects which look like the "flying saucers" seen shooting through the night skies.

Today a spokesman for the Army Corps of Engineers said his findings explain at least some of the "flying saucer" reports and might help towards solving the mystery generally.

Mr. Scott reported that by introducing molecules of ionised air into a partial vacuum in a bell jar he created the orange-red balls, discs, and mushrooms described by hundreds of excited skywatchers. These miniature masses of illuminated air can be picked up by radar, he said.

Fantastic speed

Using a jar 3ft. high and 18in in diameter, Mr. Scott pumped out air to create a partial vacuum and simulate conditions in the upper atmosphere.

Then he injected several molecules of ionised air into the jar. An ionised gas—one whose atoms have lost or gained an electron—is a conductor of electricity. The use of various gases would produce other colours.

When a magnet—and sometimes even a human hand—is moved outside the jar, Mr. Scott said, strange lights inside will dart about with fantastic speed, turning erratically, hovering, or reversing direction quickly. A magnet, or a hand containing static electricity, breaks up magnetic fields to make the objects move at extreme speeds.

A.P.

The Evening News

NO. 22,025   LONDON, SATURDAY, SEPTEMBER 20, 1952   THREE-HALFPENCE

R.A.F. SEE 'FLYINGSAUCER'

Following Meteor Jet,

Say Crews of Bombers

GOING AT 'TERRIFIC SPEED'

Air Ministry Investigate

ROYAL AIR FORCE FLIERS IN EXERCISE MAINBRACE REPORTED A FLYING SAUCER OVER BRITAIN, IT WAS REVEALED TO-DAY.

They said they saw it following a Meteor jet.

The report came from the R.A.F. station at Topcliffe, Yorks. It is being investigated.

The object was seen by about ten R.A.F. officers and men, the crews of Shackleton planes operating from Topcliffe.

A Meteor was flying at 5,000 feet and was descending when an object was spotted five miles astern of it at about 15,000 feet, moving comparatively slowly on a similar course.

It was silver in colour and circular.

GOING DOWN
Then—A Burst of Speed

Then it started to descend, swinging like a pendulum.

The Meteor turned towards Dishforth and the object, still descending, appeared to follow.

It then began a rotary motion about its own axis, but suddenly accelerated at incredible speed.

Those who saw it say its movements were not like anything they had seen in the air and that the acceleration was greater than that of a shooting star.

Those who saw it were F.-Let. Kilburn and F.-Lt. Cybulski, F.-Officer Paris, Master-Signaller Thompson and about six other aircrew members.

One report said it descended like a "falling sycamore leaf."

An Air Ministry meteorological office spokesman said: "It could have been a met. balloon. They are released daily."

Sunday Dispatch

151st Year. No. 7,872.   2½d.   SEPTEMBER 21, 1952.   4   Radio Page 8.

What Intruded Into 'Exercise Mainbrace'?

'SAUCER' CHASED RAF JET PLANE Say 6 Airmen

NOT Smoke-Ring Or Weather Balloon, Says Pilot

S.D. 21 SEP 1952

By Sunday Dispatch Reporter

SERIOUS investigation was being made last night by the R.A.F. into the mystery of a silvery-white object that chased a Meteor jet-plane over Yorkshire during "Exercise Mainbrace."

It was seen by two R.A.F. officers and three aircrew as they stood near Coastal Command Shackleton Squadron H.Q. at Topcliffe.

Here are five of the R.A.F. men who saw the Flying Saucer. Left to right standing: L.A.C. Grime, Sgt. T. B. Dewys, Master Sigs. A. E. Thompson, Flight-Lieut M. Cybulski, Flight-Lieut. J. W. Kilburn.

They had just landed after a flight and were watching a Meteor coming in to land at the neighbouring Dishforth R.A.F. station.

One of them, Flight Lieut. John W. Kilburn, 31, of Egremont, Cumberland, then spotted "something different from anything I have ever seen in 3,700 hours flying in a variety of conditions."

He told me last night:

"It was 10.53 a.m. on Friday. The Meteor was coming down from about 5,000ft. The sky was clear. There was sunshine and unlimited visibility.

"The Meteor was crossing from East to West when I noticed the white object in the sky.

"This object was silver and circular in shape, about 10,000ft. up some five miles astern of the aircraft. It appeared to be travelling at a lower speed than the Meteor but was on the same course.

"I said: 'What the hell's that?' and the chaps looked to where I was pointing. Somebody shouted that it might be the engine cowling of the Meteor falling out of the sky. Then we thought it might be a parachute.

"But as we watched the disc maintained a slow forward speed for a few seconds before starting to descend.

Pendulum Swing

"While descending it was swinging in a pendulum fashion from left to right.

"As the Meteor turned to start its landing run the object appeared to be following it. But after a few seconds it stopped its descent and hung in the air rotating as if on its own axis.

"Then it accelerated at an incredible speed to the west, turned south-east and then disappeared.

"It is difficult to estimate the object's speed. The incident happened within a matter of 15 to 20 seconds.

It Flashed

"During the few seconds that it was rotating we could see it flashing in the sunshine. It appeared to be about the size of a Vampire jet aircraft at a similar height.

"We are all convinced that it was some solid object. We realised very quickly that it could not be a broken cowling or a parachute.

"There was not the slightest possibility that the object we saw was a smoke-ring, or was caused by vapour trail from the Meteor or from any jet aircraft. We have, of course, seen this, and we are all quite certain that what we saw was not caused by vapour or by smoke.

"We are also quite certain that it was not a weather observation balloon. The speed at which it moved away discounts this altogether.

"It was not a small object which appeared bigger in the conditions of light. Our combined opinion is that it was about the size of a Vampire jet—and that it was something we had never seen before in a long experience of air observation."

Flight Lieutenant Marian Cybulski, 34, who was in a Polish squadron during the war and has flown 2,000 hours, said:

"I agree with everything that Flight Lieutenant Kilburn says about this mysterious object. There may be Flying Saucers and there may not be. But this was something I have never seen before."

'Sort Of Halo'

Master Signaller Albert W. Thomson, 29, of Abbey-road, Barrow-in-Furness, who has been with the R.A.F. for 14½ years, said: "I saw just the same. It was there in the air, a round shape which hung for a few seconds. What it was I simply don't know."

Sergt. Flight Engineer Thomas B. Deweys, 20, of Bedworth, Warwickshire, also saw the object.

L.A.C. George Grime, 22, of Salford, said: "I saw a sort of halo shining on the centre of the object. It appeared to be going round and to shine as it turned. It was a solid object with no marks on it."

A sixth flyer who saw the incident, **Flight Lieutenant R. M. Paris**, of Brighton, was on a flying exercise yesterday and could not give a personal account.

S.D. 28 SEP 1952

NOW IT IS DISCLOSED—

RAF Has Probed 'Flying Saucers' For Five Years

By Sunday Dispatch Reporter

FOR years the British public has been led to believe that the R.A.F. has regarded "flying saucers" as a joke. The "Sunday Dispatch" can reveal today that, on the contrary, ever since the first "saucer" was reported in 1947 the R.A.F. has been operating a hush-hush investigation bureau in London.

A staff of technical experts —mostly commissioned officers under the direction of a wing commander — are analysing every report of a flying saucer over British territory.

Though the exact location of the flying saucer investigation bureau—known at the Air Ministry as the D.D.I. (Technical) Branch—is secret, I can reveal it occupies rooms in a building, formerly an hotel, not five minutes' walk from the Air Ministry in Whitehall.

The building is closely guarded. No one is allowed in without a pass.

To this office will come this week detailed reports of the mysterious "something in the sky" which burst into "Exercise Mainbrace" last week-end.

Intelligence officers at Topcliffe aerodrome, Yorkshire, interrogated the two R.A.F. officers and three aircrew who, as reported in the *Sunday Dispatch*, said they saw a silvery-white object chasing a Meteor jet coming in to land.

Experts Baffled

Detailed statements by the men will be closely examined for clues to the mystery. Preliminary investigation has left experts baffled.

"Till the experts have made a thorough investigation," an Air Ministry official told me yesterday, "it is impossible to do more than guess.

"Our experts will examine this report in the same way as they have been examining every similar report of objects seen in the sky which are not aircraft and which are generally referred to as flying saucers.

"The Air Ministry examines closely every serious report of a flying saucer."

NOT FROM THE EARTH, SAYS BREATHTAKING U.S. REPORT

S.D. 28 SEP 1952

THE U.S. Air Force has a "breathtaking" report expressing belief that some mysterious flying objects seen on earth originate from "sources outside this planet," Mr. Robert S. Allen, Washington correspondent of the *New York Post*, wrote yesterday.

Mr. Allen said the report, by noted U.S. scientists and Air Force officials, was based on 1,800 "flying saucer" observations in the past five years.

Air Force authorities were considering publishing certain portions of the report.

"Chiefly deterring them is fear the sensational findings may cause public alarm," Mr. Allen continued.

'Fantastic'

"These findings were described by an Air Force official as 'fantastic but true.'"

The correspondent said the document contained two other findings:

1. In some instances flying objects that have been sighted were secret U.S. missiles undergoing tests.

2. The Soviet was profoundly mystified and worried by flying saucers, and strongly suspected they were a new American weapon.

Air Officers Watch A Glowing Disc

S.D. 28 SEP 1952

THREE Danish Air Force officers saw a glowing disc-shaped object over Karup Airfield on September 20, when Exercise Mainbrace was on in the area, it was reported from Copenhagen last night.

This was the day after five R.A.F. men saw a silvery object chase a Meteor jet over Yorkshire.—A.P.

Pictures Taken 38 Miles Up

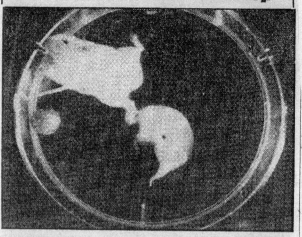

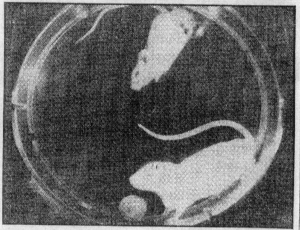

Mice Test Secrets Of
S.D. 28 SEP 1952
Gravity In A Rocket

WHAT would happen if a man were put in a rocket and fired so far from the earth that the laws of gravity no longer held?

That was the question U.S. Air Force experts set out to answer.

They put two monkeys and two mice in a rocket which was fired from testing grounds (see small picture) at New Mexico. Also in the rocket was a camera, with a shutter timed to give an exposure as the warhead came away.

As the big pictures show, the mice were in a two-sectional drum.

The top photograph, made shortly after the separation of the rocket-nose from the rest of the rocket, shows how the mouse in the rear drum can grasp the sides of his platform to maintain his equilibrium, while the mouse in the front section is floating in air in this zero-gravity period.

The rocket being fired.

Note that the rubber ball is suspended in air, away from the wall of the drum.

The lower photograph was taken when the parachute opened and the rocket began to come down. The mouse in the front compartment is standing poised and normally orientated as it follows the drum movement. In contrast with the top picture, the ball is now supported by the drum. The mouse in the rear compartment prepares to jump off the small shelf with normal agility.

After studying these experiments, and others with human pilots in jet planes, the experts believe that a man, properly secured in a plane, can function normally during brief periods of zero gravity and perform any operations necessary in piloting the aircraft.

After the tests the two monkeys and two mice were taken from the rocket alive and in good health.

The monkeys were put under anæsthetic before the rocket left the earth to prevent them from tampering with the delicate apparatus.

POINTS OF VIEW

ARE THEY REAL?

SIR, — Anyone who has studied the mass of evidence which is available will find it difficult to disagree with Reader Priest's opinion (Points of View, September 26) that flying saucers exist.

Their performance and behaviour point almost inescapably to the conclusion that they come from outside the earth. This seems to fill many people with alarm.

I do not know why, for flying saucers and their unknown crews have shown us no ill will and have so far given us far less reason to fear them than many of our fellow men.

G. H. ARMSTRONG
Petersfield, Hants.

●

YOUR correspondent argues that enough evidence has accumulated to prove flying saucers are real machines. His idea of "evidence" is quite different from that required by our leading astronomers, engineers, meteorologists and physicists.

G. E. W. GOSNELL
Coulsdon, Surrey.

☆

THERE are many difficulties in the way of accepting flying saucers as machines of solid construction. No matter from what material they were made, or by what method propelled, they would still produce the phenomena caused by high-speed flight through the atmosphere.

I have yet to hear that their reported tremendous acceleration has been accompanied by supersonic bangs, or that they have left vapour trails in their wake. They are said to be completely silent, and this seems to discount any structure capable of making disturbances in the air.

R. A. FRY
Christchurch, Hants.

●

WHEN I was a child I had a metal spinning top which I had to push up a spiral stick with a metal ring. When it flew off the stick it went up in the air until it lost its spinning momentum, then came to earth. Someone has perfected the idea. A spinning disc with enough momentum could reach unprecedented speeds and performance in the air.

F. MUDD
Bradford, Yorks.

☆

HAD the flying saucers been lethal weapons of an earth power surely one must have landed or been seen to explode in the sky? So it is clear they are expertly handled, and we must look outside the earth for their origin.

C. L. BARTON
Beckenham, Kent.

●

THE flying saucer is a phenomenon so far ahead of us that we don't like to admit it has us beaten.

A. H. JORDAN
Chessington,
Surrey.

☆

FLYING saucers are no more than was foretold by Christ. To quote His own words in St. Luke: "And there shall be signs in the sun, and in the moon, and in the stars; and upon the earth distress of nations, with perplexity . . . men's hearts failing them for fear, and for looking after those things which are coming on the earth. . . ."

P. J. HILDER
Muswell Hill, London, N.10.

Experts have said—

I AM still patiently waiting for reports of a flying saucer having landed anywhere. . . . It is very significant that most of the reports appear to have come from a country where mass hysteria is prevalent: *Sir Harold Spencer Jones, the Astronomer-Royal.*

Impossible to guess. It (picture of a flying saucer) is clearly not a meteorite. Therefore it is either a machined or cast structure: *Air Chief Marshal Sir Philip Joubert.*

Collective illusions: *Professor August Piccard, Swiss physicist who explored the stratosphere in a balloon.*

Red corpuscles of the blood passing in front of the retina: *Professor F. S. Cotton, Professor of Physiology, Sydney University.*

The approach of Mars to earth may have a definite connection with reports of flying saucers: *Professor Paul Becquerel of the French Academy of Sciences.*

If they exist, you can bet they belong to the U.S. Air Force: *Captain Eddie Rickenbacker, American fighter pilot, now a U.S. airline chief.*

WE FLEW ABOVE FLYING SAUCERS

One of the most astonishing reports of Flying Saucers in action has just been filed by the pilot and second officer of a giant American airliner.

The fact that both men have been flying for more than ten years, with vast experience of aircraft recognition, gives authenticity to a story which reads like fictional drama.

"Suddenly a red brilliance appeared (near their plane) . . . and almost immediately we saw six bright objects streaking toward us at tremendous speed," they write. And they conclude: "We are certain in our minds that they were intelligently operated craft from somewhere other than this planet."

Here is the full story, as told by First Officer William B. Nash and Second Officer William H. Fortenberry:

Nash

Fortenberry

'No pilot could conceive of any earthly aircraft capable of the speed we witnessed'

It all happened on the night of July 14. We were ferrying our plane, with ten passengers, from New York to Miami. The night was clear; visibility was unlimited. The only clouds, practically invisible to us, were reported to be thin and at 20,000 feet.

We were cruising along at 8,000 feet and had just sighted Norfolk, Virginia, when suddenly a red brilliance appeared in the air beyond and somewhat eastward. We saw it together. It hadn't grown gradually into view; it seemed simply to have appeared, all of a sudden, in space.

Almost immediately we saw that the phenomenon consisted of six bright objects streaking towards us at tremendous speed, well below us.

They looked like red-hot coals, perhaps 20 times more brilliant than any of the scattered ground lights over which they passed or the city lights to our right.

FOLLOW MY LEADER

Their shape was clearly outlined and evidently circular. Edges were well-defined, neither phosphorescent nor fuzzy.

Within the few seconds it took for the six objects to come half the distance from where we had first seen them we could see that they were holding a narrow echelon formation—a stepped-up line tilted slightly to our right, with the leader at the lowest point and each following craft slightly higher.

At about the half-way point the leader appeared to attempt a sudden slowing. The second and third objects wavered slightly, and seemed almost to overrun the leader. The fact that Nos. 2 and 3 did not react at once to the sudden change in speed indicated an element of "human" or "intelligence" error.

Diameter of the objects was about 100 feet, and they were flying at about 2,000 feet from the ground.

When the procession was almost directly under us, the objects performed an amazing change of direction.

Altogether they flipped on edge, the sides to the left of us going up and the glowing surface facing right.

While all were edgewise to us, the last five slid over and passed the leader, so that the echelon was now tail foremost. Then, without any swerve, they all flipped back to the flat altitude and darted off in their new formation.

LIGHTS BLINK OUT

Immediately afterwards two more identical objects darted from behind and under our plane at the same altitude as the others.

Then, suddenly, all the lights blinked out, and a moment later blinked on again with all eight "machines" in line speeding west. They disappeared by blinking out one by one—not in sequence, but in a scattered manner.

We stared after them dumbfounded, and then looked round the sky, half-expecting something else to appear.

12,000 m p h

The whole incident had taken 12 seconds, but we KNEW we had seen flying saucers. We couldn't both be mistaken about such a striking spectacle.

When we went back to check with passengers, most of them had been dozing and had seen nothing.

Back in the cockpit we discussed and formulated a quick report, called the Norfolk radio station and asked them to report our experience to the military.

Then, using our plane's computer and other instruments, we began to work out as many facts as possible about the saucers. We ascertained that they had made a 150-degree change of course almost instantaneously.

By reference to a chart we estimated that the saucers' track, from the locality where we had first seen them to the place where they had disappeared, covered about 50 miles, and they had travelled it in 12 seconds.

If we were conservative and allowed 15 seconds, that would mean that the objects were flying at 200 miles a minute, or 12,000 miles per hour!

If we were to be even more conservative and cut our distance estimate right in half, the speed would still be around 6,000 miles per hour!

'NOT UNIQUE'

We landed at Miami International Airport shortly after midnight, and the next day were closely interrogated by Air Force officers.

We were surprised when told at the end that our particular experience wasn't by any means unique.

In all our long and varied experience, neither of us has ever seen anything even remotely resembling the strange and unforgettable objects we saw near Newport.

Maybe there is some sort of confirmation in the fact that, following our sighting, Washington radar twice picked up unidentified objects, on July 19 and 26, and that on the second occasion a pursuing jet flyer reported being outdistanced by four disappearing lights.

'NO EARTHLY CRAFT'

What were the saucers we saw doing there? We have no idea. One of us thought that their sudden lighting up suggested that they may previously have been hovering.

In any case, whether they saw us and came to investigate or happened to move toward our position and took alarm, or rendezvoused there with the last two, or had some entirely different purpose, are about equally undeterminable guesses.

Though we don't know what they were, what they were doing or where they came from, we are certain in our minds that they were intelligently operated craft from somewhere other than this planet.

We are sure that no pilot, able to view them as we did, could conceive of any earthly aircraft capable of the speed, abrupt change of direction, and acceleration that we witnessed, or imagine any airplane metal that could withstand the heat that ought to have been created by friction in their passage through the dense atmosphere at 2,000ft.

REMOTE CONTROL?

Whether they were controlled from within or remotely, we can't say, but it is impossible to think of human flesh and bone surviving the jolt of their course reversal.

We have the usual reasons, too, for not believing that they were secret guided missiles. It is not logical that our own armed services would experiment with such devices over large cities and across airways, and another nation would not risk them here.

Nor could anybody's science have reached such a stage of development without some of the intermediate steps having become public knowledge.

One thing we know: mankind has a lot of lessons to learn . . . from somebody.—*Copyright True, the Man's Magazine*, 1952.

Two new riddles of the sky

TWO new riddles of the sky — strange objects moving at terrific speed — were reported from Southern England yesterday.

The reports—coming 16 days after airmen on an R.A.F. exercise were said to have seen a "flying saucer" over Yorkshire—were:

1—From Mrs. Jean Cobb, artist wife of David Cobb, marine painter, in their yacht White Heather, moored in Newlyn Harbour, Cornwall.

SKETCHED IT

Mrs. Cobb, who sketched the "saucer" before reporting it, said: I first saw the object, gleaming white, flying high, at seven minutes to noon.

It was making a wide, descending curve like a shooting star, and passed from east to south in four seconds.

It appeared to have a spherical body with a flat wing protruding on either side, but

Turn to Back Page, Col. 3

Two more riddles of the sky

Continued from Page One

when it swerved behind the clouds it became oval.

2—From an unnamed man who telephoned the Air Ministry meteorological office that he believed he had seen a flying saucer from a boat in the Thames at 1.30 p.m.

He said he saw a turquoise light in the sky moving downward and suddenly shooting off at an angle.

SOLID OBJECT

It was definitely a solid object, he said. Till he saw it he had been sceptical about flying saucers, but now was "considerably shaken."

He added that a man with him in the boat also saw the object.

Air Ministry officials said no weather balloons were in the air at the reported times of the sightings.

'REVOLUTIONARY' AIR PROJECTS

=8 OCT 1953

DESIGNERS TO MEET IN CANADA

FROM OUR OWN CORRESPONDENT

NEW YORK, OCT. 7

Thirteen leading British designers of jet engines and guided missiles arrived here yesterday on their way to Canada for discussions on " revolutionary " aeronautical projects with the Canadian Government and experts of the Canadian aircraft industry. Before leaving the United States they will be received by President Eisenhower at the White House and, in conjunction with the British joint services mission in Washington, will exchange views on forward planning with American naval and air force leaders.

The group is drawn from the " inner design circle " of the Hawker Siddeley complex and is led by Sir Frank Spriggs, its managing director, and Sir Roy Dobson, head of Avro Manchester and chairman and founder of Avro Canada, the largest aircraft concern in the Dominion. It includes the chief designers of five of Britain's top-priority jet engines and others who are largely responsible for the country's rocket and guided missiles programme.

It is the first time that the design council, which meets every quarter to pool ideas, has met outside Britain. Before leaving London Sir Frank Spriggs spoke of the significance of holding these consultations in Canada, which had emerged so rapidly as a primary air Power. The visit is described in Toronto as a clear sign of Canada's coming of age as a designer and manufacturer of aircraft.

Other members of the mission are Sir Sydney Camm, director and chief designer, Hawker Aircraft Limited; Mr. W. G. Carter, technical director, Gloster Aircraft Company; Mr. S. D. Davies, chief designer, A. V. Roe and Company, and its technical director, Sir William Farren; Mr. J. Lloyd, technical director, Armstrong Whitworth Aircraft Company, Mr. W. H. Lindsey, its director and chief engineer, Mr. W. J. Newman, the chief engineer of its armaments division, and Mr. H. R. Watson, its chief designer of aircraft; Mr. W. F. Saxon, director and general manager, Armstrong Siddeley Motors Limited; and Mr. J. C. Floyd, chief design engineer of Avro Canada.

WHAT MR. POTTER SAW

WHAT was it that Mr. Frank Potter saw flying over his garden at night? Was it a flying saucer? =9 OCT 1953

The first time he saw it was three weeks ago. But The Object had gone before Mr. Potter, of South Park-avenue, Norwich, could get his telescope.

But, as a member of Norwich Astronomical Society, he was curious. "Every night since I have kept watch," he said yester-day. And on Tuesday night it came again.

The time: 7.15. Mr. Potter, who is a 36-year-old window cleaner, saw it through the telescope—for three-and-a-half minutes. Then he made a sketch of it.

"It was one large dome on which was mounted a smaller one," he said yesterday. "From eight hatches—four on each side—shone powerful rays.

"Round the edge of the larger dome, which was a dark grey colour, was a much lighter band. It glowed red underneath. It moved silently at a great height."

Mr. Potter's sketch is very similar to the picture published in a book by George Adamski, an American. Mr. Adamski claims to have seen a flying saucer land and to have spoken to the occupant, who came from Venus.

Mr. Potter is sending his sketch to the British Astronomical Society.

COMMENT by the Air Ministry: "It could have been an experimental jet aircraft. There are a lot around these days."

etters to the Editor

the finished product, and thus a lower price to the consumer. These facts are often lost in the economic maze; they are nevertheless irrefutable.—Yours faithfully,

S.W.11. DAVID WILLIAMS, M.A., D.A.A.

*

Seen Over Norwich

Sir,—While observing the sky over Norwich at 7.15 p.m. on Tuesday last, October 6, I noticed a bright and very large object appear from the south-west. It appeared to be a very large yellow star. I then noticed it was travelling on a level plane, and with the naked eye it now appeared oval-shape, like a cluster of tiny stars. I waited for a favourable opportunity and focused the object in my 3½-inch refractor telescope.

On bringing the object into focus, the apparent cluster of stars took on the appearance of a dome on a large flat disc. The dome had apertures placed at intervals around it, four of which were in my field of view. Light from these apertures made the disc visible. The top dome did not rotate. There was no noise to be heard from where I was observing, and the object kept a constant altitude. Under the disc a cavity

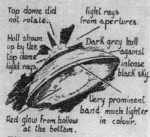

Top dome did not rotate.

light rays from apertures.

Hull shown up by the top dome light rays.

Dark grey hull against intense black sky.

Very prominent band much lighter in colour.

Red glow from hollow at the bottom.

This drawing, reproduced by courtesy of the " Eastern Evening News," was copied by a member of that paper's staff from a sketch made by Mr. F. W. Potter immediately after he had sighted the object he describes.

could be seen, and this glowed a dull red colour. I saw no traces of gas or flame.

The object travelled south-west to north-east and remained in my view for three and a half minutes. The sky was perfect, with no cloud. All the constellations were visible, and this object was seen independently by at least seven other Norwich people—members (like myself) of the Norwich Astronomical Society and the British Astronomical Association.—Yours, etc.,

Norwich. F. W. POTTER.

*

'Visitor from Venus'

Sir,—The photograph of a "space-craft" in Mr. Charles Davy's article, "A Visitor from Venus," bears a curious resemblance to that of a metal electric lampshade.

Incidentally, why do planetary visitors avoid England? Is it our climate, our cooking, or our lack of imagination?—Yours truly,

N.W.8. LESLIE CUSDEN.

*

Sir,—Surely the photograph is nothing more than a touched-up picture of a child's humming top, upside down?—Yours faithfully,

N.W.3. (Mrs.) S. L. HILL.

Sir,—To our contemporaries whose experience of the village washhouse is that of a battery of washing machines, the sight of the once familiar copper poss-stick would cause amusement. Yet an American writer has the idea that to take a slightly out-of-focus photograph of one of these utensils, say that it has been taken through a 6-in. telescope and weave a fantastic story around it, will convince the reader that a Venusian space-ship has visited the earth.—Yours, etc.,

Camberley. G. G. J. COOPER.

Michael Peto

*** Mr. Davy writes: The resemblance of the "space-craft" to an electric lamp (or to some similarly shaped object) is undoubted. I have looked at various types of lamp used in this country, and the Kodak flood-lamp shown in the accompanying photograph is the nearest match I could find in a short time. A more extensive search, particularly in America, might reveal a closer match.

I am not quite sure what the resemblance indicates. One might have thought that anyone who wanted to support a tall story with faked photographs would have managed to make them look more plausible—more like an imagined "space-craft" and less like a lamp.

*

Mr. Adamski

Sir,—In his most interesting and fair review of the book, "Flying Saucers Have Landed," written partly by Mr. George Adamski and partly by myself, Mr. Charles Davy rightly examines the possibility of a tremendous and silly hoax. I can only tell you this: that I have found Adamski to be—even to an unusual degree—a man of his word.

Just after the landings had taken place, he gave me his promise (no contract) that he would work with me. No money was mentioned, nor did any publisher seem willing to touch the book at that time. A few weeks later an international syndicate offered Adamski a large sum of money to release the story through them. Most flesh would have weakened and felt it had no *legal* obligation towards me. However, Adamski turned the offer down flat with : " I am very sorry to refuse you, but I have already promised another."

Now, my simple line of reasoning tells me that a man who keeps his word on money matters, when severely tempted to do otherwise, is likely to be telling the truth in other things. I may be wrong, but that's how it strikes me.

Many people find it hard to believe that a Venusian could look like us. But if, as Christians, we believe (concretely or allegorically) that God

made Man in His Image and Likeness, then how could that Image become a freak? The Image must have a similarity wherever Man appears. We may be the " freaks," having failed to live by His Law.

When Adamski " burned " his arm on the saucer, the Venusian made a grab to save him, scratching his own hand against the flange in the process. It bled—*red blood.* This would surely indicate a similar organic system to our own. But the visitor did complain that our atmosphere was heavier than his own and that long spells in it, unprotected, caused him discomfort.—Yours, etc.,

N.W.8. DESMOND LESLIE.

*

13 air chiefs view the 'Flying Saucer'

DOG GOES INTO AR...

12 OCT 1953

From JAMES COOPER: Toronto, Sunday

BRITAIN'S aircraft industry brains trust will consider today whether to go ahead with building the first prototype of Project Y, the secret revolutionary plane known as the "flying saucer."

The brains trust of 13 will see Project Y at Avro's factory at Malton, near Toronto.

Led by Hawker's managing director Sir Frank Spriggs and Avro chairman Sir Roy Dobson, the 13 experts will be taken past the electric-eye guard to see a 40ft. wood model of Project Y.

The design is top secret, but it is understood it embodies a gyroscopic engine revolving round a pilot enabling a plane to take off vertically, and with an expected speed of 1,500 miles an hour.

Sir Frank conceives that seeing it from some angles it might resemble "a saucer that got bent."

1,500 m.p.h.

Sir Roy says that successful experiments have been carried out in Britain in getting the air-craft into the air almost vertically. He says:—

"Something along this line will have to be perfected. We cannot go on indefinitely building miles and miles of runways."

What is certain is the Canadian company, with a big proportion of its 15,000 workers from Britain, is working on a revolutionary design.

New York cable: The New York Times correspondent said it was reported that paper work on the 1,500-mile-an-hour disc fighter had gone as far as it could go. What was needed now was money to build the prototype.

He estimated the cost of such a pilot model at £70,000,000.

Trials held

"The researchers have blue-printed a system of controls for the gyroscopic type of craft, but they face many tough and expensive hurdles before their 'baby' flies," the report continued.

"The whirling engine would provide the disc with its basic stability, and this principle has already been proven sound in wind-tunnel trials.

"Information unconfirmable officially, but believed essentially correct, indicated that surrounding the engine of the projected craft would be a circular wing which, like the cockpit, would not revolve.

"Air would be drawn in through intakes on the wing's leading edge. Part of the air would be injected into the engine and the remainder would be funnelled through a series of vanes on the wing's flat trailing edge."

the Editor

Ernstein," for example, contained advertisements for a firm of " hair restorers " and " Odonto, the Pearl Dentifrice "; Ruskin's " Love's Meine " advertised " Ball's Corsets " (with eight excellent reasons why every lady should wear a pair). Even reprints of Dickens's novels carried, in the 1880s, advertisements for a host of things ranging from tea, cornflour and sewing machines to a patent medicine called " Litholydium Zachariae."—Yours, etc.,

Norbury. HELEN MACGREGOR.

*

Mr. Adamski

Sir, — May the publisher of " Flying Saucers Have Landed " be allowed to make a few remarks on the photographs in the book?

The resemblance to lamps and other utensils had been pointed out to me while the book was being printed. I have myself noticed a likeness to the lid of an electric kettle and to my bath plug, which is at the moment unrelated to its chain. All this seems to prove that circular and dome-shaped objects resemble each other in general appearance—a conclusion so obvious as to be unremarkable.

The real point at issue, however, seems to have been completely overlooked. According to Mr. Adamski's testimony, the object he observed was 35 feet across, and it is within this context that the dispute must be confined. Here we have the opinion of two experts. Mr. Pev. Marley, a Cecil de Mille cameraman, as quoted in the book, confirms that the pictures, " if faked, were the cleverest he has ever seen, rivalling Houdini." The other expert, an English manufacturer of model aircraft, recently visited Adamski in California and inspected the telescopic camera and negatives in question. His opinion is that it would have been impossible without the expenditure of a large sum of money, and doubtfully even then, to make any model resemble the strange craft described by the author. Much more remarkable is the resemblance to the object seen by three youths over Sheffield, as reported in the " Sheffield Telegraph " on April 24, 1953, and to the Norwich sighting recently reported by Mr. Potter and others.— Yours, etc.,

WAVENEY GIRVAN,
Editor-in-Chief.

W.C.1. T. Werner Laurie, Ltd.

*

20 SAY: WE SAW FLYING SAUCERS

D.M. 29 OCT 1952

And 'thread' that melted at touch

From Daily Mail Reporter

PARIS, Tuesday.

FOR the second time in a fortnight people in the South of France today reported having seen a formation of so-called flying saucers.

About 20 townspeople at Gaillac say that at four o'clock yesterday afternoon they saw a series of white circular objects, slightly swollen at the centre, spinning across the sky; they were flying in formations of two and were grouped around something that looked like a giant flying cigar.

As the objects passed overhead they let fall a sort of string of bright white threads, which settled gently on trees and telephone lines. But when the eyewitnesses ran forward to pick up the white material, they said it disintegrated "like melting ice."

For half an hour

A police officer said: "None of my men actually saw the saucers but two of them reported picking up the strange thread-like substance. It looked like glass wool and it melted away almost as soon as it was touched."

Two other people said the saucers were over the area for nearly half an hour.

A similar occurrence was reported on October 17 from the town of Oloron, in the Lower Pyrenees. There, about a dozen people, including a schoolmaster, reported that they had seen flying saucers surrounding a long cigar-like object flying through a clear sky at about 6,000ft.

12 NOV 1952

'FLYING SAUCER' REPORT

Bexhill people who noticed a white streak pass across the setting sun yesterday believe they saw a "flying saucer." They state that the streak left a trail which disappeared after half an hour.

D.M. 13 NOV 1952

JUMPING SAUCER

COPENHAGEN, Wednesday.—For 75 minutes a "circular object" was seen flying over South Jutland last night. It changed from green to yellow and bright red, circled in "figure-six" curves, and "now and then jumped sideways."—D.M. Reporter.

We tend to think of flying saucers as a modern mystery when "circular objects," like that over South Jutland a few days ago, are reported. But queer and often frightening objects in the sky have been making news for over 100 years

D.M. 18 NOV 1952

As old as a—flying saucer

FEW will remember the series of aerial manifestations that puzzled the world 75 years ago.

Here, for instance, is a report in The Times of October 5, 1877: "From time to time the west coast of Wales seems to have been the scene of mysterious lights. . . . Within the last few weeks lights of various colours have been seen moving over the estuary of Dysynni River and out to sea. They . . . move at high velocity for miles toward Aberdovey, and suddenly disappear."

★

In 1877, too, the report of the British Association carried an account of a group of exceptionally slow - moving "meteors" . . . seemingly huddled together like a flock of wild geese.

Writing in the 500th number of Observatory, E. W. Maunder, the astronomer, recalls "a strange celestial visitor" he saw from the Royal Observatory, Greenwich, on the night of November 17, 1882. For two minutes a large greenish light was seen sailing smoothly across the sky.

This phenomenon was witnessed over a wide area—even from Holland and Belgium

Another of the baffling phenomena bears an uncanny likeness to recently published drawings of projected space-stations.

The Dutch steamer Valentijn was sailing the South China Sea at midnight on August 12, 1910, when its skipper, Captain Brever, suddenly saw a rotation of flashes above the water—"like a horizontal wheel, turning rapidly." This report was published by the Danish Meteorological Institute.

On record are dozens of similar reports on wheel-like objects.

★

On the night of February 9, 1913, appeared an equally astonishing spectacle.

Many of the observations on this were collected by Professor Chant, of Toronto, and are published in the Journal of the Royal Astronomical Society of Canada, November and December, 1913. They all confirm that on that historic night successive formations of luminous bodies were seen gliding across the sky in a south - easterly direction — with "a peculiar, majestic deliberation."

Many witnesses likened them to formations of airships.

These reports represent only a fraction of the evidence recorded on aerial phenomena during the past hundred years.

John Ellis

Mystery Object In Sky Turns Night Into Day

E.N. 21 NOV 1952

POLICE and night watchmen saw a flame of "burning light" which lit Bognor Regis early to-day.

The object was also seen over the cathedral city of Chichester, seven miles to the north.

One officer at Bognor said: "I was cycling along Chichester-road when suddenly the night became day. In the sky was a huge, candle-like shape with a blunt head travelling at terrific speed from west to east. It was as light as mid-day and the object was gone in a matter of moments."

Another officer also saw the strange object over Chichester at the same time.

At Ford Air Station the traffic controller said: "We have no reports of any unusual body being seen."

D.M. 26 NOV 1952

CHANNEL 'SAUCER'

People telephoned Hove police yesterday afternoon to report a "flying saucer," seen travelling south-west to sea at a terrific speed.

Sunday Dispatch

152nd Year. No. 7,881.   2½d.   NOVEMBER 23, 1952.   5   Radio Page 8.

Question That Is Puzzling An English Coastline

WHAT IS THAT FAST, BRIGHT LIGHT ?

It Sped Across The Sky Again Yesterday

Plane, Rocket Or Guided Missile?

S.D. 23 NOV 1952

By Sunday Dispatch Reporters

PEOPLE living on the South Coast and in East Anglia were yesterday discussing a strange white ball of light that had flashed across the sky, illuminating their towns and villages.

It bears no resemblance to any previous unidentified sky object, such as a Flying Saucer. Accounts indicate that the brilliant light may be caused by some new hush-hush type of aircraft.

First seen early on Friday, it was observed again yesterday by a Mr. Charles Henderson from his sister's home in Chichester-road, Bognor Regis, Sussex.

"It flashed across the sky almost before I'd realised it was there," he said. "It gave off a tremendous light."

Mr. Arthur Quick, of the Bay Estate, Aldwick, Bognor Regis, also saw it streak past his windows towards the sea.

Support for tne theory that it might be a new hush-hush plane was given by Mr. James Johnson, of Westerton, near Chichester.

On Friday morning he saw a sleek, powerful jet-plane, with swept-back wings, coming in over Tangmere, Sussex, Aerodrome with three "blinding lights" on its nose and wing-tips. The same mystery plane was seen by Railwayman Hardman, of Drayton, near Chichester.

"I had never seen anything like it before," Hardman said. "The plane appeared to be equipped with three powerful searchlights They were amazingly brilliant."

But both the R.A.F. authorities at Tangmere and the Air Ministry denied that any new experimental plane was based there.

An Air Ministry official said: "I know of no Service plane which carries lights of the kind described by these observers."

Early on Friday a Bognor policeman and an Isle of Wight milkman saw something that both described as a "tadpole-like object" speed across the sky.

Moving Tail

The policeman, William Keates, said: "I thought at first it was the headlamps of a car behind me. Then I turned round and realised that it was something travelling horizontally in the sky. It looked like a tadpole with a moving tail. It lit up the whole town of Bognor."

The milkman, Mr. W. Liggens, of Newport, Isle of Wight, said that while he was delivering milk just before 6 a.m. he was startled to see the whole street lighten.

For a moment he thought it was some effect of moonlight. Then he saw the "tadpole-like object" with a glowing green head and a red flaming tail. It swept across the sky and was quickly out of sight.

Another Newport milkman who saw it described it as looking like "a green beetle with a flaming tail." Both milkmen agreed that it travelled without sound.

It was seen from the mainland by Mr. "Vic" Cunningham, an ex-R.A.F. man at Bosham railway station, near Chichester. "It looked like a guided missile to me." he said.

Not Sparks

Two policemen going on duty in Chichester at 6 a.m. saw the sky light up. "We thought that sparks from an electric train must be the cause until we turned round and saw this queer thing speed across the sky to the north-east," said P.C. Tony Cox afterwards.

Mr. Frank Craft, a newsagent, saw the strange light from South-street, Chichester. "It looked just like a rocket — the sort you see illustrated in boys' magazines," he said.

"It went across the sky and seemed to break up over Tangmere Aerodrome or somewhere in that direction."

It was seen at Margate, Kent, by another newsagent, Mr. Charles Denby. He said: "It travelled much faster than a plane and made no noise."

Three Ipswich men saw something move across the sky which gave off a bluish light.

Mr. William Amos, of Kartoum-road, who saw it from Orchard-street, said it lit up the ground and buildings for five or six seconds.

Mr. Bertie Potter, who saw it from Spring-road, described it as a ball of fire with a tail of blue and green light about 4ft. long, and Mr. Phillip Farnish, who saw it from Bishops Hill, said: "It looked like a big blue ball travelling slowly south-east at a level height."

Turkeys On Way Again

THE THING

● *Puts troops on parade*

● *Has day out in Commons*

25 NOV 1953

BY DEREK DEMPSTER

THE THING tracked by a Territorial Army radar set on November 3 is helping to swell parades of part-time soldiers at the unit's drill hall in Eltham-road, Lee Green, Woolwich.

They all want to have a peep at the screen to see if they can see The Thing too.

The adjutant, Captain Fowler, said yesterday: "Attendance at the drill hall last Thursday was larger than it has been for a long time.

"We are now waiting to see what happens tonight and whether interest is sustained. We have drill parades every Tuesday and Thursday. The Thing has at least provided the men with a new interest outside the ordinary."

Bad weather

Mr. Richard Hughes, secretary of the Flying Saucer Club, complained at his home in Hove, Sussex, yesterday that the weather had been too bad for an observation expedition on the South Downs.

But, he added: "I've been burning the midnight oil, just coping with applications for membership and answering inquiries.

"Membership is now well over 300 and applications are still pouring in.

"Several members are setting up local study groups and I have appointed area representatives in South Wales, Scotland, Yorkshire, Cornwall, and other parts of the country.

"Interest is really snowballing. Last week, the bookshops were displaying ordinary travel books. This week space-travel astronomy books are overcrowding the shelves and windows."

'Balloony?'

M.P.s in the Commons asked about The Thing. And Mr. Nigel Birch, Parliamentary Secretary to the Ministry of Defence, replied:

"On November 3 two experimental meteorological balloons were observed at different times, one by two officers in an R.A.F. aircraft and the other by a member of A.A. Command. There was nothing peculiar in either of these occurrences."

The House had a laugh when Mr. George Isaacs (Soc., Southwark) asked if Mr. Birch would agree "that this story about flying saucers is all balloony."

Mr. Birch replied: "I think Mr. Isaacs's appreciation is very nearly correct."

Air control men see two 'saucers'

D.M. 2 DEC 1953

Daily Mail Reporter

FIERY objects sweeping noiselessly through the star-studded sky above Southend-on-Sea last night, were reported by frightened men and women

Many eye-witnesses said: "They must have been flying saucers. They were travelling much faster than any aircraft, and—unlike shooting stars—on a level course."

OBJECT No. 1 was spotted just after 6 p.m. by Mr. Howard Midgley, 43, on his way home to Rayleigh-road, Eastwood, Essex. "I was pretty scared," he said.

He telephoned Southend airport where a groundsman said he had seen it too.

OBJECT No. 2 was seen soon after 7 p.m. by five men in the airport control room. "It was like a large rocket and showered sparks," said one.

The Royal Observatory, Greenwich, said: "From descriptions received we feel they must have been shooting stars."

A meteor— or was it a Thing?

2 DEC 1953

WELL, what were they? Dozens of people saw them, first on Tuesday evening, then yesterday, whizzing across the sky over London and the Midlands.

At lunch - time yesterday several directors of a Birmingham firm saw "a large sheet of flame" moving north-east across the sky, afterwards disintegrating. They saw, they say, a charred piece of metal falling toward Sutton Coldfield.

Police were told to watch for wreckage.

Cloud, but . . .

At Sutton Coldfield the previous evening Mr. S. T. Warr saw a star travelling very fast north-west. That was at 6.5 p.m. —when Birmingham Observatory were recording complete cloud cover at 800 feet.

A minute later in Nottingham Mr. I. M. MacIntosh, a research physicist, saw "a small silver ball, very, very bright with a stream of light behind it."

About the same time Mr. G. Pollard, of Leicester, saw a bright disc-shaped object moving across the sky.

In East and North London five people saw unidentified "brilliant objects" between 7 and 7.30.

'Saucer-shaped'

In Leicester about 7.20 Mr. William Francis, of East Park Road, saw something "clearly saucer-shaped and with an incandescent glow" flying east. At West Bridgford, Notts, a farmer saw an object "leaving a greenish light behind."

"Probably meteors," said the Royal Observatory. An Air Ministry weather man suggested cloud haloes caused by refraction. Neither even mentioned that word—saucer.

THESE THINGS IN THE SKY CHUG THEN BURST

D.M. 3 DEC 1953 Daily Mail Reporter

STREAKS of flame speeding through the sky were seen by hundreds of people in the Midlands yesterday. In Birmingham it was said the "flaming objects" travelled at about 3,000ft. and burned out seconds after disintegrating.

Eighteen hours before this hundreds of people in Nottingham, Leicester, Southend, and parts of the Home Counties had reported seeing similar mystery objects.

Theories that they were shooting-stars, meteors, or fireballs are discounted.

Last night Professor Herbert Dingle, president of the Royal Astronomical Society, said: "I cannot explain them away scientifically. They must be man-made and part of some experiments on earth.

Charred fragment

"Fire-balls rarely come in groups. Normally they are seen singly and only on occasions. Meteorites only come very occasionally, too ; and these descriptions do not fit shooting-stars."

The fiery streaks were seen over Birmingham at lunch-time yesterday.

Mr. James Willetts, managing director of a city firm, told the police : "I and fellow-directors saw a large sheet of flame travel in a north-east direction, between two and three thousand feet up. It broke into smaller pieces then burned out."

Others said a charred fragment was seen to fall eight miles away, over Sutton Coldfield. Warwickshire.

There was no explosion, but a sound like the chugging of a World War I. aircraft.

People in Nottingham and Leicester reported seeing "silvery balls of flame shoot across the sky" on Tuesday night at about 6 p.m.

Mr. H. T. Cooledge a greengrocer. of Mansfield-road. Farnsfield, said : "I saw it for about eight seconds. It looked like a small silver ball, leaving a stream of bright light behind."

Similar objects were seen in parts of North London and the Home Counties.

CATTLE PLAGUE
Eight nations to fight foot-and-mouth

ROME. Wednesday.—Britain and seven other European countries today supported a United Nations move to wipe out foot-and-mouth disease in cattle by co-ordinated action. The eight nations agreed that the U.N. Food and Agriculture Organisation should form a European commission to fight the disease by slaughter, vaccination and emergency re-vaccination in stricken areas.—A.P.

RENT REPRIEVE

Brighton housing committee yesterday referred back a higher rents plan for putting council house rents on an economic basis.

RAF's 'Saucer' Is Still A Mystery After Eleven Weeks

S.D.   7 DEC 1952

By Sunday Dispatch Reporter

SPECIAL investigators at the Air Ministry are unable, after 11 weeks of inquiry, to explain the silvery-white object that followed a Meteor jet fighter over Topcliffe Air Station, Yorkshire, during Exercise Mainbrace.

The object was closely watched and accurately described by five trained observers.

R.A.F. Intelligence officers questioned each man separately on what he had seen. The details were impressively similar.

Two flight lieutenants, with nearly 6,000 flying hours between them—men who in the past had probably laughed at "Flying Saucer" reports—both affirmed they had never before seen anything like the Topcliffe phenomenon.

At the Air Ministry yesterday I was told: "The special branch which has been dealing with this is keeping an open mind on the subject and all reports received are still being studied."

It was noticeable that the experts are not on this occasion attempting to explain away the evidence as being "meteorological phenomena."

This is how Flight Lieut. John Kilburn described the object at the time:

Incredible Speed

"It appeared to be travelling at a slower speed than the Meteor, but was on the same course.

"**The disc maintained a slow forward speed for a few seconds before starting to descend . . . . After a few seconds it stopped its descent and hung in the air rotating as if on its own axis . . . . Then it accelerated at an incredible speed to the west, turned south-east, and then disappeared.**

"It appeared to be about the size of a Vampire jet aircraft at a similar height."

Last night Flight Lieut. Kilburn, now stationed in Northern Ireland, said: "I stick by the account of the occurrence which was given in the *Sunday Dispatch* on September 21."

News Chronicle 23 April, 1953

95

Flying saucer? This could be IT

From Canada comes latest news of the Flying Saucer—this time man made. Reports from Toronto say Avro Canada, North American branch of the famous British firm, is working on a saucer project. Reuter reports Field-Marshal Lord Montgomery saw a model of the machine when he visited Avro Canada's plant at Malton this week. First descriptions of the projected craft have been published in the Toronto Daily Star and the current issue of the Royal Air Force Review. Ronald Walker, News Chronicle Air Correspondent and Ritchie Calder, Science Editor, here analyse the news

N.C ap. 33 53

A 1,500 m.p.h. saucer like this would get you there before you'd started

By RONALD WALKER

THE Avro flying saucer is really a flying horseshoe, according to the drawing published in Canada.

It does not revolve as the phantom saucer is supposed to. But the power unit in the middle does.

Although stated to be 40 feet in width, the machine presumably is designed to carry only one pilot, housed in a stationary plastic-covered capsule in the centre of the power unit.

The horseshoe is said to be designed to fly at around 1,500 m.p.h., more than twice the speed of sound.

The rapid rotation of the disc containing the engines would provide a means of control, ensuring stability in the air. In the front edge of the machine is a row of ducts through which air is drawn.

After compression, part of the air is fed to the main engine in the revolving disc and the rest to combustion chambers ranged along the rim of the saucer.

Snags in jets

Exhaust gas from the central engine passes through ducts at the flat end. Here are movable surfaces which can act as rudders.

First hint of the flying saucer was given earlier this year in Toronto by Air Vice-Marshal D. M. Smith, R.C.A.F., when he said : " We are giving preliminary consideration to a project of this nature."

Later Mr. Crawford Gordon, president and general manager of Avro Canada, was asked whether the firm was building a flying saucer.

" Like all other aircraft companies which want to stay in business," he replied, " we are directing a substantial part of our effort toward new ideas and advanced designs.

" Like other firms, we have a number of such projects under way. One of them can be said to be quite revolutionary in concept and appearance."

Although every aircraft designer, encouraged by the progress made possible by the jet engine, has his own pet projects hidden away, he and his colleagues are realists.

There has yet to be produced a jet engine with enough power to enable an aeroplane to fly faster than sound in straight and level flight.

There is a strong school of thought among the jet engine experts that questions of size and fuel consumption will limit the use of the jet engine.

They believe that large aeroplanes or new machines, like a flying horseshoe, will not fly faster than sound until the nuclear-fission or the atomic engine can take over.

But can they be piloted?

by RITCHIE CALDER

ON the " flying saucer's " schedule, you could have lunch in London and arrive in New York in time for another lunch, the same day. By the clocks in Manhattan, you would have arrived before you started.

The flight would take 2½ hours (less than the rail journey from London to Birmingham), and New York time, according to the sun, is five hours behind Britain.

But beating the clock to this extent in manned aircraft involves scientific problems still unsolved. The idea of a circular wing is not new.

What is novel (and plausible) to the scientists with whom I discussed it yesterday is the idea of an engine rotating in a circular (or near-circular) " wing."

The aerodynamic problems of such a " set-up " have still to be resolved in the windtunnel. Recently miniature flying saucers, 40 inches in diameter, were tried out, under remote control, by the Yugo-Slav Air Force. And they operated effectively.

Take-off query

It is the speed factor about which the aviation scientists are dubious. It is not merely the question of getting the necessary power but of the stresses on the materials of a machine of this shape and diameter when it " crashes " the sound-barrier.

The other problem is the take-off (no one can even speculate on how it will land). From a stationary base, such as the suggested tripod launching gear, the aircraft would need enormous acceleration—of the order of that required to launch a rocket.

This involves problems of the fragile human body. Everyone who travels by air knows that there is no physical discomfort in sustained speed

The problem is acceleration, which among other things drains the blood from the head and gives airmen black-outs.

So high that . . .

There is also a question of height. It is estimated that such an aircraft would have to fly at, at least, 65,000 feet. At that height, without pressurisation, an airman would not live for 15 seconds. His blood would boil and his body would swell up like a cake in an oven.

The pressurised suits which have so far been devised can prevent gas-bubbles forming in the airman's blood owing to pressure changes, but even that would keep him alive for only about 10 minutes.

So everything depends on the pressurising of " the central plastic capsule "—the stationary " bubble " which is the cockpit.

AT LAST—A REAL FLYING SAUCER

D. H.   Apr. 23/53

by William Towler
Science Editor

A GENUINE "flying saucer" is nearing reality, in design at least, at the A. V. Roe Canadian works near Toronto.

Details have been published in the *Toronto Daily Star* and the *Royal Air Force Review* discusses the machine's revolutionary design in this month's issue.

This does not mean, however, that the Air Ministry is in any way involved in its production.

Its level speed is 1,500 m p h

ACCORDING to the details so far released, this disc-wing plane will be about 40 feet across and will fly at a level speed of 1,500 m p h.

This is more than twice the speed of the latest swept-wing planes.

The pilot sits in a plastic "capsule" in the centre of the saucer. This part can be ejected if the machine gets into difficulties.

Around the pilot's compartment is a jet-power plant of most unusual design which whizzes round at high speed.

This, in effect, acts like a gyroscope and gives the machine stability.

Then comes the fixed outer rim of the saucer with exhausts along its sides.

On the front are air-intake slots to feed the turbine and along the short straight back are vanes through which air can be fed to control the flight.

This disc-plane, as at present contemplated, cannot take off from a runway, but will rise straight up from a tripod launching gear.

It will have to make a gentle pancake landing on a flexible deck or platform.

Rockets help take-off

BOOSTER rockets will help the take-off, which will be made with the machine at a sharply inclined angle.

Though no prototype has been made, nor is likely to be made for a couple of years, the design is said to have reached an advanced stage.

A wooden model is believed to be hidden behind tarpaulin screens at the Canadian Avro experimental station.

When and if the saucer takes to the air, its sponsors believe it will be so revolutionary that all other types of supersonic aircraft will become obsolescent.

It outstrips everything

EXPERTS in aerodynamics with whom I discussed the machine yesterday were reluctant to comment on its feasibility before knowing much more detail.

Circular-wing planes have been designed and flown in the past. A notable experiment was the Lee Richards annular monoplane (the "Doughnut" of World War I), a model of which is in the Science Museum at South Kensington.

But this present flying revolving power house project outstrips all that has been thought of since then.

7/5/53

Flying Saucers

Sir,—I have been engaged for the last two years solely with the investigation of flying saucers, so that my colleagues and I now feel in a position to make a statement.

After studying over two thousand sightings in this century, and several hundred historic reports, plus a few score of the ancient Sanskrit books, we feel it is sure to say that:—

1. Saucers are mostly interplanetary, originating both within and without the solar system.

2. It seems that there was never a time in our planet's long history when it was not visited or passed in transit, by spacecraft of some description.

3. A recent translation of some old Sanskrit books leads us to believe that at one time a simple form of flying saucer was actually built on Earth; and that interplanetary communion was known, and practised by the great civilisation which perished in the catastrophe of circa 9460 B.C.

4. There is nothing new in the phenomena. More saucers were seen in 1846 and in 1870 than ever since 1947. The first photograph of a saucer was taken by an observatory in Mexico in 1883.

5. Above all, there is a menace, far from a blessing. This fear that saucers are a little peculiar, is in need of a little outside supervision, more to-day than ever before—particularly since Hiroshima. One asteroid belt was sufficient for any System.

These findings, and many others, liberally supported by personal testimonials, documents, and amazing photographs of saucers that landed recently, are the collected fruit of two years' unbiased, plodding research. When our findings are completed, we shall consider publishing them.—Yours, etc.

DESMOND LESLIE.

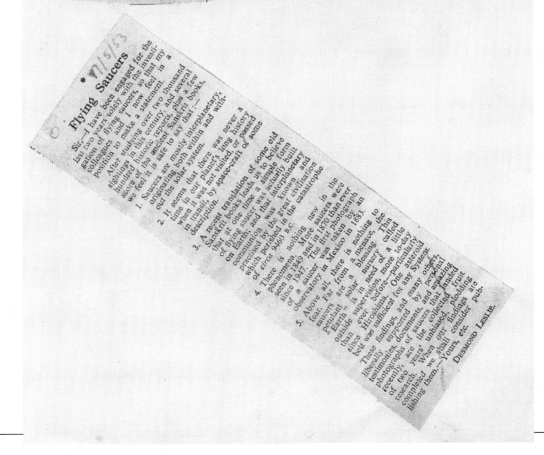

THEY'RE OFF TODAY

DOBSON   SPRIGGS   CAMM   FARREN

1 OCT 1953

to probe Flying Saucers

By FREDERICK ELLIS

A SUPER brains trust of Britain's aircraft industry sails for Canada today to discuss "revolutionary aeronautical projects" with the Dominion Government.

Among these projects is likely to be a flying-saucer plane almost circular in design.

Such a plane, driven by jets and boosted by rockets, is said to be under discussion at the Avro Canada works in Malton, near Toronto.

The speed aimed at is 1,500 miles an hour—more than twice that of Lieut.-Commander Mike Lithgow's world-beating Swift.

The flying saucer is believed to be already on the drawing board. A prototype may be built after the brains trust's visit.

The party of 13 will sail in the Queen Mary. It is headed by 58-year-old Sir Frank Spriggs, managing director of the £23,000,000

Hawker Siddeley Group, Britain's biggest maker of military aircraft.

With him go the Group's top technicians — Sir Roy Dobson, aged 62, the Avro boss; Sir William Farren (61), Avro's chief technical director; and Sir Sydney Camm (60), designer of aircraft from the Hurricane to the Hunter flown by Squadron Leader Neville Duke.

With them are nine more of the Group's leading specialists covering all design fields: aircraft, engineering, armament, and metals for high-speed flying.

From Canada the party will go to Washington for meetings with American air force and naval plane chiefs.

Two Experienced British Airline Pilots Tell

The Detailed, Expert Story Of How They Saw

THE FLYING SAUCER OVER THE CHANNEL

18 OCT 1953

Two experienced British European Airways pilots have reported to London Airport that on a recent flight to Paris they watched FOR 30 MINUTES a mysterious object in the sky that might have been a "flying saucer."

Captain Peter Fletcher, of Putney, has been a pilot for 18 years, first with the R.A.F. and, since its beginning, with B.E.A.; First Officer R. L. Lemon, of Iver, Bucks, became a pilot in the R.A.F. 14 years ago. Both are therefore trained observers as well as skilled pilots.

EACH DESCRIBED THE INCIDENT TECHNICALLY AND DISPASSIONATELY. NEITHER HAS THE LEAST DOUBT THAT HE SAW AN "UNUSUAL AIRCRAFT" OF SOME DESCRIPTION.

They agree, although they cannot prove it, that they were not deceived by a trick of light.

Here is their story, factual and unvarnished. It is told by Captain Fletcher:

OUR Elizabethan flight left London Airport at nine o'clock on the morning of October 9. There was a certain amount of low cloud and to 150 feet. I judged this other aircraft was flying at approximately 20,000 feet, and was about the same distance from me as the Constellation, or probably a further 20 miles away.

After watching the two aircraft —and I had no reason up to now to think that the other object was not an aircraft—it became

They Watched It, Measured It, Discussed It Technically For Over Half An Hour

Captain Peter Fletcher and First Officer Lemon

shallow saucers with their rims together. We noticed that:

1. Its relative position to ourselves remained completely unchanged for the whole of 30 minutes a course exactly the same without showing some variation in apparent position relative to our own aircraft, for they would be flying twice as fast.

Remember also that we could see variation in the apparent position in the Constellation.

The most striking thing to both of us was the absence of fluctuation in the intensity of the reflected light.

I admit that at one time I toyed with the idea that it might be a balloon. But it would obviously have had to be an enormous balloon and later observation confirmed the elliptical shape. In this it had the properties of an aircraft wing, being roughly one-tenth as deep as it was long.

It was impossible to estimate the size of the object because we did not know how far away it was from us. The day was so clear that it could have been an extremely large craft up to 100 miles away.

How Big?

GIVEN the size of an object one can estimate its distance away. Given the distance one can estimate size. We knew neither.

It certainly looked as big as the Constellation and was farther away from us. How far we could not judge but we estimated that it was somewhere over Northern France.

Neither of us has any doubt about one thing: *We were not deceived by a trick of light.*

WE HAVE NO DOUBT WHATSOEVER THAT THE OBJECT WAS SOLID, HAVING A SHAPE APPROXIMATELY THAT OF AN AIRCRAFT WING AND THAT IT WAS CONSTRUCTED OF A METAL SIMILAR TO THAT USED FOR AIRCRAFT CONSTRUCTION ONLY MUCH MORE HIGHLY POLISHED.

In 18 years of flying I have never seen anything like it. If it had been visible for a few seconds or even for a few minutes I would have dismissed it as an illusion or a trick of light.

But we had our "saucer" under observation for a full half-hour. We had time to consider it, to estimate its size. Our radio officer saw it and we brought along the steward to confirm what we saw.

Certainly we saw something material in the sky. Whether or not it was a "flying saucer" we cannot say.

But we will not dismiss it as a trick of imagination—not after 30 minutes of wondering what it could be.

If it wasn't another conventional aircraft, and I have given my reasons why we do not think it was, then what was it?

Maybe your guess is as good as mine but we saw it.

SUNDAY GRAPHIC

2,013   November 8, 1953   A Kemsley Newspaper

IT'S OFFICIAL NOW!

RAF AND THE SAUCERS

≣ 8 NOV 1953

"Graphic" Air Correspondent

BRITISH and American Intelligence experts are now exchanging "Top Secret" information about Flying Saucers. Air Ministry officials admitted to me last night: "Regular interchange of information between Britain and America has begun. The whole thing is in the hands of Intelligence people now.

"We can however confirm that air crews who have reported certain unidentified objects have been interrogated and that certain factors remain unexplained. We cannot say more than that."

★

The Admiralty is also known to have collated information from the Fleet Air Arm.

In America, so seriously are the Saucers being taken, USAAF crews are issued with a questionnaire before taking off. Carefully calculated questions, 42 in all, have to be answered as soon as any "object" is spotted.

AIR CREWS ARE ALSO ASKED TO MAKE SKETCHES AT ONCE. IN ADDITION A SEPARATE "ELECTRONICS DATA SHEET" HAS BEEN PREPARED FOR GROUND RADAR STAFFS WHO MIGHT GET THE SAUCERS IN THEIR

SCREENS.

The matter is now a top level staff item in Britain. Several alleged Saucer incidents have been withheld from the public on the grounds of security.

The files in which data about them has been compiled are labelled "Top Secret."

★

In an official letter accompanying a book published last week, the USA Ministry of Defence states:

"THE AIR FORCE HAS NEVER DENIED THAT THE POSSIBILITY EXISTS THAT FLYING SAUCERS ARE FROM ANOTHER PLANET."

Meanwhile in Ontario, Canada, the A. V. Roe Company are officially reported to be proceeding with Super-priority Project Y — the construction of a Flying Saucer.

Flying saucers? Someone painted them ages ago!

16 NOV 1953 EXPRESS POST

EVIDENCE and testimony about flying saucers have accumulated so much that now the thing for authorities to do is *not* just to begin believing in these craft, but to decide on how to make it safe and attractive for them to land.

We want to look over them, and get to know a little of those who man them and travel in them.

The United States Air Force has been more advanced and has watched for these craft, of which there is considerable variety, for a few years now.

But, in view of Leslie and Adamski's book having already established that these are interplanetary (space) ships and that they have been visiting our atmosphere for centuries past, it is amusing arrogation for the U.S.—if the report is correct—to begin to *suggest* that they *could* be interplanetary.

Even in one of the 14th-Century frescoes from Yugoslavian churches and monasteries, on view now at the Tate Gallery, two such space ships, round and with glowing tongues of fire *and human beings inside them*, have been boldly painted into the sky.—(Dr.) K. J. KABRAJI, Albany-street, N.W.

DETAIL of one of the "space ships" from a Yugoslavian fresco now on view at the Tate.

RAF pilot reports a Flying Saucer

10 NOV 1953

By DEREK DEMPSTER

INTELLIGENCE officers of the R.A.F. are now investigating every case of "flying saucers" reported over Britain.

The latest comes from Flying Officer T. S. Johnson and Flying Officer G. Smythe.

They were together in a Vampire jet night-fighter at 20,000ft. over Kent last week when they saw an object which at first appeared to be a star or a bright stationary light.

It was "very much higher" than they were. After a few seconds it passed over their aircraft at "tremendous" speed.

The object was maintaining level flight. It was circular in shape and appeared to be emitting or reflecting a fierce light.

Johnson and Smythe thought they would have their legs pulled when they reported at West Malling air station.

Instead, the station commander, Group Captain P. H. Hamley, put in a report to Fighter Command. Command sent for the two officers and questioned them for an hour and a half.

RADAR CHECK

Two other incidents are worrying R.A.F. Intelligence :—

1 On October 9 two B.E.A. pilots, Captain P. G. F. Fletcher and First Officer R. L. Lemon, saw an object in the sky on their way from London to Paris.

On their return to London they were told that Northolt's radar screen had been plotting an unidentified object that circled at 50,000ft. for two hours.

2 On September 7, the day Neville Duke broke the world's speed record from Tangmere, Sussex, a saucer was seen hovering over the airfield.

One of several R.A.F. men who saw it was Flight Sergeant Norster, of Portsmouth. He said : "It was a circular and whitish object. It was directly overhead in a bright blue sky.

"We thought it was a weather balloon until it moved off at a terrific speed towards the Channel."

The R.A.F. is now exchanging information with America.

And the U.S. Air Force is beginning to suggest hesitantly that flying saucers could be interplanetary.

Plane men strike

DAILY EXPRESS

No. 16,663   THURSDAY NOVEMBER 19 1953   CONTROLLING SHAREHOLDER **LORD BEAVERBROOK**   Weather: More fog

TV Eight peers to fight Cabinet plan   **CALL-UP** Forces manpower to be probed   **'SAUCERS'** War Office makes a first report   **BOYCOTT** West End ignores pro-Israel film

MYSTERY—AT 60,000 ft.

Army radar team spots the Thing R.A.F. pilots saw

19 NOV 1953 Express Air Reporter DEREK DEMPSTER

FROM the staid and unfrivolous War Office last night came a report that a "strange object" seen passing over Kent on November 3 was, in fact, tracked by an Army radar set in South-East London.

Sergeant said: Look —a flying saucer—

19 NOV 1953
Herald Reporter

KENTUCKY—1947

Hundreds saw these flying saucers. Press photographer took this picture.

BOSTON—1952

Four in formation. Spotted by a U.S. coastguard.

BULAWAYO—1953

In broad daylight. A farmer took this one.

AN object seen and tracked in the skies near London by five trained men with a radar telescope has set R A F Intelligence men on a new flying saucer "trail."

For many months, R A F and American Air Force Intelligence have been exchanging information on reported "saucers."

All reports are taken seriously until definitely disproved.

Last night, it was revealed that a senior R A F officer was sent to investigate the latest report, which came from 265 Heavy A A Regiment, at Lee Green, S.E.

35 MINUTES

The five men were testing new radar equipment when they saw something register on the screen. It was nearly motionless, apparently hovering somewhere over Essex.

One of the five was Sergeant Harry Waller, an instructor in the Royal Artillery. His story—

"It was a bright, sunny afternoon. We got this thing in our sighting telescope. It was spherical, and stayed stationary for 15 minutes at about 60,000ft.

"I called to a colleague: 'Do you believe in flying saucers? Have a look at this.'

"It moved very slowly, almost at walking speed, until a cloud came over and we lost it, after 35 minutes of observation."

SIGNALS

Sergeant Waller said that the radar signal was three to four times the strength that a heavy bomber would have created at similar height.

"The object," he said, "could not have been a balloon. It was dead white and at times it seemed to glow."

The other men who saw the object with Sergeant Waller were Mr. Ron Trew, Mr. A. J. Jeffrey, Mr. Denis Fuller, and Mr. S. Russell—all civilian staff.

Last night, an Air Ministry official said: "All reports about unidentified objects which might be flying saucers are now investigated.

"In 95 per cent. of the cases there is a natural explanation— weather balloons, or reflections on aircraft.

NO ANSWER

"But in the remaining cases there is no explanation.

"There is no conclusive evidence for saying that flying saucers do, or do not, exist."

In the past few weeks there have been several reports of "flying saucers" over England.

On October 9, two B E A pilots saw an object in the sky on their way from London to Paris.

Later, they heard that the radar screen at Northolt had plotted an unidentified object circling at 50,000 feet.

Several R A F men reported "a circular and whitish object" over Tangmere, Sussex, airfield.

WHO'S WATCHING US?
Or is it just a big balloon?

19 NOV 1953
By CHAPMAN PINCHER

WELL, what WAS the strange object—seen, reported, and tracked by radar—which passed over Kent on Tuesday, November 3?

Do we have to jump to extravagant conclusions that this was something that came to the Earth from afar? Let us see the possibilities.

Could it have been a plane?

No. The only type of aircraft which can stay "practically motionless"—as the object was reported by the radar trackers —is a helicopter.

And no known type of helicopter can get up to 70,000ft.—the height of one recorded object.

NO PLANE

Indeed, the greatest height ever reached by a jet is 6,335 feet short of 70,000.

The greatest height reached by a rocket plane is 82,253ft.— but then, a rocket plane could not be "practically motionless" in the air.

So it was NOT a plane.

Could it have been a meteorite?

No meteorite or any other kind of "celestial phenomenon" could have produced such a peculiar record on the radar screen.

Could it have been a balloon?

Possibly.

Large plastic balloons up to 200ft. in width are being released by scientists investigating cosmic rays at heights up to 20 miles.

THAT SPEED

They record well on radar screens, especially as some are coated with aluminium paint.

They can remain almost stationary for a short time at certain levels. When swept away by strong winds, they would appear to move at high speed.

They are pear-shaped when first launched, but expand to become spherical, and then look white from the ground.

And the fact that the object sighted was losing height when it "flew away" supports the theory that it was a balloon from which the gas had begun to leak.

BUT physicists studying cosmic radiation at Bristol University —a main centre for this research—said last night that no cosmic ray balloon has been sent up for the past three months.

Then maybe some other research centre in Britain or Europe is using these giant balloons.

Daily Mirror

THURS NOV. 19 1953

MYSTERY 'SPOT' SEEN ON LONDON RADAR SCREEN

19 NOV 1953

By GEORGE MORTON-SMITH

RADAR screens of a London anti-aircraft unit have twice recently picked up mysterious objects in the sky. The most recent was on Tuesday, when Sergeant-Major Ernest Stead, a radar instructor, was making a routine check at the headquarters of the 265 Regiment Heavy A.A., at Lee Green, Lewisham.

With four civilian helpers, he got on the screen "a very strong target" at a height of about 60,000ft. The object was moving slowly, and it gradually went out of range.

Sergeant-Major Stead reported the incident to his adjutant, Captain Ralph Fowler, who told Brigade headquarters.

Captain Fowler said last night: "It is impossible to say what the object was. Because of fog, it could not be seen through the sighting telescope, but the strength of the signal seemed to indicate that the object was a colossal size."

'Very Strong'

The object reported by Sergeant-Major Stead was almost exactly the same as that seen by Sergeant Waller, another radar instructor, on November 3, at about the same time of day.

In his report to Captain Fowler, Sergeant Waller said: "We got a very strong target between 2.30 p.m. and 3.15 p.m.

"The signal was extremely strong. I estimated the object's height at 61,000ft.

Two RAF pilots report 'object'

"It was stationary for some time, then moved away slowly and gradually went out of range. It disappeared at about 43,000ft.

"As soon as I lost it from the screen I went out to see if I could see it. Through the sighting telescope I saw a round or spherical object, a brilliant white in colour, still stationary.

"Although it looked small through the telescope, it must have been of great size to be visible at that height."

Two RAF pilots stationed at West Malling, Kent, saw an object that they could not identify on the same day as Sergeant Waller, but about four hours earlier.

Same People

On both occasions when the object appeared on the radar screen, there were four other people present. In each case they were the same people, Mr. A. S. Trew, a technical assistant, A. J. Jeffrey, storeman, Mr. D. Fuller, mechanic, and Mr. S. Russell, an electrician. All four are employed on the maintenance of the radar set.

For the next two or three weeks the radar set at the headquarters of 265 Regiment will be manned continuously.

● The War Office refused to comment on "The Thing" last night.

An Air Ministry spokesman said: "Reports of strange objects in the sky seen recently have been fully investigated. It has been proved that in 95 per cent. of the cases the cause was some form of natural phenomena.

"The remaining 5 per cent. have not been officially explained for the simple reason that there was not enough evidence to determine the cause."

RADAR SPOTS SAUCER

60,000 ft. up, says sergeant

19 NOV 1953

News Chronicle Reporter

SERGEANT HARRY WALLER didn't expect to see it, but when he had seen it he had to report it —and the job is now to get anyone to believe the report.

For what Sergeant Waller saw was a flying saucer. And what encourages Sergeant Waller is that he had four witnesses—and a radar set.

It's a powerful modern radar set, part of the equipment of the 265th Heavy A.A. Regiment, at Lee Green, London.

And it was the radar that saw the saucer first.

SERGEANT HARRY WALLER LAST NIGHT
" It looked about so big, on my radar screen "

A big signal

"The signal on the screen," says the sergeant, "was three or four times as large as that received from the largest airliner.

"I immediately put a telescope, attached to the set, on to the target and there it was—a circular or spherical object, white in colour, hanging motionless at about 60,000 feet for 15 minutes.

"It looked like a saccharin tablet. Every now and then it glowed."

Sergeant Waller, aged 35, lives in Carnac Street, West Norwood, S.E. He has been in the Army for 12 years.

Four other technical soldiers of the unit took turns in observing the object until it moved slowly out of range.

No comment

That was 15 days ago, but an Air Ministry announcement was not made until last night: "We are not prepared to comment on individual reports," said an official. "Every report is investigated, but 95 per cent. are found to be due to natural phenomena. About the others, the experts can reach no conclusions."

But last night came more news — from Sergeant-Major Ernest Stead, of the same regiment. He says he picked up the signal on November 17.

"We have been talking this over and we have come to the conclusion that it must be the same object. I am also fairly certain that it must be the same object that was reported by two pilots on November 3," he declared.

'FLYING SAUCER' SEEN BY RADAR OVER LONDON

19 NOV 1953   S.T.

Reports that "flying saucers" have been plotted on radar screens of anti-aircraft units have been made to R.A.F. Fighter Command. The reports are being investigated.

The most recent report came from a Territorial Army unit at Lee Green, London. The unit was testing a new radar set and suddenly received a " very large target echo.' The set was immediately locked on to the object, which was then practically motionless.

Through the sighting telescope on the set five people saw a " circular or spherical object, white in colour, about 90,000ft away." They watched it for 10 minutes until it slowly moved off.

The unit. 265 Hy. A.A. Regt., T.A., has its headquarters in Eltham Road, Lee Green. The "flying saucer" was seen by Sgt. H. Waller, radar operator; Mr. A. S. Trew, technical assistant; Mr. A. J. Jeffrey, storeman; Mr. D. Fuller, mechanic; and Mr. S. Russell, electrician.

During September mysterious objects were seen on the radar screens of A.A. Group Training Centre, Woolwich. These were picked up at heights varying from 50,000ft to 70,000ft, and the size corresponded to "a very large bomber."

The Air Ministry stated that it was not prepared to comment on individual reports. Every report is investigated.

But 95 per cent. have been found to be due to natural phenomena. In the other five per cent. the experts have been unable to reach any conclusions.

ARMY'S RADAR PLOTS 'THE SAUCER' SEEN BY RAF

'Circular and white'

A STRANGE, bright light, travelling at fantastic speed, seen by two R.A.F. officers flying over Kent on November 3, was plotted on an Army anti-aircraft radar screen.

The object was reported to the R.A.F. Intelligence officer at West Malling by Flying Officer T. S. Johnson, who, with his navigator, Flight Lieutenant Smyth, was flying at 20,000ft. in a Meteor jet. Later both officers described their experiences on a B.B.C. television newsreel, and agreed that what they had seen was not another aircraft " but something very strange."

Now the War Office has officially recorded the report of a Territorial Army unit—265 Heavy A.A. Regiment—at Lee Green, London, S.E., who were testing a new radar on that same day.

'LARGE TARGET ECHO' RECEIVED

Before the set were Sgt. H. Waller, radar operator ; Mr. A. S. Trew, technical assistant, A. J. Jeffrey, storeman ; D. Fuller, mechanic ; and S. Russell, electrician. Suddenly they received a " very large target echo."

The set was immediately locked on to the object, which was then practically motionless. Through the sighting telescope on the set, five people saw a " circular or spherical object, white in colour, about 90,000ft. away." They watched it for ten minutes until it slowly moved off.

During September other strange objects were seen on the radar screens of A.A. Group Training Centre, Woolwich, S.E. These were picked up at heights varying from 50,000 to 70,000ft. and the size corresponded to " a very large bomber."

The Air Ministry has been investigating all reports of " flying saucers " for several years, both those seen by R.A.F. flyers and by civil airline pilots.

In 95 per cent. of the cases, R.A.F. Intelligence officers have established to their satisfaction that the objects sighted were the products of " natural phenomena."

Natural ? No

" In the other five per cent. they were unable to find ' natural explanations,' " and Air Ministry officials say : " They could be anything from anywhere."

And the officials maintain there is insufficient evidence to prove that " flying saucers " do not exist.

Statements sent to the Air Ministry have included the shape of strange objects seen in the sky, estimated speed, and direction.

Conferences with meteorological officers and anti-aircraft experts have followed, and all statements have been considered alongside the weather conditions at the time. In some instances — as on November 3—radar has been used to check the object and to help in establishing an explanation.

Flying Saucers, Or Just Sorcery?

By HAROLD WALTON 19 NOV 1953

FLYING saucers, sorcery or just spots before the eyes? Close examination of all the reports in this strangest of all post-war stories gives no adequate answer to this question.

In the past few years, several thousands of people, in all parts of the world, have undoubtedly seen things which they were genuinely convinced were flying saucers. Can all of them be wrong?

The first report of something unusual in the skies came not, as many people suppose, from America but from Berlin. During the second week of October, 1946, a number of witnesses reported seeing "a fiery ball, flying from east to west, which they thought was a rocket."

NAME IS BORN

Thereafter the ball, as it were, passed to America. On June 24, 1947, a Mr. Kenneth Arnold, flying a private plane from Idaho to Washington, said he saw a number of strange aircraft weaving in and out of a chain of mountain peaks.

He described them as "strange saucer-like things."

And the phrase "flying saucer" thus was born.

And how the story snowballed. Immediately, all over America, people were seeing saucers or other similar curious objects. Many of these phenomena were soon identified as meteorological balloons, but some could not confidently be explained at all. And so it began to go around that these things were coming from Mars or from some other planet in the skies.

OVER BRITAIN

The first saucer over Britain was reported from Brighton on July 7, 1947. Two days later one apparently looked in on Rochester. People also began seeing things at Birmingham.

And on July 12, 1947, the visitation or whatever it was became sort of official. For a British ferry pilot radioed from the Bay of Biscay that he had seen a mysterious object flying at 15,000 to 16,000ft. one hundred miles off Bordeaux.

His message was considered sufficiently serious for the Air Ministry to pass a warning to the French authorities.

And look at some of the strange reports that have come in since:

January 9, 1948: An American pilot, Capt. Thomas F. Mantell, flew after a "flaming red cone" over Kentucky. As he approached the mysterious thing his plane blew up. Capt. Mantell was killed.

'MASS HYSTERIA'

March 25, 1948: A flying saucer streaked across the sky over Kent, vanishing towards the Channel near Folkestone.

March 10, 1950: The strangest story of them all. An "ultra-streamlined flying saucer" (apparently the latest model) was said to have been found wrecked on a hillside in Mexico and a man "23 inches tall" found dead inside it. What became of his body? "It was carried away for scientific investigation."

March 11, 1950: Washington comment on above: "A mild form of mass hysteria—or hoaxes."

CREW OF TWO

June 7, 1950: A Meteor fighter pilot reported to his station at Tangmere that he had seen a "shining disc-like object" revolving and travelling at very high speed.

November 6, 1950: London Airport employees reported "a white ball with a blue flame" flashing across the airport at very high speed. Saucer or something left over from the Fifth?

February 20, 1951: Nine men and two women signed an affidavit that they saw a saucer while flying in an air liner near Mount Kilimanjaro, Tanganyika.

June 29, 1952: A refugee mayor from East Germany said he had seen a flying saucer and two members of its crew in "metallic overalls" on the ground at close range in the Soviet Zone.

September 20, 1952: R.A.F. fliers in "Exercise Mainbrace" reported seeing a saucer over Yorkshire. Said the Air Ministry: "It could have been a met. balloon."

KNOCKED OUT

August 25, 1952: A Scoutmaster in Florida said an object large enough to hold six or eight men and shaped like half a rubber ball hovered ten feet above the ground near him, "knocking him out." When he recovered he found he was suffering from burns.

October 10, 1953: Two B.E.A. pilots on the 8 a.m. London-Paris flight saw a "strange oval-shaped object" at a height of 50,000 feet. They watch it for 30 minutes.

So there it is. And while some of these stories must be the result of hallucination or imagination, others could be true. What is going on in the skies?

Met. Men on Trail of The 'Flying Saucer'

19 NOV 1953 By CYRIL BIRKS

"Evening News" Air Reporter

METEOROLOGICAL officers made this report to-day to Air Ministry and War Office Intelligence staffs investigating reports by an R.A.F. crew and an anti-aircraft radar crew of a strange object over Kent on November 3:

"A 'Met' balloon was in the same area at about the same time at a height of some 60,000 feet.

A group of R.A.F. officers in an Intelligence Department at the Air Ministry have been collating and examining "flying saucer" reports.

They are now working out with the "Met" experts exact times and heights and are pin-pointing the area to establish beyond doubt that this strange object was actually a "Met" balloon.

FIRST REPORT

From 20,000ft.

First report of what they described as a "strange object" came from Flying Officer T. S. Johnson who, with his navigator, Flight-Lieutenant Smythe, was flying a Vampire jet night fighter at 20,000ft.

They reported to the R.A.F. Intelligence officer at their base at West Malling, Kent, that the object was definitely not another aircraft, that it was "something very strange," and that it was at a great height.

They also said that it was circular in shape and appeared to be emitting or reflecting a fierce light.

Then came the report from 265 Heavy A.A. Regt., a Territorial Army unit that while testing a new radar set on November 3, a very large target echo was received.

WHITE SPHERE

Five Saw It

The set was immediately locked on to the object, which was practically motionless, and through the sighting telescope five members of the unit each saw a white circular or spherical object about 90,000ft. away.

The type of "Met" balloon that it reported by the meteorological officers to have been in the approximate area about the same time is known as a Radio Sonde. It is white and 12ft. across.

This type of balloon carrier a small container in which certain instruments record and measure data in the upper atmosphere.

After a certain time the container releases itself automatically and sails to the ground at the end of a parachute.

Attached to the container is a tag asking the finder to return it to the Meteorological Department.

In 95 per cent. of the "flying saucer" cases reported R.A.F. Intelligence officers have established that the objects sighted had a natural explanation.

In the other five per cent. they could have been meteorites or other natural phenomena, but the investigating officers had not been able to prove that this was the case.

COUPLE SAVE BABY

The Day The Balloon Went Up

19 NOV 1953

"Evening News" Reporter

WHAT was the "strange object" seen by R.A.F. fliers and tracked by an Army radar unit over Kent on November 3?

That was what the intelligence departments of the War Office and Air Ministry were trying to discover to-day.

That was what people all over the country were asking.

And that was what Sergeant Harry Waller and his colleagues of 265 Heavy Anti-Aircraft Regiment were still debating at their Lee Green headquarters.

Was it a "flying saucer" such as many people still believe are spaceships from another world? Or is there a simpler explanation.

The object was first seen by Flying Officer T. S. Johnson and

Sergt. H. Waller, who saw the object on his radar screen, with Mr. A. J. Jeffrey, a civilian technical storeman.

his navigator Flight-Lieutenant Smythe in a Vampire jet night fighter flying at 20,000 feet.

It was definitely not another aircraft, they reported to intelligence officers. It was circular flying at a great height and appeared to be emitting or reflecting a fierce light.

Then came the report from the radar unit of 265 Heavy A.A. Regiment that while testing new equipment they had obtained a very large echo from something 60,000 feet up.

Not only that but several men had observed it through a telescope.

Out on the sunlit parade ground at Lee Green to-day Sergeant Waller pointed up at the clear sky and said: "It was a day like this when we saw it."

THE SERGEANT
'Quite Certain'

The object which glowed at intervals over London, was watched from Lee Green for about 15 minutes before it disappeared. Sergeant Waller and the men with him were quite certain it was a "flying saucer."

They began to wonder whether other unexplained objects tracked by their radar in the past were not "flying saucers" also.

As experienced operators they knew what sort of signal to expect from a passing aircraft. It was because this (on November 3) was so much bigger that Sergeant Waller used a telescope to try to discover what caused it.

But to-day Meteorological officers rather damped the excitement by reporting that a "Met" balloon was in the area at the same time as the unexplained object, and at about the same height.

It was released from the meteorological station at Crawley, Sussex at 2 p.m. on November 3.

Tracked by Met. office radar from Crawley travelling in a north easterly direction and passed over East Grinstead.

Then it changed direction to the south-east.

At 2.45 it was at 57,000 ft. crossing the coast near Eastbourne in a south south-easterly direction.

It then burst and observations were discontinued. It was estimated that the radio-sonde fell into the Channel at about 3.30 p.m. after descending slowly by parachute.

More than 90 per cent. of saucer sightings in the world since the scare started soon after the war have been explained in this or similar ways.

But there remain others which are still a puzzle.

'ONE LANDED'
In California

In an authoritative book on "Flying Saucers" Dr. D. H. Menzel, Professor of Astrophysics at Harvard University, ascribes the majority of sightings to "mirages" caused by the optics of the Earth's atmosphere.

This, he says, explains the speed and oblique angles at which they appear to streak off when approached by aircraft.

Many others have been explained away by photographic hoaxes.

But great numbers of people persist in believing "flying saucers" as spaceships from other worlds.

Major Donald E. Keyhoe, formerly of the United States Marine Corps, and one of America's most energetic investigators into saucer phenomena, remains convinced that some of them, at least, come from another planet.

The 'saucer' —almost certainly a balloon

By JAMES STUART

It became as near certain this afternoon as it ever will be that the "flying saucer" sighted by a Royal Air Force fighter crew and plotted by an anti-aircraft radar set on November 3 was nothing more than a weather-recording balloon.

Weather forecasters at Crawley, Sussex, released a radio-equipped balloon half an hour before a strange object was plotted on an Army radar set at Lee Green.

The balloon was tracked by the weather men's radar towards the Sussex-Kent boundary.

At 45,000ft.

It passed over East Grinstead and the fringe of Kent. At 2.30 p.m. it was at 45,000ft. A quarter of an hour later it was at 57,000ft.

The balloon crossed the coast near Eastbourne and was travelling south - east across the Channel when it burst. All this was plotted by radar.

Normally, when a weather balloon bursts, the recording apparatus comes down by parachute.

Other reports of "flying saucers" over Kent recently can be accounted by the fact that weather balloons are released from Crawley "as a matter of routine." The normal prevailing wind would carry them over East Sussex and Kent.

FRIDAY, NOVEMBER 20, 1953.

SAUCERS OR CIGARS?

MANY people have "seen" flying saucers in the past few years—usually over America. Most of these have been as ethereal as Tinker Bell or the bog lights which lure travellers into Irish morasses.

Now there is something new. A flying saucer has been picked up on radar screens. That makes it more solid than a mirage, less distant than Venus, and much larger than a metal stopper from a beer bottle.

All these explanations, and many more, have been used to dismiss the flying saucer as the offspring of too-vivid imaginations or of mass-hysteria. But when we read about those radar screens we sat up and took notice.

At last, we thought, the mystery is about to be revealed. At any moment now East and West will unite and the statesmen will come out with a Declaration to the Peoples of the World.

The balloon

ALAS!—the large object picked up by both the Army and Air Force over Kent on November 3 seems to have been another meteorological balloon. It burst—and exploded with it our hopes of the biggest news story since The Flood.

We remember writing on this subject three years ago, when there was a previous epidemic of "sauceritis" and someone said he had seen a number of "little men with red hair" from another planet.

More recently we have been told of an "interview" with a visitor from Venus who was so remarkably like ourselves that he might have walked out of London or New York—except that he needed a haircut.

It is good fun and does little harm. But when all the nonsense has been drained away there remains a sediment of observed fact which remains inexplicable.

The evidence

THAT is not our conclusion. We reach it on the authority of R.A.F. Intelligence officers who say that in five per cent. of the cases they investigate they are "unable to find a natural explanation."

What does emerge is that men of many hours' flying experience, civil and R.A.F. pilots and crews alike, have soberly and circumstantially told of things which are abnormal.

For several years the R.A.F. have been collecting and collating such evidence. We suggest the time has come to disclose it to the public—unless the national interest is involved.

It is all very well for them to say there is not sufficient evidence to prove that flying saucers do not exist. By the time we have worked out the implication of that double negative we do not know what they mean.

The thing

WHAT do they really believe? A White Paper setting out their conclusions would be more enthralling than some recent similar documents!

Why, in any case, are the objects always called "saucers"—a name destined to be at once as simple and significant as "tank"? Most of them are disks, but some are "cones" or "arrow-heads," while many are "cigar-shaped."

We should like to know more about the "silver circular object" which trailed a Meteor plane over Yorkshire and descended, "swinging like a pendulum," before moving off at high speed.

We should like to know why two U.S. pilots investigated a "bright red" thing at 17,000ft. and were forbidden to talk of what they had seen.

But, above all, we should like to know whether these "space-ships" are saucers, cigars, or—nuts.

News ✠ Chronicle
20 NOV 1953

TOP SECRET

WHEN, during duty hours, the British Army begins to see flying saucers, it is time to sit up and take notice.

It is true that these particular saucers have now turned out to be balloons. But that is not the point.

The point is contained in the fact that the mistaken report has evoked from the R.A.F. the information that it has been able to explain ninety-five per cent. of reported sightings.

This piece of news, so innocently delivered and so discreetly left unamplified, might easily qualify as the calmest understatement of the year. What, in the name of heaven and earth, are we to think about the other five per cent.?

Whatever we think, we are to be left to do it without official guidance.

It is hard to see why this must be so. If the so-called saucers are some new defensive weapon, would they not be a more effective deterrent if proclaimed?

The U.S. Air Force now says America is making no such thing. But suppose they are thought to be hostile, would forewarned not still be forearmed?

Or are the authorities just afraid of looking silly if they start discussing visitors from outer space? If this is the trouble, they should take the risk and tell us what they make of all these rumours.

That troublesome five per cent. is making it hard to believe that there is nothing more behind them than balloons.

---

and eiderdowns, clean the   Surrey.

SAUCERS OVER SCOTLAND

I SAW and reported a flying saucer over Dunoon on June 21 at 11.5 a.m. I doubt whether anyone in Britain has had a closer view of one in daylight than I had.

I also had sufficient experience of aircraft during the war to know that I wasn't looking at an observation balloon or any of the natural phenomena that the powers that be try to tell others they have seen. The cold light of day gives the lie to all those explanations.

S. CALLOW.
Johnstone,
Renfrewshire.

frantically for a pittance.

A LIGHT THAT FAILED

PATRIOTIC imaginations were undoubtedly uplifted yesterday by the news that a Territorial unit had plotted a Flying Saucer on a radar screen. Here was something material—no mirage or mass hallucination—hovering in the upper air of Britain. The town council of Boise, Idaho, who have announced fees for non-scheduled Flying Saucer landings at their airport, could consider themselves rebuked for presumption. It is, of course, somewhat disappointing that this British Flying Saucer, like so many others, was probably a meteorological balloon. On the other hand the Air Ministry admission that five per cent. of the reports have not been conclusively explained away provides a gleam of hope after this particular light has failed.

Not every Saucer has been seen by observers in their cups. Meteorites and rockets, air-bubbles and reflections do not account for all the phenomena. There is nothing scientifically absurd in the supposition that unknown aircraft have been built by unknown beings and propelled by unknown forces from the planets. The limited interest which the beings who, it is claimed, emerge from these vessels take in us is, however, disconcerting. The long-haired celestial tourist who recently conveyed to a human observer, partly by gestures and partly by telepathy, that he himself came from Venus need not have given such a brief connotation to his flying visit. Moreover the person in a space-ship who "quite distinctly" addressed an Italian farmer with the words "Verren Urg Much" was positively abrupt. Why should we be sauced from Saucers?

U.S.A.F. REPORT ON "FLYING SAUCERS"

WASHINGTON, Nov. 19.—A new United States Air Force report on "flying saucers" discredits the existence of such mysterious objects as the "saucer" which the British Air Ministry to-day said was seen over London recently. The report is to be issued next month. A draft, examined at defence headquarters to-day, says most of the strange objects sighted in the United States since 1947 have proved to be conventional objects, such as balloons and aircraft, or have been meteors or planets.

Other sightings which were tracked on radar screens but which could not be explained were almost certainly caused, it adds, by other natural phenomena, including temperature inversion (the reflection of images of ground objects on layers of warm air high above the earth), ionized clouds, thunderstorms, birds, ice formations in the air, and other types of reflections from the ground.—*Reuter.*

※ The sighting of a "strange object" over south-east England on November 3 is reported on page 5.

'STRANGE OBJECT IN SKY'

INVESTIGATIONS BY AIR MINISTRY

BY OUR AERONAUTICAL CORRESPONDENT

The Air Ministry are investigating reports of the sighting of a " strange object " in the sky over south-east England on the afternoon of November 3. Sightings were reported by an R.A.F. night fighter pilot and his navigator, who were flying from West Malling, Kent, and by the crew of a Heavy Anti-Aircraft Regiment radar unit at Lee Green, in south-east London.

It is known that a meteorological balloon with a radio-sonde instrument attached, released at Crawley, Sussex, was floating in the area on that afternoon.

SEEN ON RADAR SCREEN

Flying Officer T. S. Johnson and Flying Officer C. Smythe were in a Vampire night fighter at about 20,000ft. when they saw an unidentified object which appeared to be moving very fast high above them. Anti-Aircraft Command received a report that, at about the same time, an object was picked up on a radar set by No. 265 Heavy Anti-Aircraft Regiment, R.A., a Territorial Army unit, at Eltham Road, Lee Green.

The report stated: " On the afternoon of November 3 a radar set was being tested at this location at 2.30 p.m. A very large target echo was received on bearing S.E., angle 42deg., slant range 30,000 yds. The radar was locked on to follow the target automatically. It was then noticed that the target was practically motionless. On being observed through the sighting telescope the object appeared to be circular or spherical and white in colour. After approximately 10 minutes the object began to move away very slowly, its bearing remaining constant. Finally, it passed beyond the radar tracking range at 3.10 p.m."

This report indicates that the object was at one time as high as 60,000ft. but that it was down to 43,000ft. when it disappeared. Other unidentified objects were picked up on radar sets at Woolwich on three occasions between September 14 and 22.

BALLOON'S PROGRESS

The Air Ministry reported yesterday that a radio-sonde balloon was released from the meteorological station at Crawley at 2 p.m. on November 3. It was tracked by radar from that station as follows: It ascended, travelling in a north-easterly direction, and passed over East Grinstead. Then it changed direction to the south-east, and at 2.30 p.m. was at 45,000ft. At 2.45 it was at 57,000ft., and crossed the coast near Eastbourne travelling in a S.S.E. direction. It then burst, and observations were discontinued. After the balloon had burst, the radio-sonde would have descended slowly by parachute, and it is estimated that it would have fallen into the Channel at about 3.30 p.m.

An Air Ministry spokesman said yesterday that there was insufficient evidence upon which to base an opinion as to the existence or non-existence of so-called " flying saucers." For about four years, whenever reports were received of the sighting of unusual objects, they were investigated. In 95 per cent. of the cases a simple explanation had been found. This might well apply to the other 5 per cent., but proof could not be obtained. Some reports undoubtedly referred to natural phenomena. " Sightings " had proved to have been meteorological balloons, light reflected from the wing of an aircraft as it banked, or unusual cloud or other weather. All reports were investigated by the Intelligence Department in consultation with the Meteorological Office.

DIFFERENT SHAPES

Every day Meteorological Office stations in the United Kingdom release at least 32 large radio-sonde balloons, as well as about 100 smaller ones, which are observed visually. The radio-sonde balloons carry a special reflector to enable them to be tracked by radar, and they give as strong a radar response as would be obtained from a four-engined aircraft. Such balloons have been known to reach a height of 100,000ft., though the normal is about 60,000ft. Because of the thinner air at great heights, as the balloons rise they expand to a diameter of about 12ft. At great altitudes, in particular, they reflect the sunlight. Meteorological observers say that they appear to assume different shapes, depending on the angle from which they are observed in relation to the position of the sun.

NEWS CHRONICLE, FRIDAY, NOVEMBER 20, 1953

U.S. DENIES SECRET WEAPON, REJECTS ENEMY MISSILES

Flying saucers? 'There's no such thing'

20 NOV 1953

'CLUE' OF A BALLOON

NEWS CHRONICLE REPORTER

FLYING SAUCERS meet with a setback from both sides of the Atlantic today.

POINT 1.—The Air Ministry suggested last night that the "unidentified object" reported by the War Office as having been tracked by a radar team in South-East London on November 3 was probably nothing more or less than a weather balloon.

POINT 2: A new U.S. Air Force report issued in draft form in Washington, goes further. It says *there is no such thing as a Flying Saucer.*

Let us start with the **Air Ministry.** They say a radio sonde balloon was released from the weather station at Crawley, Sussex, on November 3.

Burst over coast

It drifted south-east, rising to at least 57,000 feet. It burst near Eastbourne and the instruments it was carrying are thought to have come down—by automatic parachute—in the Channel.

These balloons, which provide information for weather forecasts, carry metal reflectors which give a radar response at least equal to that of a four-engined plane.

They reflect the rays of the sun and often appear to assume misleading shapes. Sometimes, in fact, they look like saucers. Their actual maximum size is only 12 feet.

WASHINGTON is told by the U.S. Air Force that most of the strange objects sighted in the United States since 1947 have proved to be conventional objects, such as balloons and aircraft, or meteors or planets.

Other unexplained sightings tracked on radar screens were, it is stated, "almost certainly" caused by other natural phenomena, including temperature inversion (reflection of images of ground objects on layers of warm air), ionized clouds, thunderstorms, birds, ice formations in the air, and other types of reflections from the ground.

No 'space ships'

"The unidentified aerial phenomena (observed in the United States) are not a secret weapon, missile or aircraft developed by the United States.

"None of the three military departments nor any other agency in the Government is conducting experiments, classified or otherwise, with flying objects which could be a basis for the phenomena.

"By the same token, no authentic physical evidence has been received which could establish the possible existence of space ships from other planets."

The third possibility—missiles or "flying saucers" sent by an "enemy" country—is not discussed, but military authorities reject this suggestion.

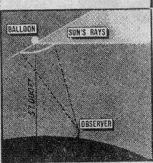

How it works

BALLOON SUN'S RAYS

57,000 FT.

OBSERVER

THIS is how a balloon becomes a "flying saucer." The sun's rays reflect on the convex surface of the balloon and give an enlarged image to the observer. According to the angle of the sun's rays in relation to the observer's position, the image of balloon, enlarged many times, may be spherical, eliptical, or saucer-shaped

THE WHOLE WORLD IS WONDERING

E.N. 20 NOV 1953

FLYING saucers . . . balloons . . . or meteors, or . . . Well, read on from here:

FROM WASHINGTON: A new U.S. Air Force report on flying saucers is to be issued next month, reports Reuter.

A draft examined at Defence Headquarters to-day, says most of the strange objects sighted in the United States since 1947 have proved to be conventional objects, such as balloons and aircraft, or have been meteors or planets.

Other sightings not explained were almost certainly natural phenomena—including ionised clouds, thunderstorms, birds, ice formations and reflections from the ground.

The report says : "Unidentified aerial phenomena are not a secret weapon, missile or aircraft developed by the United States."

'NO EVIDENCE'

None of the three military Departments or any other agency in the Government is conducting experiments with flying objects which could be a basis for the reported phenomena.

And "No authentic physical evidence has been received which could establish the possible existence of space ships from other planets."

More than 275 "flying saucer" reports were investigated in 1949, 1,700 in 1952 and 250 this year.

FROM PRETORIA: Reuter says Defence H.Q. reported to-day that mysterious objects have been seen by experienced South African Air Force officers and "other reliable observers."

A spokesman declared: "We have had some very clear descriptions of the phenomena by experienced officers trained in the detection of rockets and other objects moving at high speed."

They had accumulated a great deal of information. There was a regular exchange of information with the Royal Air Force and reports had also been referred to Military Intelligence.

FROM CAPE TOWN: A senior Air Force officer said the reliability of several reports sent to the South African Air Force was beyond question.

A mysterious radar contact with an unexplained phenomenon over the Cape Peninsula was now being investigated, he stated. The contact was "undoubtedly with something solid."

Latest report was made in May by a doctor in Uppington, North Cape Province. For security reasons no details were given.

AN ILLUSION?

Dr. R. H. Stoy, Royal Astronomer at the Cape, said: "My own opinion is that there is some sort of phenomenon which has not yet been adequately explained."

FROM CANBERRA: The Air Minister, Mr. William McMahon, told the House of Representatives to-day that he believed the matter was a problem for psychologists rather than for the defence authorities, says Exchange Telegraph.

The Air Force had received many reports but were unable to identify the cause of the phenomena.

Each report recorded that the sighting was preceded by a meteorite flashing across the sky. It was possible that some optical illusion might be the cause.

The Air Force advised that the aero-dynamic features related to flying saucers remain unsolved. "It is possible to fly such machines in circles using round gas engines, but I believe this is far in the future," he declared.

All the World Watches the Skies, and Now—

M.P.s TO ASK ABOUT SAUCERS

E.N. 20 NOV 1953

FLYING saucers . . . balloons . . . or meteors, or . . . Well, read on from here:

IN LONDON: Official statements will be made in the Commons next week about Kent's flying saucers, now believed to be meteorological balloons.

Lieut.-Colonel W. Schofield (Con., Rochdale) will ask the Parliamentary Secretary to the Defence Ministry for a statement on reports his department has received of the flying object seen by two airmen over London or other parts of the United Kingdom and reported to him.

Mr. F. Bellinger (Lab., Bassetlaw), a former War Minister, will ask the War Minister whether he has been able to identify the flying saucer object reported by one of the members of anti-aircraft Command.

Mr. R. T. Paget (Lab., Northampton) will ask the Under-Secretary of State for Air whether he has any statement to make with regard to the flying object reported over Kent on November 17.

SECRET? NO

FROM WASHINGTON: A new U.S. Air Force report on flying saucers is to be issued next month, reports Reuter.

A draft examined at Defence Headquarters to-day, says most of the strange objects sighted in the United States since 1947 have proved to be conventional objects, such as balloons and aircraft, or have been meteors or planets.

Other sightings not explained were almost certainly natural phenomena—including ionised clouds, thunderstorms, birds, ice formations and reflections from the ground.

The report says : "Unidentified aerial phenomena are not a secret weapon, missile or aircraft developed by the United States."

'NO EVIDENCE'

None of the three military Departments or any other agency in the Government is conducting experiments with flying objects which could be a basis for the reported phenomena.

And "No authentic physical evidence has been received which could establish the possible existence of space ships from other planets."

More than 275 "flying saucer" reports were investigated in 1949, 1,700 in 1952 and 250 this year.

FROM PRETORIA: Reuter says Defence H.Q. reported to-day that mysterious objects have been seen by experienced South African Air Force officers and "other reliable observers."

A spokesman declared: "We have had some very clear descriptions of the phenomena by experienced officers trained in the detection of rockets and other objects moving at high speed."

They had accumulated a great deal of information. There was a regular exchange of information with the Royal Air Force and reports had also been referred to Military Intelligence.

FROM CAPE TOWN: A senior Air Force officer said the reliability of several reports sent to the South African Air Force was beyond question.

A mysterious radar contact with an unexplained phenomenon over the Cape Peninsula was now being investigated, he stated. The contact was "undoubtedly with something solid."

Latest report was made in May by a doctor in Uppington, North Cape Province. For security reasons no details were given.

AN ILLUSION?

Dr. R. H. Stoy, Royal Astronomer at the Cape, said: "My own opinion is that there is some sort of phenomenon which has not yet been adequately explained."

FROM CANBERRA: The Air Minister, Mr. William McMahon, told the House of Representatives to-day that he believed the matter was a problem for psychologists rather than for the defence authorities, says Exchange Telegraph.

The Air Force had received many reports but were unable to identify the cause of the phenomena.

Each report recorded that the sighting was preceded by a meteorite flashing across the sky. It was possible that some optical illusion might be the cause.

The Air Force advised that the aero-dynamic features related to flying saucers remain unsolved. "It is possible to fly such machines in circles using round gas engines, but I believe this is far in the future," he declared.

SIX REPORT 'SAUCER' HOVERED OVER TOWN

'A balloon? It was far too big'

D.M. 21 NOV 1953

A LARGE metallic spherical object was seen in a clear blue sky above Newton Le Willows, near Warrington, Lancashire, it was claimed yesterday.

Mr. P. P. Bowers, assistant manager of a sugar works, of Eccles, was watching jet planes manœuvring when he saw the bright metallic-looking object.

He called Mr. Russell Welsh and Mr. George Turner, works chemists. They were joined by three others, and all watched the object for about ten minutes.

Mr. Bowers said: "I sighted it between 2.15 and 2.30 p.m.—the sky was a clear lucid blue. We saw it above the jets."

'No evidence'

"It could not have possibly been a weather balloon of only 12ft. in diameter."

The authorities at the nearby American air base at Burtonwood said emphatically that the object was none of the jets from their airfield, and they had not released any weather balloon.

Washington cable: Most of the strange objects sighted in the United States since 1947 have proved to be conventional objects, such as balloons and aircraft, or have been meteors or planets, says an Air Force report.

"No authentic physical evidence has been received which could establish the possible existence of space ships from other planets," it states.—*Reuter.*

"ROUND OBJECT" SEEN ABOVE JETS

D.M. 21 NOV 1953

BALLOON DENIAL

A "large, metallic, spherical object" was seen in a clear blue sky above Newton-le-Willows, near Warrington, Lancs, on Thursday, by Mr. P. Bowers, assistant manager of a sugar works. Two chemists, two assistant chemists and a joiner at the works also saw the object, Mr. Bowers stated yesterday.

He said: "I sighted it between 2.15 and 2.30 p.m." It was above two or three jet planes which were manœuvring. "We thought it was moving, but discovered that its apparent motion was caused by the passing of clouds which, after about 10 minutes, hid it from sight."

The object was at an angle of between 55 or 60 degrees from the horizontal. It was "at least six or eight times" the size of the jets. The authorities at the nearby American air base at Burtonwood said it was not a jet from their airfield, nor had they released any weather balloons.

THE THING RADAR MEN TO MAKE OWN TEST

D.M. 21 NOV 1953

With their own balloon

By DEREK DEMPSTER

THE Army radar men who tracked the Strange Object over Kent on November 3 were far from impressed yesterday by the Air Ministry's explanation—that it was a weather balloon.

So unconvinced were they that at Lee Green, S.E.—where the Thing was tracked—they planned an experiment.

These men of the 265th Heavy A.A. Regiment are to send up a weather balloon themselves.

They hope to show that it will not have the same radar effect as the speeding, spherical, flashing object of November 3.

I COULDN'T—

Sergeant Harry Waller, the operator who tracked it and saw it through a telescope, said yesterday: "I could never have seen a 12ft. balloon 12 miles high."

The object was also seen by two R.A.F. officers in a Vampire jet, and they reported it the same day.

Since then the growing speculation has led M.P.s to put down questions to be asked in the House next week.

Mr. F. J. Bellenger (Soc., Bassetlaw) will ask Mr. Antony Head, the War Secretary, on Tuesday whether he has been able to identify "the flying saucer object reported by one of the members of anti-aircraft command."

WHAT REPORTS ?

On Tuesday too Lieut.-Colonel Schofield (Tory, Rochdale) will ask Mr. Nigel Birch, the Parliamentary Secretary to the Ministry of Defence, what reports his department has received "of the flying object observed by two airmen."

And on Wednesday Mr. R. T. Paget, Q.C. (Soc., Northampton), will ask Mr. G. R. Ward, Under-Secretary for Air, if he has any statement to make "with regard to the flying object reported to him by two airmen."

Are we being watched...

BY ANOTHER WORLD?

By ROGER LAWRIE

THERE is one remarkable FACT that stands out in all this hullaballoo about the Flying Saucers. Not one of the men who have specialist knowledge to do so will come straight out and say: "It's all rubbish."

Take, for instance, the story of Sir Miles Thomas's experience. He and Group-Captain Cunningham were up in an experimental Comet, when they saw an object. "It was an impressive-looking object," he told me, "and though it was at great height we decided to give chase.

"When we got close enough we saw that it was just a weather balloon." That, you might think, would have turned Sir Miles into a sceptic, convincing him that his was a typical experience. But it hasn't.

Makes you wonder

"It would be foolish to be sceptical about these Saucers," he said. "Although like the man from Missouri, 'I want to be showed' before I believe in them as a hard fact, I do not disbelieve in them."

And this is what makes ordinary feet - on - the - ground people wonder.

The U.S.A. Air Force went on record last week with a "draft" statement that Saucers did not exist.

But, as the Sunday Graphic revealed a fortnight ago, they are still issuing 42-point quest'onnaires to air crews to be filled in as soon as an "object" is spotted.

SO WHO BELIEVES WHAT?

The Canadians have just built a scientific observatory "for detecting fast - moving objects at great heights."

'Keep open mind'

And what about the scientists? These men spend their lives digging into the nature of things and the facts of the Universe. Almost to a man their final word is:

"We must keep an open mind on the subject."

The available evidence, they told me, did not convince them yet that we were being watched by unearthly creatures in strange machines. But none ruled it out as impossible.

As Professor Bronowski put it:

"We would be very vain creatures to believe that we are the only human beings in the Universe."

Life is possible

Where are these creatures, if they exist? There are two kinds of possibility:

1 In star systems near our own, there are 22 planets on which astronomers believe life like ours could exist. And they think it reasonable to suppose that life DOES exist on them.

2 Even on planets which are too hot or too cold to support life as we know it, scientists believe that there might be creatures of a completely different kind who could live under conditions impossible to us.

Nor has the Church in this country or America denied the possibility of life in outer space.

Then we come to another fact. A group of American scientists have just completed the plans and tested the gear for rocket-ships capable of making the journey to the moon in five days.

No one denies it can be done.

So, the interplanetary men ask, if we can go out into space, why should we refuse to believe that people on another planet, who could and probably do exist, can come and visit us?

Near home the most likely bet is Mars.

Scientists say it is possible that intelligent beings there could have retired from the bleak surface to underground cities.

And Canadian researchers wonder if it is significant that reports of flying saucers come in periodic flurries when Mars reaches its closest point to earth.

Older civilisation

Suppose there were an older civilisation on Mars, or some other planet.

Is is unreasonable to think that they might have progressed as far beyond us as the jet plane is beyond the first box-kites of aviation? That THEY can swoop through space as easily as WE can fly the Atlantic?

It may sound fantastic—but how would a forecast of TV have sounded to a man of the 17th century?

An advance of three centuries in knowledge brought television with it. It is possible there are people in space three centuries in advance of us.

Low-level survey

HOW WOULD WE GO ABOUT INVESTIGATING ANOTHER PLANET ONCE WE HAD THE MEANS?

Major Keyhoe, a leading investigator of the Saucer mystery in America has answered that one:

We will launch small manned craft from the mother ship and begin a low altitude survey. If they are intercepted by Martian planes they will zoom away out of danger.

Does this not tally perfectly with the function and description of Saucers?

For convenience, says Major Keyhoe, we would set up bases on the moons which circle Mars so that we would not have to travel all the way from earth each time.

Those who think we are having "visitors" point out that men from other worlds could equally well have established a base on our moon—on the side which is always turned away from us.

As if there was not confusion enough in the mystery, there is always an element of muddle in official announcements on the subject.

Last week the War Office disclosed that a "strange object" had been seen over Kent and had been tracked by radar. The object was seen on November 3.

The disclosure was not made until November 19. The authorities had had 16 days to think it over. Yet a few hours after the news was released they suddenly "discovered" it was a balloon.

Men were sure

The men who saw the object and tracked it seem sure it was not a balloon.

And now the whole business is to be raised in Parliament.

One thing is fairly certain. No one is panicking about these "visitors."

The general feeling seems to be their presence might well do us a lot of good!

23 NOV 1953

FLYING SAUCER IS THEIR CUP OF TEA

A BUREAU of scientists and technologists has been set up in Britain to investigate flying saucers. The secretary is Mr. E. L. Plunkett, ex-Army captain, who was British representative on the International Flying Saucer Bureau in the U.S. for 18 months.

The British bureau has 33 members and was established because the International bureau was wound up several months ago. It has its headquarters at Bristol.

Dr. Irving Bell, of Oakwood-road, Bristol, is president and Mr. G. Knewstub, an electronics expert, who works for the Bristol Aeroplane Co., is vice-president.

Mr. Knewstub said last night the bureau had a lot of information on the subject.

LOOK
MA

FLYING SAUCERS? IT'S ALL BALLOONEY

E.N. 24 NOV 1953

Evening News Parliamentary Reporter

IT'S all ballooney. That is how the recent flying saucer story was described in the Commons this afternoon.

Lieut.-Col. Schofield (Cons., Rochdale) asked Mr. Nigel Birch, Parliamentary Secretary to the Defence Ministry, what reports his department had on the "flying objects" seen by two airmen over London or other parts of Britain.

Mr. F. J. Bellenger (Lab, Bassetlaw) asked whether Mr. Birch had been able to identify "the flying saucer object" reported by one of the members of Ack Ack Command.

A Large Echo

Mr. Birch replied that on November 3 two experimental meteorological balloons were seen —one by two R.A.F. officers in an aircraft and the other by a member of Ack Ack Command.

"There was nothing peculiar about either of these occurrences," Mr. Birch said.

Mr. Birch said that meteorological balloons were fitted with a special device in order that they should produce a large echo on a radar screen.

There was laughter when Mr. George Isaacs (Lab., Southwark) asked whether the Minister would agree that this story about flying saucers was all ballooney.

Mr. Birch: Mr. Isaacs' appreciation is very nearly correct.

NEW U.S. 'SAUCERS' REPORT

15 per cent remain a mystery

From Daily Mail Reporter

NEW YORK, Monday.

MORE reports about "flying saucers" have quietly been coming to the United States Air Force for investigation, it was learned in Washington today.

Some 200 sightings of mysterious objects in the sky have been reported in this country so far this year, bringing the total figure up to 3,600 during the past six years.

The Air Force has been at great pains to keep these reports out of the headlines and is preparing another special White Paper on the matter. The U.S. Navy has also established a research agency.

The Air Force will again take a "yes and no" position in its forthcoming report. Claims and rumours about spaceships from other planets and secret foreign aircraft will not be confirmed. Neither will they be categorically rejected.

No answers yet

Most of the reports after thorough study have turned out to be either weather balloons, astronomical and climatic phenomena, birds, light reflections, planes, or radar and other electronic disturbances.

But 15 per cent. of the sightings do not fall into these categories and the experts have no answers for them yet.

The Air Force's large flying saucer research staff includes the best scientists and technicians in the country, assisted by the latest equipment. Newest additions are a number of sighting stations with high-speed cameras.

Air Force authorities are still debating whether to publish anything produced by these stations. They are located in strategic sectors of the country, particularly in the vicinity of atomic plants where sightings are frequently reported.

NOW...BURY THESE FLYING SAUCERS!

DURING the past six years there have been frequent reports of unusual objects being seen in the sky—some in the daytime, shining like silver in the sunlight, others at night, glowing brightly.

Some have been described as moving with tremendous speed, others as practically stationary.

Many of the reports have mentioned objects of a flat disc-like shape, giving the appearance of a large saucer flying through the air; the description of such objects as "flying saucers" appeared appropriate.

The saucer shape was the most common but it has become customary to describe every object or apparition seen in the sky, which seemed to be something out of the ordinary and for which there was no obvious explanation, as a flying saucer irrespective of whether it was saucer-shaped or not.

They DO exist

THESE reports have become so frequent and persistent that we cannot explain them as figments of the observer's imagination.

Some of the objects have been tracked by radar, so that their reality cannot be queried. Flying saucers undoubtedly exist. What, then, are they?

The frequent reports of these strange apparitions soon gave rise to many rumours. There were all sorts of suggestions to account for them. For some time the reports came only from the United States, then the saucers began to be seen in this country, in Sweden and elsewhere. . . . *Perhaps they were some new and secret aircraft that were being tested; perhaps they were some Russian device sent over to spy out the secrets of atom bomb developments; perhaps they were some unknown type of aircraft visiting us from interplanetary space.*

The hoaxes

THIS last idea caught the popular imagination. The time was ripe for it. The rapid development in long range rockets during the later years of the war and since have aroused widespread interest in the possibilities of space flight.

Rockets have been sent to heights of up to 250 miles. It does not seem beyond the bounds of what is practicable to send a rocket to the moon.

The youth of to-day eagerly devour tales about space travel and interplanetary wars. Reports emanating from the United States referred to some of the saucers having come to earth and of little men having come out of them, though it was significant that no photographs of these reputed visitors from another planet have been obtained. In these matters we have to be on guard against deliberate hoaxes to see how much a gullible public would swallow.

But not Venus

I CAN say quite definitely and with absolute assurance that none of the flying saucers can have come from another planet.

Venus and Mars are the only two planets from which they might conceivably have come.

Sufficient is known about conditions on VENUS to be able to say that life of any sort on that planet is quite out of the question. Mars, on the other hand, does show some traces of a primitive type of vegetation, akin to rock lichens on our Earth; but the conditions are so near to the limit at which life ceases to be possible that it is doubtful whether there can be any animal life at all on Mars, and there can certainly not be any of the higher forms of animal life. Life on MARS appears to be in its last phase and to be on the verge of extinction.

THE MOON can be ruled out of consideration as it is a completely dead world. Reports of little men having come from flying saucers are therefore nothing but humbuggery.

Secret weapons

ON various occasions I have given it as my belief that most of the reports of flying saucers can be attributed to observations of meteorological balloons.

One of these balloons when at considerable height appears like a flat disc or saucer; it may move rapidly or slowly according to the velocity of the wind; the instruments attached to it will give a radar reflection.

The United States Air Force have recently announced officially that most of the flying saucers can be accounted for by these balloons and that none is attributable to tests of secret weapons.

There is a small minority of reports that cannot be explained in this way, but for which various natural explanations can be found.

Some are real phenomena, such as bright fireballs, ball lightning, distant airplanes, vapour trails from aircraft, peculiar clouds, even bright planets such as Venus or Jupiter.

Some of the reports can be explained by searchlights playing on thin clouds or banks of mist. Others can be accounted for by various optical or

THE MASSACHUSETTS VERSION
Four round objects with bars of light extending forward and behind passed over a U.S. air station at Salem, Massachusetts, in August, 1952. A coastguard snapped this picture through a window.

☆ **The Astronomer Royal conducts an inquiry into strange objects in the sky and concludes that it is time the question was closed for ever**

by
SIR HAROLD SPENCER JONES, FRS

meteorological phenomena, such as the reflection of sunlight by ice crystals in the atmosphere, mock suns and haloes, mirages, reflections in mist.

Many of these phenomena would give rise to rapid and erratic movements of bright patches of light, which could easily be interpreted as due to a flying object.

Flying saucers of these types have been recorded throughout history. There is nothing new in them. There was published in 1646, for instance, a book entitled Strange Signes from Heaven, in which were described appearances that would now be called flying saucers.

No mystery

IT is high time that the flying saucers should be allowed to lapse into obscurity, as the Loch Ness monster has done. Let us be finished with them, for there is nothing mysterious about them.

All the reported appearances are capable of a natural explanation. Flying saucers are not secret weapons undergoing test; they are not spying craft from a potentially hostile power; they are not space craft from a neighbouring planet.

When these facts are generally realised interest in flying saucers will die a natural death. WORLD COPYRIGHT RESERVED

Keeping Track Of The Flying Saucers

TO THE EDITOR OF THE RECORDER — 26 NOV 1953

Sir,—Is it mere co-incidence that the advent of the sight by earth men, of unidentifiable objects in the sky, commenced almost immediately upon the birth of the atomic age?

That the so-called Flying Saucers exist, in that particular form or another is without doubt. The public of the world, and America, and Britain in particular (in their case as world leaders in the scientific field) have for too long been treated rather as an impatient parent treats an inquisitive child. Not content to even make a credulous statement, they obligingly refer to sundry meteorological balloons, and similar.

Is it really possible that a trained radar operative can mistake what must surely by now be a well-known "track" on radar screens, for something that is new and unexplained?

Could it be unthinkable that the inhabitants of another planet, during the past ten years, have become aware of life on this planet, through the medium of atomic explosions, and in doing so have in fact decided to send preliminary investigations?

In answer to the obvious question of why do we not pick up the intelligence of atomic experiments on other planets, is, I think based on time.

Even if we can record the last two hundred years in means of scientific fact, it is not unlikely that the other planets within our universe have discarded the use of atomic energy as outmoded or uneconomical, several thousands of years ago, or in fact beyond all measurable time! The history of civilisation on this planet is an infinitesimal drop in the ocean of space time.

I respectfully submit that The Recorder can be the first to attack this problem in a sane manner. Sifting the true information from the sensationalism prevalent today, is a challenge to the Press, and what better champion to fight the cause, than the fresh independent, and most important, young idea-conscious paper, The Recorder.

To keep a close watch on reports coming in from all over the world, and to reduce them to a form of understandable pattern, if indeed such a pattern exists. To invite such experts as necessary, to try and evaluate the importance of occurrences that are so often dismissed as imagination or "post jet neurosis."

It is up to The Recorder to give the members of the public, who are not content to be ignored or starved of intelligent facts, that are after all of paramount importance to us all, a lead in the matter of The Earth and?

LOUIS F. PEEK, F.R.S.A.
72, Peterborough Road,
Hurlingham, S.W.6.

Photo that baffled the experts

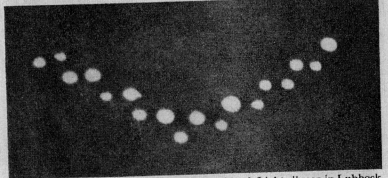

No one has been able to explain the "Lubbock Lights," seen in Lubbock, Texas, in 1951. This photograph was taken by eighteen-year-old Carl Hart

THE THING Fooled a Village And Almost Fooled Whitehall

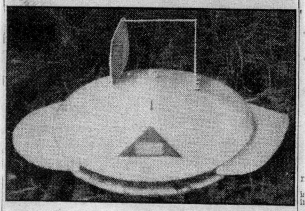

The Thing.

This Flying Saucer Put The Lid On It

E.N. 27 NOV 1953
By CYRIL BIRKS
"Evening News" Air Reporter

THERE was The Thing, a circular-shaped metal object with a slight dome to it, with the early morning mist swirling round it.

A gardener walking along the road just outside the little Sussex village of Birch Grove, several miles from Haywards Heath, spotted it lying half-buried in the undergrowth at the side of the road.

The police were summoned. While they consulted a higher authority rumour began to sweep through the village. A flying saucer had been found.

A message was sent to Whitehall by the police.

Security officers from the Air Ministry and other Government departments drove down. The operation was cloaked in the greatest secrecy.

Air Ministry officers got there first. They found a hole in a tree, apparently made by the object crashing through it as it sped earthwards.

Twigs from the tree were scattered over The Thing.

PHOTOGRAPHS

The Air Ministry security officers rushed back to Whitehall with the precious object.

A preliminary examination revealed that it appeared to have jets that had been burning some kind of fuel. It had a highly polished surface, suggesting it was capable of very high speeds.

In the villages around Birch Grove the rumours grew thick and fast . . . A flying saucer more than 26ft. in diameter had been found . . . Little men 18 inches high crossed some minds.

At the Air Ministry only a handful of people were let into the secret . . . The Thing was photographed, a minute was written about it . . .

Certain features about the object, puzzling at first, began to make sense.

It was handed over to Air-Marshal Sir Victor Goddard, at that time Member of the Air Council for Technical Services, and to Air-Marshal Sir Colin Weedon, the then Director General of Technical Services.

They began to chuckle as they examined the object which was about 3ft. in diameter. Their conclusion: it was something made out of a dustbin lid!

THEN—SMILES

A solemn Air Council meeting were shown The Thing. Grave faces broke into broad smiles.

The Flying Saucer Hoax of Birch Grove had been discovered.

But who was responsible has never been discovered by the authorities.

Air Marshal Sir Victor Goddard, now Principal of the College of Aeronautics at Cranfield, chuckled when I spoke to him. Yes, he admitted, it was a grand hoax. For a short time it caused "quite a flap."

By the way the object had been constructed it was obvious to him that it was the work of someone who had served in the R.A.F. and knew something about aeronautical gadgets.

Air Marshal Goddard is right.

THE PLOT

It was the work of two ex-R.A.F. men. I have traced one of them who told for the first time the full story of the Flying Saucer of Birch Grove.

This is it:

"With all the talk of flying saucers we decided to make one and plant it in the vicinity of the village.

"We made it with a dustbin lid, a length of copper wire, a vaporiser unit from an oil lamp, a tuning knob and a plunger from an acorn switch.

"We covered the interior with sheet metal, gave it stubby wings with a double tail unit, two copper jet tubes, painted on the nose a yellow identification triangle with the markings GM/12345.

"We blackened the rear of the thing with an oily rag to give the impression that it had been burning fuel.

"We collected twigs from the tree and scattered them around the object, which we placed in a half-buried position giving the impression that it had dived out of the sky at terrific speed, tearing through the trees.

"The village, and other villages round about, had plenty to talk about."

Mystery Noise in the Atmosphere

11 JAN 1954

Call for Full Inquiry

To the Editor of The Daily Telegraph

SIR—I have been engaged for some years in collecting information and investigating an "unidentified vibratory noise in the atmosphere" very similar to that complained of by Chalfont St. Giles residents. My very extensive correspondence, and personal experience, confirm that this vibratory noise is heard, or sensed, all over the country.

It is frequently described as at Chalfont, as a "high-pitched whine," a "monotonous throbbing," or "humming like a gigantic machine." It is worse at night, and neither burrowing your head under the pillow, or stopping up your ears eliminates it

The noise has been reported from Chesham Bois, Berkhamsted, and I myself have always heard it when visiting the Amersham district.

My wife and I first became aware of this noise in 1942 (at West Hampstead) and inquiry showed that other people were picking it up locally. It is quite impossible to give it any sense of direction, it is just "everywhere" in the atmosphere, nor is any screening effective.

Incidentally it is heard in a coal mine 2,400ft below surface, and I myself have sensed it just as clearly in a deep chalk cave under Guildford Castle as in the town.

By various means of publicity, including two notices in the Personal Column of THE DAILY TELEGRAPH, in 1947-8, I have received a very large correspondence ranging from Cornwall, and the South Coast, to the North of England, besides some information from Scotland. The severity of the impact varies according to the individual.

It is usually more noticeable indoors, but can be heard out of doors when not temporarily blanketed by traffic, and such ordinary sounds. It by no means follows that all members of a family will hear it, and those who are immune cannot pick it up however hard they may try.

So far, no firm explanation has been forthcoming as to the exact origin of this noise. The time is long overdue for a really serious scientific investigation into this most persistent and irritating phenomenon. Yours faithfully,

RALPH B. COX.

London, N.W.6.

∴ Correspondents report the noise from Kensington, Streatham, Kew Gardens, Grimsby, Bexhill and Brentwood, Essex.

A U.S. Coastguard photographer at Salem, Mass., Air Station made this phenomenal photograph. He was in the station's photo lab preparing to clean a camera, when he noticed several brilliant lights in the sky. He grabbed the camera, clicked the shutter and this photograph is the result.

Flying Saucers No Joke To Australian Air Force

STORIES of "flying saucers" and "strange objects in the sky", are being taken seriously by Australian authorities. "We do not regard this business as a joke," Mr. Seymour, superintendent of air traffic control of the civil aviation department, said. "People are definitely seeing objects which have not been explained."

Captain Douglas Barker, a veteran airways pilot, gave an impetus to public and official interest when he reported seeing, on New Year's Day, "a semi-transparent object, shaped like a mushroom with a stalk, oscillating rapidly in and out of the thick cloud, and travelling faster than any jet."

He reported it to the Civil Aviation Department's flight control.

"They said I should take more water with it," he said.

Later the department's regional director, Mr. A. R. McComb, said he believed that what Captain Barker had seen were reflections of a Convair aircraft in the area, but added: "Captain Barker is a very experienced pilot and unlikely to imagine things. His report will be fully investigated."

Captain Barker, a pilot for 17 years, with nearly 14,000 hours of flying to his credit, remarked, "I could not possibly confuse this with any plane."

Fear Of Ridicule

When he discussed it with senior fellow-pilots, they reported they had seen "flying saucers and things." They added they had been "too scared to mention them for fear of ridicule."

Mr. Seymour appealed through the Press to all who saw unidentified aerial objects to tell his department.

Since then reports have flowed into the air departments. The Civil Aviation Department alone received 50 in one week, including one from Mr. J. W. Boyle, vice-president of the Victorian Branch of the British Astronomical Association.

Reports run to a general pattern of "discs," "saucers," "rockets" and "balloons." They differ only in detail.

Investigation

Most of the objects are said to have travelled at terrific speed across the sky, leaving a trail of vapour or brilliant light. Others hovered and rotated before flashing out of sight.

---

15 JAN 1954

'MISSILE MILE' CAR HAS CLUE

News Chronicle Reporter

EIGHTY-THREE times the mystery of the Surrey "missile mile" at Cobham, near Esher, has been repeated. But yesterday a clue which may solve the riddle of shattered car windscreens and dented coachwork lay in Cobham police station.

It was a sample of white powder picked up from two dents on the roof of the eighty-third victim's car which was struck opposite a large nursery on the stretch of road near Fairmile.

Sent to the Yard

For the last three years that mile has a history of broken windscreens and dents in car bodies. Every reasonable—and unreasonable— theory has been investigated without success.

Now Mr. Bernard Sawkins, of Green Lane, Ockham, Surrey, has brought in the sample of powder.

"It looks like minute pieces of white paper," he said, "but when you touch it it feels rough —like ground-up seashells." It has been sent to Scotland Yard.

Mr. V. D. Hopper, senior lecturer on cosmic ray research at Melbourne University, said that these objects could be cosmic ray balloons released by his staff for research, or moving clouds of grass seeds—or the planet Venus.

Others have suggested meteors, falling stars, patches of fog or cloud lit by light deflected from the setting sun, or an aftermath of atomic explosions.

One high-ranking Royal Australian Air Force officer said his Service had been investigating "flying saucers" since 1947.

21 Are Blank

The Australian flying saucer investigation committee, formed before unexplained objects developed official status, has received 28 reports from Australia. It exchanges reports with the New Zealand body, the civilian saucer investigation, and has sent reports to England, the United States and France.

The committee, which consists of four engineers, two industrial chemists, two clerks, a banker and a journalist, could explain seven of the reported objects, which were meteors or aircraft.

But they are blank on the other 21.

The secretary, Mr. D. K. Thomson, said: "We are satisfied that there is something new and strange in the skies, but as yet we have not enough first class evidence to draw any conclusions."

Do Flying Saucers really exist, or is there a quite natural explanation? In this first of four articles the author gives some idea of the nature and extent of the "sightings" and how they are treated in this country by the authorities.

Britain Saw the First 'Saucers'—in 1290

by J. STUBBS WALKER

THEY are not called flying saucers any more. Since Government Departments have been investigating these fascinating phenomena at high level the saucers have been officially named U.F.O.s—Unidentified Flying Objects—by the British Air Ministry.

Their renaming may be accepted as a measure of the official interest now being taken in a subject which, since the war, has produced more world-wide controversy and speculation than any other topic except perhaps the prospects of peace or war.

Flying saucers are by no means new. Although the first "sighting" generally accepted as the beginning of the major interest in the subject was in 1947, when ten shining circular discs were seen dodging in and out of the peaks of Mount Rainier, Washington, at 1,000 m.p.h., there was a sighting centuries earlier in Yorkshire.

Documents relating to Byland Abbey, Yorkshire, dated 1290 tell of a round, flat silver object like a discus which flew over the monastery, exciting, the report says, "*maximum terrorem*" among the brethren.

Half in America

FLYING saucer reports have been intelligently studied—and occasionally very unintelligently !—for little more than six years. In that time, it is safe to estimate, there have been at least 10,000 sightings all over the world.

American reports account for approximately half of these, and there have been many hundreds from Europe, including some 300 from Britain. India, Australia, New Zealand, South Africa, and Japan have added their quota.

The sightings work out at an average of at least four a day, and the most surprising thing is that the only territory in the world which seems to be missing from the saucer-reporting list is Russia.

In Britain and the United States U.F.O.s have been taken seriously. In both countries Air Force Intelligence organisations have carried out quite surprisingly meticulous surveys of reports, and in both countries personnel of the Armed Forces have been warned that detailed reports of sightings must be given to Intelligence departments.

The result of these inquiries is producing almost as much controversy as the flying saucers themselves. American official sources, while not flatly turning down the theories of visitors from space or secret weapons of a foreign Power, have shown that of the thousands of cases investigated all but 15 per cent. are explainable by orthodox things.

In Britain the percentage of saucers left unexplained is even lower : the Air Ministry say that only five per cent. cannot be accounted for.

Thrilling foretaste

MOST people experience at least the temptation to believe in flying saucers. There seems no doubt that in the foreseeable future mankind will have solved the problems of space travel, and the idea of the saucers gives a thrilling foretaste of the future.

Firm believers in the saucers complain, both in America and here, that there has been a great hushing-up of official information. They argue that because the Governments now realise that the U.F.O.s come from another planet the facts are being hidden from the people to prevent the danger of panic. Others argue that the full facts are not being given to the public because the saucers are highly effective secret weapons belonging to an unfriendly Power.

'Cannot agree'

AFTER a comprehensive investigation into flying saucers in Britain, I cannot agree with this accusation of unusual secrecy. Official investigation into U.F.O. reports frequently entails correlating the reports to other questions which affect national security ; consequently a fair degree of secrecy is necessary.

Recently the Air Ministry and the War Office have issued instructions that personnel involved in saucer sightings must not make statements to the public

Two journalists took this picture off the coast of Brazil over a year ago. Flying Saucer or . . . ?

without high-level permission. Throughout my inquiries, however, I have been given a most reasonable degree of co-operation.

Some of the saucer-sighting witnesses I have interviewed have hinted darkly that they have been advised not to talk too much about their experiences, but in no case could I find reasonable confirmation that there had been any attempt by officialdom to restrict the descriptive powers of civilian witnesses.

There was one case in which the "saucer" turned out to be a piece of secret experimental equipment (and most unsaucerlike) which the Government Department concerned were not happy to have discussed publicly.

What happens to U.F.O. reports in Britain ?

Almost every one that has sufficient factual background is studied by a special technical intelligence section of the Air Ministry. Remember that the Air Ministry have *not* denied the existence of flying saucers ; they have merely indicated that of the several hundred cases investigated 95 per cent. have an explanation.

Of the other five per cent. "doubtfuls." some, at least, are so lacking in detail that full inquiry cannot be made into them.

Treated seriously

EACH report is treated as seriously as if it were the only one. Most detailed checks are made on the time, date, location, and direction of the U.F.O., and these factors are then related with the known movements of aircraft, weather balloons, and the meteorological conditions at the time.

Many of the sighting reports are convincing, and it would be foolish, whatever the investigation figures indicate, to accept flatly the assumption that there is no such thing as a flying saucer. Some of the eyewitnesses are most unlikely to have imagined their experience. Others are trained observers —one an experienced amateur astronomer—while in several cases there is confirmation by other witnesses.

At least one of the officially investigated saucer reports, written off in the Air Ministry files as a weather balloon, still leaves room for some doubt.

Photographs

ON the other hand, with the thousands of sightings made all over the world, it is strange that in the period of more than six years there has never arisen any absolutely convincing proof of the reality of the saucer.

Photographs have been produced. The most remarkable were those taken by Mr. George Adamski and published in his book "Flying Saucers Have Landed" (Werner Laurie), in which he claims to have had a personal interview (conducted by telepathy) with the pilot of a flying saucer which landed in the California desert in November 1952. These photographs and several others, however, have never been proved.

Tomorrow : Strange tale from Norwich.

Mrs. Cubitt and her husband—they say they saw an object over Norwich looking like a child's humming top, coloured with white and blue bands

Astronomer Frank Potter, of Norwich, uses a telescope in the garden of his home. He claims he watched a disc in the sky for over three minutes

An amateur astronomer saw it through his telescope last October. It wasn't a meteor . . . or a weather balloon. Could it be . . .? This is the problem posed in this second of four articles on the Flying Saucer mystery.

Was it a 'Saucer' They Saw over Norwich?

by J. STUBBS WALKER

WHETHER you are a saucer enthusiast or what the "saucerers" call a heretic, you have to admit that the evidence of some of the sightings is sufficiently impressive to justify fully the detailed study the Air Ministry still give to the subject.

Take the case of Mr. F. W. Potter, a 34-year-old amateur astronomer, who runs his own window-cleaning business in Norwich.

For nearly 20 years Mr. Potter has been interested in astronomy. He is a member of the British Astronomical Association and of the Norwich Astronomical Society. His wife also is a member of the Norwich society, and their interest in astronomy is sufficiently alert for them to have bought, for their own personal use, a 3½in. refracting telescope—an expensive piece of equipment.

One night early in October last year Mr. and Mrs. Potter were leaving their home near Norwich to attend a meeting of the local society. It was a dark, clear night, and the time was about 15 minutes after seven o'clock.

This artist's drawing is based on a verbal description and a sketch made by Mr. Potter of the mysterious object he saw in the sky.

A habit

AS they stepped from their porch, turning towards the garage, Mr. Potter looked up into the sky. "I always do," he says, "more or less out of habit."

He saw something which he first took to be a bright yellow star in a position where it should not have been. Then he noticed that it was moving, so he called to his wife to fetch from the house the big telescope, which they then set up in the front garden.

The object, however, was moving over their house, and they had to fold up the cumbersome telescope and its tripod and carry it through the house to set it up again in the back garden. There, for three and a half minutes, both Mr. and Mrs. Potter were able, they say, to make a close study of the "object."

"We were both pretty excited," Mr. Potter admits. At the same time, however, he was able to keep the telescope trained on the U.F.O., and his observation of detail was confirmed by his wife.

It was a dark grey hull against an intensely black sky, dome-shaped and with the curve of the dome hanging towards the ground. The flat side emitted a pulsating light which was much stronger when the object was stationary, dulling as the object moved. At the centre of the curved dome there was a kind of conning tower with eight windows through which light was beaming.

Excitement

"I HAVE seen hundreds of meteors," Mr. Potter told me, "and there was no question that this was one. Neither could it have been a weather balloon."

The Potters went on to their meeting at the Norwich Astronomical Society, arriving late and in a flutter of excitement.

Mr. W. E. Bennett, the honorary secretary of the society, confirms their state of excitement and confirms, too, that when members questioned the Potters their stories coincided in all detail. Mr. Potter immediately sketched for the members what he had seen. His wife agreed that the sketch was as accurate as she could remember.

Now, here is a strange thing about what the Potters saw and what Mr. Potter drew. The whole of his description is very much like the much-questioned photographs of a flying saucer supposedly taken at short range by Mr. George Adamski and published in his book "Flying Saucers Have Landed," except for the vital fact that Mr. Potter drew what he saw in his refracting telescope, *which reverses the image.*

Adamant

HIS flying saucer was not flying the same way up as those of Mr. Adamski, and no amount of arguing will make him change his mind. Mr. Potter had previously seen a representation of the Adamski saucer and was consequently aware that what he saw might be expected to be flying the other way up.

So far as I am aware, Mr. Potter's sighting has never officially been investigated. He himself refuses to call it a flying saucer, despite his detailed sketch of it. He and his wife have received scores of insulting letters, ridiculing and reviling them. As Mr. Potter points out, none of those letters of ridicule seems to have been written by anyone with any scientific training.

 **Mail**

9. 1954

THREE HALFPENCE

What is it?
BOYS SET RIDDLE

COULD this be another unidentified flying object, otherwise known as a Flying Saucer? Here, for you to decide, are the picture, the strange story of Stephen John Darbishire and Adrian Sabur Myers (right), and the comments of J. Stubbs Walker, *Daily Mail* Science Correspondent.

This is the story:—

Stephen, 15, and cousin Adrian, eight, set out from Torver, Lancashire, on Monday to photograph bird life on the slopes of nearby Coniston Old Man.

☆

At about 2.30 p.m. Adrian drew Stephen's attention to something in the sky about 300 yards away. Stephen took two photographs. One is reproduced above.

Adrian says that the object seemed to rise from a valley and circle before making off.

It made no noise.

So much for the boys' story. Stephen's father, Dr. S. B. Darbishire, rounds it off by reporting that on Monday there was broken cloud over the snow-covered hills with the sun shining through.

☆

Which, says J. Stubbs Walker, are just the sky conditions to produce a " mock sun " effect.

He adds: " The shafts of sunlight through the clouds could refract on ice crystals in the atmosphere, producing apparently solid shapes."

With that, the story rests.

As a witness Mr. Potter is good. He is unshakeable in his facts. His local astronomical society members have a good opinion of him as an observer.

If you believe his story in complete detail there would seem to be something in flying saucers. There is, however, always the possibility that both Mr. and Mrs. Potter were innocently and subconsciously influenced by the fact that three weeks previously Mr. Potter's brother (another amateur astronomer) had seen unidentified lights in the sky and that they had been on the look-out for something unusual.

Both Mr. and Mrs. Potter deny this strongly. They say, quite reasonably, I believe: "We didn't *want* to see a flying saucer, anyway!"

'Flaming tadpole'

ONE of the best-authenticated series of sightings in Britain recently was the "flaming tadpole" seen streaking over the Isle of Wight, Bognor, and Chichester in the dark early morning of a winter day, when it lit up the streets and seemed to dodge in and out of cloud.

At least half a dozen people saw this phenomenon at widely spaced parts of the South Coast, and there were even stories that very soon afterwards it was seen in the Norwich area. The stories from the South Coast witnesses match remarkably well in timing and description.

Two milkmen in Newport (Isle of Wight) were probably the first to sight it. They were delivering milk in different parts of the town and told their separate stories before they had an opportunity of comparing notes.

Mr. Walter Liggins, 31, was in a street in the town when he saw the roadway and buildings brilliantly illuminated. He thought at first that it was some effect of moonlight, but then he saw his "tadpole," with, he says, a brilliantly green glowing head and a red, flaming tail.

Very large

THE light from it seemed to undulate (how frequently U.F.O. observers agree on that undulation of light), and, though he admits the impossibility of judging its height, he did not think it was very high because it seemed to pass through cloud and appeared very large.

Danny Breen, another milkman, saw very much the same thing from high ground near Parkhurst Barracks, just outside Newport. It was very brilliant, he said, and seemed to have a small head, a larger body, and a tapering tail of light.

Intense light

JUST about the same time Police Constable William Keates, 43 years old, with 18 years' service in the force, was cycling to Bognor police station to take over the 6 a.m. duty.

"I suddenly saw all the road illuminated from behind me, and I thought it must be a car with brilliant headlamps," he says. "I drew into the side of the road and looked over my shoulder and saw an intense white light in the sky travelling from west to east.

"There was no apparent beam of light from the object. It was just a mass of light with a long moving trail, travelling horizontally. I saw nothing fall from it."

Colleagues agreed

AS soon as he reached the police station he telephoned Chichester police. Two of his Chichester colleagues had seen the same thing, and their descriptions tallied with the rest. The only difference in any of the "tadpole" sightings was in the descriptions of colour. This, however, could have changed to some degree with the type of cloud through which the object was observed.

No one claimed that these South Coast sightings were flying saucers, and the descriptions fit in very well with the classical picture of a fireball, except for the reports that it appeared to pass through cloud. A fireball is normally many miles high in the atmosphere, though it may appear much nearer.

Tomorrow: What the R.A.F. observers saw.

In his third article on the Flying Saucers mystery the writer describes a strange incident during a Coastal Command exercise off the Yorkshire coast.

90,000-feet Radar 'Target' set 'Ack-Ack' a Puzzle

12 FEB 1954

by J. STUBBS WALKER

SIGHTINGS of Unidentified Flying Objects by men of the Royal Air Force and by crews of airliners are treated with considerable respect by the official investigators for the reason that the men reporting are trained to observe, accustomed to the difficulties of making intelligent estimates of things seen in the sky, and should be aware of the strange visual effects that the weather can have.

Five R.A.F. Coastal Command aircrew were at Topcliffe air station, Yorkshire, during "Exercise Mainbrace" towards the end of 1952 and were watching a Meteor approach to land at the nearby aerodrome of Dishforth.

Behind a Meteor

AS they watched they all noticed t h a t about five miles behind the Meteor and at some 10,000ft. above it there was a white object in the sky apparently following the Meteor but, as the men on the ground first saw it, travelling at a slightly slower speed.

The airmen had the white object under observation for approximately 20 minutes. They watched it lose height with a "falling leaf" movement and then saw it appear to hover, spinning on its own axis, before speeding off to the west, changing course to the south-east and disappearing at an extremely rapid speed—"as fast as a shooting-star," the witnesses said.

This group of observers, two officers, a master signaller, a sergeant, and a leading aircraftman, all insisted that what they had seen was a solid object and they did not believe it was a balloon because of its manoeuvring, change of direction, and speed.

The following day, it was reported, three Danish Air Force officers saw a very similar thing happen over Karup airfield.

Tracked on radar

THE ace of well-authenticated sightings by experts, however, must be that of a group of radar experts at a Territorial heavy anti-aircraft regiment H.Q. in South London. Here the U.F.O. was not only seen through a telescope by a group of technical men but was also tracked for 15 minutes on a modern Army radar set which was able to give an accurate record of its distance and bearing and its speed of movement.

Even though this sighting has been officially explained away as a meteorological balloon there are some facts worth studying.

Sergeant Harry Waller, 35-year - old permanent-staff radar instructor at 265 Heavy Anti-aircraft Regiment, Lee Green, a man holding a "B.2" radar certificate in the Army, indicating a high degree of training, was making a routine test on a radar set early in the afternoon when on the radar screen he saw a very large response from a target. Because of its depth he at first thought that it must be something "very big and very low."

For five minutes

BUT when he checked on his instruments he realised he was wrong. His target was at a height of 60,000ft. and the "slant range" from his radar set—the straight-line distance from the aerial to the target—was 90,000ft.

Modern radar equipment can be "locked on" to the target, which means that, without any manual help from the operator, the instruments will keep the target in the centre of the radar beam.

For five minutes Sergeant Waller had his set "locked on" to his very large target and from his instruments saw that its movement was negligible—possibly a movement of 100 yards in 30 seconds.

He went outside, expecting to see something quite big in the sky, and was surprised to find that he could see nothing with the naked eye. On the radar equipment, however, lined up on the moving aerial array is a low-p o w e r sighting telescope used for testing the alignment of the set.

Through this—which, of course, was automatically "looking" at the s a m e target as the radar beam— he was able to see with some difficulty a white ball—"not merely reflecting sunlight, but seeming to glow of its own accord."

Now Sergeant Waller is an experienced, practical man. The response on his radar was three times as large as any signal he could expect from even the largest aircraft at that range. The response was completely steady, and because he has had experience with the fluctuating, rhythmic response from the reflecting aerials of weather balloons he now has difficulty in believing that explanation.

Idea of size

SOME time before he had had the radar set lined up on a big four-engined Valiant jet bomber at a range of little more than a third of that of his mysterious target. Though he could only just see his "balloon," which at that height would have measured only a dozen or so feet, it was just as big as the Valiant had appeared at 35,000ft. range compared with the 90,000ft. range of the "balloon."

"I cannot understand how at that range I could have

This photograph was taken by a U.S. coastguard at an air station after he had seen four unknown objects in the sky. Bars of light seem to extend in front and behind.

seen a weather balloon measuring some 12ft., even if it were brilliantly illuminated by the sun," says Sergeant Waller.

"Imagine what a six-foot target on a 300-yard rifle range looks like in your sights and compare that with an object only twice as large and 100 times as far away.

"Besides, the extremely large radar response, as steady as a rock, has to be explained away."

Every detail of his story is confirmed by a group of half

a dozen technicians at the regimental headquarters, including Mr. A. S. Trew, a civilian radar engineer. They all saw the radar response and in turn looked at the "target" through the telescope.

Another interesting feature in Sergeant Waller's story was the fact that he took the trouble to search the sky for cloud movement in order to estimate wind conditions. His target had moved out of range towards the south-east, but a small patch of high cirrus cloud was moving easterly.

An explanation

THIS, however, may well be accounted for by the unexpected movements that are to be found in the upper air. In fact, the Meteorological Office report for that day shows that at 55,000ft. the wind was north-westerly (blowing to the south-east, the same direction as the very slight movement of the sergeant target) while at 30,000ft. was blowing from the south west, which would have carried the lower-lying cloud to the north-east.

The discrepancy there that the 55,000ft. wind, according to the weather men, was blowing at 35 miles an hour, while the radar target had very little movement.

These tricks of wind at varying heights are well known to the weather men, and it is to make a more complete study of them that well over 100 met. balloons are released in Britain daily. Both speed and direction can sometimes vary enormously in different layers of the atmosphere.

T o m o r r o w : What the scientists think.

Air Force Still Mum

5 to 10 Saucer Sightings Nightly

By JIM G. LUCAS Scripps-Howard Staff Writer

Commercial airline pilots report between five and 10 flying saucer sightings each night, it was learned today.

Representatives of major airlines will meet Wednesday in Los Angeles with Military Air Transport Service (MATS) intelligence officers to discuss speeding up saucer reporting procedures. The idea will be to "get the reports in the quickest way possible" so that the Air Force can send fast jet fighters to investigate.

Heretofore, commercial pilots have landed and then reported to MATS thru their companies. By that time, the trail usually is cold. Now, pilots are instructed to flash reports direct from the air to MATS intelligence here in Washington or to the nearest Air Force base. However several "bugs" have been found in this plan. Some pilots, for example, don't know how to contact MATS intelligence. Others don't think it important enough. That's one angle to be discussed at the Los Angeles meeting.

ASK SECRECY

Airline pilots are asked not to discuss their sightings publicly or give them to newspapers.

Navy Capt. Bernard Baruch Jr., MATS intelligency officer, is in charge of the project. Capt. Baruch's headquarters are in New York, but MATS intelligence also maintains a large staff at Andrews Air Force base.

One well-informed source said that until recently the largest number of sightings were from the Southwest Pacific. Saucer sightings have been particularly numerous around Australia, where the British maintain a guided missile range.

Recently, however, there has been an increase in saucer sightings in the North Atlantic, this source said. Simultaneously, the number of oil slicks and submarine sightings in this area has increased. However, associate these sightings with the establishment of an Air Force B-36 base at Thule, Greenland.

'FAIRLY COMMON'

The same source said flying saucer sightings are "fairly common" thruout the non-communist world. They invariably are made at night. Frequently, several independent sightings of the same "saucer" are reported from different spots along a plane's route.

Two reports made this week by commercial airline pilots were cited as typical.

● In the first, a Colonial Airlines pilot, en route here from Richmond, said he saw a saucer descend from the stratosphere, approach his ship, hesitate for a moment and then reverse its course. He said it appeared to re-enter the stratosphere.

The pilot was described as a "man of mature judgment, a college graduate and an attorney as well as a pilot."

● In the second, two Northwest Airlines pilots en route from Seattle to Anchorage reported a strange object with several portholes which exuded a "blueish light" flew alongside their ship most of the journey, disappearing as they were about to land in Anchorage. The pilots tried several times to close the gap between their ship and the strange object, but could not. They said the object was "definitely under someone's control."

They were questioned for two days in Alaska before going on to Tokio.

From the Scientists, This Sobering Reminder—

THE SKIES CAN PLAY SO MANY TRICKS ON US

13 FEB 1954

Concluding article in his series on the mystery of the Flying Saucers

by J. STUBBS WALKER

THE atmosphere can do some very strange things—things which even the scientists and the astronomers do not properly understand—and it can be responsible for all manner of "visions" that can easily be confused with reality. The perfect example, of course, is the mirage which shows the thirsty desert traveller an entirely imaginary oasis.

The greatest of all "flying saucer" stories is vouched for by some of the most eminent astronomers of their day. It was meticulously observed and reported by Dr. E. Walter Mander, of the Royal Observatory, Greenwich.

His report is supported in detail by such men of science as Dr. J. Rand Capron, the spectroscopist, and the Dutch scientist, Zeeman, a Nobel Prize winner.

Unexplained

YET this early flying saucer, sighted on the night of November 17, 1882, is still a mystery to the astronomers. They are certain that it was a natural occurrence, but they cannot give an adequate explanation for it.

Sir Harold Spencer Jones, the Astronomer Royal, quotes the "saucer" of 1882 as an example of a happening which is certainly natural but which defies adequate scientific explanation.

"On saucers generally," he told me, "one is forced to the conclusion that the reports result from observations which have a natural explanation, though it is not always possible, in our present state of knowledge, to give the complete explanation."

It was the Astronomer Royal who drew my attention to the remarkable report written by Dr. Mander on the 1882 observations.

Mander was expecting a particularly brilliant auroral display because earlier in the day a violent magnetic storm had broken out. He took up his position on the roof of the Royal Observatory at Greenwich and immediately after sunset he watched the expected display.

Moved smoothly

"WHEN the display was quietening down," he reported, "a great circular disc of greenish light suddenly appeared low down in the E.N.E., as though it had just risen, and moved across the sky, as smoothly and steadily as the sun, moon, stars, and planets move, but nearly a thousand times as quickly.

"The circularity of its shape when first seen was evidently merely the effect of foreshortening, for as it moved it lengthened out, and when it crossed the meridian and passed just above the moon its form was that almost of a very elongated ellipse, and various observers spoke of it as 'cigar-shaped,' like a torpedo, or a spindle or shuttle.

"This torpedo-shaped beam of light," Mander continues, "was unlike any other celestial object that I have ever seen. The quality of its light and its occurrence while a great magnetic storm and a bright aurora were in progress seem to establish its auroral origin. But it differed very widely in appearance from any other aurora I have ever seen. . . . It seemed to be a definite body."

There is no doubt at all that a great number of U.F.O. reports are caused by fireballs and meteorites. Fireballs, for instance, were almost certainly the reason for the "flaming tadpole" report from Bognor and the Isle of Wight mentioned earlier in this series.

The fireball is larger than a shooting star and smaller than a meteorite. It is caused by a small piece of matter about the size of a tennis ball, probably part of the debris of a disintegrating comet.

Fireballs do not, in fact, often reach the earth. They explode and disintegrate. But meteorites, which very roughly are the same thing only larger, reach the surface of the earth much more frequently than most people imagine, an average of about half a dozen a day. Most are fortunately quite small, but one that landed in South-West Africa weighed 60 tons.

There are complicated problems of reflection and refraction in the earth's atmosphere which inevitably must take some of the blame for flying saucers.

'Mock' suns

THE formation of ice crystals high in the air can look very solid at times, while "mock suns" and "mock moons" that can be formed by the reflection from the ice crystals can add to the confusion.

These formations in the atmosphere can also lead to faulty radar sightings. A meteor or fireball can produce a patch of ionised air which will give quite a solid response on a radar set. In fact, radar is used by the astronomers in the study of meteor showers.

Then there are the problems of the mirage. This is caused by two layers of air of different temperatures being in contact. This forms the atmospheric equivalent of an optical lens and can play all kinds of visual tricks.

You cannot blame the scientists for being generally sceptical of flying saucer reports. Added to the large number of natural explanations, they are always a little unhappy about the frailty of the most honest and conscientious observer, particularly if he is inexperienced.

Sir Harold Spencer Jones pointed out to me that if you ask two people how large they think the moon appears, one is likely to say as large as a dinner plate, the other describes it as being as large as a sixpence. Neither description is of any value because it is a "measurement" related to nothing factual.

Unknown power

THERE is, of course, no real reason why we should accept the certainty that life on other planets is impossible. There could be different forms of life from our own; the scientists are not *absolutely* certain, for instance, whether the atmosphere on Venus could support life, although they have reason to be very doubtful.

If, however, the flying saucers are from another planet they must obviously be driven by some power outside our own knowledge.

"To suppose that space craft from another world have the power to enter the earth's atmosphere and then return against the pull of our gravity is ridiculous. It is against all aerodynamic principles. You must realise that to get a six-ton rocket to the moon requires a starting weight from the earth's surface of some 24,000 tons, consisting mostly of propellent," the Astronomer Royal says.

Gravity theory

BUT whatever the scientists say, they cannot damp the ardour of the flying saucer enthusiasts. They point out that in the most serious scientific circles the theory of making use of gravity to produce power and diverting gravity to give movement in space is being considered. The new Einstein theory is believed to support this idea.

Why should not the people of another world have succeeded in solving that problem before we have?

As Professor J. Bronowski says: "We would be very vain creatures to believe that we are the only human beings in the universe."

TANFIELD'S DIARY

★ Fighter pilots are lectured on Flying Saucers

24 MAR 1954

PILOTS at Horsham St. Faith's fighter station were lectured recently on flying saucers. Air Chief Marshal Sir Dermot Boyle was there. The talk went on until midnight because of the great interest and questions.

Mr. Colin Hodgkinson, prospective Conservative candidate for S.W. Islington, gave this piece of news to a meeting of 300 people in London last night during a discussion on flying saucers. He said the problem was occupying the minds of the Air Ministry and many leading officials.

Mr. Hodgkinson—he lost both legs in a flying accident before the war, but, like Douglas Bader, flew Spitfires until 1942, when he was captured—said Mr. Desmond Leslie, ex-Spitfire pilot and co-author of the book "Flying Saucers Have Landed," gave the lecture.

Missile mile

At the discussion I noticed Lord Dowding, Fighter Command chief in the Battle of Britain, sitting in the front row.

I spoke to Mr. Humphrey Gilbert, a civil pilot who has been flying for 15 years. His compass was shattered recently over "the missile mile" on the Portsmouth road. He tells me that another pilot flying another plane on the same course with him at the time said a silver disc was over Mr. Gilbert's plane.

Throwing trains

The pilot of a Halifax bomber told me of an experience when he bombed Hanover in October 1943:

"My mid-upper gunner, 'Fussy' Davis—I last heard he was living in Brockworth, Gloucester — said: 'I think they're throwing trains at us.'

"I looked out and saw a thing that was like the illuminated coach of a railway train passing my Halifax at a terrific speed."

BOYS TELL ABOUT 'SAUCERS'

AND THE CELEBRITY IS?

24 MAR 1954

By JOHN RYDON

TWO schoolboys faced six fighter pilots, the ex-chief of Fighter Command and 300 people at Britain's first public flying saucer meeting last night.

Thirteen - year - old Stephen Darbyshire craned up before a microphone to tell his story of a saucer near his Lake District home at Coniston.

And his eight-year-old cousin, Adrian Myers, stood up among the audience and shouted: " It's true, I saw it, too."

Stephen, four other speakers and the six pilots on the platform, faced a barrage of theories from the questioning 300 in a hall in Holloway-road, N.

" Could they be thunder-

And fliers swop yarns

bolts . . . result of sex repression . . . indigestion? "

Air Marshal Lord Dowding. war-time Fighter Command chief, sat silent with his wife in the second row.

Stephen said he photographed the saucer near his home. His pictures, blown up to a large size, showed a mushroom shape in the sky over the brow of a hill.

When the photographs were passed among the audience someone said he could see a face looking out of the saucer. And the picture was grabbed from hand to hand.

The first speaker an un-

In your garden

named ex-bomber pilot, said: " In 1943, returning from a raid over Hanover, we saw a long red object with lighted windows shooting past us."

Civil pilot Humphrey Gilbert, whose compass shattered recently over Surrey's " missile mile," said: " A fellow pilot flying near me said afterwards he saw a small shining disc flying over my plane."

Desmond Leslie, who wrote a best-seller about flying saucers, said: " There have been about 10,000 reports of people sighting flying saucers.

" I'm prepared to discount 80 per cent. of these reports. The remaining 20 per cent. are unquestionable."

Jet fighter pilot Derek Dempster read out a letter from ex-B.B.C. Air Correspondent Charles Gardner, whose 12-year-old son said he saw two saucers for 30 seconds.

After the meeting ended crowds stormed the platform. And Lord Dowding. pushing through the crush, murmured: " Very interesting, very interesting. This has given me a lot to think about."

out | **Stephen had a hunch— he took his camera**

Flying Saucer snapshotter, schoolboy Stephen Darbishire, tells what he saw. His audience (left to right) : Humphrey Gilbert, Colin Hodgkinson and Desmond Leslie. Below : The evidence from Stephen's camera of what he had seen

Stephen, thirteen, drew these sketches before the photograph (left) was developed. Right : Stephen and his cousin, Adrian Myer, snap the object

NEWS CHRONICLE, WEDNESDAY, MARCH 24, 1954

Boy steals 'flying saucer' show

DOWDING SEES 'EVIDENCE'

24 MAR 1954 By **MICHAEL MOYNIHAN**

LORD DOWDING, Commander-in-Chief of Fighter Command in the Battle of Britain, last night asked a 13-year-old schoolboy to pass round the photographs he says he took of a flying saucer.

Sitting in the second row at a public meeting in Islington, Lord Dowding was among 290 people who heard four Battle of Britain pilots and two civil air line pilots state a case for saucers.

The star turn was the schoolboy, Stephen Darbishire, who had been given leave by his headmaster to describe what he had seen—and photographed—on the slopes of Coniston Old Man in the Lake District.

Lord Dowding looked at the photographs with close attention. But after the meeting he hurried away.

"I have no views to express," he said. "I have a train to catch."

Stephen said he had a hunch to go up to the fells one morning last month. He took his camera.

And he first saw the Thing when his eight-year-old cousin nudged him and said: "What's that coming through the clouds."

Four portholes

THAT, according to Stephen, his photographs and the drawings he made, was a space-ship with four portholes and a hatch.

It was about 40 feet across and it hovered 150 yards away, metallic and shining, before flying away at tremendous speed.

And, said ex-Spitfire pilot Desmond Leslie, co-author of "Flying Saucers have Landed," it bore a remarkable resemblance to the craft supposedly seen in Arizona in 1952 by George Adamski.

Other flying saucer descriptions from last night's eye-witnesses:

A cigar-shaped object with lit-up windows flashing by at 18,000 feet like an express train —witness a B.E.A pilot on a war-time raid on Hanover;

A dark blue cigar-shaped object, 30,000 feet over Marseilles two years ago—witness civil pilot Humphrey Gilbert.

Compass smashed

Mr. Gilbert also said that his compass was smashed three weeks ago when he was flying over the mysterious "missile mile," where many car windscreens have been inexplicably shattered.

Since 1946, said Mr. Leslie, there had been 10,000 reports—some of which could be explained—of flying objects, most from Australia.

'We shall

Duke Wanted To Know More About Saucer

Dispatch Diary

S.D. 28 MAR 1954

THE boy who photographed a flying saucer with his box camera made a secret journey last week.

He went to Buckingham Palace to talk to one of the Duke of Edinburgh's secretaries. It was all very hush-hush.

At four o'clock that afternoon

This is Stephen's drawing of his "saucer."

young Stephen Darbishire was being interviewed by reporters. But, despite the barrage of questions, he kept his secret.

Half an hour later he was on his way to the Palace in a hired car.

Special Report

IT SEEMS THAT the Duke read about Stephen and wanted to know more.

So it was arranged that the 13-year-old schoolboy should talk it over with someone at the Palace and that a report of the conversation should be sent to the Duke in Australia. Hence Stephen's appointment at the Palace.

It was about four weeks ago that he photographed the flying saucer over Cumberland. Since then many people have examined the snapshot and agreed that it is one of the most convincing pieces of flying-saucer evidence yet produced.

Stephen's doctor father took him to London, ostensibly for a public meeting called to discuss these strange objects. Nobody mentioned the question of a visit to the Palace.

"Down with Nasser."—A.P.

2 APR 1954

SONNY SEES HIS FLYING SAUCER

ALICE SPRINGS, Australia, Thursday.—Sonny, an Aborigine, employed on a sheep station near Alice Springs, says that a strange object—about 35ft. long and flying low—nearly knocked him off his horse. He has never heard of a flying saucer, but describes the object as a round ball with a tail. Four columns of smoke came from each side of it.—B.U.P.

JEWEL SNATCH AS FAMILY DINES

Oval light seen off coast

D.M 28 APR 1954

A mysterious round green oval-shaped object was seen in the sky off Bexhill, Sussex, yesterday.

Mrs. W. Hammond, of De La Warr-road, said she heard a loud noise and then saw a brilliant light. It circled for about a minute. Police and coastguards also reported seeing the object.

TAKING OVER

---

tion in painting in water-colours.

E.N. 6 MAY 1954
Believe It

AUTHOR Desmond Leslie reiterated at Caxton Hall last night that flying saucers *have* landed.

Very tall, dark and handsome in evening dress, maroon bow tie and cummerbund, this ex-Spitfire pilot gave a much too convincing lecture, illustrated with very genuine lantern slide photographs, to a full house.

Eager believers, wearing bronze flying saucers in their buttonholes, were still more certain; hardened cynics stopped laughing; and the general mass of "Don't Knows" found themselves faced with majestic apprehensions.

Leslie said his co-author, American George Adamski, would be here in September to describe in detail the man from Venus he claims to have met 18 months ago.

This photo, by Stephen Darbishire, is claimed to be the first of a saucer over Britain. Left: Artist John Richards's impression of the saucer

'Meteor' Comes to Earth In North California Hills

By the United Press

SAN JOSE, Calif. May 17.—Astronomers said today that a giant green fireball spotted over the San Francisco Bay area Saturday night was a "spectacular meteor" technically known as a bolide.

The meteor flashed across the sky shortly before midnight and apparently exploded or struck the earth in the rugged country behind Mt. Hamilton, on which Lick Observatory is located.

Dr. Olin Eggen, of the observatory, said witnesses reported the meteor was greenish in color, then faded into an orange glow as it neared the earth.

Lick astronomers said the meteor apparently broke into pieces in the Isabel Valley behind Mt. Hamilton. It appeared to set off 14 or 15 short-lived brush fires.

However, George Britton, local chief of the State Division of Forestry Rangers, made an aerial survey of the region by daylight and found no evidence of fires.

The chances are, authorities said, the fires were actually glowing pieces of the disintegrating meteor. The last one did not go out until 2 a.m. yesterday, or about 2 1/2 hours after the meteor was first observed in the sky.

Saucer Stories

Flying saucers come into the Light programme on May 20. People who have written to the BBC about their personal stories of flying saucers will take part. Other contributors include Douglas Bader, W. J. Brown, an aircraft designer, an author of a book on the subject and Professor A. C. B. Lovell of Manchester University.

'SAUCER HIT COMET? —THAT'S BALDERDASH'

By J. STUBBS WALKER, Daily Mail Science Correspondent

"UTTER balderdash." This is the Ministry of Civil Aviation's opinion of a statement by an American author that the British blamed a flying saucer for the Comet crash in India last year.

Said a Ministry official last night: "There has never been any such suggestion and neither we nor the Air Ministry made any statement that the Comet might have been struck by an 'unidentified flying body.'"

"Unidentified flying objects" (UFOS) are the official British and U.S. Air Forces' descriptions of flying saucers.

The man who connects one with the Comet crash, which killed 43 people, is Major Donald Keyhoe, a retired officer of the U.S. Marines.

Today his book "Flying Saucers from Outer Space" is published in Britain. In it he says: "Several times these weird machines have come dangerously close to planes.

"One such approach, the evidence shows, led to a tragic disaster."

Then he details the take-off of the BOAC Comet from Dum Dum Airport, Calcutta, in bad weather during May last year.

"Six minutes later," he writes, "something hit the Comet.

"For days experts analysed the strangely battered wreckage. Then the Air Ministry gave out a guarded statement. The Comet had been hit by an unidentified flying body."

That is Major Keyhoe's story.

In fact, there was no sign of collision and the official on-the-spot investigation showed that the Comet broke up either through severe strain in the storm or loss of control by the pilot.

'Oval shape' shot over his home

MELBOURNE, Sunday.—Fourteen people have reported seeing an object like a flying saucer over Melbourne suburbs in the past 24 hours. One said an "oval-shaped thing as big as a railway carriage" shot over his house with a loud buzzing sound.—*Reuter.*

'GLOBE IN THE SKY'

A mysterious light was seen in the sky over Canvey Island, Essex, last night. It appeared as a small globe that gained height, and disappeared rapidly in the

MANY believers in the extra-terrestrial origin of flying saucers feel that a more general recognition of this fact is slow in coming because they have been so ridiculously named. I cannot agree. Nicknaming something which is strange, if not menacing, to us is our traditional way of approaching it. In the first Great War our soldiers soon found that they could face the enemy with stouter heart if they called him "Jerry"; and a quarter of a century later we felt we knew all we wanted to know about the first of Hitler's secret weapons by dubbing it "buzz-bomb."

We are reminded in *Flying Saucers from Outer Space*, by Major Donald E. Keyhoe (Hutchinson, 10s. 6d.), that they were so called when Ken Arnold, an Idaho pilot flying his own 'plane, reported sighting nine saucerlike discs over Mount Rainier, Washington; and so the Americans must take the credit for this bit of inspired flippancy. But as in these things the Americans are so like us, what difference does it make? Flying saucers they are and flying saucers they will remain.

Like most nicknames, this one is singularly appropriate: they *do*, we are told by those who claim to have seen them, look like saucers (except when observed from an angle which changes them into spheres or "cigars") and they fly at a speed of anything from one mile to five miles a second.

MAJOR KEYHOE'S previous book, *The Flying Saucers Are Real*, published three years ago, contained the results of his first investigation into these phenomena and he reprimanded the information service of the U.S. Air Force for issuing contradictory and deliberately evasive statements to the Press. Now he tells us of the 1952 "scare" when saucers were seen "flying singly, in pairs, or in group formation" all over the world.

As more and more reports reached the U.S. Intelligence Department in Washington official uneasiness grew. The U.F.O.s (unidentified flying objects) were being seen not only by mere citizens, whom officials everywhere regard as little better than half-wits, but by military and airline pilots, radar teams and civil defence aircraft spotters. But what really shook the Service chiefs was what happened on July 20th.

On that day, just after midnight, the men at the Air Traffic Control Centre at Washington National Airport who "reach out by long-range surveillance radar to track 'planes 100 miles away" tracked on their "scopes" some strange aircraft flying at a speed later estimated at 7,200 miles an hour. These machines circled Washington *for two hours*. They vanished when jet fighter 'planes went up to intercept them, but the moment the jets left, they reappeared, and at five-thirty a radio engineer saw "five huge discs circling in a loose formation. As he watched, dumbfounded, the discs tilted upward and climbed steeply into the sky."

Six days later, at Key West, "a red-lighted saucer flashed over the Naval Air Station" and was seen by hundreds of people, to be followed by more saucers over Washington and no cessation of reports of sightings from other parts of America. So, under pressure from Congressmen and the Press, General Samford, director of U.S. Air Force Intelligence, called a Press conference. But an astronomer's "temperature-inversion theory" with which the General tried to explain the phenomena satisfied neither the Press nor leading scientists—nor Major Keyhoe. Moreover, the radar men who had tracked the machines and the air pilots who had seen them felt disgruntled. One of the Control Centre men told Major Keyhoe:

Every man in here knows temperature-inversion effects. When an inversion's big enough, it picks up all sorts of 'ground clutter'—water-tanks, buildings, shore lines and so on. But anybody here can recognize it. You'll see huge purplish blobs, but nothing like those things we tracked. In the six years I've watched the scopes, absolutely nothing—high-speed jets, storms, inversions, or anything else—has ever caused blips that manœuvred like that. . . .

Eventually Major Keyhoe told the Air Force that he intended to investigate further and to publish his views and findings, and asked if they would take him into their confidence because he did not want to mislead people if he were on the wrong track. Their answer was to give him access to the secret Intelligence analysis of sightings and to welcome his co-operation. A list of sightings officially cleared forms an appendix to his book, together with a

SAUCERS OVER AMERICA

By REGINALD MOORE

– 4 JUN 1954

facsimile of the incredibly comprehensive "Technical Information Sheet" which air pilots have to fill up when they see a saucer. It is all very factual and conclusive, this book—a valuable addition to our present knowledge of the subject.

If you are new to all this, and want to know how long people on earth have been seeing strange things in the sky which are neither meteors, fireballs, light refractions nor spots before the eyes; and how the craft may be energized (have you heard of the magnetic lines of force?)—you could not do better than read *Flying Saucers on the Moon*, by Harold T. Wilkins (Peter Owen, 16s.). It has a useful index; an appendix

in which very recent sightings are summarized; a bibliography; and eleven photographs of actual saucers which will surely give you pause!

And if it seems outlandish to you that the moon should be dragged into it, remember that another Mr. Wilkins—Percy Wilkins, author of *Our Moon* (Muller, 12s. 6d.)—has observed some very odd things on the face of our satellite. The Americans have a Project Bluebook, which is the special section of the U.S. Air Force investigating saucers. With schoolboys taking photographs of saucers in the Lake District, and the B.B.C. doing a programme on them, isn't it time *we* had an investigation too? My suggestion is that the "cloak-and-dagger boys" borrow Superman's cloak. That should settle everything!

Page FIVE
Tie Comet

'Oval shape' shot over his home

MELBOURNE, Sunday.—Fourteen people have reported seeing an object like a flying saucer over Melbourne suburbs in the past 24 hours.

One said an "oval-shaped thing as big as a railway carriage" shot over his house with a loud buzzing sound. He and five friends clearly saw "dark shapes" in it.

"If I had seen the same shapes in an aeroplane, I would have said they were people," he added.—Reuter.

WAILING WORRIES TOWN

TOWNSFOLK at Eastleigh, Hants, are worried about a wailing noise. They describe it as "eerie," "sinister" — and nobody knows from where it comes. **2 JUN 1954**

It is mostly heard at midnight, when it wakes householders and alarms their children. The town council is asking factories to help to trace the noise.

---

as reported yesterday owing to a train...

2 JUN 1954

MYSTERY AIR OBJECT
Travelled Against Wind

Capt. C. J. Kratovil, pilot of a Trans-World Airliner from Paris, reported to-day having seen an unidentified object in the sky about 10 miles north of Boston. A number of jet planes were sent up to chase it, but gave up when a report came through that a weather balloon released by the Air Force was soaring in the Boston area.

"It's the first time I ever saw a weather balloon travelling against the wind," Capt. Kratovil said later. He described the object as "large and white and disc-like." He was, however, unable to get a good look at it because it kept disappearing into cloud.

THE THINGS PEOPLE SEE...

A CANADIAN miner, 25-year-old Ennio La Sarza, has seen a flying saucer with a crew of three—"each of them 13 feet tall with ears like spurs and three sets of arms," he told the Royal Canadian Air Force.

He said the saucer—"a huge disc"—came from the sky near Garson (Ontario) on Friday —the day the planet Mars was nearest to the earth's orbit. He shouted, asking the crew who they were and "they fixed me with a hypnotic stare until I fainted; when I came to they and the ship had vanished."

The R.C.A.F. is checking the story, but declines to comment.—Express News Service,

8 JUN 1954

SAUCER SEEN

DUSSELDORF, Wednesday.—Airline officials at the airport here claimed today to have seen a "flying saucer" travelling at high speed at about 13,000ft.—Reuter.

D.M. 9 JUN 1954

Pulman's Weekly News

1 JUN 1954

Mystery of The Air

Somerset Youth's Strange Story

[BY A STAFF REPORTER]

What did 18 years old Nigel Frapple, of High-street, Bruton, Somerset, see "hovering in mid-air" over the Redlynch area of Bruton, about 2 a.m. on Thursday?

He makes no claim to be numbered among those who assert that they have seen a "flying saucer," but his description, in an interview with me as to what he is quite confident he did see, cannot be explained away very easily except that he saw something which answers to no known description. This is his story, which he accompanied with a rough sketch in my notebook.

He was cycling home from a visit to Wincanton and on reaching the area of Redlynch crossroads says the air became illuminated with an orange light. Travelling along slowly at a height he estimates at about 75 feet was what he first thought must be a balloon on fire. He then saw that it was an object, he thinks about 30 to 40 feet across moving along more or less in front of him. This object hovered over a field. Dismounting from his bicycle he got to within about 50 yards of it and crouching behind a hedge had a good view.

The object, which made no sound, says Mr. Frapple, had a cockpit in its centre, with "sort of glass panels" and this was surmounted by a small revolving light. At one end was another orange light, which for want of a better description, he describes as a tail light, although he could see nothing connecting it with the main body, so that it seemed "suspended on nothing."

He endeavoured to get a closer look and the object commenced to move away slowly in a northerly direction and then vanished upwards at a terrific speed still making no sound except for a "whooshing noise." There seemed to him to be a kind of blue vapour coming from the craft.

Young Frapple is quite resigned to having no believers in his story, and was quite frank as to the difficulty of giving credence to what he is quietly quite confident that he saw.

Sunday Dispatch, JUNE 13, 1954   5

Youth Sees 50-Foot 'Saucer' Hovering Only 30 Yards Away

By Sunday Dispatch Reporter

WHAT was the huge, circular flying machine, surrounded by a brilliant, flame-coloured light, which was seen silently hovering over hamlets in Hampshire and Somerset? 13 JUN 1954

Last week Air Ministry experts were puzzling over this extraordinary phenomenon which has been described as "a perfect example of a flying saucer," and which was observed in one case from a distance of only 30 yards.

So far no natural cause has been found to account for it.

It was seen by 18-year-old Nigel Frapple, of High-street, Bruton, and by Miss Doreen Heffer, of Shobley, near Ringwood, Hampshire, on the night of May 19-20.

Hovered Gently

Both independently describe surprisingly similar features.

Both agree that it was circular, emitted a brilliant flame-coloured light from a central cockpit, and was at least 50ft. across;

That it hovered gently for more than a minute and then made off at great speed;

That it was practically silent except for a slight swishing;

That it had associated with it another and smaller light a little distance away from it.

Nigel Frapple had the nearest view while cycling home at 2 a.m. on May 20. "There was a terrific light in a field nearby," he said.

Only 20ft Up

"About 80ft. away was a huge object hovering up and down about 20ft. above ground.

"I watched for more than a minute. Then it moved off."

Miss Heffer saw a similar object about three hours earlier.

'Object' Over Zurich

REPORTS of an illuminated object said to have been observed circling over Zürich early on Friday are being studied by the Swiss Air Ministry.

About 50 people in the industrial suburb of Oerlikon have given the police descriptions of it.

Mars Nears: Earth Will Look For Signs of Life

GUS

"Just my luck, Benson, Mars only 40,000,000 miles away for the first time in years and I've brought my wrong glasses."

"Evening News" Reporter

NEXT week we may know if there are such things as Martians. Astronomers all over the world are at the ready with their telescopes and other instruments to try to solve this age-old mystery.

Favourable opportunities for observing Mars occur every 15 or 16 years, when the earth and Mars move nearer each other. The maximum distance between them is 63 million miles. (The moon is 238,857 miles and the sun 93 million miles from the earth.)

Next week the earth and Mars are expected to pass, at a distance apart of only 40 million miles, on or about Friday.

Astronomers in Britain and elsewhere in the Northern Hemisphere are not expecting useful results.

IN SOUTHERN PART OF ORBIT

The planet will be in the southern part of its orbit. This means they will see Mars lifting only briefly over the southern horizon in the middle of the night.

South Africa is expected to provide the best vantage point. A number of astronomers, including several leading American authorities, have gone to Lamont-Hussey Observatory at Bloemfontein, which is equipped with a 27-inch refracting telescope.

They will be looking for firm definitions of the canals and belts of vegetation bordering water-courses that have been reported from time to time.

They will be looking for supporting evidence of claims that the water being poured along chan-

nels suggested it was the work of intelligent beings with engineering knowledge such as exists on the earth.

They will be looking for clear definitions of Martian seasons.

They will be looking for clearly defined signs of life.

ENTHUSIASTS HOPE TO SEE 'SAUCERS'

And if they don't succeed this time there will be 1956, when despite the longer cycles of the past Mars and the earth will pass even closer—35 million miles.

It is estimated that after that approaches will not be as close until some time in 1970.

Flying saucer enthusiasts in New Zealand calculate that there will be a greater number of sightings from to-day when Mars and the earth "start to move closer to each other."

The New Zealand calculations have prompted the British Flying Saucer Club to record that "many believe there will be a great number of sightings."

SKY "OBJECTS" SEEN FROM PLANE

B.O.A.C. PILOT REPORT

Daily Telegraph Reporter

Capt. J. R. Howard, pilot of a Stratocruiser airliner which landed at London Airport from New York yesterday, reported that between New York and Goose Bay, while flying at 19,000ft, he saw a number of dark objects in the sky.

He flew his British Overseas Airways Corporation plane on a parallel course, and the objects, one large and the others smaller, remained about five miles away. It was "highly improbable" they were birds—he put their speed at about 260 m.p.h.

His first officer, to whom he pointed out the objects, said he thought it might be smoke from anti-aircraft shells. The rest of the crew, eight in number, saw the dark spots. Capt Howard radioed Goose Bay and a fighter was sent up.

At Goose Bay he was met by a United States Air Force intelligence officer, and gave a report. He was told that a fighter control radar operator had picked up a large number of dark objects on his screen. Capt. Howard lives at Bristol.

"MYSTERIOUS OBJECTS" OVER ATLANTIC

STRATOCRUISER PILOT'S REPORT

1 JUL 1954

Mysterious objects flying 19,000ft. over the Atlantic were reported by the pilot of a B.O.A.C. Stratocruiser early yesterday. The pilot, Captain Howard, radioed that the objects, one very large—looking rather like a burst of "flak"—and six smaller ones, flew parallel to him for 80 miles, not less than five miles away.

Captain Howard radioed to Goose Bay, Labrador, that he had sighted the objects at about 150 nautical miles south-west of Goose Bay. A jet fighter from the United States Air Force at Goose Bay took off to intercept the objects, but as the fighter approached the Stratocruiser the objects faded.

Captain Howard and all his crew, except one steward, saw the objects, as did some of the passengers. On landing at Goose Bay the crew were interviewed by an intelligence officer of the United States Air Force. A second fighter aircraft was dispatched to continue the search, but was unsuccessful.

The Stratocruiser was on the B.O.A.C. Monarch service from New York to London Airport, where it arrived about midday. The objects were sighted at 1.15 a.m. G.M.T. yesterday. They disappeared at 1.23 a.m. The aircraft was flying at 19,000ft. at 238 knots, above a layer of thin cloud. Visibility was excellent.

S.D. 27 JUN 1954

VICAR: I WATCHED FLYING SAUCER OUTSIDE WINDOW

IT was midnight when the Rev. Cedric Wright, vicar of Seighford, near Stafford, saw a bright light through the curtains of his home. He looked out and—claims he saw a flying saucer.

He said: "It was a great illuminated crab-like thing with feelers hovering like a helicopter about 80 feet in the air. It threw out a light like burnished gold and kept moving back and forwards.

"I called my wife and 22-year-old son and we watched it for nearly an hour. I have always been sceptical about flying saucers. Now I am a believer in them."

It happened on Thursday last week. The son described the object as a dome like half an orange about 25 feet wide. There was a halo above and a noise coming from it, he said.

Canada Looks For 'Flying Saucers'

AT the same time as the eclipse of the sun on Wednesday, Mars will be at the nearest point to the earth for 13 years. And, taking no chance on a surprise Martian "invasion," Canada has set up a flying saucer look-out post.

Explained an official: "Most flying saucer reports are made at 18 month intervals, coinciding with the times that the earth and Mars are in closest proximity."

Mystery of the flying jellyfish over Atlantic

BLOBS 'ESCORT' AIRLINER

By Daily Mail Reporter

CAPTAIN James Howard, piloting a BOAC Stratocruiser from New York to London yesterday, reported that a formation of weird flying machines had flown parallel to him for more than 80 miles.

Two United States Air Force Sabre jets took off to investigate the formation.

Captain Howard told American Intelligence officers that the formation consisted of six small, black objects and one larger machine, which he described as a "flying jellyfish."

All 11 members of the Stratocruiser's crew and many of the 51 passengers aboard watched the formation in the clear, evening sky for about 30 minutes.

Captain Howard, aged 33, said in London: "There was one large flying machine which constantly appeared to change shape—so that we dubbed it the 'flying jellyfish' — surrounded by six smaller objects.

Like a fighter escort

"These kept station round the larger machine, rather like a group of fighters acting as a bomber escort.

"My co-pilot, Lee Boyd, a Canadian of immense experience as a pilot, and I thought that the big machine might be a delta- or swept-wing bomber.

"But it changed shape several

MISS DAPHNE WEBSTER.
"We are quite certain."

times. Once it looked like a dart. Then like a dumbell.

"Mr. Boyd called Goose Bay radio immediately they were sighted to ask if there was a formation of aircraft in the area. Goose Bay replied that we were the only aircraft on their screen. Nothing else was being recorded.

Miss Daphne Webster, 28, the stewardess, said : "The objects appeared to be not less than five miles away. It was difficult to assess their size because there was nothing in the sky at the time to measure them against.

"We are quite certain that the machines were in flight, and were something solid."

Flying Saucers?

YES
Says the captain

YES
Says the crew

YES
Say the passengers

Express Staff Reporter

A FORMATION of strange objects tracked the B.O.A.C. Stratocruiser Centaurus over Labrador for 18 minutes, the airliner's captain reported yesterday.

Just another flying saucer story? Perhaps—BUT:—

Captain James Howard, the 33-year-old ex-R.A.F. pilot, was sufficiently impressed to write 800 words about it in his routine flight report ;

His crew of 11 saw the same objects — a large one attended by six smaller ones—and all agreed about what they saw ;

A dozen of the 51 passengers flying from New York to London saw the "formation"; and

The airliner's radio flash to Goose Bay, Labrador, sent a Sabre jet fighter speeding to intercept it.

Base ship?

As the fighter approached, the satellite objects—in the words of First-Officer Lee Boyd —"appeared to return to their base ship." Then all faded away.

IT HAPPENED—said Captain Howard's report — 170 miles south-west of Goose Bay, just after sunset on Tuesday evening.

For 80 miles the objects flew parallel to the Stratocruiser, "keeping station not less than five miles away."

The large black object changed shape slightly from time to time; the six smaller objects did not.

WERE THEY AIRCRAFT ? Goose Bay had no reports of any in the area—except the airliner — and its radar confirmed that. Captain Howard said there were no vapour trails or lights.

WERE THEY BIRDS ? Might explain it (said the captain's report) IF they were birds which could fly at 274 miles an hour, at 19,000ft., and keep formation for 80 miles. . . .

WHAT DO THE WITNESSES THINK ? Slim Miss Daphne Webster, 28-year-old stewardess who lives at King's Heath, Birmingham, and lodges at Hounslow between trips, said last night :—

"I have never seen anything like it before. The one big black object, roughly roundish, kept changing shape like a jellyfish swimming in the sea."

'Controlled'

Mr. Lee Boyd, 33-year-old Canadian and ex - squadron leader in the wartime Pathfinder force, said at Bristol :—

"It was the greatest thrill of my life. I am willing to swear that what we saw was something solid, something manoeuvrable, and something that was being controlled intelligently."

Mr. George Allen, 31-year-old navigation officer: "I am absolutely convinced that the objects we saw were a base ship of some kind with a number of satellites linked with it."

And Captain Howard, at home in Sea Mills, Bristol : "I just can't formulate a theory of *any* kind."

SKYNOTE : Mars is closer to the earth this week—less than 40,000,000 miles—than at any time since 1939.

WE SAW 'MOTHER' OF FLYING SAUCERS

1 JUL 1954—say BOAC crew

'DAILY MIRROR' REPORTER

TEN members of a B.O.A.C airliner crew said yesterday that they watched "a formation of strange objects" in the sky for twenty minutes.

"It was like a mother flying-saucer with chicks," one of the crew told me. "They flew alongside us during a flight from New York to London."

Several passengers also said they spotted the objects.

Captain J. R. Howard, of Southwood-drive, Sea Mills, Bristol who captained the airliner, told me: "We saw the objects quite clearly—a large one with a formation of smaller ones round it.

"The whole of the crew saw them."

Co-pilot Lee Boyd, of Lavington-road, St. George, Bristol, said: "The smaller objects kept changing in number, as though they were being taken aboard the mother ship."

IN BRIEF

¶ Mrs. Violet C⸱ ard, mother playwright N⸱ COWARD, d⸱ her flat in square, We⸱ aged 91.

Valerie Bromle⸱ BULL⸱ SHO⸱ B 1 ⸱ ⸱ pic⸱ w⸱

Pilot draws 'flying jellyfish'

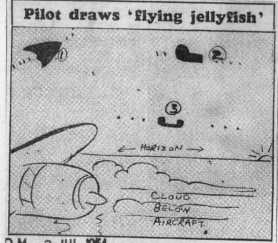

D.M. 2 JUL 1954 by Daily Mail Reporter

THIS sketch of seven mysterious flying objects was drawn exclusively for the *Daily Mail* yesterday by Captain James Howard, 33-year-old pilot of the BOAC stratocruiser, who saw them at 19,000ft. over Goose Bay, Labrador, on Wednesday.

The centre machine he described as a "flying jellyfish" because it appeared to be constantly changing shape. His sketch shows the three main shapes. The six smaller blobs —"they were dots in comparison"—altered their positions, sometimes three ahead and three astern, at other times one or two ahead and the rest astern.

At his Bristol home, Captain Howard said: "I'm still sceptical of the flying saucer theory, of piloted aircraft from other planets, and all the other tales. All I am willing to believe is what I saw and what my crew saw. Whether these objects were piloted craft or what they were I refuse to speculate. They were not like any plane I have seen before except for one short time when the larger object took on the shape of a delta-wing aircraft.

"In my 7,500 hours in the air, nothing like this has ever happened before. I am certain these objects, were not the result of reflected light or mirages or any other usual phenomena one meets at high altitude. This really was something different."

These are what the BOAC pilot saw and drew at the time

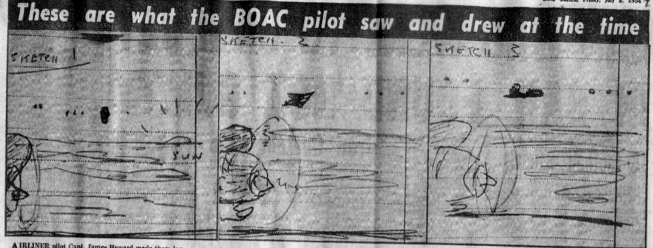

SKETCH 1 SKETCH 2 SKETCH 3

SUN

AIRLINER pilot Capt. James Howard made these log-book sketches of the mystery objects as he watched them track his plane over the Atlantic. Sketch No. 1 shows how he first saw them—one large, six very small. Then (centre) they changed shape and position. In his third sketch (right) the largest object has changed shape again.

-2 JUL 1954
Daily Sketch Reporter

NOW RAF ASKS ABOUT THE SAUCERS

—after seven years

THE Royal Air Force are prepared—for the first time — to believe there ARE flying saucers.

Yesterday they took official action on the sighting by a veteran B.O.A.C. pilot, his crew and 51 passengers of seven "mysterious black objects" over the Atlantic.

They examined the pilot's drawings of the objects. They analysed the Strato-cruiser's log. They went over statements by the crew.

And they asked 33-year-old Captain James Howard to call at the Air Ministry to tell high-ranking intelligence officers his story.

Captain Howard, matter-of-fact, play-it-down, ex-R.A.F. bomber pilot has 7,500 flying hours and 265 Atlantic crossings in his log books.

Lampton Park-road, Hounslow, said last night: "It was the most exciting sight I've ever seen—but a little creepy.

"I was making tea at 19,000 feet when I saw the objects. The big one was constantly changing its size and shape—one minute like a cigar, then an orange, then a mushroom.

"The smaller ones kept changing formation but not their shape. Every one of us was far too intrigued to be afraid."

First reports of flying saucers came from America in 1947.

DAPHNE WEBSTER
She saw them, too.

DAILY EXPRESS FRIDAY JULY 2 1954

Express Science Reporter checks up on yesterday's Page One story

Flying Saucers ▶ NO *SAYS CHAPMAN PINCHER* NO *SAYS CHAPMAN PINCHER* NO *SAYS CHAPMAN PINCHER*

'A SHINY PLANE REFLECTED'

Express Science Reporter CHAPMAN PINCHER

THE formation of "flying saucers" reported over Labrador by Captain James Howard, pilot of the B.O.A.C. Stratocruiser Centaurus, was—I believe—nothing more than a reflection of the aircraft itself from a wavy layer of air.

This would be broken up into separate parts—a large object and six smaller ones were seen—like a reflection from rippled water.

Consider these facts from Captain Howard's official report :—

1 The "saucers" accompanied the airplane for 80 miles, travelling at exactly the same speed, at the same height, and the same distance from it.

2 They could not be picked up by radar though the airplane was clearly detected by the Goose Bay radar station.

3 They repeatedly changed their shape and size as happens with reflections from ripply water.

Flying Saucers?
YES
Says the captain
YES
Says the crew
YES
Say the passengers

—Page One, yesterday.

ON-THE-SPOT SKETCH —BY THE CAPTAIN

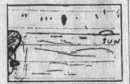

SUN

SIX small black objects and a larger one—a "flying jelly-fish" that appeared to change shape constantly. . . . Captain Howard's impression of the first glimpse of "unidentified flying objects"—taken from his actual voyage report.

THE NEXT PHASE

The "objects"—sketched after they had changed position and the large one its shape . . .

has never seen anything comparable before.

Third, why did the formation follow the plane for 80 miles and then disappear when a fighter was coming up to investigate ?

"Inversions" sometimes stretch for hundreds of miles, so the reflection would seem to travel with the plane. The disappearance of the "saucers" may have been due to a change of light—remember the sun was setting—or the "inversion" may have petered out.

Mirages, too

Could a layer of air in which there was no cloud act as a mirror in this way? Yes, especially as the Stratocruiser is an exceptionally shiny plane.

At various levels in the atmosphere there are regions called "inversions" where the air temperature suddenly changes.

Boundaries between layers of warm and cold air are such good mirrors that they cause mirages in the desert.

Because of the turbulence of the atmosphere, the boundary is sometimes rippled and breaks up an image into several parts which, after reflection, can be seen at eye-level.

The artist's sketch shows how this could have happened to the Centaurus.

If my theory is right, the "saucers" could have been seen only in the direction of the sun's rays — through the port-side windows of the aircraft which was travelling north-east while the sun was setting in the north-west.

They *were* seen through the port-windows.

Three against

I discussed my theory with Captain Howard last night. He agreed that it is feasible, but raised three points against it.

First, he thought the "saucers" looked too solid to be reflections. (They were not solid enough to reflect radar, and their constant change of shape argues against solidity.)

Second, though he has flown the Atlantic 265 times and knows all about "inversions," he

—AND A THIRD

Still another — and later — impression by Captain Howard, drawn for the voyage report.

WHAT PINCHER THINKS THEY SAW . . .

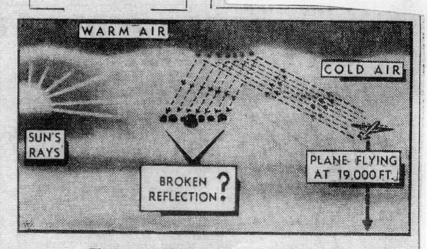

WARM AIR   COLD AIR

SUN'S RAYS

BROKEN REFLECTION ?

PLANE FLYING AT 19,000 FT.

There are regions called "inversions." . . .

No wonder

ARE we, in this age of many marvels, losing our faculty of wonder? At about 11 p.m. last Thursday I was lying in bed in a house on the Sussex downs when a brilliant light suddenly appeared in the southern sky.

My first thought was that an aeroplane had caught fire—but the light remained stationary at a height that I estimated as 5,000 feet.

Even with field-glasses I could not make out the shape of the object; but the blaze of white light continued, with an occasional crimson glow at what might be called its bows.

I woke my sister and a woman guest in the house. They had the same impression as myself. Might it be the planet Mars, they suggested, now unusually close to the earth? But it was too large and bright to be a star.

The next night it was there again, motionless at the same spot in the southern sky. The only difference was that a green light replaced the crimson gleam.

Many must have shared this experience, but we seem to be losing the capacity for being surprised.   **G. Ward Price.**
London, E.C.4.

D.M. 2 JUL 1954

---

blame—juvenile delinquents.

3 JUL 1954

Saucer 13

Johannesburg, Friday. — A flying saucer bearing the figure "1" followed by "3" or "B" has been seen near Kimberley.

EXPERT PROBES 'FLYING JELLY'

Capt. James Howard, B.O.A.C. Stratocruiser skipper, who says he saw seven "flying jellies" over the Atlantic, has been questioned by an Air Ministry flying saucer expert.

So far no conclusion has been reached about Capt. Howard's report.

But the Air Ministry says: "We do not believe in flying saucers."

3 JUL 1954

D.M. 3 JUL 1954

HIGH IN SKY

Three see flying object going at great speed

Three men who saw a crescent-shaped object in the sky over Wallsend-on-Tyne think it may have been a "flying saucer." Mr. John Poole, 40, of Chester-le-Street, said yesterday: "It was at a great height and we thought it was a jet plane.

"But when we saw it turning circles almost on its own nose we realised no jet plane could turn so quickly and in such a small circle. It spun several times and then shot off at a high speed. There was no sound at all."

---

3 JUL 1954

Six Witnesses

Golly—Was It A Flying Saucer?

By CYRIL BIRKS
"Evening News" Air Reporter

ANOTHER "flying saucer" report is to be added to the growing dossier in the Technical Intelligence Branch of the Air Ministry.

Six people say they watched a strange object in the sky for 1½ hours from a top-floor flat near Regent's Park.

Five of them—Miss Eve Becke, her brother, Mr. Colin Becke, Miss Adriana Colle, an Italian, Mr. Jo Wisman, a Dutchman, and an American woman—told the strange story to-day in the room from which they watched the object.

They also drew for me their impressions of it, and all agreed that at times the shape had a "bowler hat" appearance.

Miss Becke said: "I was resting on a couch near the window last Saturday night. It was about 9 p.m. and the sun was going down. I glanced through the window and exclaimed: 'Golly, a flying saucer.'"

Her brother came to the window with their friends. "They all said they could see it and we all watched it."

TWO LINES

It was a long way off and high in the sky. It appeared to hover and at times moved slowly and was surrounded by a very bright light.

Suddenly, she said, two lines shot out from each side. At the end of each was something like a shimmering plate.

As it moved it seemed to change shape. "It was definitely not a star or an aircraft."

Mr. Becke said: "The impression I got was that of a luminous base with an object on top of it that looked like a ball of light. It seemed to be shooting off sparks."

The American observer declared: "After a time the object seemed to divide into two equal parts and from the point of division silver rays appeared to be emitted."

Miss Colle, the Italian girl, thought that little objects were coming off the main body but she could not define them. She saw the main object suddenly speed up and disappear.

FOOTNOTE: Later in the week B.O.A.C. crew reported seven strange objects over the Atlantic.

Jet crashes after 'interception'

3 JUL 1954

NEW YORK, Friday.—A jet fighter crashed in New York State today after it had been sent up, armed with rockets, on an "active air defence intercept mission."

The interception was successful, but U.S. Air Force officials said they did not know what the object intercepted was.

The cockpit of the crashed plane became unbearably hot during the flight and the pilot told his observer to bale out.

Then he baled out himself, at about 7,000ft., over Utica, New York State.

The plane crashed into a car and two buildings, killing four people.

It hit the car, wrecking it and itself. Then the remains ploughed into two houses, setting both alight.

The pilot and observer both landed alive and were taken to hospital. A second plane which took off on the interception landed safely.—B U P.

RIDDLE OF CRASHED AMERICAN FIGHTER

Unidentified object was intercepted: Air Force

D.M. 3 JUL 1954

The following story was sent out last night by British United Press:

NEW YORK, Friday.

A JET fighter crashed near Utica, New York State, today after it had been sent up on an "active air defence intercept mission."

The U.S. Air Force said: "There was a successful intercept." But officials did not know what the object intercepted might be.

The plane, a Starfire jet fighter, crashed into a car and two buildings, killing four people.

Air Force headquarters in Washington said that the plane was armed with rockets because its mission was active.

Cockpit hot

The cockpit of the plane which crashed became unbearably hot during the flight, said a spokesman, and the pilot ordered his radar observer to bail out as the plane was heading towards Rome, New York State. He then bailed out himself from about 7,000 feet.

At the Griffiss base, it was said both the pilot and radar operator were under treatment at a hospital.

The plane which crashed was one of two that took off from the 27th Fighter Squadron base.

RIDDLE OF THE ROCKETS JET

NEW YORK, Friday.

A JET fighter crashed today after it had been sent up on an "active air defence intercept mission" near Utica, New York State.

The U.S. Air Force said the plane was armed with rockets and made a successful interception. But the Air Force spokesman said he did not know what the object intercepted was.

The plane, a Starfire, crashed into a car and two buildings, killing four people.

The pilot later said the cockpit became unbearably hot during the flight and he ordered his radar observer to bale out. He then baled out himself.

Both men are now in hospital.

The crashed plane was one of two that took off from the 27th Fighter Squadron at Griffiss Air Force Base, New York State, on the mystery mission.—B.U.P.

BERLIN SEES 3 SAUCERS —REGULARLY

U.S. experts begin investigation

From Daily Mail Reporter

BERLIN, Sunday.

ALLIED officials in Berlin are investigating the appearance of mysterious flying objects over the city.

German eye-witnesses claim a formation of three fast-moving objects can regularly be seen whenever the sky over Berlin is clear.

D.M. 5 JUL 1954

The objects, described as "small and disc-like," are said to appear between 10 and 11 p.m. and fly at extremely high altitudes.

U.S. experts have interrogated dozens of people, and a long "flying saucer" questionnaire for people who claim to have seen the objects is being prepared.

Sceptical

Radar operators at Berlin's Tempelhof Airport, who are keeping close watch on all air movements in the Berlin area, refused to say whether they have been able to trace the objects.

But a German flying control official said today : "We are still sceptical. Many Russian jet fighters are stationed around Berlin, and their night activities are not always known to us."

I CHALLENGE PINCHER says the airline pilot who started it all . . .

EXPRESS POST
- 6 JUN 1954

I AM the pilot concerned in the recent sighting of sky-objects over Labrador, and I challenge Mr. Chapman Pincher's "explanation" that this could have been merely the reflection of my own aircraft.

An inversion can act as a mirror and reflect, or sometimes refract, distant objects—true.

But not in the way illustrated by Mr. Pincher. Had an inversion existed above us at the time (highly unlikely with the high temperature) we *might* have seen a reflection of the sunset, nothing more ; certainly not six small black dots and one large variable shaped thing.

Was it a *shadow* that we saw ? Plausible, maybe, but shadows are thrown *away* from the light source, not towards it.
—J. R. HOWARD (Capt., B.O.A.C.), Arthur-road, Wokingham, Berks.

CHAPMAN PINCHER says : Reflections through the air over long distances become blurred and broken up. Desert mirages caused by distant buildings have looked like waving palms to thirsty travellers. The "saucers" seen by Captain Howard were said to be between five and 50 miles away.

Fantastic !

I CANNOT understand why a "flying saucer" report invariably triggers off a chorus of denunciation. People labour to prove that "flying saucers" are anything from ion-ised air pockets to a deranged liver.

Some of the explanations are more fantastic than the subject they seek to disprove.—RALPH GREEN (Second Officer), Royal Fleet Auxiliary Seafox.

PINCHER says : I find the desire to believe that flying saucers are real objects from another world far less understandable.

D.M. 7 JUL 1954.

IS THIS A FLYING SAUCER?

Cameraman in air-liner says: I photographed it at 13,500ft

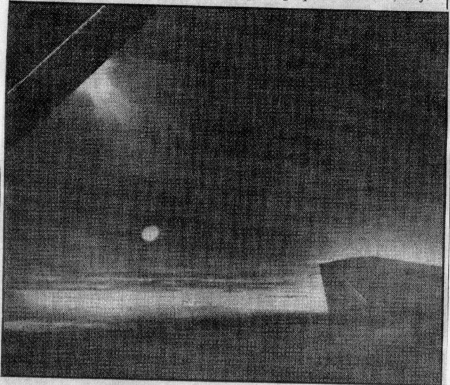

*T*HIS picture of what appears to be a "flying saucer" was taken by Norwegian cameraman Johnny Bjornulf through the window of an airliner flying at 13,500ft. above the Hardangervidda mountain plateau during last week's eclipse.

In the centre is a white disc which, he says, "moved across the horizon at great speed." The rays of the sun can be seen (top left).

Bjornulf was taking a colour film of the eclipse. The film was flown to London for processing and shown to a small audience.

Two other photographers in the plane had similar results when their pictures were developed.

The colour film is now back in Oslo, from where this picture was wired to the Daily Mail last night.

D.M. 7 JUL 1954

CAMERA LOGS TWO FLYING SAUCERS

OSLO, Tuesday.

"*F*LYING saucers" were filmed by a Norwegian photographer, Johnny Bjornulf, who took pictures from an airliner during the eclipse last week.

The photographs were taken at 13,500ft. as the plane sped eastward over the Hardangervidda mountain plateau following the shadow of the moon over the earth's surface.

The film shots were developed in London and shown to a small audience there yesterday, and a discussion arose over the origin of the two shining spots, moving from one side of the horizon to the other at very high speed.

One of them had a condensed vapour tail.—B.U.P.

D.M. 8 JUL 1954

They Saw It

I SAW the "wonder" to which Mr. Ward Price referred in his letter, also on that Thursday and Friday. It was after midnight and I called a friend to see it. She thought it was Jupiter. Certainly not Mars, which always seems to have a reddish glow. She now thinks it was Venus.

(Mrs.) E. Davies.
Bognor, Sussex.

▲ Other readers, from London, Norfolk, and Enfield, have written to say they saw the illuminated objects.

Fantasy

D.M. 8 JUL 1954

'THAT SAUCER'

Cosmic research balloon starts two scares

The cosmic research balloon which alarmed thousands of Londoners yesterday caused a second flying saucer scare as it drifted over Hereford, Gloucester, and other West Country towns last night.

It was released in the morning at Cardington, Bedfordshire, by Professor C. F. Powell, of Bristol University, and rose to a record 80,000ft. Last night the professor was searching near Reading for the photographic equipment parachuted from the balloon.

SHINING OBJECT PUZZLE IN SKY

8 JUL 1954

BALLOON AT 70,000FT

Daily Telegraph Reporter

For an hour before lunch yesterday Londoners were puzzled by a shining object which appeared at a great height over the City. It was a cosmic radiation research balloon, the largest ever released in Britain, belonging to Bristol University.

Because of its altitude, which at noon was 70,000ft, it was visible to the naked eye only as a brilliant white dot, almost stationary. Street crowds speculated on whether it was a "flying saucer."

Prof. C. F. Powell, of Bristol University, said the balloon, 100ft in diameter and 150ft long, was released from Cardington, Beds, at 10.24 a.m., it carried automatic apparatus to release photographic plates.

Search was being made for the plates late last night. At 9 p.m. the balloon was reported over Hereford.

RESEARCH BALLOON OVER LONDON

8 JUL 1954

THOUSANDS OF TELEPHONE INQUIRIES

An object floating at a calculated height of 70,000ft. over London yesterday morning resulted in thousands of telephone calls jamming the switchboards in the Air Ministry, the Meteorological Office, and the police, and observers studied it for some time from the roof of the Air Ministry in Kingsway.

An official explanation issued at noon identified the object as a balloon released by Bristol University from Cardington, Bedfordshire, connected with cosmic radiation research. It was released just after 10 a.m.

The balloon carried photographic plates for research purposes, and just after 4.30 p.m.—the time planned—a special "cut out" apparatus released the photographic equipment.

Later Professor C. F. Powell, of Bristol University, stated that it was the biggest balloon they had ever launched, and that it should reach 106,000ft. "We are making the flight at this altitude because we want, first, information on the performance of these big balloons, and second, we want information about the primary radiation coming into the high atmosphere."

Asked what happened to the balloon when the equipment was released, Professor Powell said, "We lose it—it drifts on, and becomes flying saucers over half a dozen different countries."

D.M. 8 JUL 1954

News of Salome

THERE must be an omen in this somewhere—especially in view of "flying-saucer" reports that ran around London yesterday. Over lunch the Hungarian - born actress Miss Agnes Bernelle, handed me a cable from her husband, Mr. Leslie Desmond, saying :

"Delighted with news of Salome. Ten minutes ago saw my first flying saucer, so everybody's happy."

Saucer explanation: Author Leslie Desmond co-operated with George Adamski in writing

the book "Flying Saucers Have Landed"; both are now in the Californian desert doing research work on those elusive objects.

Salome explanation: Miss Bernelle (pictured here) goes to St. Martin's Theatre in two weeks' time to play the title-rôle in Oscar Wilde's "Salome."

FLYING SAUCERS AND CIGARS

S.D. 11 JUL 1954

LUMINOUS objects described as "flying saucers" and "flying cigars" have been seen in Southern Finland. Several people reported a cigar-shaped rocket flying from a westerly direction, leaving a streak of fire behind.

One man reported a brilliant blue-green ball. Others say they saw a green object "like a plate." A Helsinki photographer has taken a picture, claimed to be the best ever seen of a flying saucer.

(See "I Believe In Flying Saucers," by Lord Dowding—Page SIX.)

I Believe In Flying Saucers

S.D. 11 JUL 1954

By
Air Chief Marshal
LORD DOWDING,

Air Officer Commanding-in-Chief
Fighter Command In The
Battle of Britain

I HAVE never seen a "Flying Saucer," and yet I believe that they exist. I have never seen Australia, and yet I believe that Australia also exists. My belief in both cases is based upon cumulative evidence in such quantity that, for me at any rate, it brings complete conviction.

More than 10,000 sightings have been reported, the majority of which cannot be accounted for by any "scientific" explanation, e.g., that they are hallucinations, the effects of light refraction, meteors, wheels falling from aeroplanes, and the like.

Best Evidence

THE best available evidence, perhaps, is contained in Major Donald Keyhoe's recent book, "Flying Saucers From Outer Space."

I say this because most of the incidents which he records have been checked by the Intelligence Branch of the United States Air Force. They endorse the accuracy of the evidence, but they put forward no explanation. The critics who deny the existence of these objects must produce some alternative theory which will account for the observed facts.

In a brief article I cannot deal at length with the suggestion that they are new types of aircraft under development by Russia or the U.S. They have been tracked on radar screens in America—on one occasion by three screens simultaneously—and the observed speeds have been as great as 9,000 miles an hour.

No earthly materials that we know of could be forced through the air at such a speed without getting too hot to allow human occupants to exist. The accelerations which they develop in starting, changing course, and stopping would also make human life as we know it, impossible.

I say then that I am convinced that these objects do exist and that they are not manufactured by any nation on earth. I can therefore see no alternative to accepting the theory that they come from some extra-terrestrial source.

And why should this be considered to be such a ridiculous idea? In ten

This is the outstanding picture in the Flying Saucer debate.

years' time we shall probably have shot a rocket to the moon. In a hundred years we may have made the return trip with a manned projectile. In 500 years we may have reached the nearer planets. Are we so arrogant as to maintain that the inhabitants of no planet are as much as 500 years ahead of us in scientific development?

Principal Questions

PLEASE do not tell me that scientists affirm that life is not possible on other planets. They assume that "life" must necessarily exist in earth-type bodies. But it is only reasonable to suppose that bodies would be conditioned to the physical conditions existing on each planet.

Now that is as far as my "convictions" take me; beyond this my ideas are frankly speculative. The principal questions which arise are: Where do these objects come from? And what are the motives of the

occupants in visiting the Earth's atmosphere?

I think that we must resist the tendency to assume that they all come from the same planet, or that they are all actuated by similar motives. It might be that visitors from one planet wished to help us in our evolution from the basis of a higher level to which they had attained.

Another planet might send an expedition to ascertain what have been these terrible explosions which they have observed, and to prevent us from discommoding other people besides ourselves by the new toys with which we are so light-heartedly playing.

Other visitors might have come bent solely on scientific discovery and might regard us with the dispassionate aloofness with which we might regard insects found beneath an upturned stone.

A Warning

IF I say that I believe that the majority of our visitors are actuated by friendly and helpful motives, I cannot produce the same volume of evidence in support of my opinion as I have done for the physical reality of the Saucers; but the fragmentary and uncorroborated evidence which I have is reinforced by the reasonability, if not the probability, of the idea that, if the inhabitants of other planets are so far ahead of us in making use of the (to us) unknown forces of nature, they may well be equally far ahead of us in spiritual evolution, and may have better methods of spreading their wisdom than by killing those who disagree with them.

But this hypothesis is not universally accepted, particularly in the U.S., where fighters sent up to intercept the visitors have sometimes had unpleasant experiences. In the case of Captain Mantell, who was sent to investigate a "huge round glowing object," his machine disintegrated in mid-air and his body was found among the wreckage.

This brings me to the most important thing which I have to say. It is to give a warning against attempts to open fire either with guns or aeroplanes on these objects. Looked at from the purely selfish aspect, such gratuitous folly might well turn neutral curiosity into active hostility, and it may be assumed that those who visit us from outer space can well look after themselves and will have the means of making us sorry that we compelled them to defend themselves.

But it is not on this note that I wish to finish. It seems possible that for the first time in recorded history intelligible communication on the physical level may become possible between the earth and other planets of the solar system.

Such a prospect is epoch-making in the literal sense of the word, and we should be guilty of criminal folly if we were to do anything to hinder a contact which may well bring untold blessings to a distraught humanity.

The 'things' from space are coming, says Rector

5 AUG 1954

Express Staff Reporter

THERE'S a touch of Jeff Hawke* about the Rev. Ronald Cartmel—he *knows* that flying saucers exist, he *knows* that "things" from outer space are moving in on the earth.

He has told his 10,000 parishioners so, and he said so again, yesterday.

At 54 ("I'm old enough to know better, you may think") he believes also that flying saucers are signs and portents prophesied in the Bible.

But his approach to them is strictly practical: he has a new nine-inch reflector telescope in his rectory garden at Aldridge, Staffordshire.

And he has been a Fellow of the Royal Astronomical Society for 30 years.

'FIND OUT'

"I am encouraging my parishioners to take a practical interest in flying saucers and astronomy," he said.

In the current issue of his parish magazine he has written: "Don't believe everything the Government tells you about flying saucers. Read the facts and find out for yourself. . . .

"Although thousands of sane, ordinary folk have seen them, we are told they are mirages, spots in front of the eyes, or what-have-you.

"As the days of this age run out, the Bible tells us of many signs in Heaven and earth which are to precede the next.

"I believe that we are on the threshold of those days and that these visitors are the forerunners of many more."

SWOOP, ZOOM

The article advises parishioners to read two recently-published books on flying saucers.

Several times the rector has talked of flying saucers from his pulpit. He has lectured his parishioners at a weekly study class.

"Several have told me of objects that swoop down from the skies and zoom up again out of sight," he said. "They can't *all* be meteorological balloons, you know. These other creatures from o u t s i d e are moving in, mark my words !"

Had he ever seen a flying saucer himself? "No," he confessed.

For the further adventures of Jeff Hawke, see Page Six.

Look out for space visitors, warns rector

'IT'S NOTHING TO SMILE AT'

D.M. 5 AUG 1954

By Daily Mail Reporter

THE Rev. Ronald Cartmel, who watches stars from his rectory, is warning his 9,000 parishioners to watch for visitors from outer space. Further, to help his parishioners prepare for any such visitors, he is recommending them to read two books on flying saucers.

"Don't smile," writes Mr. Cartmel in his Aldridge, Staffordshire, parish magazine. "It is nothing to smile at. Although thousands of sane, ordinary folk have seen them we are told they are mirages and spots in front of the eyes."

Mr. Cartmel, who is 54, believes that people from another planet are watching us from flying saucers. They may well land here within 50 years, he said yesterday.

Several reports

In his magazine he accuses the authorities of concealing information about Outer Space visitors. He adds: "Experts can tell us nothing about life on other worlds.... But the much despised Bible has always spoken of principalities and powers in the Heavenlies."

Mr. Cartmel is a Fellow of the Royal Astronomical Society. He is building a 9in. lens telescope to study reports of atomic explosions on Mars and flashing lights on the moon.

He said yesterday: "It is possible that Mars and the moon are bases from which people of other planets are studying us in flying saucers. I have never seen a flying saucer, but I have had several reports from parishioners who have seen different types of craft in the skies.

"If a space craft landed here I would, as Rector of Aldridge, welcome the visitors to our world. They seem friendly enough."

← The Rector expects an invasion from Space...

SEEN ANY GOOD SAUCERS LATELY?

By JOHN LEE

ALDRIDGE (Staffs), Saturday.

PEERING nervously over my shoulder, I sidled up to the only man in the deserted street. "These flying saucers," I said. "Are you worried?"

"WHAT flying saucers?" he said.

"You know—these flying saucers your rector keeps talking about. Reckons any week now they're going to invade the earth. Here—look what he says in the parish magazine:

'As the days of this age run out, there will be signs in Heaven, and Earth ... These visitors are the fore-runners of many more...'

"New one on me," said the man. "Mind you, I'm new round here. Try the pub."

In the pub

I tried the pub. After all, the rest of Britain was talking about the Rev. Ronald Cartmel (left) and his flying saucers. Surely his own parishioners *MUST* be worried about it.

But this is how my time-table went:

11.45: Entered bar. Holiday-makers playing dominoes in silence. Two old ladies whispering together. I inched over to them and listened for saucer talk. They were discussing the weekend joint.

12.15: Flying saucers still not mentioned. I put a copy of the parish magazine on the bar, saucer page facing upwards. While I wasn't looking a man put his glass on it.

1.15: A domino player went to the window and looked up nervously. Was he looking for saucers? I moved over quickly. "I think," he said, "it will be fine after all."

Direct approach

1.45:—Decided to try the direct approach. "About these flying saucers your rector is arning us about ..."

"Flying *saucers*?" said the landlord. "Ah. Yes. He's a good man, you know. Funny you should mention it. Can't remember one of my customers saying a word about 'em."

I tried the drapers. No ★ luck. I listened at street corners. Not a saucer.

Five hours, and still no saucers. In desperation, I tried the rectory . . . and found one man who *would* talk: the verger, Mr. Bevan.

"The rector first started talking about flying saucers six years ago, from the pulpit here," he said. "There are people who laugh, but I challenge anyone to defy what he says.

"It is frightening when you come to think of it. That's why so many people brush it aside. But if you could have half an hour with the rector you'd say: *He's right.*"

But I couldn't have half an hour with the rector. He had just gone off to Cornwall on holiday.

Perhaps, for my peace of mind, it was just as well.

Did it spot a saucer?

Ottawa, Monday.—The gravimeter at the Canadian Government's flying saucer sighting station has made its first recording since installed last October. The meter detects changes of gravity and mass in the atmosphere.

"There may have been a failure in the instrument," said the engineer in charge. "But we cannot say it was not a flying saucer."—Reuter.

Mystery of Stratocruiser With 50 Aboard

Airliner Windscreen Shatters at 10,500 ft.

IT RETURNS TO LONDON

A MYSTERIOUSLY shattered windscreen on the flight-deck of a B.O.A.C. Stratocruiser caused the 62-ton airliner to put back to London Airport to-day.

The plane, with 50 passengers aboard, had taken off for New York. Forty-five minutes out at 10,500 feet, the windscreen on the right-hand side of the flight deck in front of the second pilot suddenly shattered.

Just like a car windscreen it splintered and frosted over completely. Neither the second pilot nor the commander, Captain Liles, could see any apparent reason for the shattering. Both are convinced it was not caused by impact with birds.

Radio messages were flashed to London Airport and the Stratocruiser returned.

The stratocruiser will take off again as soon as the windscreen has been replaced.

DUMPED WHEAT STOCKS

D.M 25 AUG 1954

'SAUCER CIGAR'

Three watch it flying for 45 minutes

PARIS, Tuesday.—Three people have reported seeing a "flying saucer" attached to a huge cigar-shaped object over the Seine at Evreux, north-west of Paris.

The "saucer" left the "cigar," fell vertically, shot out horizontally and then leapt upwards. It was watched for 45 minutes early on Sunday.—*D.M. Reporter.*

MAN IN A FLYING SAUCER

D.M. 25 AUG 1954

We spoke to him, women claim

OSLO, Tuesday.

TWO Norwegian sisters claim to have spoken to a man who landed by flying saucer, said a police chief in Mosjoen, Central Norway, today.

This, according to the newspaper *Helgeland*, is their story :

The sisters, aged 24 and 32, were out in the hills picking berries. A dark, long-haired man wearing a kind of khaki overall without buttons appeared. He motioned them to a hollow.

He seemed friendly enough, so they went. There on the ground was the flying saucer, about 16ft. in diameter. The man tried vainly with words, gestures, and drawings to explain himself.

Three languages

The women tried French, German, and English without success. Then the stranger climbed into the saucer. It started up with a slight humming sound like a bumble bee, rose at great speed straight into the air—and vanished.

Police are to visit the spot to-morrow to see if they can find any trace of the saucer.—*Reuter.*

D.M. Paris cable : Three people have reported seeing a "flying saucer" attached to a huge cigar-shaped object over the Seine at Evreux, north-west of Paris. It was watched for 45 minutes.

Man in the flying saucer was U.S. airman

AND THE SAUCER WAS A HELICOPTER

D.M. 25 AUG 1954

From Daily Mail Correspondent and Agencies

OSLO, Wednesday.

IT was not a man from outer space that two sisters found behind a blackberry bush yesterday. It was an American airman.

Furthermore it was not a flying saucer that the man climbed into and flew away. It was a helicopter of the Norwegian Air Force.

Those statements came today from an Air Force spokesman. Police added : "The sisters had been reading a book on the invasion of the earth by space ships from another planet."

But one of the sisters was unconvinced by Air Force or police. She shrugged. She said : "We met a Martian and it was a wonderful experience."

Undisturbed

The sisters are Miss Edit Jacobsen, 24, and Mrs. Aasta Solvang, 32. They reported that they offered the man blackberries. Said one : "He refused in some incomprehensible babble. We tried to shake hands with him. He just laughed and climbed into his ship. It rose straight up in the air with a whirring sound.

"First we thought he was a lunatic, but he looked like an ordinary earth man."

Today the Air Force spokesman said that a big helicopter manned by an American had been operating in the blackberry-bush area. It was, like the sisters' "saucer," blue-grey.

Later, police said that they had visited the place from which the "saucer" took off, and had found not even a broken blade of grass.

LOTS of people believe in flying saucers—and lots of others don't. Maybe the saucers are just another form of spots before the eyes. Or perhaps they really are space ships carrying strange beings from other planets. It is one of the world's biggest controversies.

● That is why we are publishing this amazing prediction by Agnes Bernelle, one of the believers.

● We hope that you will enjoy the article, whether you believe in flying saucers or not.

THE EDITOR

FLYING SAUCERS WILL LAND HERE NEXT YEAR!

— says —

AGNES BERNELLE
West End stage star

"**IF** all goes well there will be flying saucer landings in England next year. . . ."

Those are the words of my husband, Desmond Leslie, written from the Californian desert, where he and an American investigator, George Adamski, are watching the sky in search of flying saucers.

Last year, you may remember, Desmond wrote a book with George, entitled : "Flying Saucers Have Landed,"

which was widely publicised in the English Press.

At that time he had never seen a saucer. But now he has.

A few days ago he cabled me: SAUCER SCORE NOW 12. And in a letter to me from their lookout point he wrote :

"Coming into San Diego we saw a beautiful, golden ship in the sunset, but brighter than the sunset.

"I had ten-power binoculars with me, and was able to study it for a half a minute from the halted car.

"It slowly faded out, the way they do."

That letter reached me in my London flat as I was rehearsing for Salome, the rôle that Rita Hayworth made famous in Hollywood.

I felt a chill of fear inch its way up my spine. I knew Desmond would never exaggerate, and the space ship sounded horribly eerie.

But Desmond assured me that we have nothing to fear from the men in the saucers. He and Adamski have been in close contact with them, and have learned many of their secrets.

"We have been given their simple philosophy," he told me. "It runs parallel to the original teachings of Jesus."

And Desmond explained to me that the space visitors do not seek trouble.

"If attacked, they would prefer to let themselves be destroyed rather than kill," he wrote.

How will we make contact with these beings ?

Desmond wrote, excitedly, on July 4 :

"They have little discs which

5228 ESCONDIDO CALIF 22 16 1150A 36 SOUTH LODGE

LT LESLIE   GROVE END RD

    CUNNINHAM 4615 LONDON   1D 0   8ᵒ
                                                   NW8.

    SAUCERSCORE NOW TWELVE —— ALL LOVE

                                     DESMOND

DESMOND'S CABLE

can pick up our thoughts, and others which translate our vibrations and tones into their own language ! "

[In his book " Flying Saucers Have Landed," Adamski said he had been able to communicate with spacemen by telepathy.]

He described their ships too.

"The first one I saw was oval, with a dome on top," he told me. And in the same letter he gave me the amazing news that he and George have actual knowledge of the interior of the saucers.

"**We now have plans and blueprints,**" he wrote, "**of the interior layouts of four or five different types of craft.**

"And we have details of the landing arrangements and instruments which, believe me, are out of this world ! "

Perhaps you are wondering if I myself believe in flying saucers ? Yes, I do.

I have thought it all out, and, from what I have learned from my husband, I think there is no doubt that they do exist.

D e smond has told me :

" Everything the spacemen say is so very true. Their description of events is beyond our wildest science fiction."

Until Desmond had had actual contact with the men from the other worlds I doubted their existence. But his letters are full of facts which have amazed and shaken me.

What is more, I share my husband's belief that the present "cold war" conditions in the world may flare up at any time, and that the saucer men will probably be our only means of salvation.

'100 landings'

In his letters from California Desmond has told me of landings already made on the earth.

"Altogether over a hundred landings have taken place," he wrote me on July 17.

"Slowly, other 'contactees' (space people wanting to contact us) are linking up with us.

"A ship has landed in Canada containing four beautiful men from another solar system altogether!"

So the saucers may be a means of escape in time of world destruction.

For Desmond is convinced that the atom and hydrogen bomb warfare may not only end our earth's existence but could throw the whole universe off balance.

All this sounds incredible, I know. Unless, like Desmond and I, you have studied the saucer men.

But perhaps we will all receive proof sooner than we think. And I hope we will be ready for it when it comes.

Birmingham E.Despatch, August 27,1954.

DID A THING FROM SPACE HOVER OVER BIRMINGHAM?

WAS the strange object seen over Birmingham last night a flying saucer?

Several people saw it at about 9.30. Mr. J. S. H. Johnson, of 71, Vicarage Road, Aston, was riding his motorcycle combination along Witton Road when it startled him.

"It was a bright bluishwhite light, and appeared about the size of an orange," he declared today. "It made no sound, and it seemed to leave a trail of sparks. It looked as though there was some experimental work going on."

Flying types scoff

But flying types in the Midlands scoffed at the idea. Elmdon Airport did not record the intrusion of a "thing from space." An official remarked drily: "It strikes me as being more than coincidence that there was night-flying from Honiley last night."

But an officer at Honiley was on the control tower at the same time. Gazing into the beautiful clear night, he, too, saw something unusual.

"It was undoubtedly a shooting star, but in level flight," he said. "It was a remarkable sight. And it could have given the impression of being near the ground."

One unofficial observer saw a "pinky-blue ball with a blue tail."

"Reflection of navigation lights on cloud," was the Honiley officer's unhesitating explanation of this phenomenon.

So far, Birmingham police have received no reports of an unkown aircraft or spacecraft on ground or above ground in the Birmingham area.

Birmingham ... gust 31.1954.

They All Say They Saw The 'Saucer'

I HAVE just read the paragraph in your paper about the "Flying Saucer." I saw the object while waiting to cross the road in the centre of West Bromwich. The time was 9.45 p.m. As soon as I got home I told my husband about it and he suggested it was an aircraft, but I said it could not have been because it was not many yards away from me and it was so low it appeared to fly between the buildings in St. Michael's Street. It was travelling at no great speed.

M. P. GOODING (Mrs.)
West Bromwich.

. . . As my mother, father and I were coming home, and within a few doors of our house, we noticed what we thought was a shooting star, and then realised that it lasted far too long in the sky.

It was, as reported, "round like an orange brilliantly white, with a tail of definite sparks in various colours."

We realised it was not a shooting star, for it travelled at speed, keeping level, and, as far as we could see, did not drop.

Perhaps this confirms what other observers saw on Thursday night at 9.30.

E. PEARSALL (Miss)
Oldbury.

. . . My daughter, Frances, aged 19, and grandson, George, aged 13, saw the peculiar object in the sky at 9.35 p.m. They were standing by our front gate in Sunningdale Road, Tyseley, at the time.

They describe it as a circular object. It was a vivid green, with a white circle around it, and it left a white trail behind with bright red

sparks flashing from it. It appeared to be slowly descending to earth in a spinning fashion. My daughter estimated its speed at about 40 miles per hour.

Tyseley. A. THOMPSON

. . . The same bluish-white light, leaving a trail of sparks, passed over Victoria Park, Leamington, in the direction of Birmingham at 9.30 p.m. on the 26th. It passed over at about 300ft in level flight, and it was entirely silent.

A. J. WILKINS.
Leamington Spa.

. . . I was travelling with my wife and son from Bridgnorth (Salop) to Stourbridge on Thursday night. Around about 9.30 p.m. we saw this light in the sky. It was bluewhite, tinged orange, and was travelling towards Bridgnorth, fast and rather low.

By the time I had stopped the car it had vanished without any noise or reflection.

I have never seen anything like it before.

G. W. HANDLEY.
Belbroughton.

⁂ Possible explanations of the strange object are that it was either a shooting star or a reflection of navigation lights on cloud. Night flying was going on at the time.

Getting ...

of waiting for a ho... should buy one.

If our own Brum... to do this, it is al'... so nice and...

Gillott Road,

Birmingham E.Despa...

Just a star

MAY I tell you what the strange object was which your readers saw? It was an ordinary shooting star. My wife and children and I saw it start and finish in the sky, for we were actually watching it as it started to shoot.

C. W. BLOOMFIELD
King's Heath. 8/9/54

Flying saucer?

I READ in the *Evening Despatch* about a man and woman seeing a strange bluish-white object in the sky on Thursday night. I saw it, too, and the time was 9.20.

It was going dead straight across the sky. It was very plain and solid. It was no shooting star or aircraft. I've never seen anything like it before.

A READER
Village Road,
Witton.

DEATH-TOLL SOARS—
FLOOD PERIL

Broken dam swamps hamlets

10 SEP 1954 ORLEANSVILLE, Algeria, Thursday.

THOUSANDS of people fled in panic tonight from the "dead town" of Orleansville, fearful that a second earthquake would follow the one that hit Central Algeria earlier today, killing about 1,000 people according to official estimates. About 5,000 are believed injured.

Orleansville, a thriving modern French town of 35,000 people, was the centre of the twelve-second earthquake, and 600 dead are believed to have been buried under its rubble. Already 450 bodies have been recovered.

Where it struck

Tonight the town is deserted but for the troops, Foreign Legionnaires, gendarmes, and Government workers using bulldozers and cranes to dig out the dead and wounded.

A constant watch was being kept on the 160ft. wall of the mighty Fodda River dam, which cracked but did not break. If it does, millions of gallons of water will flood the ravaged area. A smaller dam, the Lamartine, collapsed in the initial shock, swamping villages, and killing 200 people.

But more than 200 people are believed to have died in smaller towns and villages in the 60-mile radius around Orleansville. Some hamlets are reported to have been completely razed.

NEW TREMORS
Terrorise villages

Tremors are still being felt tonight. In the village of Tachta, where 100 people are missing, the new tremors sent the population in terror into the desert.

Orleansville looks as though it had been pulverised in a 1,000-bomber raid. About half the town was razed—including its three hotels, hospital, prefecture, railway station—when the earthquake shook the area early this morning.

The Governor-General, M. Roger Leonard, flew from the capital to take charge of the rescue operations.

A French commercial traveller, M. Marcel Coste, was returning to his hotel after a late film when the shock came. "It was like being blown up by an atomic bomb," he said.

A street-cleaner, Mohammed Bougra, said: "Just before the shaking started a great ball of fire appeared in the sky over the mountains. It was orange and yellow and red, with a sort of violet light around the edges. The

clouds were thick and the moon shone red."

A great shudder ran through the sleeping town. Wide fissures opened in the streets and homes. Nine-storey blocks of flats and solid public buildings folded up like a pack of cards.

One of the first to go was the Fifth Century Christian cathedral. It crashed in the market place. 10 SEP 1954

Underground gas pipes were thrown up above the lurching soil, splitting and throwing out streams of gas which caught alight and sent flames roaring into nearby houses.

Men, women, and children rushed screaming from their beds naked or in night clothes. They scrambled through the littered streets, fighting to reach the safety of the open fields outside the city's walls.

rn to Page 2, Col. 4

Saucer sighting station closes

D.M. 1 SEP 1954

MONTREAL, Tuesday.—Mr. J. R. Baldwin, Deputy Transport Minister, announced today that the flying saucer sighting station at Shirleys Bay, 10 miles north-west of Ottawa, has been closed.

"We have decided that nothing has so far come out of the station's operations to merit further expenditure," he said. The station has sighted nothing since it was built in October 1953. —D.M. Cable.

Now, a 'saucer' with sparks

D.M. 1 SEP 1954

NORTH BAY, Ontario, Tuesday. —Henry Durdle, mess orderly at the Air Force station here, saw a "great glowing ball of light" hovering above the station before dawn yesterday. It was circular, he said, with a 15-ft. wide rect-angular box underneath, and was shooting out "tremendous sparks, like knitting-needles of lightning." Three other men said they also saw the "thing."—Reuter.

SKY 'BUBBLE'

"Two bubble-shaped objects" crossing the sky over Rye at "an incredible speed" were reported last night by Mr. W. G. Kitchener, of Rye, Sussex.

D.M. 1 SEP 1954

'Flying saucer' hung on balloons

1 SEP 1954

DARMSTADT, Germany, Wednesday.—Darmstadt police at last have the first authentic report about a flying saucer, repeatedly reported sighted.

It was a wooden disc, suspended from children's balloons, and illu-minated by torchlight bulbs.

The mysterious object was identified for what it was by a motorist, who saw it during a night drive, and turned his search-light on it.—Reuter.

FLYING FEATHERS
He heard them too

1 SEP 1954

AFTER the flying saucers—the flying feathers. The observer this time is Mr. W. K. Kitchener, of Ivy Cottage, Rye, Sussex. He said yesterday:

"I was sitting reading in my garden. I looked up to see two objects like giant feathers floating towards the ground.

"Then there was the drone of accelerating engines. The two feathers shot away in the direc-tion of London. Their speed was terrific, perhaps 2,000 miles an hour and they travelled with a swirling zig-zag motion."

Mr. Kitchener is no novice as an observer. He was an aircraft spotter during the war.

The Air Ministry said last night: We have heard nothing.

Did they see our Flying Saucer?

D.M. 8 SEP 1954

Four railway workers yesterday saw "a silver ball" in the air at Derby—where work was done on Britain's new vertical take-off "Flying Saucer."

"It shot up vertically at a fast speed after being stationary for a time," said one of the men, Mr. D. Shaw, of Arridge-road, Chad-desden, Derby.

Yesterday's picture of Wing Commander Shephard—who flew the "Flying Saucer" on its first test—is in BACK Page.

TWO LITTLE MEN
FROM A SAUCER

E.N. 13 SEP 1954

THEY LANDED IN MY GARDEN, POLICE TOLD

QUAROUBLE (Northern France), Monday.

POLICE here are investigating a claim by a 34-year-old steelworker that a flying saucer carrying two little men landed at the bottom of his garden.

The steelworker, Marius Dewilde, told them: "I saw two small beings, about a metre (three feet) tall but with very wide shoulders. Their heads were encased in enormous helmets and both were wearing overalls.

"A brilliant green light shot out from the object and dazzled me. I seemed to be paralysed Then the object rose into the air."

The saucer, he said, looked like "a circular cake cover" about 9ft. high and 15ft. across.—Reuter.

2 men from Mars!

M. 1 4 SEP 1954

At the bottom of his garden

By Henry Kahn

PARIS, Monday.

HIS dogs began barking at night so M. Marius Dewilde went outside. And this, he says, is what he saw:—

● A flying saucer parked on the railway line at the bottom of his garden in Quarouble, near Lille;

● Two Martians—in overalls— walking along the line.

The men were about three feet tall, had no arms but " enormous shoulders and were wearing vast divers' helmets," says M. Dewilde.

DAZZLED

He claims he tried to head them off. But a brilliant green light from the saucer—it looked more like a cheese dish cover, really— dazzled him.

Then The Thing rose from the railway, hissing out black smoke.

M. Dewilde, a 34-year-old steel-worker, told his story to the police. They were sceptical—but then someone noticed strange markings on the railway and found scorched stones.

Tonight the police, security men and special air police joined the investigation and part of the railway track and some gravel were removed for examination.

Look what Marius the Serious saw down the garden!

Cummings

'They were both little men'

From JOAN HARRISON

PARIS, Monday.

IN the bistros and the bakers' shops they are all asking the same question — Did Marius *really* see a flying saucer and two men from Mars at the bottom of his garden?

Marius Dewilde is a 34-year-old steelworker, what the French call "serious."

He does not drink or gossip, and has never been known to have any sense of drama.

Yet Marius the Serious has just told the police at his village of Quarouble, in Northern France, of a strange sight which he swears he saw at the bottom of his garden on Friday night.

No one else saw it, and the police have been unable to confirm it. But this is Marius's story :—

It was around 11.30 last Friday night. Mrs. Dewilde had just gone up to bed, and Marius was in the kitchen reading. Suddenly his dog Kiki, who was tied up in the yard, began to howl.

The dog howls

"There is a railway line that runs at the bottom of my garden," said Marius today. "I saw what I thought at first was a cart at the side of the rails.

"Suddenly I heard footsteps. My dog was straining at the leash and howling his head off.

"I shone my torch and saw two figures some three or four yards away, one walking in front of the other. My torch shone on the leading figure, which seemed to have a metallic shine. I got the impression that whoever it was was wearing a diving helmet.

"They were both little men with enormous heads.

"I started to walk towards the strange pair. Then from the shape on the railway line came a strong arc light. It seemed to be a green ray and it paralysed me. I found I could not move my legs.

Cloud-smashing doctor does it by brain-power

Express Staff Reporter

TORONTO, Monday. — Three small clouds disintegrated over Orillia, Ontario, last night as 63-year-old physician Dr. Rolf Alexander told watchers he was "blasting" them with his brain.

Alexander says that the prefrontal lobe of the brain radiates some unknown form of energy.

Spectators said other clouds disappeared without the doctor blasting them. Said the doctor : "I doubt if any broke up as rapidly as my target clouds."

The Thing rises

"The two men continued to walk towards it. The green light was turned off and The Thing began to rise like a helicopter. There was no other noise but a swishing sound as clouds of black smoke began to come from it.

"The Thing gained height and went towards the west. It was semi-circular in shape, like a meat cover, and seemed about six yards wide and about three yards deep.

"As it disappeared it seemed to glow like a red light."

Now Marius is such an unimaginative, hardworking man that police next day examined the railway track.

And, *voila!* They found the ballast of the tracks slightly dented and the stonework pitted as if some strong heat had been applied.

This is not regarded as proof, as the marks could have been made with a sleeper screw. But Marius sticks to his story.

'ANOTHER THING'

KAMPALA, Uganda, Monday— A "strange golden ball," smaller than the moon but bigger than a star, was reported over Kampala early today.—Reuter.

Shake Hands With a Man From Mars

E.N. 14 SEP 1954

From FRANK TOLE
PARIS, Tuesday.

M. ANTOINE MAZAUD walked down a footpath near Clermont Ferrand, Central France, and shook hands with a man from Mars, he says.

And M. Mazaud is a very angry man to-day because, when he told the police about it, they just smiled a sceptical smile and said: "Tiens!" which is French for "Well, would you believe it?"

It all happened near the quiet country town of Ussel, and is the best story of the flying saucer season which has now opened in France.

It beats the story told by Marius Dewilde 34-year-old steel-worker from Quarouble near Lille, who saw two spacemen only three feet high at the bottom of his garden.

They took off in a flying saucer and did not even shake hands, which for a Frenchman, is hardly la politesse.

THE MEETING

This is what Antoine Mazaud says happened to him in the twilight of a September evening as he was returning to the lonely hamlet where he lives.

He took a footpath across the fields. And there he met the Man from Mars.

He wore a helmet and appeared of normal height. Not only did he shake hands but he kissed M. Mazaud on both cheeks in truly French fashion.

He spoke some strange words which M Mazaud could not understand, then he jumped into a cigar-shaped object, about 12ft. long which rose vertically at great speed and disappeared westward.

Meanwhile in the North of France they were still looking for the spacemen seen by Marius Dewilde.

To-day he pointed to marks on a railway sleeper. They could have been caused by the flying saucer—but they could also have been caused by plate-layers repairing the line.

'WE SAW IT'

M. Dewilde's neighbours, who saw nothing of the little men or the saucer, pulled his leg about it until two men came forward to say they also had seen it.

They were Emile Renard, a 27-year-old builder and his assistant, 23-year-old Yves de Guillerboz, who live 50 miles away from M. Dewilde.

Three days previously they were cycling along a country lane when they noticed a queer looking machine in a stubble field.

It was a metal disc, blueish-grey in colour, about 30ft. long and nine feet high, they said.

It took off at about the speed of a helicopter and they could see smoke coming from an exhaust pipe. But the machine made no noise and disappeared into the clouds.

Thousands Saw Mystery 'Cigar in the Sky'

E.N. 18 SEP 1954

ROME, Saturday.

THE Italian Air Force announces that one of its radar stations had tracked for 39 minutes a big cigar-shaped object seen by thousands of Romans.

The Air Force said the object was shaped like a cigar cut in half, with a big antenna amidships. A trail of luminous smoke poured from the pointed rear.

The object flew slowly before making off at great speed and disappearing at a height of 3,600 feet, along a 15-mile stretch of coast, west of the capital.

The radar station at Pratica di Mare, 40 miles south-west of Rome, picked up the object.—Reuter.

Thousands See 'Flying Cigar'

S.D. 19 SEP 1954

THOUSANDS of people were startled to see a big cigar-shaped object flying at about 3,600ft. along a 15-mile stretch of coast west of Rome.

The Italian Air Force radar station at Pratica Di Mare, 40 miles south-west of Rome, yesterday reported tracking the object for 40 minutes on the screens.

Technicians at Ciampino Airport said the object at one time appeared to plummet towards the earth for 1,000ft., then it rose vertically, and vanished in a north-west direction at tremendous speed.

It was silver-coloured on one side and red on the other, and it had a big antenna amidships. A trail of luminous smoke poured from the pointed end.

Hundreds of people who saw it phoned police stations and newspaper offices.—Reuter and A.P.

FLYING SAUCER DIDN'T KEEP THE 'APPOINTMENT WITH VENUS'

20 SEP 1954

'DAILY MIRROR' REPORTER

TWO coach-loads of men and women spent an hour in a windswept field yesterday waiting for a flying saucer.

They were trying to get in touch with one by telepathy. And they all concentrated their thoughts on the planet Venus.

But no visitors from outer space joined the party, who had driven from London to the field near the Wiltshire village of Avebury.

The trip was the result of a suggestion made at a London lecture by Mr. Foster Forbes.

Mr. Forbes, in white gloves and bow tie, told me: "Flying saucers appear to have a tremendous telepathic range.

"We hoped one of them might pick up our thought vibrations.

"But I'm not disappointed. I think if further experiments are held on the same lines we will get somewhere."

'Telepathy'

He added: "If some of the people here have grown sceptical, they are not seriously interested in the subject."

Although no flying saucers appeared, one of the party, Mr. George King, of Clifton-gardens, Maida Vale, said that he got into telepathic communication with Venus.

A dozen people told me that as Mr. King went into his "trance" these words came from his lips:

"Some of you would be frightened if we came to-day. There is too much difference of opinion here."

Mr. Kenneth Kellar, of Stoneydown-avenue, Walthamstow, said: "I heard the voice 'using' Mr. King quite plainly.

"It seems there were too many of us and conditions were not suitable.

"The Venusians will not come apparently if anyone is going to be frightened of them.

"There must be complete friendship between us and the visitors from outer space."

Mr. King said: "In earlier communications with Venusians, they have told me they are not out to hurt us.

"But they want to help because they are frightened at the damage we may do to ourselves with atomic research."

Those Dogs

A disappointed woman in the party said: "Of course a flying saucer didn't come.

"If some people will bring their dogs, how can we possibly project our thoughts into space?

"Just think what harm a few yapping dogs would do to such an experiment."

THREE WHO WATCHED

Three of the party watching, waiting . . . but no flying saucer appeared.

E.N. 28 SEP 1954.

Theatre Chief 'Snapped a Flying Cigar'

"Evening News" Reporter

PARIS, Tuesday.

AN important clue about the "flying cigars" a lot of people have reported seeing lately may be in our hands in a couple of days

Rene Valery, the sober and sane art director of the Olympia Theatre here says he photographed one last week-end.

He said to-day that he was driving near Lyons with his wife and son around 10 p.m when all three of them spotted the peculiar, noiseless object in the sky, trailing a cloud of smoke—jet like—behind it.

Valery jumped out of the car and photographed the object on movie film. Weather conditions were excellent, he said. The film will be ready shortly.

A Flood of Flying Saucers Now

E.N. 29 SEP 1954

"Evening News" Reporter

PARIS, Wednesday.

A "FLYING SAUCER CIRCUS" has visited the sky over France, according to a flood of reports to-day.

One report came from a Chambery doctor, formerly an artillery observer, who was backed up by 15 witnesses.

The doctor, M. Martinet, said he saw a dark grey mass hovering over mountains at an altitude of about 6,000 feet. He stopped his car to watch it and was soon joined by other motorists.

LIKE A PLATE

When the grey mass lost height it appeared " in the shape of a plate bottomside up," light in colour with dark patches all round.

Then it " shot away like lightning and disappeared," Dr. Martinet said.

Near Feyzin a man said he saw an apparatus shaped like a dome, flying rather close to the ground. It gave off a bright light, like burning magnesium, he said, and rose vertically without sound.

A report of a disc which had landed on the ground came from a woman who lives in Valence. She said she saw the "saucer" as she was walking in the country near Chabreuil.

ONE LANDED

It made a whistling noise. She rushed to find witnesses, but the object had disappeared when they returned. A circle of crops nine feet across was broken down, as if something had landed there.

A young French labourer, Yves David, living near Chatellerault, reports a "meeting" late at night with a sort of "diver" on a lonely country road.

The "diver," said David, came and took him by the arm, uttering unintelligible sounds.

He then withdrew towards a machine, which David could not describe, but from which a ray shot out fastening him to the spot, he said.

This machine then rose silently and vertically into the sky and vanished.

David said he kept this encounter to himself at first because he was "afraid of being laughed at."

Finally he confided to a friend, who repeated the story to others in the town.

The newspaper *Le Parisien* today gave the names and addresses of five readers who telephoned from different parts of Paris around the same hour to report seeing "strange objects" over the city.

HOT WORK

A 'Circus' of Flying Saucers Now

E.N. 29 SEP 1954

"Evening News" Reporter

PARIS, Wednesday.

A "FLYING SAUCER CIRCUS" his visited the sky over France, according to flood of reports to-day.

One report came from a Chambery doctor, formerly an artillery observer, who was backed up by 15 witnesses.

The doctor, M. Martinet, said he saw a dark grey mass hovering over mountains at an altitude of about 6,000 feet. He stopped his car to watch it and was soon joined by other motorists.

LIKE A PLATE

When the grey mass lost height it appeared " in the shape of a plate bottomside up," light in colour with dark patches all round.

Then it " shot away like lightning and disappeared," Dr. Martinet said.

Near Feyzin a man said he saw an apparatus shaped like a dome, flying rather close to the ground. It gave off a bright light, like burning magnesium, he said, and rose vertically without sound.

A report of a disc which had landed on the ground came from a woman who lives in Valence. She said she saw the "saucer" as she was walking in the country near Chabreuil.

ONE LANDED

It made a whistling noise. She rushed to find witnesses, but the object had disappeared when they returned. A circle of crops nine feet across was broken down, as if something had landed there.

A farmer, 28-year-old Yves David, of Chatellerault, insisted that a creature, dressed up like "a sort of diver," came up to him on a lonely road, caressed his arm and burbled unintelligible noises at him

Then the creature went off towards his "saucer." A green ray was directed at the farmer, temporarily paralysing him, while the machine shot off silently into the sky.

MORE 'SAUCERS' REPORTED

E.N. 30 SEP 1954

AND A 'FLYING CIGAR' OVER ALGERIA

LINZ, Upper Austria, Thursday.

TWO policemen reported seeing a "flying saucer"—an oval, light object racing across the sky—at Steyregg, Upper Austria, yesterday.—Reuter.

A B.U.P. cable from Casablanca says that many people in Morocco have reported seeing a "red flying saucer" at Kouriga, 90 miles from Casablanca last night. It was "spitting out blue and green flames." At Safi, in neighbouring Algeria, "a flying cigar surrounded by a luminous blue mist hurtling through the night sky" was seen.

The Saucer Pilot in a Plastic Bag

E.N. 1 OCT 1954

PARIS, Friday.

THREE pilots of "flying saucers" have landed in France in the past 24 hours—one in a Cellophane bag, the second dressed like a deep-sea diver and the third wearing a plain khaki suit.

All arrived in luminous unearthly machines.

So say Frenchmen in various parts of the country in reports to the police.

The Cellophane pilot—the height of a boy—was reported by Mme. Leboeuf, of Drome.

"At first I thought it was a new type of plastic scarecrow," she said. "But when it moved towards me I ran and hid behind a hedge."

She said the man got back into his "saucer" and took off vertically. "It sounded like a musical top," she said.

'TOUCHED ME'

The man in the diver-type of dress was reported by Yves David, a farmer of Vouneuil. He said the man touched his arms and said something to him in an unintelligible language.

The man in khaki was reported by Mme. Geoffrey, a widow of Diges, a little town near Auxerre. Her story was repeated by a shepherdess, Gisele Fin.

"I saw an engine, dark in colour, about 18ft. long, pointed at one end and rounded at the other, which rested on what looked like sleigh runners," she said.

"I took fright and left the wood. Three minutes later I looked back and the clearing was empty. I heard no sound at all."

She said she later found in the early morning dew traces of two slim runners.

The Saucer Pilot in a Plastic Bag

E.N. 1 OCT 1954

PARIS, Friday.

MORE and more mysterious objects were reported to-day as France's "Spot the flying saucer" season continued in full swing.

Police received reports of "a cigar-shaped object surrounded by a dozen smaller cigars" and "a bright red luminous object with things like sticks standing up all round it."

And three "flying saucer" pilots were said to have landed—one in a plastic bag, the second dressed like a deep-sea diver, and the third wearing a khaki suit.

All arrived in luminous unearthly machines.

The plastic pilot—the height of a boy—was reported by Mme Leboeuf, of Drome.

"At first I thought it was a new type of plastic scarecrow," she said. "But when it moved towards me I ran and hid behind a hedge"

She said the man got back into his "saucer" and took off vertically. "It sounded like a musical top," she said.

The man in the diver-type of dress was reported by Yves David, a farmer of Vouneuil. He said the man touched his arms and said something to him in an unintelligible language.

Flying Saucers Dance a Ballet In the Sky

E.N. 1 OCT 1954

"Evening News" Reporter

PARIS, Friday.

TWO thousand and twenty-one Frenchmen can't be wrong—or can they?

This is the tally of witnesses who are claiming to-day to have seen flying saucers over France in the last few hours.

One is a child of 12, the son of a farmer living near Premanos.

He says he heard his dog barking in the fields and found "a three-legged saucer" six feet high. "I threw stones at it," he says, "and it rose in the air and quickly disappeared."

Ten Satellites

A farmer at Tournon reports that while working in the fields he saw a bright green light moving rapidly. He called his daughter, and together they saw 12 more saucers "dance a ballet in the sky."

At Mulhouse two hard-headed Alsatians say they looked at a "luminous flying cigar" through field-glasses. The cigar was surrounded by ten satellites "like cigarettes."

Saucers (or cigars) are also reported from Besseges, Nevers and Perpignan, while at Pau 2,000 people watched for some time a "flying cigar" and two "saucers."

---

no-one knows."

E.N. 2 OCT 1954

'BEER BOTTLES'

Flying in the Sky

Halifax (Nova Scotia), Saturday.—Mr. Ruben Coolen—a teetotaller—has reported seeing flying shapes "like quart beer bottles with yellow tails." The "bottles" flew ten times faster than aircraft, he said.—Reuter.

Now 267 say 'We've seen the saucers'

- 3 OCT. 1954

Sunday Express Reporter

PARIS, Saturday.

THE French Air Ministry is taking this week's reports of flying saucers so seriously it has ordered an official investigation.

In the past few days 267 people in widely separated areas of France have "seen" flying saucers. They include meteorological experts, doctors, seamen, and loco-drivers.

The Government weather station at Morvan reported an oval-shaped craft moving with remarkable speed at 2,000-3,000ft.

Cigar-shaped

Other people have reported cigar-shaped objects and at Coulommiers, 60 miles south of Paris, police have photographed marks left by a mushroom-shaped object.

Mme. Simone Geoffroy, of Diges, 100 miles south of Paris, says she saw " a curious engine " that looked like a cigar " pointed at both ends " near a field.

" Standing beside it was a tall, dark-skinned man in a khaki hat. He looked at me but said nothing. I was terribly frightened and ran away. When I came back two hours later there was nothing there."

From Calcutta it is reported 800 people living in three adjoining villages in the Manbhum district of Bihar claim to have seen a flying saucer which descended to within 300 feet of the ground.

Sunday Dispatch

154th Year. No. 7,978.   2½d.   OCTOBER 3, 1954.   Radio Page 8.

What *Is* Going On In The Skies Over France?

'FLYING SAUCER' SIGHTS
AMAZE THOUSANDS

Fantastic Stories Of Mushrooms, Cigars

By ROLAND ATKINSON
'Sunday Dispatch' Paris Reporter

3 OCT 1954

FROM all over France in the past few days have come reports of people saying they have seen strange craft in the air — flying saucers, cigars, half-cigars, even men from another planet. Thousands say they have seen them, among them doctors, mayors and people whose word can be trusted.

These are some of the phenomena of the skies which are exciting all France and turning the eyes of French people upwards:—

Near **Grenoble** farmer Joseph H a b r a t saw a luminous engine moving at great speed.

His daughter, Yvette, said it came to within 600 yards with " a gentle snoring sound."

A little later 2,000 people saw a d o z e n of them " dancing a ballet " in the sky.

Two people at **Rixheim**, near Mulhouse, watched a cigar-shaped luminous engine surrounded by 12 smaller satellite cigars.

Three holidaymakers on **Carry-le-Rouet** beach saw a half-cigar over the port. Three women who also saw it described it as leaving a trail of smoke.

Mushrooms Too

A flying mushroom was reported by a lorry-driver and his friend at **Faremontiers.** It was in a field and had three tripod-like legs.

" I tried to approach it," he said, " but about 400 feet away I was stopped by a ray. I felt little prickings. My head swam. I had a cold sweat. I could not move."

The mushroom then rose slowly and flew off.

Dr. Martinet, skin disease specialist at **Chambery**, watched a flying saucer manœuvring in the sky for four minutes.

At Sea

In the **Gulf of Gascony** the mate and two seamen of a cargo boat saw a moving disc with a greenish glow.

Actress Michele Morgan saw a luminous disc over the Invalides air terminal in **Paris.**

There have been three reports of men from another planet landing in France.

At **Vienne** a farmer said the visitor, who wore a kind of diving suit, caressed his arm.

A woman at **Drome** saw " a being about the size of a child, and with a human face. He seemed to be wrapped in a transparent sack."

Both visitors to France returned to their saucers and took off vertically.

A little helmeted and booted man with a revolver firing " luminous and paralysing rays " was seen by the foreman of a quarry at **Marcilly-sur-Vienne** and six of his workmen.

Rose Vertically

A whistling sound drew the attention of two men at **Blanzy** to a cigar-shaped machine in a freshly ploughed field.

The men said the machine was about 6ft. in length. The pointed tip was yellow, the rest of the cigar brown.

As they a p p r o a c h e d the machine it rose vertically.

A policeman, a grocer, and eight other people saw an incandescent " cigar " at **Agen.**

A " brilliant ball " appeared to a stallkeeper at **Belesta.** He said it left a trail of grey smoke as it shot through the sky.

Objects spotted by a ferryman at **Grandcouronne**, near Rouen, also took a spherical form.

A flying cigar noticed by a butcher at **Marmande**, in the valley of the River Garonne, was flying very high, and seemed to be using the river as a terrestrial guide.

A French M.P., M. Jean Nocher, yesterday asked the French Secretary of State for Air, M. M. Catroux, to set up a commission " to study this phenomenon objectively by extracting the truth from among the mistakes and possible hoaxes."

The latest " flying saucer " report to reach Paris today said villagers at Plouguenast, near St. Brieuc, in Brittany, had seen a low-flying, noiseless cigar which gave off brilliant flashes " like a camera-man's flash-bulb."

The authorities are perturbed at the spate and variety of the strange sights which have been seen in the past week.

FLYING SAUCERY

ANOTHER outbreak of flying saucery brings stories ranging from the plausible to the childish. That mysterious aircraft of eccentric shape may have been seen is not disputed. There are secret lists, and not all of those who suggest space-ships are necessarily irresponsible. Nor are circular aircraft without precedent. There was an American disc-winged aeroplane, and over forty years ago Capazza designed a lenticular airship which would have qualified as either a saucer or a cigar, according to one's viewpoint. Indeed, there is scarcely a limit to the shapes and sizes of these alleged machines.

4 OCT 1954

All down the centuries people have reported prodigies in the sky. They usually have been what they expected, or feared, to see—devils, murdered emperors, departed relatives, unpleasant animals, and, under threat of war, embattled armies among the clouds. One can see things clearly in a dream, and can even hear complex yet recognisable music. Intra-cerebral illusions may persist, or exceptionally occur, while the subject is awake. Nowadays people still fear war and dread curious flying machines for what they may bring. Without denying the possibility that various odd aircraft exist, unknown to millions and undescribed in technical papers, it is fair to assume that most stories of flying saucers, dishes, beer bottles, cigars and "luminous engines" are the ghost stories of to-day.

Those Very Shy Men in the Flying Saucers

F.N. 4 OCT 1954

From "Evening News" Reporter

PARIS, Monday.

WITNESSES in two widely-separated parts of France to-day reported encounters with "flying saucer" crews. But the strangers were shy. . . .

Angelo Dinardeau, aged 55, said that on his way to work near Bressuire he saw a luminous "machine" parked on the ground. A "being" dressed in "a kind of diving suit" was moving around.

He said the "being" fled into the machine, which took off at great speed.

And two youths of Vron (Somme) said they were walking along the national highway between Crecy and Ligescourt when they saw a "curious machine" with strange creatures. It took off as the youths approached.

In other reports two women of Cerisier, near Chateauroux, told police they saw a "luminous bowl" about 9ft. in diameter just over the rooftops.

At Corbigny several people said they saw a luminous orange disc moving about the sky.

A pilot and many other people reported a brilliant "machine" moving about the sky for more than one hour to-day between Mount Lachat and Mount Blanc.

THE WIDER WORLD

Six fiery red discs

4 OCT 1954 E.N.

INHABITANTS of Foederlich, Austria, reported seeing six glowing red discs flying in a perfect semi-circle over the Karawanken Mountains early on Saturday.

Josef Rudl, a Civil servant, said he watched the discs for some minutes. Suddenly one of them turned back and zigzagged to the south. The rest, still in perfect formation, disappeared to the north-east.—Reuter.

* * *

100 SEE 'CRAB-SHAPED SAUCERS'

PARIS, Monday.

SEVERAL "crab-shaped" flying saucers are reported to have been seen by more than 100 people over Lille to-night.

A miner dashed into a café shouting that one of the machines, about three feet high, had landed in his garden. Café customers ran outside and watched it "hovering in the sky with several others for about 25 minutes."

4 OCT 1954

And, according to another report, the "saucers" have appeared in darkest Africa.

M. Vernhet, administrator of Danane territory, 300 miles north-west of Abidjan, Ivory Coast, said that he and his wife saw a "luminous, egg-shaped object in the sky for 30 minutes, before it flew silently out of sight."

HE SEEKS FLYING SAUCER SPOTTERS

5 OCT 1954

Daily Sketch Reporter

MR. EDWIN R. DAVIES, 35-year-old electronic engineer, wants to form a flying saucer club.

The club would collate information on flying saucers seen over Britain and the Continent and submit it to the Air Ministry for investigation.

Mr. Davies, of Woodland-rise, Highgate, N., claimed that he saw what appeared to be a flying saucer over Hampstead Heath.

"I saw a luminous object, which seemed to be similar to the magnesium-like light which observers saw over Paris recently.

NO SET COURSE

"It appeared to be manoeuvring without any set course over the Heath," he said. "It eventually ascended to a great height and disappeared."

Other people saw the "flying saucer"—or whatever it was—at the time. Mr. Davies wants them to get in touch with him.

● *Candidates for the club —people of Foederlich, in Austria, who saw six glowing red discs flying over the Karawanken mountains on Saturday.*

admit
rror

nitted a
erday.
d stated
a court-
missing
eorge
Service

r S. J.
istant
the
state-
y in-
said,

, of
was
ing
se.

FLYING SAUCER HOAX BY MINER

LILLE, Northern France, Tuesday.

Many of the flying saucers reported recently in the sky near here were built for a joke by a miner of the village of Beuvry-les-Bethune, said the police to-night. He made them out of strong grey paper on the fire-balloon principle.

After paraffin-soaked rags had been lit, hot-air lifted the "saucers," some of which were about 10ft in diameter, and off they went into the wind, displaying orange and yellow lights. The miner claimed that he made over 1,000 of them.

His name has not been disclosed. The police found him out after one example landed near a haystack.—Reuter.

6 OCT 1954

Out of This World

More Flying Saucers Reported in France

By Robert N. Sturdevant

A cardboard-box salesman, Pierre Allouis, told Paris reporters that he spotted a huge silver saucer in the sky around 4:30 p.m. yesterday as his taxi stopped for a red light near the Porte Dorée, at the eastern outskirts of the city.

Two other persons, Gilbert Bacon and Paul Julien, reported seeing the same thing but thought it looked more like a flying wing. All witnesses spoke of a screeching sound and a smoky tail which followed the object.

These were the latest reports of out-of-this-world manifestations which have been pouring in from all parts of France for the last two weeks. A Deputy in the National Assembly has asked the Air Ministry what it is doing to explain the so-called phenomena.

In fact, there was some evidence to show that people were spoofing their neighbors in all kinds of ways.

From Lille, it was reported that a retired miner, known as a local wag, had fabricated some hot-air balloons three yards in diameter which went aloft with the aid of gasoline-saturated straw attached to the bottom.

When the balloons went up and got caught in the wind they gave off a yellowish flare, to the consternation of people who saw them in the middle of the night. Unfortunately for the jokester, one almost set a haystack on fire on landing, and the miner was arrested. He is charged with what French law calls "dangerous amusement."

A road-mender in middle France also was caught for playing a joke. He had reported seeing a flying cigar alight in a field near his work, and claimed that when he approached the object he was paralyzed by a strange light. Afterward he pointed out three holes in the ground which he said were made by the object.

Gendarmes picked him up a couple of days later and perceived that the holes had been made by the road-mender's own hands. He was held for further disciplinary action.

THE MAYOR SAW IT

ATHENS, Wednesday.—A "flying saucer" hovered over the village of Vryssa, on the island of Mytilena, this afternoon for 15 minutes. The village mayor vouched for its appearance.—*Exchange.*

'FLYING BARREL' RIDDLE FOR THE AIR POLICE

From FRANK TOLE

PARIS, Wednesday.

FRENCH special air police are studying reports on the many strange objects seen in the sky in recent weeks. This follows a question to the French Air Minister by an M.P., who wants to know if "flying saucers" really exist.

The latest report is of a "flying barrel," about six feet high, seen near Angouleme, South-West France, by a 22-year-old motorcyclist, M. Jean Allary.

IN THE GRASS
20ft. Long

He says the object left a mark 20 feet long in the grass beside the road as though someone had rolled a heavy object.

Near Lille, Northern France, 100 people watched three crescent-shaped objects perform "a dance" in the sky before disappearing. They were visible for 25 minutes. Police took statements from eye-witnesses.

The only "official" flying saucer was claimed by a man on duty at a meteorological station at Le Morvan, Brittany. He reported a brilliant green oval shape, which disappeared in clouds at a height of 3,700ft.

Many of the reports which are now being checked by the air police show that the objects are seen at about dusk. These are explained as tricks of light caused by the setting sun.

Daily Sketch, Wednesday, October 13, 1954

Junior SKETCH

FLYING SAUCERS— FACT OR FICTION?

TO-MORROW!

NEXT year sees the start of a regular helicopter taxi service in London. Space travel draws closer every day. The Monorail Silver Streak is on its way. Can we really say flying saucers are airy-fairy nonsense?

These things are part of To-morrow. Look at this page, with its X-ray view of a flying saucer. See the Firebird on Page 8. To-morrow? We can hardly wait!—SALLY and SIMON, The Sketch Twins.

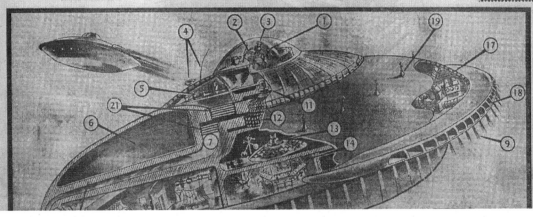

DAVID'S DUCK IS A WINNER

Eight - year - old David Hartnell, of Hill-street, Kingswood, Gloucestershire, proudly led his pet duck Donald into the ring at the Pets' Show at Kingswood.

Thirty minutes later David led him out prouder than ever.

He had a ribbon and medal around Donald's neck because Donald had won a prize for being the most unusual entry in the show.

David said afterwards: "Donald will get a lot of worms for his next meal as a reward. I thought he might stand a chance of winning because I gave him a nice soapy bath."

Strange sights seen in skies of France

IMAGINATION? Truth?

Millions of Frenchmen seek the answer. From every part of France have come reports of strange machines of all shapes flying through the air.

There have been so many separate accounts of these unexplained spectacles that many people in France are tempted to believe in the existence of the mystery machines.

The most astonishing story of all is told by a French metal worker, Marius Dewilde, who lives in a cottage near the railway line at Quarouble, in Northern France.

Dewilde was in his kitchen one night when he heard his dog howling terribly.

He ran outside and saw two men between the railway lines. He thought they might be burglars or dynamiters and he ran forward, shining his torch.

He was dumbfounded to see that the "men" were only two feet high with their heads encased in a transparent turret. And they had no arms.

A bigger surprise was a Flying Saucer sitting on the rails only 50 yards away.

The little robot men ran towards the saucer. As Dewilde gathered his courage to run after them a ray from the saucer struck him in the face, temporarily paralysing him.

The men entered the saucer through a trap door, and the saucer disappeared in the darkness.

The French Government have been asked to investigate the strange happenings in the skies of France.

MARIUS DEWILDE, who claims to have seen two crew members of the Flying Saucer, points to the exact spot where they stood between the railway lines (above). The picture (right) shows the chalk-like circles left on the wooden sleepers by the mysterious, armless men.

JUNIOR SKETCH PAGE ONE: THE PAPER WITH ITS EYE ON TOMORROW AND ITS WONDERS...

'FLYING SAUCERS' AND . . .

The Earth is being watched, he says

By a REUTER CORRESPONDENT

VISITORS from outer space are probably observing and mapping the Earth, and have been directing their recent attentions to East Africa. That, at any rate, is the considered opinion of one of the leading astronomers in the Nairobi area, the vice-president of Kenya Astronomical Association, Mr. G. Duncan Fletcher.

He put forward this startling and eerie suggestion after a deluge of reports from scores of observers throughout East Africa, who claim to have seen " flying saucers." These reports have flooded newspaper offices in the three East African territories of Uganda, Kenya and Tanganyika.

Europeans, Asians and Africans have all variously claimed to have seen objects in the sky: Stationary; zooming over the horizon; changing colour from white to red, blue and green; elliptical in shape; and elongated with upright projections at either end.

First reports of " flying saucers " came from Dar-es-Salaam, capital of Tanganyika on the Indian Ocean coast, and were quickly followed by " sightings " at Mombasa and Kampala.

In Nairobi, citizens telephoned local police-stations to say that they had spotted " saucers " circling the suburbs. More than one police patrol car, sent to investigate, reported following the course of " mysterious bright objects " in the sky.

* * *

Two Europeans on duty at the international airport observed an " aerial object " through binoculars.

Mr. Fletcher says that he has recently observed something in the sky over Nairobi from his well-equipped observatory.

" It was about 7.40 p.m. that I had four friends in my observatory," he says. " Very low and towards the east there was a large light in the sky which had no relationship to anything astronomical, to Very lights or to the aircraft which had just landed at the airport."

The altitude of Mr. Fletcher's " object " was about 2,000ft., was stationary when first spotted by himself and his four companions and " emitted a bright orange light." This light brightened to a yellowish colour and the object rose, dropped and then rose again, finally disappearing through the clouds, he states.

Mr. Fletcher says that he thinks that there is no question about the genuineness of reports about " flying saucers," which " have been given by very experienced observers " in all parts of the world.

* * *

" Not all the American and British people who have seen these unidentified flying objects have been suffering from hallucinations," he declares.

The most encouraging thing about reports of unidentified flying objects (or UFO as they are labelled officially in Nairobi), Mr. Fletcher avers, is that " they seem to be friendly towards the people of this planet."

" From all the information which is available they are steadily mapping every part of our Earth," he concludes.

Countless reasons, he believes—and he cites Dr. F. Hoyle, Professor of Astro-Physics at Cambridge, and Sir James Jeans—can be offered as to why there should be many more planets, or bodies, in the universe capable of supporting life.

Probably this life would differ enormously from life as known on Earth. " It is possible that whereas we need oxygen and other elements to support life on this planet, entirely different elements may be supporting life on others," Mr. Fletcher declares. " Indeed, the forms of life could be completely different from any that we can imagine."

Whether the beings now visiting the Earth from outer space are short or tall, have blood in their veins, or whether they have veins at all, will have to await their contact with human beings here, he says, inferring that " Outer Space Men " will one day decide to land their " machines " and attempt to communicate with Earth men.

It may be sheer coincidence, Mr. Fletcher says, but he points out that these other beings seem to have been interested in activities on Earth since the time of the first atomic explosion about seven years ago.

" There does not seem to be any doubt that they are miles ahead of us in their methods of propulsion, and reports have been made by observers who have seen these unidentified flying objects over atomic plants, dockyards, airfields, naval bases and some of the larger cities of the world," he says.

* * *

" Their approach to us is, I suggest, similar to what our own approach would be if the boot were on the other foot. Suppose we were to visit Venus. I do not think that, until we had made every possible investigation, we would land.

" The obvious thing is that we should map, photograph if possible, and carry out a thorough investigation before we wantonly risked life by hasty landings. It is not unreasonable, therefore, that whatever controls the unidentified flying objects is doing exactly that."

Mr. Fletcher is convinced that the objects come from outer space and declares that " their behaviour cannot be mistaken for a meteorite which, on coming into contact with our atmosphere, is pulled at an ever-increasing velocity by gravity towards the earth. This velocity becomes so great that the object burns up because of the intense heat generated by friction with our atmosphere.

" A meteorite does not rise or hover in the air. Its path is a parabolic curve similar to that of a shell fired from a gun. Therefore, the things which we have seen are undoubtedly unidentified flying objects."

Mr. Fletcher does not pretend to know how the objects operate, what they contain or where they come from. But he gives this advice: " Vigilance and a friendly approach to their overtures would appear to be the best course to follow."

Morning Advertiser

THURSDAY, OCTOBER 7, 1954

A FLYING SAUCER COMES TO EARTH

The Man from Mars Left No Address

by J. Stubbs Walker

D.M. 11 OCT 1954

ALONE, along the wild Morayshire coast between Lossiemouth and Buckie, in Scotland, an Englishman has met, photographed, and interviewed, he says, a man from Mars.

His interview, carried out in sign language, helped out by sketches in a notebook, may have solved age-old problems about Mars and given the answer to the mystery of the flying saucers.

The interview took place less than 50 miles from Loch Ness, where other remarkable and unworldly things have also been seen. Details are given today in a book written by Mr. Cedric Allingham, wealthy amateur astronomer and, under an assumed name, a writer of thrillers.

Abroad

IT all happened in February of this year, but Mr. Allingham has only just made his report public. Yesterday when he might have expected a bombardment of questions on what must be one of the most remarkable experiences a man has ever had, he was unfortunately out of England.

He is touring America, according to his publishers, and is going to interview Mr. George Adamski, an Arizona café proprietor, who claims to have interviewed a man from Venus two years ago.

Mr. Allingham's story is simple. In **Flying Saucers from Mars — the Facts** (Frederick Muller, 10s. 6d.), he says he was walking along the coast when he saw his first flying saucer. He was studying bird life at the time.

The flying saucer vanished, but Mr. Allingham resolutely stuck around. He was rewarded, he says, for after more than three hours the saucer came back.

"There was no doubt about its intention. It was going to land," he reports. It did land ("with a soft but audible thud") 50 yards from where he stood.

The "quick snap" of the man from Mars.

It was about 50ft. in diameter, perhaps 20ft. high, the colour and lustre of polished aluminium, with two groups of portholes. That, for a writer of thrillers, might have been good enough, but Mr. Allingham had a lot more coming.

A sliding panel in the saucer moved back, and a man leaped lightly and gracefully to the ground.

He and Mr. Allingham both raised their right arms in salute. The space-man was tall, graceful, with short brown hair, a high forehead, and skin deeply tanned. He would have passed anywhere as an earthman, but his voice was liquid— "the clear liquid of a hillside spring."

Sign language

AT first Mr. Allingham felt certain that the man came from Venus. After all, he had read Mr. Adamski's book, and everything so far was very similar. But when they got to their sign language conversation and Mr. Allingham had made a rough sketch of the solar system he pointed to the planet Venus on the sketch, and the space-man shook his head (a delightfully worldly way of indicating the negative). In turn he picked out Mars on the map of the planets.

Mr. Allingham asked the Martian about the canals on Mars, which still cause bitter argument among astronomers, and he learned that they are man-made canals built to irrigate the arid deserts of the planet.

It seems from the interview that the Earth is far behind Mars and Venus in the way of interplanetary travel. The men of Mars and Venus, using flying saucers that look very similar, manage to see quite a lot of each other. They also apparently use the Moon as a take-off point for studying the Earth.

Only at the end of the interview did Mr. Allingham realise that though he had photographed the saucer—with the driver's permission—he had failed to get a picture of the Martian. By then, however, the visitor from space was walking back to his flying saucer, and the best Mr. Allingham could do was a quick snap in poor light of the retreating back of the man.

Vital witness

THE interview lasted half an hour, and as it ended Mr. Allingham claimed to have found a local fisherman, James Duncan, who was willing to write a statement in the astronomer's notebook, solemnly swearing that he had witnessed the conversation from a distance and had seen the pilot get in his flying saucer and take off.

Most unfortunately no one has been able to trace Mr. James Duncan. A representative of the publishers visited the area and could find no such man, and when Mr. Allingham was sent back by the publishers to Lossiemouth, he also failed to find Mr. Duncan.

During the week-end *Daily Mail* inquiries in the area were equally unsuccessful.

A representative of the publishers said yesterday: "This James Duncan, the vital eye-witness, is the one thing we have been unable to check. The rest of the book and the pictures have been examined by scientists, astronomers, and photographers. Mr. Allingham says that he was so flummoxed by the whole affair that he forgot to ask the man for his address."

162

'SAUCERS FLY IN FORMATION'

E.N. 8 OCT 1954

VIENNA, Friday.

THOUSANDS of people watched a formation of luminous "saucers" fly over the town of Ried, Upper Austria, yesterday, police report.

The "saucers" flew at a great height from east to west.—Reuter.

---

2 SS   *The Evening News,*

E.N. 12 OCT 1954

Venus and Her Friend Drop In From Mars

PARIS, Tuesday.

A SCHOOLMASTER on leave from a French colony, M. Martin, said he met two young women from Mars on the island of Oloron, off the French Atlantic coast.

They were about 5ft. 7in. tall, wore leather helmets, gloves and boots and were very good-looking, he declared.

A Message

They borrowed his fountain pen and scribbled some mysterious signs with it which he has kept as evidence.

Flying discs, balls and "cigars" have again been reported everywhere, from the Pyrenees to Alsace and back to Brittany, in the past 24 hours.—Reuter.

E.N. 13 OCT 1954

FLYING BELL NOW

With Red and Green Sparks

Paris, Wednesday.—A "flying bell" is the latest shape to be reported in the flying saucer epidemic now sweeping France. Three workmen at Louviers, Normandy, claimed to have seen a bell-like object, seven to nine feet tall, hovering about a foot above the ground. Red and green sparks came out of it and then an orange light from the base made it jump 25 to 30 feet. After about an hour the "bell" rose vertically and flew away.—Reuter.

OBSERVATORY TO START PROBE INTO 'SAUCERS'

REPORTS of "mysterious bodies" in the sky are to be studied at Belgium's Observatory. 10 OCT 1954

Professor L. Tadwell, who is in charge of the investigation, has appealed to the Belgian people to report anything unusual they see.

Meanwhile a "flying cigar," which can stop cars and put out their lights, was reported by a Le Mans, France, milkman yesterday.

Flying Mushroom

He said he was driving his lorry along a road when suddenly the engine stopped and the headlights went out. As he got out to see what was wrong a shining red and blue "cigar," about 3ft., long, sped over his vehicle.

A few minutes later his engine started and the lights worked again.

Other reports of strange objects seen in the sky over France included a "flying illuminated mushroom," a bright smoking orange disc and a grey machine making a loud whistling noise.—*Reuter, B.U.P.*

Two observatories in Alexandria last night reported seeing what appeared to be a cylindrical "flying saucer." coloured red and green, says an *Exchange* message from Cairo.

MYSTERY OBJECT SEEN OVER EYNSFORD

13/10/54

WAS IT A FLYING SAUCER ?

A MYSTERY object, believed by some residents to have been a flying saucer, was watched by at least three men for five to six minutes at two vantage points at Eynsford and Romney Street on Monday.

Mr. Barry Boulton, of Broadview, St. Martins-drive, Eynsford, told a *Kentish Times* reporter that he and Mr. A. H. Smart, also of St. Martins-drive, Eynsford, were working at Mr. Bruce Dolling's yard at Priory-lane, Eynsford, when they sighted an object moving swiftly against the wind in a north-easterly direction about 4.20 p.m.

He said it was spherical in shape. The top half resembled very highly polished aluminium and had a dark underside. It was flying much higher than an American jet plane travelling across the wind at the same time.

About half-a-dozen jet fighters then came in view travelling in the same direction as the first plane and the object suddenly began to climb rapidly and disappeared.

On Tuesday morning, Mr. Tom Knight, of Otford, discussed the object with Mr. Boulton and Mr. Smart. Mr. Knight said he was working at Mr. Matthew Barclay's farm at Romney Street, when he noticed the object and the American jet plane.

KENT

THE SAUCERS AGAIN

by DIOGENES

THE only sensible approach to the problems presented by this strange world and this mysterious universe is the tentative and conditional. It seems to have been constructed on the principle of assembling a million pairs of opposites and letting the positive in every pair live in constant combat with its negative. The result is never dull and is often fascinating.

This arrangement of things in pairs of opposites extends to human minds. In this field we have the credulous which will believe anything, however absurd, and the incredulous which will believe nothing, however well documented and attested. Flying Saucers are in the news again—both disreputably and respectably.

IN FRANCE some 230 people in the neighbourhood of Paris have testified recently to having seen Flying Saucers. They seem to be a fair cross-section of the population —doubtless they include some scoundrels, but also doubtless some honest, if possibly misguided, people. Anyway they all testify to the same thing.

Then there bobs up a French engineer, who affirms that he made dozens of balloons, some ten feet in diameter, filled them with gas, heated the gas and released the balloons, which were then taken by simple people for Flying Saucers. Astronomic orthodoxy promptly sat back with a smug smirk on its face. One could almost hear them saying, with St Thomas, 'And *that* will settle the Manichees!'

BUT THE more I look at this engineer's story the less I like it. I have noted that there is no fun in practical jokes unless you can witness the effect. Thus to put a banana skin in the path of a pompous politician and witness his skid and fall may be amusing. But merely to drop a banana skin, go away and never see the upshot of the act, would not, I imagine, convey any sense of fun at all. When I was a schoolboy a favourite recreation of myself and my fellow gangsters was to tie a string to the knocker of a house and then, allowing some 'slack', to tie the other end to the knocker of the house opposite. Then we would knock one of the knockers and retreat to a safe distance. This would bring the householder to the door, which he opened, thereby lifting the knocker of the house across the road. Finding no one at the door, he would close it and so the knocker opposite fell and brought that householder to *his* door. This . . . but I need not go on.

Two householders, who grew increasingly angry, were repeatedly brought to their respective doors by knocks accountable for by no apparent human agency. It was great fun, we thought, to watch their rising wrath. But the fun was in the watching. Our French engineer, since the movements of a balloon are controlled by nothing but the incalculable wind, whose urges differ at different heights, could not have selected victims to deceive and then derived fun at their mystification.

NEXT I have noted that, while the French have a lively sense of fun, it is usually directed at the authorities of this world and is concerned with some practical thing. This was illustrated some time ago, when the French Customs authorities decided that the making of apple brandy in baths and other containers by farmers in Normandy, who thus evaded paying excise duty, must stop.

The farmers then organized a system under which one man kept watch from the church tower with orders to ring the bell at the appearance of the *douanier*. One day the bell rang. Instantly the farmers, equipped with pitchforks, advanced to meet the invading *douanier* and surrounded him. As an agent of the Government bent on collecting taxes he merited instant death; but he was also a man and possibly a brother. So they did not hurt him. They merely removed his trousers and sent him back, *sans-culotte*, through the countryside, thereby exhibiting both their contempt for Governments which rob a man of the reward of his labours and their sense of humour (doubtless a little coarse) simultaneously. I have often thought that a modified version of what happened there might be very useful in England.

I find it difficult to conceive of a French engineer, to safeguard nothing at all, sitting up o' nights spending much labour and money on materials to stage an act which, I have said, could gratify no one's sense of humour. But that's the story. And it is disreputable.

BUT IF disreputability prevails in France, respectability is the order of the day in Kenya, where, it is to be noted, the atmosphere is particularly clear. Mr G. Duncan Fletcher is a leading astronomer in the Nairobi area and Vice-President of the Kenya Astronomical Association. It seems that white men and black men have been seeing lots of Flying Saucers and their reports have flooded the local newspapers. Mr Fletcher does not think their reports have all come from men 'suffering from hallucinations'. For he, from his observatory, has been seeing things too.

He now thinks there is no doubt about the genuineness of reports about Flying Saucers which 'have been given by very reputable observers' in all parts of the earth. He takes comfort in the fact that these things, whatever they are, 'seem friendly'. He accepts that none of them have landed (though Mr Adamski of America affirms that he has seen them land and has actually talked with the Venusians they carried) but thinks this entirely natural. If we were able to reach Venus he does not think that we should land either until a prolonged and thorough examination of the planet and its inhabitants had been made from the air. Of these visitants from outer space he expresses the view—'From all the information which is available they are steadily mapping every part of our Earth.'

HE THINKS that these beings have been interested in activities on the earth since the first explosion of an atomic bomb seven years ago. Well, if I inhabited one planet and saw the beings on a nearby planet playing monkey-tricks which might destroy not only their own planet but the balance of the whole solar system, I too should be 'interested'.

But Mr Fletcher *is* wrong here. I have a collection of records of the appearance of strange things in the skies going back before the atomic bomb arrived, even before the aeroplane was invented. Still, maybe the atomic bomb has increased interest which was only desultory.

ANYWAY MR FLETCHER is important. He represents something like the heresy of a Bishop of an established Church: he thinks that there are many heavenly bodies capable of bearing life. That itself is a considerable heresy. Until quite recently it was held that, since other planets had no atmosphere, or because their atmosphere was differently constituted from that of Earth, they could not bear life.

But I know of no planet of which it has not been asserted at various times (*a*) that it had no atmosphere and (*b*) that it *had* atmosphere. As for the idea that there can be life only where conditions make possible the production of the kind of food we live on, that is a characteristic example of the vanity of man.

It is scientific orthodoxy to explain away everything which seems to be a Flying Saucer. Such things are 'specks of dust in the air', 'reflections on clouds of the lights of cars', 'specks in the eyes', the

Police Told To Look For 'Saucers'

S.D. 17 OCT 1954

As more reports of flying saucers streamed in from the Continent at the week-end, Vienna police chief Josef Holavbek ordered all his men to keep a special watch for unidentifiable flying objects.

In Italy a motorist and other people in Modena reported that an incandescent cigar-shaped object shot past him at terrific speed.

People in 15 parts of the Po river valley have given reports of flying cigars or saucers in the past 48 hours.

Eight farm workers said they saw a luminous disc land and then shoot away again with a blinding light.

Reddish Machine

A Norwegian farmer described objects he saw over his farm as "mauve coloured and triangular."

In France a retired Customs inspector said that a strange reddish craft landed only 40 yards from him at Perpignan.

A man "in a sort of diving suit" walked round the machine but was scared by barking dogs.

The mysterious visitor got back into his machine and took off at high speed.

Saucer man left propaganda

D.M. 19 OCT 1954

Rome, Monday.—A shepherd in Sardinia, Giuseppe Milla, claims that he saw a "flying saucer" land and an aviator, "clad in luminous overalls," alight from it. The aviator is said to have fled when Milla approached, but to have left a package, which the local police say contained — anti-Communist propaganda printed in Hungarian.—D.M. Cable.

FLYING SAUCERS —'THEY'RE BRITISH'

E.N. 20 OCT 1954

Milan, Wednesday.

A NOTED Italian airman, Signor Maner Lualdi, speculated to-day on the origin of flying saucers and concluded: "If I had to bet (on their nationality) I would bet on Britain."

Signor Lualdi, who last year flew over the North Pole, said he himself saw a flying saucer on September 17. He expressed his views to-day in a magazine article.—A.P.

ABOUT THOSE LITTLE MEN FROM MARS...

Monkeys make a monkey of them

OCT. 19 - 1954

By W. A. WATERTON

THOSE "two-foot Men from Mars" who made monkeys out of many observers on Earth were—it turned out—monkeys themselves.

This becomes clear from growing evidence disclosed in America.

The first report of a "two-foot-high Spaceman" came in 1950, when one was reported dead in the wreck of his "flying saucer."

This "saucer" had crashed on a Mexican hillside.

Similar reports followed from other parts—mostly in an area south-west of the United States.

Thousands sent

People who claimed to have seen these little "Spacemen" were dismissed as cranks and crackpots.

It seems now that they had seen real creatures—common monkeys.

For the Americans, who announced a year ago that they were sending up monkeys in rockets for research purposes, have also sent them up *in balloons.*

The purpose: to probe the stratosphere.

These monkeys have been flown out of India in tens of thousands, mostly to America, where they have been used for all kinds of research.

A main branch of this research has been on cosmic radiation. This radiation could harm human tissues at the height at which men can now fly.

Miles high

And so the monkeys have been sent up more than 10 miles to record the effects.

The Americans have shaved the monkeys—hair would interfere—and have attached electrical leads to them to probe upper space.

The monkeys have been given oxygen masks and helmets—and the little aeronauts have gone aloft to stay for many hours.

And vital information about blood pressure, temperature, and other conditions has been returned by radio to scientists on Earth.

But occasionally balloons and gondolas with monkeys in them have returned to Earth—and been found by folk not in the know.

Hence—"two-foot Men from Mars."

FLYING SAUCERS TO BE IMPOUNDED

French Mayor's Decree

From our own Correspondent

28 OCT 1954 PARIS, OCTOBER 27.

The Mayor of Châteauneuf-du-Pape has banned flying saucers and flying cigars throughout the length and breadth of his commune. His decree, issued to-day, is no frivolous declaration of intention, but a municipal measure drafted with due consideration for the laws of the Republic and based on the Statutes of April 5, 1884, and May 31, 1924. It reads:

Article 1: The flights, landings, and take-offs of airships called "flying saucers" or "flying cigars" of any nationality are forbidden on the territory of the community of Châteauneuf-du-Pape.

Article 2: Any such airship which lands on the territory of the community of Châteauneuf-du-Pape will be immediately impounded.

Article 3: The rural constable is charged with carrying out the present decree.

This last provision is of greater importance than may at first appear. There has already been a case of a farmer (not on the territory of Châteauneuf-du-Pape) who excused himself for having fired a shotgun at a benighted traveller on the ground that he had taken him for a Martian. Henceforth, the farmers of Châteauneuf-du-Pape at least will know that it is not for them thus to take the law into their own hands.

FLYING SAUCERS STOP THE TRAFFIC

E.N. 29 OCT 1954

"Evening News" Correspondent

ROME, Friday.

PEOPLE jumped out of cars and brought traffic to a standstill in one of the central squares of Rome when a "formation" of flying saucers, nine in all, swept across the sky.

The saucers came down in a straight dive and then climbed again. Witnesses said they were obviously powered for vertical flight, although they made no sound.

A Diplomatic Incident From Mars

E.N. 29 OCT 1954

ROME, Friday.

THE flying saucers are over Italy in droves. Even America's woman Ambassador, Mrs. Clare Boothe Luce, has seen "something."

It zoomed over the city, she says. "But I don't know what it was."

Romantics, however, declare it was like the moon dashing across the sky.

In Florence a football game was held up for half an hour while 15,000 people gaped upwards.

For there were disc and cigar-shaped objects, say eye-witnesses. And they shed what appeared to be a wispy trail, rather like a spider's web.

This substance was picked up and analysed. A professor said it contained calcium and magnesium.

THE MARTIAN

But all these stories fade into nothingness beside the experience of 60-year-old Ermelinda Lanzilla, who stepped out of her house 60 miles north of here last night to look for her cat.

And there, she says, stood a pot-bellied figure with metal arms hanging like a chimpansee's and a helmet like a deep-sea diver.

She rushed screaming into the house, but when her son went outside there was nothing to be seen.

FROM FRANCE comes a story of a "thing" about 15 inches in diameter like a "small saloon car with wheels."

A farm labourer says he saw it. And, he says, a four-foot-high creature in leather overalls and helmet jumped in.

Then it took off.

Game Held Up

29 OCT 1954 N.Y.H.T.

'Flying Saucers' Observed By Italian Football Crowd

By the United Press

FLORENCE, Italy, Oct. 28. — A flight of "flying saucers" held up a local football game for 30 minutes yesterday and sent 15,000 fans home convinced the mysterious disks are more than an optical illusion.

The "saucers," some disk-shaped and other cigar-shaped, had been reported to police by other citizens some minutes before they appeared over the soccer stadium. Fans at the practice game between Fiorentina and Pistoiese league teams got so excited that the players stopped the game.

Eyewitnesses said the objects were bright silver in color and flew at a very high altitude. Even more mysterious, they shed a wispy trail like a spider's web, part of which drifted to the ground and was picked up in bundles by passers-by.

The mysterious substance was analyzed tonight by Prof. Giovanni Canneri, director of the Chemical Institute of Milan University.

His report said that the substance had a fiber-like structure with considerable mechanical resistance to traction and torsion.

Prof. Canneri heated the substance, which became brown and left transparent ashes. He then examined them and reported:

"The ashes contain a predominant quantity of borium, silicon calcium and magnesium, similar to borosilicate glass."

Local experts suggested the filmy substance might have been spiders' webs, which they said sometimes get wafted in a mass to great heights by the wind.

The Florence "saucers" were the first observed by a mass of people. Other reports continued to pour in from all parts of Italy, particularly from Emilia Province, in the region of Bologna, and the Pescara region of the Adriatic coast.

LOOK OUT—

30 OCT 1954

It's a Martian!

Express Staff Reporter

PARIS, Friday. — Martians, messieurs, have eyes like pigeons' eggs, a hairy face, and leathery skin.

Or sometimes they look like the picture above. Or that Jeff Hawke version at the bottom of the page.

All France knows it. Well—half of France. The other half doesn't believe it.

For the latest crop of stories about touch-and-go landings by Martians in flying saucers is the subject of nation-wide debate.

The anti-saucerites are winning, with repeated proofs that story after story has been due to hoaxers and mass hysteria.

THEY SAW . . .

Their latest victories :—

1. A newspaper sent two reporters into the countryside dressed in diving suits, and then analysed the other newspaper accounts which followed.

Scores of eyewitnesses gave graphic descriptions — all different — of the flying saucer in which they saw the two "Martians" land and take off. . . .

2. A French railway worker, Georges Ollivier, of Creil, sallied forth in a home-made Martian suit, topped with green lights in a helmet made from an oil can.

That's Georges in the picture.

He so frightened North France that as far as Boulogne, Dunkirk, and Lille, it was reported that Creil (pop. 9,476) was in the hands of Martians.

"MARTIANS WITH TRUNKS" HOAX

30 OCT 1954

10 ITALIANS CHARGED

From Our Own Correspondent

ROME, Friday.

Ten young men at Tradate, Northern Italy, were charged by the police to-day with causing public unrest, after they had hoodwinked a Milan journalist into publishing a fictitious account of how they had conversed with "Martians from a space machine." The report appeared to-day at length in Rome and Milan newspapers.

It described how the machine, with coloured lights, landed in a field. The "Martians," wearing transparent helmets, "had trunks like elephants and voices like the gobbling of a turkey."

Crowds gathered in the streets of Rome and Florence to-day, watching "flying saucers" crossing the sky. It is stated that the luminous objects which caused public excitement were a spun plastic substance used in air exercises for eluding radar detection.

LONDON LAUGHS (No. 6,039) *By LEE*

"Gosh! The papers *are* short of space to-day.
No room even for *US* !"

LINCOLNSHIRE ECHO
TWOPENCE   Nov. 12th 1954.

Flying Saucers as seen in the film "Stranger from Venus."

SEEING THINGS?

NORMAN FRISBY INVESTIGATES

SO FLYING SAUCERS are zooming over Lincolnshire again.

The first of this winter's saucer reports came in from South Carlton last week. A farm worker and his wife heard a noise like a humming top, looked up and saw . . . The Thing.

"It was definitely a flying saucer," said 42-years-old Mr. Albert Smith when he phoned the Echo office in the cold light of next morning.

What would you do if you saw a saucer?

Get another witness? Mr. Smith had his wife with him, and as he was watching his saucer disappear, two American drove up.

Late At Night

Had they seen it? They agreed they had seen something fading away into the clouds.

Hardest job of every saucer-spotter is to find corroboration of his story. Usually they are seen late at night, and in the country.

The more sophisticated souls of the cities are too busy watching neon signs to bother about visitors from outer space.

And Lincoln's street lights are enough to dazzle any would-be saucer observer.

But some confirmation of Mr. Smith's story has come in.

Over to Nettleham. Thursday night about 11 o'clock — just at the time The Thing was seen at Carlton — two men were sitting indoors.

"We heard this weird humming-top noise outside. We had no idea what it might be, but we went outside to look.

"We could hear it . . . but we couldn't see anything."

Mr. Smith said his saucer sounded like a humming-top. And he saw it come through a break in the clouds. At about the same time on the same night.

COULD Lincolnshire's "saucers" be new-type planes from R.A.F. research stations in the county?

The Echo understands that the Cabinet has decided that a greater proportion of defence effort should be devoted to the R.A.F. "particularly to the speed-up of the development of new aircraft."

There is also likely to be a speed-up in the production of such weapons as guided missiles.

It is widely believed that the Government has already decided to scale down the production of orthodox weapons which are now out dated.

Defence Minister, Mr. Harold Macmillan, will make a statement on new air defence plans in the next few weeks.

Now to Saxilby. A housewife was getting ready to go to the weekly meeting of the Women's Institute on the night the Carlton saucer was seen.

"Everything was quiet, and then I heard an unusual chug-chug noise in the sky. It did not sound like an aeroplane to me.

"I could not see anything when I went outside. The sound seemed to travel from west to east.

"I'll Believe . . ."

"My neighbour was not about, or I would have asked him to listen. He was in the R.A.F. and knows more about plane engines."

Could she too have heard the Carlton saucer?

People who see saucers all react in the same way. "Yes, I have read about them. But I have never believed in them . . . not until now". Which is just what Mr. Smith said.

It is hard on those who have seen saucers for those of us who have not to say: "I'll believe in 'em when I've seen one."

Hard, and pretty unreasonable too, I suppose.

Problem Of
. . . . . an

NOT A SAUCER— BUT WHAT WAS IT?

IT was NOT a flying saucer . . . "I am not going to tell anybody I saw a flying saucer," said 32-years-old ex-fighter pilot Neville Berryman, of Nettleham-road, Lincoln, today, "because I don't believe in them."

"But," he told Echo reporter Norman Frisby today, "I saw something through my bedroom window this morning — a most peculiar thing I can't explain away."

It appeared at 7.45 a.m., when Mr. Berryman was sitting up in bed drinking his early-morning tea.

He said, "To my surprise I suddenly saw this spherical object, golden in colour, like a little sun.

Fantastic Speed

"I was in the R.A.F., and I'm interested in heights and speeds. Judging by the cloud-base this morning, the object would be about 5,000 feet up. It passed across my bedroom window at a fantastic speed. It was in sight about 2½ seconds. 13.11.54.

"I have always scoffed at people who claim to have seen saucers. I had a good laugh at a Scampton R.A.F. officer this week who told me he had seen one I tried to reason out what I had seen.

"It couldn't possibly have been a balloon. No balloon could have travelled at that speed — about 1,500 miles an hour. It couldn't have been the sun shining on the mist or a rain halo.

"It was a most peculiar thing."

Mr. Berryman's object passed from north-east to south-west, at a height of about 5,000 feet, about 12 miles from Lincoln He heard no sound from it.

Saucer Pictures Being Tested

Lincolnshire Echo, Nov. 9th. 1954.

CIVIL aviation authorities in Sydney have telegraphed to Wilcannia in New South Wales for the negatives of three photographs of a "flying saucer", claimed to have been seen there last week.

A worker on a sheep station, Mr. G. J. Porter, sent the photographs to the Civil Aviation Department after a report of "an object" seen at the station moving slowly across the sky, 500 feet high, and making a "terrific" noise.

Mr. Porter wrote that if the photographs were proved genuine, they were not for publication.

The Department's regional director, Mr. A. Hupburn, said today: "The pictures which to 99 per cent. of the population would seem genuine, show an object like an inverted saucer with an inverted teacup on top. In the foreground is a landscape of trees and paddocks."

The photographs have been microscopically examined by experts, but they are not yet regarded as 100 per cent. genuine.

DAILY SKETCH
Nov. 12.1954.

'Saucer' breaks a dish

A WHOLE town saw a "flying saucer" yesterday. At 4.55 p.m. the "saucer" was seen over Whitstable, Kent. It was described by ex-Army Sergeant Michael Randall, as a small round ball of fire flying up and down and glowing with a flashing red light.

He said: "It was travelling at average aircraft speed. At 5,000 to 7,000ft. it disappeared into cloud, flying towards Southend."

Many people gave similar descriptions. Mr. J. Foreman said: "It was nothing like an aircraft." Mr. Randall's mother, drying dishes in her home at Wave-crescent, felt them rattle in her hands. One fell and broke. She went out, saw the "saucer" and ran inside again—"in case it lands."

Page ONE
Daily Mail,
14.11.54.

300 soldiers see flying saucer

BERNE, Sunday.—Three hundred Swiss soldiers saw a "flying saucer" last week, the Swiss Army announced today. The men, on manoeuvres near Grandvillard, south-western Switzerland, say it was a disc-shaped object with a red glow on its silvery surface. It was 10,000ft. up and motionless.
—B.U.P.

SPACEMEN "BECOMING LESS SHY"

But Manchester Remains Unnoticed

n/c 6.   By our own Reporter   25-11-54

"We are living in an exciting and dangerous time," said the chairman introducing a lantern lecture on flying saucers to a closely packed, attentive audience at the Milton Hall, Deansgate, Manchester, on Wednesday. Shortly after this introduction a man in the audience fainted and was carried off past the platform where the lecturer, Mr Desmond Leslie, had been recounting the story of an American truck-driver who had spent nearly an hour in one of these machines from behind the beyond, with every hospitality shown, and American spoken.

There was no crew in this particular saucer—it was apparently manoeuvred by remote control—but the truck-driver had told how he had been able to talk by voice-pipe with a seemingly friendly voice at the other end. His employer had testified to having seen the machine, to-day from a distance.

The truck-driver's account of the interior structure of the saucer, Mr Leslie said, tallied with those of other Americans who had seen them at close quarters. They had a double compartment, with a cylindrical magnetic pole, the power-source, running down the centre, and circular windows around the walls. The last words reecived from an American fighter pilot who had collided with a "flying object," added Mr Leslie, were: "My God, it's got windows." The planetary beings, he explained, had probably learnt earthly languages from radio programmes they had picked up.

There were stronger nerves and more scepticism elsewhere in the audience as some questions showed. A clergyman who said he had been impressed by the photographs of the saucers shown by Mr Leslie—they were all, though from different places, of the now familiar "lampshade" type—wondered why we had no photographs of their crews. Mr Leslie said such a picture was about to be published; the men from outer space were apparently becoming less shy.

What planets were they from? From nearly all the best-known ones, was the answer. In one saucer alone had been representatives from Mars, Venus, and Saturn. Had they shown any interest in Manchester yet? Mr Leslie said he could not promise landings in this country, as there had been in America and other countries; and while Mancunians had reported sightings, there was no evidence that the "spacemen," for their part, had noticed Manchester.

Another American, an engineer from the West, had told Mr Leslie of a similarly exciting saucer experience; even a "grilling" by the F.B.I. had failed to shake his story, which was that he was invited into the machine by means of a trapdoor, as it hovered low near his home, by the crew of "spacemen" and they had taken him for a ride, at prodigious speed, to New York and back. His description of the machine and its occupants—"like normal human beings, but smaller"—tallied with the account given by Mr George Adamski of his meeting with a Venusian in California a year ago. At least 10 per cent of the thousands of reports of sightings proved, Mr Leslie thought, that interplanetary craft existed.

Yorkshire Post, 15.11.54

300 soldiers see a Flying Saucer

BERNE, Sunday

Three hundred Swiss soldiers saw a Flying Saucer on Thursday, the Swiss Army announced today.

The men were on manoeuvres near Grandvillard, South-Western Switzerland, with an anti-aircraft unit, when a disc-shaped object with a red glow on its silvery surface appeared about 10,000 feet above them and remained motionless.

"It was first thought it was some kind of balloon," said an Army spokesman. But suddenly it moved away very quickly in a southern direction and disappeared behind the clouds. The quick horizontal movement showed it could not have been a balloon . . . .

"Everybody left his position at the guns to gaze at the object through telescopes and other instruments at the observation post of the battery."

Unidentified flying objects have been seen over Switzerland repeatedly in recent years, said the spokesman.—British United Press.

SAUCER GLASS

Catania, Tuesday. — Feathery stuff fell from a "vast formation of flying saucers" reported by Sicilians over Gela. It was analysed and found to be spun glass.—A.P.

E.N. 16 NOV 1954

---

by the team until several months later, back in England. n/c 6. 25-11-54.

Saucers Over France

Spotting of inexplicable objects in the skies over France is having a business sequel. Though some newspaper commentators have associated the spotting with excessive eating or drinking, three films with flying saucers as main theme are to be made. One will tell a story of a reporter who tries to win a prize of £10,000 offered for the first photograph of a genuine celestial saucer. The producers will follow some of the actual spotting that has been reported, including the case of a young photographer who spent a night away from his spouse during their honeymoon. He preferred to go saucer-hunting with his camera.

Another remarkable authentic nocturnal incident to be included in the film will be the attempted shooting of a Frenchman by a friend who took him for a Martian. The producers intend to interview a hundred people who vow they have seen flying saucers, cigars, bananas, and other phenomena in the skies.

---

by
The prospect is ala

FLYING SAUCERS START PANIC

RIO DE PANEIRO, Sunday.—The pilot of a Brazilian airliner said to-day a fleet of 19 flying saucers flew at tremendous speed less than 300 yards from his plane. His passengers panicked. Members of the crew had to act "most violently" to overcome their fears.

"FLYING SAUCERS" IN AUSTRALIA

MIc G 16/12/54

An Inquiry Ordered

MELBOURNE, DECEMBER 15.

The Australian Navy Minister, Mr Josiah Francis, said in Brisbane to-night he would order an immediate inquiry into two unidentified objects which a naval pilot said accompanied him in the air after dark. According to the "Sun News-Pictorial" of Melbourne naval authorities to-night confirmed that the objects had been recorded by radar at the Nowra naval air station on the New South Wales coast.

Another Melbourne newspaper, the "Argus," claimed the navy report to be the "first authenticated information in the world on the existence of flying saucers."

The pilot reported that about three months ago he was flying at 15,000 feet when two lighted objects flashed past him. The Nowra radar screen traced the objects until they disappeared, but naval officers said they had been unable to identify them.—Reuter.

Reply to Reporter 16/12/54 N.Y.H.T.

Saucers Not Inter-Planetary As Far as President Knows

From the Herald Tribune Bureau
Copyright New York Herald Tribune, Inc.

WASHINGTON, Dec. 15. — The best information he has about flying saucers, President Eisenhower said today, is that they are not of inter-planetary origin.

The President did not indicate what information he has on the precise nature of the phenomena.

A reporter asked Mr. Eisenhower:

"Recent news reporters indicate that some European governments are investigating quite seriously the flying-saucer problem. And not too long ago there was a book published in this country that purported to show that our Air Force thought that some of these flying objects, at least, might be of extraterrestrial origin. I wonder if you could tell us if our authorities really do suspect something of that kind or, if not, what is the form of the things."

The President said that nothing had come to him at all, either orally or in written form, with regard to the recent reports.

The President recalled that the last time the subject was discussed with him was when an Air Force man whom he trusts said that so far as he knew it is completely inaccurate to believe that the objects came from any outside planet.

A recent report by the Air Force showed it had investigated a total of 254 flying-saucer reports during the first nine months of this year, compared with 429 such reports last year and more than 1,700 in the peak year of 1952. More than 80 per cent of the sightings are explainable as known objects, such as balloons, aircraft, astronomical bodies, atmospheric reflections, or even birds.

The Air Force has not completed its study of a photograph made recently in Sicily, showing two disk-shaped objects in the sky and Sicilians gazing at them. The photograph, made by a Sicilian, was distributed by the United Press, which made a copy available to the Air Force.

MAILbag

S. D. M. 20-12-54

Well, where do flying saucers come from?

SIR,—In Melbourne the Australian Navy Minister, Mr. Hosiah Francis, said: "Two objects identified as 'flying saucers' by a Royal Australian Navy pilot were track on radar sets; the pilot was joined in the air by two strange aircraft while he was flying back to base after dark.

"He reported to the air controller at Nowra, whose radar showed three aircraft flying together; the pilot identified himself on the radar by moving according to a pattern."

In Washington, U.S.A. President Eisenhower said that an Air Force official told him the so-called "flying saucers" do not come from outer space. As one who has seen U.F.O.s, over Europe and the States, may I ask: "Then where do they come from—the sea?"

C. Harrison Campbell.
Moffat.

E N 21-12-54   P.C. 477A.

The Flying Tray

I SAW an extraordinary object fly across the sky between 11 and 12 on the night of December 9. It was like a circular tray, pale pink-yellow in colour and seemed solid, which made me certain it was not a moon rainbow or some reflection. It flew like an aeroplane and was not a shooting star or meteor. My daughter also saw it just before it finally disappeared.

(Mrs.) Margaret Waters.
Newbury. Berks.

THESE ARE THE SKETCHES
CAPTAIN HOWARD DREW IN
HIS LOG BOOK

The 'things' as Captain Howard
first observed them. On the left
is the wing-tip of the *Centaurus*

Now the central object becomes
a huge flying wing. "It looked as if
it was turning to close with us"

Constantly changing shape, the central
object now looks like a giant telephone
on its back, as long as an ocean liner

WE WERE SHADOWED FROM OUTER SPACE

by CAPT. JAMES HOWARD, a B.O.A.C. pilot, as told to Graham Fisher

I was always sceptical about those reports of flying saucers. But not any more. Not since I saw one for myself

MAYBE it wasn't exactly a flying saucer. What I saw, on a recent New York to London flight, was more of a flying—arrow, I guess you'd have called it at one stage. It seemed to keep changing its shape as it flew beside me, very much like a jellyfish assumes varying patterns as it swims through the water. Or maybe the apparent changes in shape were due to the different angles we viewed it from as it banked and turned about five miles off.

Whatever it was—a giant flying wing, jellyfish or saucer—of these things I'm quite certain: It wasn't a trick of light or a figment of the imagination. It wasn't any sort of electrical, magnetic or natural phenomenon. And it certainly wasn't a mirage.

No, it was something real and substantial; something that kept station with me for eighty miles and only sheered off when I got a radio call from the Sabre-jet fighter which had been sent up from Goose Bay to intercept the thing. It was something—the idea gives me slight goose-pimples when I think of it—which was keeping my Boeing Stratocruiser, *Centaurus*, under observation.

The date was June 29 this year. Just before sunset. Over Labrador. The sky was crystal-clear.

I had taken off from Idlewild airfield at five o'clock, New York time, on what we British Overseas Airways Corporation pilots have nicknamed the 'champagne and caviar' run—the North Atlantic crossing from New York to London. It's a luxury flight used by film stars, stage personalities, diplomats and not-so-tired businessmen who can

chalk it up to the expenses account.

Normally, we do the trip non-stop, but on this occasion there wasn't very much of a tail-wind and I had a pretty heavy load aboard—fifty-one passengers and a deal of freight—which meant a touchdown some place for refuelling.

The Great Circle Route which we follow takes us roughly midway between Gander airfield in Newfoundland and Goose Bay in Labrador. Gander, this time, was out as a refuelling base on account of foggy weather. But Goose Bay was wide open. So I was headed north-east across the St. Lawrence River. Dinner had been served on board about an hour earlier, and some of the passengers had already taken to their sleeping berths.

We crossed the St. Lawrence and flew over Seven Islands, the small settlement rapidly becoming a latter-day boom town on account of the new railway being constructed from there to the mining centres of Labrador. There was low cloud at about 5,000 feet, but up where we were at 19,000 feet, cruising along at about 270 miles per hour, it was perfectly clear. The sun was just beginning to set, away to the left. At that height there is very little coloured tint on account of the rarefied atmosphere. The sky was almost silver in its clearness—perfect visibility.

It was 9.05 p.m. Labrador time and we were about twenty minutes' flying time north-east of Seven Islands when I first sighted the thing.

At first it looked like no more than an indeterminate dark blob in the distance, with several smaller blobs dancing attendance on it. The whole set-up looked, at first glance, like a cluster of flak-bursts such as I had encountered several times over

It was from the cockpit of a Boeing Stratocruiser such as this that Captain Howard saw the mysterious flying objects

Europe during World War II while bombing invasion barges lined up along the Dutch and Belgian coasts.

But the biggest blob was much bigger than any flak burst I had ever encountered, and in some strange way it seemed to have definite shape. It didn't look, somehow, as though it was going to disintegrate into thin air, the way flak-burst does. As near as I can describe it, it was something like an inverted pear suspended in the sky.

I was on the port side of the control cockpit, looking out of the window nearest the thing. Beside me was my co-pilot, First Officer Lee Boyd, a 33-years-old Canadian from Saskatchewan who flew with the famous Pathfinder Force during World War II. I gave Lee a nudge.

"What do you make of that?" I asked.

"I just noticed it," he said. "What in tarnation is it?"

As near as I could judge, the group of things was about five miles off, stretched out in a line parallel with our own line of flight. The big one was roughly centre of the group, with the smaller ones extended fore and aft like a destroyer screen convoying a battleship.

Watching, puzzled—the Stratocruiser was flying by auto-pilot at the time—I realised something else, too.

"The damn things are moving," I said.

Even as we watched, the big central thing began to change shape—or maybe it altered its angle of flight, giving the appearance of changing shape. I wouldn't know. What I do know is that during the entire eighteen minutes it flew along with us it changed shape continually while the smaller attendant things switched position around it.

This is something lots of people are going to want to know a deal about later, I told myself. There's going to be a lot of questions fired at me once I make my report. I'd better know some of the answers. How many small ones, for instance.

I counted, re-counted, counted again. Six. Always six. Sometimes there were three stretched out in front of the main thing and three behind. Sometimes five stretched out in line ahead and only one behind. I had the impression that just before I got round to counting them there were more than six, which ties in with Lee Boyd's idea that they were flying in and out of the large central object like aircraft entering and leaving a flight hangar.

Lee said, as though he didn't believe it himself: "There's a lot of Air Force traffic in and out of Goose Bay some days. Maybe it's a formation of fighters way out in the distance. Want me to call up Goose and check?"

It didn't look like any formation of fighters I'd ever seen, but I told him to go ahead.

He called up Approach Control at Goose Bay —told them what was going on.

"Hold it a moment and we'll check," they said. A minute later they reported back. "No other traffic in your area."

"Well, there are a number of very strange objects flying parallel with us some distance off," Lee said. "There's one large one and about six smaller ones."

"Can you identify them?"

"No."

"Okay. We'll send a fighter up to take a look-see."

Now, from the inverted pear-shape the big thing had looked when I first saw it, it turned into what looked like a flying arrow—an enormous delta-wing plane turning in to close with us.

There was a nasty moment as we watched the thing seeming to grow larger as though drawing closer.

"It's coming towards us," I said.

But it wasn't. We watched, tense, expectant, but it didn't come any closer. Suddenly the delta-wing appearance started to flatten down, stretching out, until it was now like a giant telephone receiver lying on its back in the sky, still with the smaller objects changing formation around it. Stretched out like that, assuming it was about five miles off, it looked about the size of an ocean liner.

I grabbed paper and began to sketch. My memory might play tricks with me later about this.

The four other members of the crew in the cockpit with us had got the gist of what was going on, had caught something of our own expectancy and tenseness. They crowded forward now to look out of the windows with us: George Allen, navigating officer; Doug Cox, radio officer; Dan Godfrey, engineering officer and a grizzled old veteran flyer; and Bill Stewart, the other engineering officer.

They all saw it. So did the steward and Daphne Webster, the stewardess, a twenty-seven-years-old Londoner. They both popped their heads inside the cockpit to tell us that some of the passengers had seen it too and wanted to know what it was.

Their guess was as good as mine.

The objects were still parallel with us, still keeping station with us at the same altitude. George Allen, angling himself so that he could line them up with the window-frame, said that at one time they went a little ahead of us and then dropped back exactly parallel again.

I was tempted to change course and take a closer look at the things, but I didn't. After all, I didn't know what the blazes they were and I had fifty-one passengers to consider. I also had a hunch that the things might sheer off if we showed too much interest, and, with a fighter coming up to intercept them, I wanted to be in the audience to see what happened.

Soon the pilot of the intercepting fighter came

Continued on page 47

through on the radio: "Those things still with you?"

I said they were.

"Okay. I'm about twenty miles off, heading towards you at a slightly higher altitude."

I looked out of the cockpit window again. The things were still there.

"How do they look now?" the fighter pilot radioed.

Even as he said it, I realised that the things were no longer there—not all of them. The half-dozen attendant things had suddenly vanished.

"What happened to the smaller ones?" I asked.

George Allen, who had had his eyes on them the whole time, said: "It looked to me as though they went inside the big one."

At that moment the big one itself began to get rapidly smaller as though it was sheering away from us at terrific speed.

"They're getting smaller," I told the fighter pilot over the radio.

I looked out again. The big central thing was streaking away into the distance —getting smaller and smaller. In a matter of seconds it was no more than a pinhead. Then it was gone altogether.

And that was that.

What was it? Search me. It wasn't anything natural, I know that. And we had the whole group clearly in view for a full eighteen minutes—entered in the navigation log as appearing at 0105 Greenwich Mean Time and disappearing again at 0123, a flying distance of eighty miles —the strangest eighty-mile journey of my life.

Twenty minutes later we landed at Goose Bay where a U.S.A.F. Intelligence Officer interviewed Lee Boyd, George Allen and myself. We told him what I have told you here.

IT has been suggested that what we saw was no more than a mirage caused by an inversion layer, a layer of warm air out of place. Normally, air gets colder the higher you climb. But occasionally you find a warm layer on top of a cold layer. This acts as a kind of reflecting mirror and produces the sort of mirages you get in the desert in early morning.

But at 19,000 feet, a mirage of what? Our own aircraft? No, that would be a reflected shadow. A shadow must fall *on* something to be visible—and there was nothing. Anyway, the light from the setting sun couldn't possibly throw a shadow *towards* itself. No, I don't believe that one.

Plenty of pilots have been flying longer than I have, but with 7,500 flying hours and 265 Atlantic crossings chalked up, I've never seen anything like it anywhere before. Nor has any member of my crew, all veteran flyers with a good many thousand hours between them.

I know, too, that the things, whatever they were, were not picked up on the radar screen at Goose Bay. There's no reason why they should have been. My own Stratocruiser wasn't picked up on the screen when the things first caught up with us.

Yes, I've read all the theories put forward to account for what twenty-two of us —eight crew and fourteen passengers—saw that night. None of them add up.

It was a solid thing. I'm sure of that, manoeuvrable and controlled intelligently —a sort of base ship linked somehow with those smaller attendant satellites.

There is no rational explanation— except on the basis of space ships and flying saucers. On that basis, it must have been some weird form of space ship from another world.

If so, then another world was watching the *Centaurus* as it flew over Labrador that night in June—watching, waiting maybe, for what? One day we shall know and that day, I'm sure, will be pretty important for the human race. I hope I'm here to see it.

period. This figure included 306 on the roads. 7-7-52 ~Tel~

"Flying Saucer Seen"

Four United States airline pilots to-day reported seeing a "flying saucer" hovering over the Hanford atomic plant at Richlands, Washington State. Capt. John Baldwin, who has had 7,000 hours' experience as an airline pilot, said that the object was perfectly round and still at first. Then it became flat, gained speed and disappeared slowly. It did not register on the plane's radar apparatus.

U.S. PILOTS SEE EIGHT '1,000 MPH GLOWING DISCS'

From Our NEW YORK Reporter

EIGHT "glowing red-orange discs," appearing for at least 12 seconds, have been reported by two Pan American Airways pilots.

The pilots—W. B. Nashid and W. H. Fortenberry—said that the objects passed beneath their New York-Miami plane near Norfolk, Virginia, travelling at "far over 1,000 m.p.h." Six were in formation.

Nashid added: "There was no doubt in our minds that we saw missiles of some kind operating under 'intelligent control. No one from here could take that centrifugal force. We feel they must be from some extra-terrestrial source."

He continued: "As they neared us they appeared to be solid bodies of light, and they glowed like hot coals. They made a sharp turn which amazed us. It was almost instantaneous."

Experts Told of 'Flying Saucers'

By CYRIL BIRKS
"Evening News" Air Reporter

A REPORT by a B.O.A.C. pilot that he saw seven strange objects in the sky as he was heading for London 19,000ft. above the Atlantic yesterday is being sent to the Air Ministry's Technical Intelligence Branch.

In this branch are officers especially detailed to collate and study all "flying saucer" reports.

This latest sighting was made by Captain James Howard, one of B.O.A.C.'s most experienced Atlantic skippers. Members of his crew, and a number of passengers said they, too, had seen the seven strange objects.

According to the report there was one big central object, followed by six smaller ones. All were black.

JET FIGHTER
Sent to Intercept

Captain Howard called up Goose Bay, Labrador, over the radio-telephone, and an American jet fighter was sent up to "intercept."

The seven mysterious objects disappeared rapidly when the jet fighter pilot called up Captain Howard.

The Air Ministry's Technical Intelligence officers are expected to compare one peculiar feature of this report with the circumstances in which a "flying saucer" was reported several weeks ago by a woman living in the New Forest and by a youth in Somerset.

There was a three-hour gap between the reports which both described a circular object, followed by something smaller.

Drama of Seven Strange Objects In the Sky

The Log of Capt. Howard

By CYRIL BIRKS
"Evening News" Air Reporter

INTELLIGENCE officers of the R.A.F. and the U.S. Air Force were studying a report to-day by a B.O.A.C. captain that he saw seven objects in the sky yesterday.

The pilot, Capt. J. Howard, aged 33, of Coombe Dingle, Bristol, was flying from New York to London. He is one of B.O.A.C.'s most experienced Atlantic captains.

The full story of what the airliner's crew and some of the passengers saw 19,000ft. over the Atlantic is told in these dramatic extracts from Capt. Howard's log-book :

At 01.05 G.M.T. on June 30, about 150 nautical miles south-west of Goose Bay, height 19,000ft., flying in clear weather above a layer of low cloud, noticed on our port beam a number of dark objects at approximately the same altitude as our aircraft.

I drew the attention of the First Officer to them. He said he had just noticed them also.

SHAPE CHANGES

I jokingly said that they reminded me of flak bursts. He agreed.

It then became apparant that they were moving along on a track roughly parallel to ours and keeping station with us.

The First Officer then called Goose Approach to ask if there was any aircraft in our area. Time 01.07 G.M.T. They said "no."

During this time the shape of the large object changed slightly, also the position of the smaller ones relative to the big one. Some moved ahead, some behind.

The First Officer then told Goose Bay what we were watching and they said they would send a fighter to investigate.

The shape of the large one continually changed, but its position relative to us did not. It was always about 90 degrees to port.

The distance from us appeared not less than five miles, possibly very much more.

During this time both engineers, both navigators, the radio officer, the two stewards and the stewardess watched it, and all of us agreed on its shape.

A number of small objects accompanying it, usually six, were visible. All were agreed that they had never seen anything like it before.

At about 01.20 G.M.T. the fighter reported that he was approaching us.

SMALLER, SMALLER

The objects immediately began to grow indistinct until only one was visible. This grew smaller and finally disappeared at 01.23 G.M.T. still at the same bearing from us.

I reported to the fighter which direction to head for and then commenced descent to Goose, landing at 01.45 G.M.T.

As we taxied in another fighter was dispatched to take over from the first.

A U.S. Air Force intelligence officer met us and we gave him the full story. I spoke to the Fighter Control radar operator and he said he picked us up at 01.13 G.M.T. when we saw the objects, but there was nothing else on his screen.

All who watched the objects are sure that the large one, at any rate, was no sort of winged aircraft. The small ones were just dots.

They left no vapour trails, no lights were seen, just black silhouettes.

THEY SAW NOTHING

The visibility at this altitude was unlimited with no cloud other than the low overcast. The sun had just set.

A large flock of birds might explain it if they were birds that could fly at a true air speed of 238 knots at 19,000 feet formating on a Boeing (the Stratocruiser airliner Captain Howard was commanding) for about 80 miles.

Another company's aircraft had flown over the same route 25 minutes earlier but had seen nothing.

Footnote: Mrs. A. Jack, headmistress of Gillock School, Caithness, and her 22 pupils were watching the eclipse yesterday when 12-year-old George Farquhar pointed to a swiftly-moving object near the sun and said, "It's a flying saucer." The others saw a silvery starlike object shoot up into the sky, then it disappeared.

8 Daily Sketch, Monday, September 20, 1954

GREY FOX FAILS TO FIND A FLYING SAUCER

uxury look for new cars

toring Correspondent

last year's austerity
n at next month's
W.
most customers
ed-down basic
screen wiper

d. One-
s with
ught.

But strangest seance hears of 'air cigars'

Daily Sketch Reporter

IN a blustering wind on the sun-drenched Wiltshire hills yesterday, 15 people took part in the strangest seance.

They were a section of the 70-strong group of archæologists, spiritualists and psychical students who journeyed from London to Avebury determined to make contact with flying saucers—and perhaps a creature or two from outer space.

When they arrived at the 6,000-year-old Neolithic stone temple on the hills skirting Avebury, they split up into two groups.

Most sauntered across the fields, led by 66-year-old archæologist Mr. John Foster-Forbes, whose Wigmore Hall lecture on flying saucers last June inspired the outing.

["It was felt that closer contact with space craft might be possible in open country," Mr. Forbes explained.]

The rest, led by 35-year-old student of the occult George King, of Clifton-gardens, N.W., headed for a hill dominating the countryside.

The party sat down in a ring. Mr. King assumed a cross - legged posture with hands on his knees.

He breathed hard several times—then went into a trance.

Soon his Indian guide voice, Grey Fox, was speaking, answering questions hesitantly but clearly.

Fair-headed Mrs. Christine Scott, a London secretary, asked: "What are the possibilities of making contact with space craft to-day?"

Grey Fox replied that owing to the diversity of opinion and the subconscious fear in the mind of some of those present, contact was not possible.

Bristol radio student, 33-year-old John Jones, asked the purpose of the cigar-shaped space ships said to have been seen recently in Rome.

The deep-throated voice answered that Rome is a centre of world religion.

MEDITATION . . .

The objects, it added, are the mother craft from which flying saucers are released.

As Grey Fox spoke the other group stood or sat in silent meditation, hoping that a saucer might manifest itself. But nothing happened.

Afterwards nine-year-old John House, the only child in the party, said: "I thought I was going to see a man from Mars or a couple of flying saucers. It was jolly disappointing."

But Mr. Forbes said: "It was well worth doing. Everybody felt spiritually uplifted."

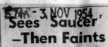

**Sees 'Saucer'
—Then Faints**

A woman fainted after claiming to have seen a luminous flying object land near the roadside at the village of Saptagram, in Assam, and take off within a few minutes, BUP cables.

Others, including the village policeman, said that they saw the object—shaped like a dinner plate with a bright tail.

Rain-dear

Sunday Dispatch

154th Year. No. 7,983.　　2½d.　　　NOVEMBER 7, 1954.　　　　　　　6　Radio P

Six Times In A Few Weeks—

STRANGE SIGHTS IN SKY BAFFLE WAR OFFICE

Picked Up On Many Radar Screens

By Sunday Dispatch Reporter

RADAR operators over a large part of Britain are watching their screens closely for the next appearance of a mystery formation in the sky which has the defence experts baffled.

Six times in the past few weeks a strange pattern of dots—the radar men call them "blips"—have been plotted on their screens, moving from East to West.

Look-Out In Africa

SOUTH AFRICANS were asked yesterday to report immediately any strange object seen in the sky. The South African Air Force said research was being conducted on a world scale.

Neither the War Office, which controls inland radar, nor the Air Ministry can say what these "blips" represent.

A careful check has shown that they have not been caused by any identifiable aircraft.

Two Miles Up

The most recent appearance was last Monday.

They appear from nowhere, usually about midday, flying at a height of 12,000ft. in an East-to-West direction.

First seen by a civilian radar scientist, they have since been plotted by all the radar sites in the area. They have been seen both on fine and on cloudy mornings and always in the same form.

'Z' Formation

This is how a War Office spokesman described them to me:

"We cannot say what they are.

"They first appear in a 'U,' or badly shaped hairpin, formation. After a time they converge into two parallel lines and then take up a 'Z' formation before disappearing.

"They are invisible to the human eye, but on the radar screen they appear as lots and lots of dots formed by between 40 and 50 echoes. They cover an area in the sky miles long and miles wide.

Area Kept Secret

"Every time they have been seen they followed the same pattern. It was always around midday.

"We have checked and found that our sets are not faulty. We are still maintaining a watch. All our sets in the area have picked them up."

I was told that the area over which these objects are seen must remain a secret.

What can they be?

When I spoke to one man who has seen them he told me he had been given very high-level orders to maintain the utmost secrecy.

'Worried'

"And even if I did know what they are, I am too worried myself to say anything," he explained.

At the Air Ministry I was told that there are many objects, such as meteorological balloons, experimental aircraft, carrier pigeons with metal rings on their legs, and even toy kites, which could form an image on a radar screen.

There are also many natural phenomena, such as electrical storms, lightning, and meteorites, which puzzle the operator.

Not Birds

But the radar specialists know all about those things, and none of them produces such regular and repeated patterns.

Even birds which fly in formation would not show on a radar screen.

Whatever the objects are, man-made, from space, or a freak of nature, they do exist.

And they have been seen on many different radar screens over a large area. On facts, they cannot be dismissed as coincidences.

UFO Headlines In America

Leased Wire
Associated Press

Roswell Daily Record

RECORD PHONES
Business Office 2288
News Department 2287

ROSWELL, NEW MEXICO, TUESDAY, JULY 8, 1947

Movies as Usual

GRAND

Levees broke and flood waters rolled into the town of Grand Tower, Ill., but while the manager of the movie theater sweeps out the water that has entered the lobby these youngsters are standing in line for tickets for the night's performance. (AP Wirephoto).

Some of Soviet Satellites May Attend Paris Meeting

Roswellians Have Differing Opinions On Flying Saucers

Claims Army Is Stacking Courts Martial

Indiana Senator Lays Protest Before Patterson

House Passes Tax Slash by Large Margin

Defeat Amendment By Demos to Remove Many from Rolls

American League Wins All-Star Game

RAAF Captures Flying Saucer On Ranch in Roswell Region

Security Council Paves Way to Talks On Arms Reductions

No Details of Flying Disk Are Revealed

Roswell Hardware Man and Wife Report Disk Seen

Ex-King Carol Weds Mme. Lupescu

Former King Carol of Romania and Mme. Elena Lupescu relax aboard the S. S. America bound for Cuba and Mexico in May, 1941. A member of his companion for 23 years in reign and exile were recently married at their hotel Copacabana Palace suite. (AP Wirephoto)

Miners and Operators Sign Highest Wage Pact in History

185

This article was published in the daily newspaper Time News, of Twin Falls, Idaho, USA, on August 15, 1947.

"Saucer" Seen Flying Down Snake Gorge

Heads Up, Folks! The Discs Are Flying Again

SIDE VIEW   BOTTOM VIEW   END VIEW

This is an artist's conception of the flying disc that A. C. Urie saw sweeping through Snake river canyon six miles west of Blue Lakes ranch. It seemed to be powered by jets emitting a fiery glow on both sides, and could well be the inspiration for something new in hats, such as a "flying saucer" creation. (Drawing by V. staff engraving)

Flying Saucer Reported Flashing Down Canyon At 1,000 Miles Per Hour; Two Others Are S

By JOHN BROSNAN

Just as Magic Valley and the nation were starting to let go of lampposts after reeling under a letter of flying saucer reports, two more Twin Falls county men received speculation on the mystery, with vivid descriptions of discs they saw.

From A. C. Urie, who operates the Auger Falls Trout farm, six miles west of Blue Lakes, came the most detailed account of any of the fast-flying objects the nation has yet produced.

The flying saucer Urie saw was skimming along through Snake river canyon at a height of about 75 feet at 1 p.m. Wednesday. At 9:30 a.m. the same day, L. W. Hawkhead, Twin Falls county commissioner and former county sheriff from Filer, also saw two circular objects moving along at a great speed near Salmon dam 40 miles southwest of Twin Falls.

Here is Urie's eye-witness description of the flying discs seen by him and his son, Keith, 8, and Billy, 10:

"I obtained a close-up view of the flying saucer as it passed by the trout farm at 1 p.m. Aug. 13 going down Snake river canyon at a height of about 75 feet from the canyon floor. I would estimate the speed at about 1,000 miles per hour."

Urie explained that the incident occurred while the two boys were coming across the river from the north side in a boat. He had become concerned about them playing there, and had gone toward the river to see if all right.

"I had a side view of about 300 feet And it level with the thing," continued. "Two of my b and Billy, were below also saw it at about angle. They both got a side view, and we ing at it from the south a

(Continued on Page 6, Co

Heads up, folks! The disks are flying again

Flying Saucer Reported Flashing Down Canyon At 100 Miles Per Hour

By John Brosnan

Just as Magic Valley and the nation were starting to let go of lampposts after reeling under a wave of flying saucer reports, two more Twin Falls county men revived speculation on the mystery with vivid descriptions of discs they saw.

From A. C. Urie, who operates the Auger Falls Trout Farm, six miles west of Blue Lakes Ranch to Snake River Canyon, came perhaps the most detailed account of any of the fast flying objects the nation has yet produced.

The flying saucer Urie saw was skimming along through Snake River Canyon at a height of about 75 feet at 1:00 pm Wednesday. At 9:30 am the same day, L. W. Hawkins, Twin Falls county commissioner and former county sheriff, also saw two circular objects soaring along at great speeds near Salmon Dam 40 miles south west of Twin Falls.

Here is Urie's eye-witness description of the flying discs, seen by him and his son, Keith, 8, and Billy,10:

"I obtained a close-up view of the flying saucer as it passed the trout farm at 1:00pm August 13th going down Snake River Canyon at a height of about 75 feet from the canyon floor. I would estimate the speed about a 1000 miles per hour."

Urie explained that the incident occurred while the two boys were coming across the river from the north side in a boat. He had become concerned about what was delaying them, and walked toward the river to see if they were all right.

"I had a side view of a distance of about 300 feet and almost was level with the thing," he continued. "Two of my boys, Keith and Billy were below me and they also saw it at about a right angle. They both a lower and a side view, and we and we were staring at it from the north side of the facing toward the north. The boys saw it coming from about a half a mile up the canyon, and we all lost site of it in less then a mile."

While the impression was still vivid in their minds, the three all got together and made rough sketches of what they had seen. These in turn were the basis of the artist conception of the strange affair by Vic Goertson of Twin Falls for the Times-News.

"The canyon floor underneath at that particular point was that it rode up and down over the hills and hollows at a speed indicating some type of control faster then the reflexes of man. It is my opinion it is guided by some type of instruments and must be powered by atomic energy, as it made very little noise-just a s-w-i-s-h when it passed by."

Urie described the size as about 20 feet long by 10 feet high and 10 feet wide, giving it an oblong shape. It might be described as looking at an inverted pie-plate, or broad-brimmed straw hat that been compressed from two sides.

Pressed for his opinion of just what it was, he said he was convinced there was something to this "flying saucer" situation. "I know a number of people who have also seen them, and I know now that they're not just imagining seeing these things or trying to get their names in the paper.
"I do know that it scared the boys, and made me feel uneasy," he added.
Tracing down a rumor that county commissioner Hawkins had seen an unusual object in the air on the same day as Urie's experience, the Times-News called him at his Filer home.

"Yes I did," he replied without hesitation. "I'll have to admit, I've been skeptical all along until I saw it with my own eyes. I can't say what it was, but I can say there is something in the air."

Hawkins related that while at Salmon dam Wednesday morning, a sound resembling that of an echo of a motor caused him to look upward, and there he saw to circular objects that reflected light. They were traveling at a great speed, and higher then most airplanes, according to Hawkins. Aside from this, he declined to add details, except to say, "there's something in the air."

His general description however, corresponded closely to hundreds of persons who reported seeing "flying saucers" after Kenneth Arnold, Boise business man, touched a deluge by telling of coming upon nine disc-like objects while he was flying in his private plane in Washington.

Thereafter the nation became increasingly "flying saucer" conscious creating a state of mind for four teen age Twin Falls boys to cause a mild sensation when they built a model flying disc and tossed in a local yard July 10th. This was subsequently revealed as a hoax, following the investigation by the army and the F.B.I.

There after the saucer reports tapered off into a few scattered incidents until the question was revived by this week's occurrences.

Speculation has ranged from mention that the discs could be army navy guided missile experiments, or they could be experiments by some foreign country, to something out of this world.

What ever they are, a lot of people have seen something.

Fiery Saucer Makes 'Passes' At Air Base

OAKLAND, Cal. (P)—The Oakland Tribune said a "disk-shaped object" roaring at an estimated speed of 1000 to 1300 miles an hour made five "passes" near Hamilton Air Force Base early yesterday.

The newspaper quoted three Air Force noncommissioned officers who said the "flying saucer," shooting blue flame and with a "roar like thunder" dived near a beacon just north of the field.

Hamilton field is 25 miles north of San Francisco.

Cpl. Roger G. Pryor, a control tower operator at the field, said he saw a blue flame shooting out as the saucer flashed by from the southwest and headed northeast.

The Tribune said Pryor's observation was verified by Staff Sgt. Ellis R. Rimer, another control tower operator, and Staff Sgt. Virgil Cappuro, member of the airways communications staff.

They said the saucer returned from the northwest and made another pass north of the field, then later made three more approaches.

The Tribune said the airmen described the object as circular, thick in the center and tapering to the sides. They used binoculars in following its course.

The men said the disk was accompanied by a roar like thunder and the blue flame looked like an acetylene torch. They described its approach altitude at between 2000 and 5000 feet.

The men said the sky was clear over Hamilton Field, although high fog prevailed elsewhere in the San Francisco Bay area.

Fiery Saucer Makes 'Passes' At Air Base

Oakland, Cal. (AP). -- The Oakland Tribune said a "disk shaped object" roaring at an estimated speed of 1000 to 1300 miles and hour made five "passes" near Hamilton Air Force Base early yesterday.

The newspaper quoted three Air Force noncommissioned officers who said the "flying saucer," shooting blue flames and with a "roar like thunder" dived near a beacon just north of the field.

Hamilton field is 25 miles north of San Francisco. Capt. Roger G. Pryor, a control tower operator at the field, said he saw a blue flame shooting out as the saucer flashed by from the southwest and headed northwest.

The Tribune said Pryor's observation was verified by Staff Sgt Ellis R. Rimer, another control tower operator, and Staff Sgt. Virgil Cappuro, member of the airways communications staff.

They said the saucer returned from the northwest and made another pass north of the field, then later made three more approaches.
The Tribune said the airmen described the object as circular, thick in the center and tapering to the sides. They used binoculars in following its course.

THE NEW YORK TIMES, JULY 9, 1947:

'Disk' Near Bomb Test Site Is Just a Weather Balloon

Copyright, 1947, by The New York Times Company.

NEW YORK, WEDNESDAY, JULY 9, 1947.

'Disk' Near Bomb Test Site Is Just a Weather Balloon

Warrant Officer Solves a Puzzle That Baffled His Superiors—'Flying Saucer' Tales Pour in From Round the World

By MURRAY SCHUMACH

Celestial crockery had the Army up in the air for several hours yesterday before an Army officer explained that what a colleague thought was "a flying disk" was nothing more than a battered Army weather balloon.

This denouement closed the New Mexico chapter in the "flying saucer" saga that already had contributions from forty-three other states in the Union as well as from Australia, England, South Africa, Mexico and Canada.

However, none of the previous or subsequent reports of strange heavenly bodies created as much confusion as the startling announcement from an Army lieutenant that "a flying disk" had been found on a ranch near Roswell, N. M., near the scene of atomic bomb tests. The officer, Lieut. Warren Haught, public information officer of the Roswell Army Air Field, made no bones about the discovery in his detailed report as carried by The Associated Press.

"The many rumors regarding the flying disk became a reality," his statement began. He told which Intelligence Office of what Bomb Group of the Eighth Air Force had passed "the flying disk" along "to higher headquarters."

Then phones began to buzz between Washington and New Mexico and the "disk" was well on the way to showing how the circle could be squared. One by one, as the rank of the investigating officer rose, the circle lost arcs and developed sides until it was roughly octagonal.

Within an hour after Lieutenant Haught had given new impetus to the "flying saucer" derby, his boss, Brig. Gen. Roger Ramey, had a somewhat different version of "the flying disk."

He said that while it was true it had been found on a ranch, no one had seen it in the air; it was "of flimsy construction," apparently

Continued on Page 10, Column 4

Warrant Officer Solves a Puzzle That Baffled his Superiors - 'Flying Saucer' Tales Pour in From Round the World

By MURRAY SCHUMACH

Celestial crockery had the Army up in the air for several hours yesterday before an Army officer explained that what a colleague thought was a "flying disk" was nothing more than a battered Army weather balloon. This denouement closed the New Mexico chapter in the "flying saucer" saga that already had contributions from forty-three other states in the Union as well as from Australia, England, South Africa, Mexico and Canada.

However, none of the previous or subsequent reports of strange heavenly bodies created as much confusion as the startling announcement from an Army lieutenant that "a flying disk" had been found on a ranch near Roswell, N.M., near the scene of atomic bomb tests. The officer, Lieut. Warren Haught [sic, Walter Haut], public information officer of the Roswell Army Air Field, made no bones about the discovery in his detailed report as carried by the Associated Press.

"The many rumors regarding the flying disks became a reality," his statement began. He told which Intelligence Officer of what Bomb Group of the Eighth Air Force had passed "the flying disk" along "to higher headquarters."

Then phones began to buzz between Washington and New Mexico and the "disk" was well on the way to showing how the circle could be squared. One by one, as the rank of the investigating officer rose, the circle lost arcs and developed sides until it was roughly octagonal.

Within an hour after Lieutenant Haught had given new impetus to the "flying saucer" derby, his boss, Brig. Gen. Roger Ramey, had a somewhat different version of "the flying disk."
He said that while it was true it had been found on a ranch, no one had seen it in the air; it was "of flimsy construction," apparently

Disk Near Bomb Test Site
Just a Weather Balloon

made "of some sort of tin foil." Subsequently, it was reported being flown to a research laboratory at Wright Field, Ohio.

In Washington, Lieut. Gen. Hoyt Vandenberg, Deputy Chief of the Army Air Force, hurried to his headquarters' press section. Atomic experts in the capital were certain that whatever had been found was not any of their doing, but no one seemed to know just how to dispose of the object. Finally, a lowly warrant officer, Irving Newton, a forecaster at the Fort Worth, Tex., weather station, solved the mystery. He said it was just part of a weather balloon, such as is used by eighty weather stations in the country to determine the velocity and direction of winds at high altitudes. Several hours before the New Mexico mystery had been solved, a Canadian meteorologist suggested the same answer in connection with rumors of "flying saucers" in Circleville, Ohio. This was soon after a couple in the Ohio town has jubilantly proclaimed their "capture" of a mysterious disk.

However, the Midwest was spurred in its hunt by offers of $3,000 rewards for "proof" that America was not succumbing to an epidemic of hallucinations. One of the first to put in a claim for the prize was an Iowa salesman, who produced a steel disk, nearly seven inches in diameter. He said he found it in his yard in the morning after hearing it "crash through the trees." According to The United Press, reporters thought the disk was playing truant from an ashtray.

Then there was the Nebraska farmer who added a bucolic touch to the story. He said the heavenly bodies were "flaming straw hats," that careened through the night, sometimes pausing for a rest.
Michigan's contributor for the day was a toolmaker from Pontiac. According to the United Press, he turned over to the newspaper a picture showing two circular objects against a black background. Examinations showed holes in the disks.

Also in the act was Wisconsin, where it has been reported that state's Civil Air Patrol would take off in search of "flying saucers."

'Disk' Found on New Mexico Ranch Is Just an Army Weather Balloon

Continued From Page 1

made "of some sort of tin foil." Subsequently, it was reported being flown to a research laboratory at Wright Field, Ohio.

In Washington, Lieut. Gen. Hoyt Vandenberg, Deputy Chief of the Army Air Forces, hurried to his headquarters' press section. Atomic experts in the capital were certain that whatever had been found was not any of their doing, but no one seemed to know just how to dispose of the object.

Finally, a lowly warrant officer, Irving Newton, a forecaster at the Fort Worth, Tex., weather station, solved the mystery. He said it was just a part of a weather balloon, such as is used by eighty weather stations in the country to determine velocity and direction of winds at high altitudes.

Several hours before the New Mexico mystery had been solved, a Canadian meteorologist suggested the same answer in connection with rumors of "flying saucers" in Circleville, Ohio. This was soon after a couple in the Ohio town had jubilantly proclaimed their "capture" of a mysterious disk.

However, the midwest was spurred in its hunt by offers of $3,000 rewards for "proof" that America was not succumbing to an epidemic of hallucinations. One of the first to put in a claim for the prize was an Iowa salesman, who produced a steel disk, nearly seven inches in diameter. He said he found it in his yard in the morning after hearing it "crash through the trees." According to The United Press, reporters thought the disk was playing truant from an ash tray.

Then there was the Nebraska farmer who added a bucolic touch to the story. He said the heavenly bodies were "flaming straw hats," that careened through the night, sometimes pausing for a rest.

Michigan's contributor for the day was a toolmaker from Pontiac. According to The United Press, he turned over to newspapers a picture showing two circular objects against a black background. Examination showed holes in the disks.

Also in the act was Wisconsin, where it was reported that on Monday 250 pilots of that state's Civil Air Patrol would take off in search of "flying saucers."

Proof that "flying saucers" were not indigenous to the United States and Canada began coming in late in the afternoon. Two residents of Johannesburg, South Africa, said, according to Reuters, that they not only saw the objects, but that these "traveled at tremendous speed in V-formation and disappeared in a cloud of smoke."

In England, a clergyman's wife, who said she had kept her discovery secret for fear of derision, finally came forth yesterday with a story about seeing "a dark ring, with clear-cut edges," that sped across the sky on Monday.

The Australian variations of "the flying saucer," though reported by six persons in Sydney, were quite ordinary. Observers said they were a bit brighter than the moon, seemed to prefer an altitude of about 10,000 feet and moved along rather briskly.

It may have been the weather, but the only allusion to "flying saucers" in New York City were a few skeptical remarks by Admiral William H. P. Blandy, commander in chief of the Atlantic Fleet. Said the admiral, in response to questions:

"I remain to be convinced there is any such thing. I am convinced that they are nothing the Army and Navy is concerned with. I am curious, like everybody else, to see what's behind it."

Proof that "flying saucers" were not indigenous to the United States and Canada began coming late in the afternoon. Two residents of Johannesburg, South Africa, said, according to Reuters, that they not only saw the objects, but that these "traveled at tremendous speed in V-formation and disappeared in a cloud of smoke."

In England, a clergyman's wife, who said she had kept her discovery secret for fear of derision, finally came forth yesterday with a story about seeing "a dark ring with clear-cut edges," that sped across the sky on Monday.

The Australian variations of "the flying saucers," though reported by six persons in Sidney, were quite ordinary. Observers said they were a bit brighter than the moon, seemed to prefer an altitude of about 10,000 feet and moved along rather briskly.

It may have been the weather, but the only allusion to "flying saucers" in New York City, were a few skeptical remarks by Admiral William H.P. Blandy, commander in chief of the Atlantic Fleet. Said the admiral, in response to questions:

"I remain to be convinced there is any such thing. I am convinced that they are nothing the Army of Navy is concerned with. I am curious, like everybody else, to see what's behind it."

Floating Mystery Ball Is New Nazi Air Weapon

SUPREME HEADQUARTERS, Allied Expeditionary Force.

A new German weapon has made its appearance on the western air front. It was disclosed today.

Airmen of the American Air Force report that they are encountering silver colored spheres in the air over German territory. The spheres are encountered either singly or in clusters. Sometimes they are semi-translucent.

SUPREME HEADQUARTERS Dec. 13 (Reuters)

- The Germans have produced a "secret" weapon in keeping with the Christmas season.

The new device, apparently an air defense weapon resembles the huge glass balls that adorn Christmas trees. There was no information available as to what holds them up like stars in the sky, what is in them or what their purpose is supposed to be.

Floating Mystery Ball Is New Nazi Air Weapon

SUPREME HEADQUARTERS, Allied Expeditionary Force, Dec. 13—A new German weapon has made its appearance on the western air front, it was disclosed today.

Airmen of the American Air Force report that they are encountering silver colored spheres in the air over German territory. The spheres are encountered either singly or in clusters. Sometimes they are semi-translucent.

SUPREME HEADQUARTERS, Dec. 13 (Reuter)—The Germans have produced a "secret" weapon in keeping with the Christmas season.

The new device, apparently an air defense weapon, resembles the huge glass balls that adorn Christmas trees.

There was no information available as to what holds them up like stars in the sky, what is in them, or what their purpose is supposed to be.

ADMITAL DUFEK DOES NOT THINK THE EXISTENCE OF FLYING SAUCERS CAN BE DISCOUNTED:

Published in the daily newspaper: The New York Times, USA, on March 12, 1959.

"SAUCERS' POSSIBLE, ADMIRAL DECLARES

WELLINGTON, New Zealand, March 11 (Reuters)—Rear Admiral George Dufek said today that he did not think the existence of flying saucers could be discounted.

"I think it is very stupid for human beings to think no one else in the universe is as intelligent as we are," he said.

Admiral Dufek, retiring as commander of the United States research and exploration program in the Antarctic, is returning home.

He said it was not beyond possibility that meteors that exploded in the earth's atmosphere were "saucers driven from Venus or other planets by intelligent creatures."

"SAUCERS" POSSIBLE, ADMIRAL DECLARES

WELLINGTON. New Zealand, March 11 (Reuters) -- Rear Admiral George Dufek said today that he did not think the existence of flying saucers could be discounted.

"I think it is very stupid for human beings to think no one else in the universe is as intelligent as we are" he said.

Admiral Dufek, retiring as commander of the United States research and exploration program in the Antarctic is returning home.

He said it was not beyond possibility that meteors that exploded in the Earth's atmosphere were saucers driven from Venus or other planets by intelligent creatures."

THE NEW YORK TIMES,1959:

This article was published in the newspaper: The New York Times, USA, on February 26, 1959.

PILOT REPORTS SAUCERS

Says Airliner Passengers and Crew Saw Lights

DETROIT, Feb. 25 (AP) — The pilot of an American Airlines DC-6 passenger plane said today that three mysterious objects that looked like shining saucers appeared to accompany the plane for forty-five minutes last night on its nonstop flight from Newark, N. J., to Detroit.

Capt. Peter Killian of Syosset, L. I., said other members of the crew and the thirty-five passengers also saw the flying objects. The plane left Newark at 7:10 P. M.

Captain Killian and Co-pilot John Dee of Nyack, N. Y., said they lost the three objects in the haze.

Captain Killian said he radioed two other American Airlines planes flying in the vicinity of his ship to make sure "I wasn't seeing lightning bugs in the cockpit." He said both other captains radioed back that they had seen the flying objects too.

PILOT REPORTS SAUCERS

Says Airliner Passengers and Crew Saw Lights

DETROIT, Feb. 25 (AP) -- The pilot of an American Airlines DC-6 passenger plane said today that three mysterious object that looked like shining saucers appeared to accompany the plane for forty-five minutes last night on its nonstop flight from Newark, N.J., to Detroit.
Capt. Peter Killian of Syosset, L.I., said other members of the crew and the thirty-five passengers also saw the flying objects. The plane left Newark at 7:10 P.M.
Captain Killian and Co-pilot John Dee of Nyacek, N.Y., said they lost the three objects in the haze.
Captain Killian said he radioed two other American Airlines planes flying in the vicinity of his ship to make sure "I wasn't seeing lightning bugs in the cockpit." He said both other captains radioed back that they had seen the flying objects too.

UFOs AT WHITE SANDS MISSILE TEST RANGE, USA, 1957:

This article was published in the daily newspaper: The Washington Post, USA, page 4, on November 5, 1957.

Patrols Report Sighting 'Object' at White Sands

WHITE SANDS PROVING GROUND, N. M., Nov. 4 (AP) — The White Sands Proving Ground announced today that a huge, oval object "nearly as bright as the sun" was spotted Sunday hovering near bunkers used in the first atomic bomb explosion.

The sightings were made 17 hours apart by two different military police patrols on this southern New Mexico missile testing-range. The first atomic bomb was touched off on the northern edge of the area July 16, 1945.

The commanding officer of the MPs said none of the men had heard radio reports or seen newspaper accounts of similar sightings in Texas.

Both sightings were in the area of abandoned bunkers used by technicians who observed the world's first atomic explosion. The bunkers are of until it was about 50 yards above the A-bomb bunkers, when it went out.

A few minutes later "the object became real bright, like the sun, then fell in an angle to the ground and went out," the patrol reported.

Penney said he had accompanied some of the MPs to the site today but found no physical evidence of the object's visit.

Neither jeep patrol had motor trouble. Some drivers who saw similar phenomena in Texas reported engine trouble.

Officials at White Sands said the phenomena had nothing to do with any activity of the base.

Patrols Report Sighting 'Object' at White Sands

WHITE SANDS PROVING GROUND, N.M., Nov. 4

The White Sands Proving Ground announced today that a huge, oval object "nearly as bright as the sun" was spotted Sunday hovering near bunkers used in the first atomic bomb explosion.

The sightings were made 17 hours apart by two different military police patrols on this southern New Mexico missile testing range. The first atomic bomb was touched off on the northern edge of the area July 16, 1945.
The commanding officer of the MPs said some of the men heard radio reports or seen newspaper accounts of saucer sightings in Texas.
Both sightings were in the area of abandoned bunkers used by technicians who observed the world's first atomic explosion.

Until it was about 50 yards above the A-bomb bunkers, when it went out. A few minutes later, "the object became real bright, like the sun, then fell in an angle to the ground and went out," the patrol reported.
Penney said he had accompanied some of his MPs to the site today but found no physical evidence of the object's visit.
Neither jeep patrol had motor trouble. Some drivers who saw similar phenomena in Texas reported engine trouble.
Officials at White Sands said the phenomena had nothing to do with any activity of the base.

A Windmill Demolishes It.

Aurora, Wise Co., Tex., April 17.—(To The News.)—About 6 o'clock this morning the early risers of Aurora were astonished at the sudden appearance of the airship which has been sailing through the country.

It was traveling due north, and much nearer the earth than ever before. Evidently some of the machinery was out of order, for it was making a speed of only ten or twelve miles an hour and gradually settling toward the earth. It sailed directly over the public square, and when it reached the north part of town collided with the tower of Judge Proctor's windmill and went to pieces with a terrific explosion, scattering debris over several acres of ground, wrecking the windmill and water tank and destroying the judge's flower garden.

The pilot of the ship is supposed to have been the only one on board, and while his remains are badly disfigured, enough of the original has been picked up to show that he was not an inhabitant of this world.

Mr. T. J. Weems, the United States signal service officer at this place and an authority on astronomy, gives it as his opinion that he was a native of the planet Mars.

Papers found on his person—evidently the record of his travels—are written in some unknown hieroglyphics, and can not be deciphered.

The ship was too badly wrecked to form any conclusion as to its construction or motive power. It was built of an unknown metal, resembling somewhat a mixture of aluminum and silver, and it must have weighed several tons.

The town is full of people to-day who are viewing the wreck and gathering specimens of the strange metal from the debris. The pilot's funeral will take place at noon to-morrow.   S. E. HAYDON.

About 6 o'clock this morning the early risers of Aurora were astonished at the sudden appearance of the airship, which has been sailing around the country.

It was traveling due north and much nearer the earth than before. Evidently some of the machinery was out of order, for it was making a speed of only ten or twelve miles an hour, and gradually settling toward the earth. It sailed over the public square and when it reached the north part of town it collided with the tower of Judge Proctor's windmill and went into pieces with a terrific explosion, scattering debris over several acres of ground, wrecking the windmill and water tank and destroying the judge's flower garden. The pilot of the ship is supposed to have been the only one aboard and, while his remains were badly disfigured, enough of the original has been picked up to show that he was not an inhabitant of this world.

Mr. T.J. Weems, the U.S. Army Signal Service officer at this place and an authority on astronomy gives it as his opinion that the pilot was a native of the planet Mars. Papers found on his person -- evidently the records of his travels -- are written in some unknown hieroglyphics and cannot be deciphered.

This ship was too badly wrecked to form any conclusion as to its construction or motive power. It was built of an unknown metal, resembling somewhat a mixture of aluminum and silver, and it must have weighed several tons. The town is today full of people who are viewing the wreckage and gathering specimens of strange metal from the debris. The pilot's funeral will take place tomorrow.

UFOs in Latin America

THE TRINDAD ISLAND CASE, 1958:

Published in the daily newspaper Diario de Sao Paulo, Brazil, on February 22, 1958.

Diario de S.Paulo

Diretor: ALVIMAR CALDAS

2 SECÇÕES
EDIÇÃO DE
18 PAGINAS

ANO XXX | Telefone: 34-4181 (Rêde interna) End. Telegr.: { Redação: MATUTINO { Administr.: DIARPAULO | S. PAULO, SABADO, 22 DE FEVEREIRO DE 1958 | Redação e Administração: RUA SETE DE ABRIL, 230 Caixa Postal 3006 | N. 8.841

DEPOIMENTO DO COMANDANTE PAULO MOREIRA DA SILVA

"NÃO FOI BALÃO SONDA, NEM TELEGUIADO, O OBJETO SURGIDO NA ILHA DA TRINDADE"

Estão sendo feitos estudos sigilosos pela Marinha — Equipe de tecnicos do Serviço Aerofotogrametrico da "Cruzeiro do Sul" assinou um laudo declarando ser normal o negattivo do disco voador, não tendo sido constatada qualquer fraude — Anexado o laudo ao relatorio que será enviado ao Conselho de Segurança Nacional   (Leia na 3.ª pagina)

FLAGRANTE DO "DISCO VOADOR" — Com o testemunho de toda a tripulação do navio-escola Almirante Saldanha, o fotógrafo Almiro Baraúna conseguiu quatro fotografias do "disco-voador", quando sobrevoou a Ilha da Trindade. Na foto, não obstante a super-exposição, percebe-se o estranho engenho nas suas evoluções em torno do pico Desejado. (Foto da Meridional)

STATEMENT OF COMMANDANT PAULO MOREIRA DA SILVA

"IT WAS NOT A BALLOON, NOR SOMETHING OPERATED BY REMOTE CONTROL, THE OBJECT THAT APPEARED IN THE ISLAND OF TRINDAD"

Careful studies have been made for the Navy - The team of technicians of the Aerophotogrametric Service of "Cruzeiro do Sol" signed a declaration that they found the negative of the flying saucer to be normal, with no evidence of any fraud - the study and the conclusion will be sent to the National Security Council.

PROOF OF THE "FLYING SAUCER"

With the testimony of all the crew of the school-ship Admiral Saldanha, the photographer Almiro Barauna obtained four photographs of the "flying saucer," when it flew above the island of Trinidad. In the photo, not showing double exposure, a strange device can be seen evolving around Desejado Peak.

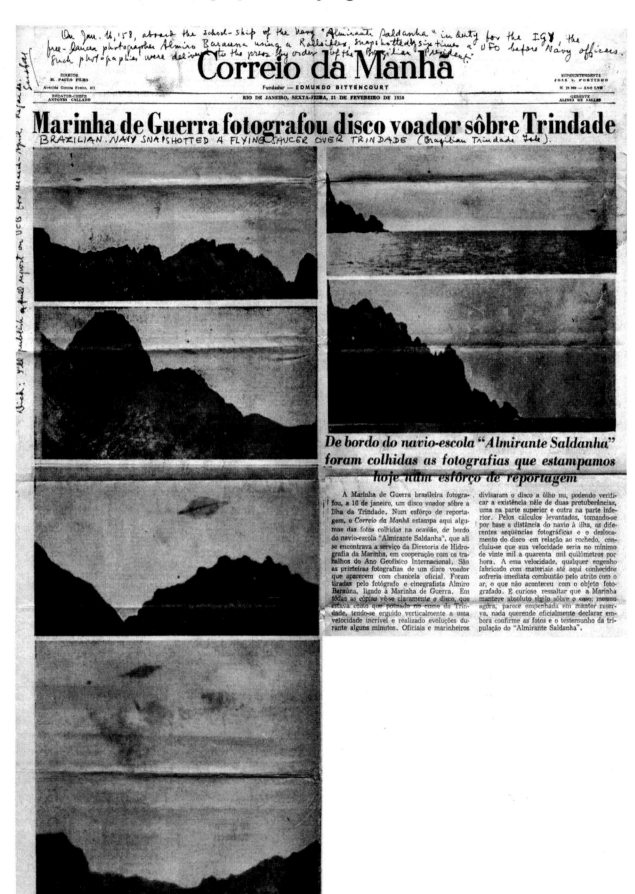

On Jan. 16, '58, aboard the school-ship of the Navy "Almirante Saldanha" in duty for the IGY, the free-lancer photographer Almiro Baraúna using a Rolleiflex, snapshotted six times a UFO before Navy officers. Such photographies were delivered to the press by order of the Brazilian President.

Note: YES published a full report on UCB trs Minas - April similar.

Correio da Manhã

Fundador — EDMUNDO BITTENCOURT

RIO DE JANEIRO, SEXTA-FEIRA, 21 DE FEVEREIRO DE 1958

Marinha de Guerra fotografou disco voador sôbre Trindade

BRAZILIAN NAVY SNAPSHOTTED A FLYING SAUCER OVER TRINDADE (Brazilian Trinidade Isle).

De bordo do navio-escola "Almirante Saldanha" foram colhidas as fotografias que estampamos hoje num esfôrço de reportagem

A Marinha de Guerra brasileira fotografou, a 16 de janeiro, um disco voador sôbre a Ilha da Trindade. Num esfôrço de reportagem, o Correio da Manhã estampa aqui algumas das fotos colhidas na ocasião, de bordo do navio-escola "Almirante Saldanha", que ali se encontrava a serviço da Diretoria de Hidrografia da Marinha, em cooperação com os trabalhos do Ano Geofísico Internacional. São as primeiras fotografias de um disco voador que aparecem com chancela oficial. Foram tiradas pelo fotógrafo e cinegrafista Almiro Baraúna, ligado à Marinha de Guerra. Em tôdas as cópias vê-se claramente o disco, que estava certo que pousado no cume da Trindade, tendo-se erguido verticalmente a uma velocidade incrível e realizado evoluções durante alguns minutos. Oficiais e marinheiros divisaram o disco a ôlho nu, podendo verificar a existência nêle de duas protuberâncias, uma na parte superior e outra na parte inferior. Pelos cálculos levantados, tomando-se por base a distância do navio à ilha, as diferentes sequências fotográficas e o deslocamento do disco em relação ao rochedo, concluiu-se que sua velocidade seria no mínimo de vinte mil a quarenta mil quilômetros por hora. A essa velocidade, qualquer engenho fabricado com materiais até aqui conhecidos sofreria imediata combustão pelo atrito com o ar, o que não aconteceu com o objeto fotografado. É curioso ressaltar que a Marinha manteve absoluto sigilo sôbre o caso, mesmo agora, parece empenhada em manter reserva, nada querendo oficialmente declarar embora confirme as fotos e o testemunho da tripulação do "Almirante Saldanha".

The Military Navy photographed a flying disc over Trinidad

The photographs that we print today in a news article effort have been collected on board of the shoal-ship "Admiral Saldanda."

On the January 16, the Brazilian War Navy photographed a flying disc on the Island of Trinidad. In a news article effort, *Correio da Manhã* is printing here some of the photos harvested in the occasion, on board of the school-ship "Admiral Saldanda," who was on duty for the Direction of the Hydrography of the Navy there, in cooperation with the works of the Internation Geophysical Year. They are the first photographs of a flying disc that appear with official seal. The photographs were taken by cameraman Almiro Baraúna, who was under contract with the Military Navy.

In all the copies, the disc is seen clearly, as it settled on the top of Trinidad, having elevated itself at an incredible speed and having carried out maneuvers during some minutes. Officers and sailors have distinguished the disk with their naked eyes, and were able to verify the existence of two protuberances on it, one on the superior part and another one in the bottom part.

As for the calculations, which were done using the distance between the ship and the island, the different photographic sequences and the displacement of the disc in relation to the rocks, it was concluded that its speed would be at the very least of twenty thousand to forty thousand kilometers per hour.

At this speed, any device manufactured with materials known here so far would suffer immediate combustion due to the friction with the air, something that did not happen to the photographed object. It is strange to note that the Navy kept absolute secrecy on the case; exactly now, they seem pledged in keeping silent, refusing to state anything officially and refusing to even confirm the photos and the testimonies of the crew of the "Admiral Saldanda

UFOs In France

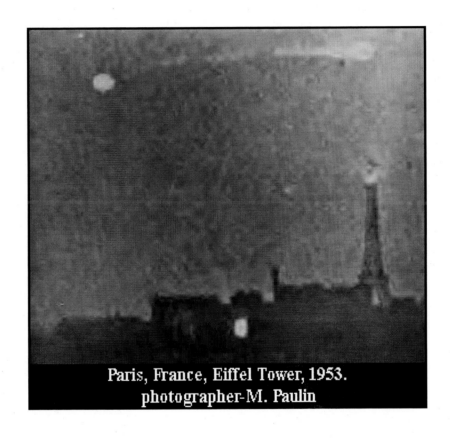

Paris, France, Eiffel Tower, 1953.
photographer-M. Paulin

L'AFFAIRE D'ORLY DANS LA PRESSE MONDIALE, 1956:

This article was published in the daily newspaper: The Sunday Mirror, England, on March 11, 1956.

Paris Radar Tracks Flying 'Object'

PARIS, France (UP).—An unidentified flying object, described as twice as large as a normal commercial airliner, has been tracked on radar screens here, Orly Airport officials reported recently.

Traveling at an estimated 1,500 miles an hour, the object appeared over the Paris region in the late evening, and seemed to hover a few moments before disappearing at high speed.

The object was also sighted by an Air France pilot flying to London who reported seeing an intermittent red flame in the sky above him.

Paris Radar Tracks Flying 'Object'

PARIS, France (UP). -- An unidentified flying object, described as twice as large as a normal commercial airliner, has been tracked on radar screens here, Orly Airport officials reported recently.

Traveling at an estimated 1.500 miles an hour, the object appeared over the Paris region in the late evening, and seemed to hover a few moments before disappearing at high speed. The object was also sighted by an Air France pilot flying to London who reported seeing an intermittent red flame in the sky above him.

AIR MYSTERY IN PARIS

Unidentified Object, on Radar, Flew at 1,500 M.P.H.

Special to The New York Times

PARIS, Feb. 19—Aviation circles were speculating today on the identity of a strange object, alternately hovering and flying at speeds in excess of 1,500 miles an hour, picked up Friday night by radar operators at Orly International Airport.

The object made a "blip" on the radar screen approximately twice as large as that of the average airliner, according to technicians. It appeared to be at an altitude of about 5,000 feet and was seen to follow aircraft taking off or coming in for a landing at Orly.

A radio beacon station southwest of Paris also reported the object but neither the radar at Le Bourget Airport nor the Paris Observatory reported contact. A spokesman at the observatory suggested that it might have been a United States weather balloon launched in Germany and blown west by the "jet stream" air currents.

AIR MYSTERY IN PARIS

Unidentified Object, on Radar
Flew at 1,500 M.P.H

PARIS, Feb. 19 -- Aviation circles were speculating today on the identity of a strange object alternately hovering and flying at speeds in excess of 1,500 miles an hour, picked up Friday night by radar operators at Orly International Airport.

The object made a "blip on the radar screen approximately twice as large as that of the average airliner, according to the technicians. It appeared to be at an altitude of 5,000 feet and was seen to follow aircraft taking off or coming in for a landing at Orly.

A radio beacon station southwest of Paris also reported the object but neither the radar at Le Bourget Airport nor the Paris Observatory reported contact. A spokesman at the observatory suggested that it might have been a United States weather balloon launched in Germany and blown west by the "jet stream" air current.

UFO SEEN AND PHOTOGRAPHED ABOVE SEDAN, FRANCE, 1954:

Published in the daily newspaper: L'Ardennais, France, on October 19, 1954.

Deux documents exceptionnels :

LA "SOUCOUPE"

qui a plané samedi soir

sur SEDAN

a été photographiée

Ces deux photos ont été prises avec un « Sem Flex » 6×6, ouverture 3.5 ; temps de pose : 1 seconde pour l'une et 2 secondes pour l'autre ; pellicule « Per Omnia » 23.

La tache plus petite est la lune qui atteignait hier soir son deuxième quartier. Le disque lumineux nettement plus gros que la lune a impressionné fortement la pellicule.

Sur les agrandissements on distingue nettement un noyau central obscur au milieu du disque lumineux.

Une photo avait été prise par un amateur du côté du « Moulin à Vent ». Malheureusement, le temps de pose trop court : 1/40e de seconde, n'a rien donné au développement.

NOUS avons signalé hier que plusieurs personne ont aperçu dans la soirée de samedi une tache lumineuse de forme ronde, au-dessus de la région de Sedan. Nous n'avons pas voulu donner une importance exagérée à cette nouvelle, à un moment où les esprits sont influencés par les récits concernant d'étranges apparitions.

Mais le fait que cette tache lumineuse a pu être fixée sur la pellicule nous oblige à sortir de notre réserve.

Les documents que nous publions sont absolument authentiques et il ne s'agit nullement d'un montage photo. Ces deux photos ont été prises samedi vers 22 h. (les témoins dans leur émotion ont oublié l'heure exacte) d'une fenêtre d'un immeuble de la rue Jean-Jaurès à Sedan. Deux témoins étaient à côté de l'opérateur. C'est ce dernier qui, voulant prendre l'air à la fenêtre de sa chambre, aperçut le premier cette lueur anormale qui a intrigué d'autres témoins, en des endroits différents. Deux gardiens de la paix, en faction au Palais des Sports, ont aperçu un disque lumineux, vers 21 h. 30. Plusieurs jeunes gens, venant de la direction de Vrigne l'ont aperçu également. Lorsque les photos que nous publions ont été prises, celui qui en est l'auteur ignorait tout des constatations faites par ailleurs.

THE "SAUCER" which hovered Saturday evening above SEDAN has been photographed

We announced yesterday that several people saw a luminous spot of round form, above the area of Sedan, Saturday in the evening. We did not want to give an exaggerated importance to this news, at a time when minds are influenced by the accounts related to strange appearances. But the fact that this luminous spot could be fixed on photographic film obliges us to come out of our reserve.

The documents, which we publish, are absolutely authentic and they are by no means about trick photographs. These two photographs were taken Saturday at about 10 P.M. (the witnesses, in their emotion forgot the exact time) from a window of a building of Jean-Jaurès street in Sedan. Two witnesses were with the photographer. It is this latter who, wanting to take some air at the window of his room, was the first to see this abnormal gleam which intrigued other witnesses, in different places.

Two policemen, in faction at the Sports Stadium, saw a luminous disc, at about 09:30 P.M.. Several young people, coming from the direction of Vrigne also saw it. When the photographs, which we publish, were taken, their author was unaware of any of the other observations.

These two photographs were taken with a "Sem Flex" exposure time: 1 second for the first and 2 seconds for the other; "Per Omnia" 23 filmstrip. The smaller spot is the moon, which reached its second district yesterday evening.

Unfortunately, the exposure time was too short: 1/100th of a second, it did not provide anything of value when developed.

Published in the regional daily newspaper: Nice-Matin, France, on Saturday, October 16.

Et voici les "soucoupes volantes" dans le ciel du Midi !...

L'une d'elles se serait posée jeudi soir à la tombée de la nuit, sur la route de BIOT et aurait décollé à l'approche d'un cycliste...

Presque à la même heure, un engin semblable (le même sans doute) a été aperçu au-dessus de Grasse, Saint-Raphaël, Opio, Gourdon Bar-sur-Loup et Roquebrune-Cap-Martin

Sur une planche à dessin improvisée, José Casella trace la forme de la soucoupe posée au sol (dessin du bas), sa forme vue de dessus (au centre) et sa trajectoire de décollage qu'il montre du doigt.
(Photo Biondo-Bonhomme).

Voici que les « soucoupes » font leur apparition dans notre ciel, s'il faut en croire du moins les témoignages très nombreux — et parfois contradictoires — qu'on lira ci-dessous.

Nous nous bornerons à enregistrer, en nous gardant de conclure dans le débat « brûlant » qui oppose les « pro-soucoupes » et les « anti-soucoupes ».

« NEZ A NEZ » AVEC UNE SOUCOUPE POSÉE SUR LA ROUTE DE BIOT

Hier matin, à Biot, tout le village, sur la place des Arcades, ne parlait que soucoupes et apparitions et, déjà, les deux clans, désormais classiques en pareil cas, se formaient.

Or, dans le courant de l'après-midi, notre correspondant d'Antibes a pu découvrir, grâce à la complicité de son chef de service, M. Courbey, receveur municipal d'Antibes, le témoin oculaire de cette aventure qui troubla depuis jeudi soir la quiétude du village biotois et de ses habitants.

Car si à Biot les témoins sont nombreux à avoir vu évoluer un engin dans les airs, vers 18 h. 15, un seul eut la chance de le voir au moment du « décollage », alors qu'il rentrait de son travail.

José Casella est un garçon de 19 ans, natif de Biot, et y demeurant avec ses parents, rue de la Passonnerie, son père travaillant à la Compagnie des Eaux de la ville. Tous les jours, matin et soir, il effectue, par la route d'An-

tibes à Biot, le trajet aller et retour, afin de se rendre à son travail, à la Recette municipale, boulevard d'Aguillon, à Antibes.

L'événement n'a pas troublé le service de comptabilité et lorsque nous entrâmes, hier après-midi, dans les locaux de la recette, chacun s'occupait à son travail quotidien. José Casella, lui-même, lorsque nous donnâmes le but de notre visite, ne leva même pas la tête. Cependant, après avoir refusé de donner son nom, refusé même la moindre indication, de crainte de « rumeurs désobligeantes de la part de ses concitoyens », nous l'amenâmes à quelques confidences, puis à une description complète de l'engin, ou, tout au moins, de ce qu'il avait eu le temps de voir.

« Il était donc 18 h. 15, je roulais vers le village et allais prendre le virage de la route de Biot, au chemin Neuf, longeant le mur clôturant l'ancienne propriété du sculpteur Bouraine. Soudain, je me trouvais face à face avec une masse de forme ovale, couleur aluminium... et instinctivement comme je l'aurais fait devant n'importe quel autre objet ou véhicule me barrant la route, je freinai.

« A cet instant précis, sans un bruit, mais à une rapidité indéfinissable, la soucoupe — car il fallait bien le convenir, je venais d'en voir une, moi qui n'y croyais pas — la soucoupe s'éleva verticalement, puis disparut dans le ciel.

« Je me trouvais alors à six mètres et j'ai parfaitement distingué la forme circulaire de l'objet, dont la surface supérieure était légèrement renflée, tandis que la partie inférieure reposant sur le sol était de la forme d'une demi-sphère, je ne vis rien d'autre, aucune vie, aucune aspérité, aucun hublot, l'objet étant totalement lisse et brillant sous les derniers rayons lumineux.

« D'après la largeur de la route, l'engin pouvait avoir 5 à 6 mètres de diamètre et un peu plus d'un mètre de hauteur.

« Après son départ, aucune trace ne put être relevée sur la route et lorsque je revins du village seul aurait pu laisser supposer qu'une soucoupe volante s'était posée là.

...and here are the "flying saucers" in the sky of Midi!...

One of them is said to have landed Thursday at the fall of night, on the road to BIOT and is said to have taken off at the approach of a cyclist...

Almost at the same time, a similar machine (the same one undoubtedly) was seen above Grasse, Saint Raphael, Opio, Gourdon, Bar-sur-Loup and Roquebrune-Cape-Martin.

On an improvised drawing board, José Cassella traces the shape of the saucer landed on the ground (drawing on the bottom), its shape seen from underneath (in the center) and its takeoff trajectory which he is pointing at. (Photo Biondo-Catch)

Now the "saucers" make their appearance in our sky, if one believes the very large number of testimonies - sometimes contradictory - about them that one can read below.

We will restrict ourselves to record them, we will not conclude in the "hot" debate which oppose the "pro-saucers" and the "anti-saucers."

"FACE TO FACE"
WITH A LANDED SAUCER
ON THE ROAD TO BIOT

Yesterday morning, in Biot on the place of the arcades, all the village spoke only saucers and appearances and, already, the two clans, now inevitable in such a case, were formed.

Indeed, in the current of the afternoon, our correspondent in Antibes had discovered, thanks to the complicity of his chief of service, Mr. Courbey, tax collector of Antibes, the eyewitness of this adventure who disturbed since Thursday evening the quietness of the village of Biot and its inhabitants.

Because, if in Biot the witnesses are numerous, who have seen a craft evolving in the air, at 06:15 P.M., only one had the chance to see it at the time of the "takeoff" whereas he was returning from work.

José Cassella is a 19 year old boy, native of Biot and remaining there with his parents, in street of the poissonerie, his father working with the Water-company of the city. Every day, morning and evening, he goes down the road from Antibes to Biot to go to his work in place, at the Town Receipt, boulevard of Aguillon in Antibes.

The event did not disturb the accounting department and when we entered in the buildings of the receipt yesterday afternoon, everyone was busy with his daily work. As for as of José Cassella, when we indicated the purpose of our visit, he did not even raise his head. However, after having refused to utter his name, refused even the least indication, of fear of "ridiculous rumors" on behalf of his fellow-citizens, we led him to some confidences, then to a complete description of the craft, or, at least, of what it had had the time to see.

"So it was thus 06:15 P.M. I drove towards the village and I was going to take the turn of the road of Biot, at the chemin Neuf ["New driveway"], skirting thewall enclosing the old property of the sculptor Bourayne. Suddenly, I was face to face with an oval shaped mass, of aluminum color... and instinctively, as I would have done in front of any other object or vehicle barring me the road, I slowed down."

"A this precise moment, without a noise, but with an indefinable speed, the saucer - for I had to admit it, what I had just seen is one of those - the saucer rose vertically, then disappeared in the sky."

"I was then within six meters and I perfectly distinguished the circular shape of the object, of which the higher part was slightly illuminated while the lower part resting on the ground was the shape of a half-sphere. I did not see anything else, no asperity, no porthole, the object was completely smooth and shone under the last luminous rays."

"Based on the width of the road, the machine may have had 5 to 6 meters in diameter and a little more than a one meter height."
"After its departure, no trace could be found on the road and when I returned from the village a little later nothing could let anyone find out that a flying saucer had landed there."

Published in the daily newspaper: L'Yonne Républicaine, France,
September 28, 1954.

UNE SOUCOUPE VOLANTE
s'est posée dans l'Yonne

A Diges, deux personnes ont aperçu quelques instants, un mystérieux engin et son pilote dans une clairière

Seules preuves : deux traces dans la rosée du matin

(De nos envoyés spéciaux)

Notre ciel icaunais a déjà eu l'avantage d'être zébré de diverses apparitions diurnes ou nocturnes. Jamais encore un de ces engins mystérieux ne s'était posé sur le sol de notre département.

Il semble bien que ce soit chose accomplie désormais, puisque deux personnes de Diges ont aperçu, vendredi matin, à 9 heures environ, un engin de couleur foncée et terne, tapi à l'angle d'une clairière. Sans bruit, l'appareil a disparu avec rapidité et discrétion.

HALLUCINATION OU VERITE ?

Bien que nous ayions accueilli cette information avec beaucoup de circonspection, nous avons été obligé de nous rendre à l'évidence. Un engin inconnu de la technique volante moderne répandue sur notre planète s'est posé, vendredi matin, à Diges.

Reprenons les déclarations recueillies. Vous suivrez plus facilement la logique de notre enquête.

Notre collaborateur Jean-Claude CHARLET a reconstitué pour vous l'image vue par Mme veuve GEOFFROY et Mlle FIN.   (Cliché L'Yonne Républicaine).

A FLYING SAUCER LANDED IN THE YONNE

In Diges, two people have glanced for a moment, on a mysterious craft and its pilot
in a clearing
Only evidence: two traces in the morning dew

Our sky already had the privilege of being streaked by various diurnal or nocturnal appearances. None of these craft had landed on the ground of our department.

It does seem that this took place now, since two people of Diges saw a craft of dark and dull color, hidden in the angle of a clearing on Friday morning, at 9 hours approximately. Without noise, the apparatus disappeared with speed and discretion.

HALLUCINATION OR TRUTH?

Although we had received this information with much circumspection, we were obliged to face the obvious fact. An unknown machine, different from modern flying technique of our planet was landed, Friday morning, in Diges.

Let us take again the collected statements. You will more easily follow the logic of our investigation.

Remaining article not available.

Published in the daily newspaper: The Newark Star-Ledger, New York, USA, on September 24, 1954.

THE RAGE IN FRANCE

'Saucer' buzzes Napoleon tomb

PARIS ⁗—To be anybody at all in France these days you practically have to have seen a flying saucer, preferably one of the iridescent ones that change color like a juke box.

Being able to down gallons of champagne, or owning a slightly rundown chateau or even attending an opening at the theater hardly counts.

Flying saucers, and now flying cigars, are "sighted" practically daily by witnesses who are upstanding citizens, models of probity and sobriety and pillars of the community.

Latest to report the phenomena was movie star Michel Morgan who said she sighted a luminous disc hovering over the dome of Les Invalides, where Napoleon is buried. *1784*

* * *

"AN OLD man near me also saw it," Miss Morgan said. "But he ran away."

Rainbow flying saucers are the rage in central France where draughtsman Jean Besse said he watched one Friday night through powerful binoculars. He said it changed color three times in a few seconds. *9-17-54 1754*

At Le Puy, west of here, hotel owner Marcel Maillet said he saw an iridescent saucer changing color like a juke box. *#1734*

Louis Moll, a railway crossing guard at Oberdorff said he saw a saucer "land" last Sunday. *SEPT. 19 1954*

"It was about 7:15 P. M.," he said. "My eyes were blinded by a great luminous mass which seemed to touch the ground near the village of Tromborn. As it neared the earth, the color changed in what looked to me like Neon tubes. It was the shape of a small bus. *#1729*

* * *

"IT TOUCHED the ground for about 40 seconds... Finally it flew off, straight up in the air, lighted by an orange glow which changed to red. I heard nothing."

At Origny - en - Thierache, Robert Chovel, his wife and brother-in-law were driving along Tuesday night when, he said, they practically ran down a flying saucer. *9-21*

"It hovered several meters in front of us," he said. "An enormous orange disc at just about tree level. It was immobile for several seconds and then swooshed straight upward with dizzy speed."

THE RAGE IN FRANCE

'Saucer' buzzes Napoleon tomb

To be anybody at all in France these days you practically have to have seen a flying saucer, preferably one of the iridescent ones that change color like a juke box.

Being able to down gallons of champagne, or owning a slightly rundown château or even attending an opening at a theater hardly counts.

Flying saucers, and now flying cigars, are "sighted" practically daily by witnesses who are upstanding citizens, model of probity and sobriety and pillars of the community.

Latest to report the phenomena was movie star Michèle Morgan who said she sighted a luminous disc hovering over the dome of Les Invalides, where Napoleon is buried.

"An old man near me also saw it," Miss Morgan said. "But he ran away."

Rainbow flying saucers are the rage in central France where draughtsman Jean Besse said he watched one Friday night through powerful binoculars. He said it changed color three times in a few seconds.

At Le Puy, west of here, hotel owner Marcel Maillet said he saw an iridescent saucer changing color like a juke box.

Louis Moll, a railway crossing guard at Oberdorff said he saw a saucer "land" last Sunday.

"It was about 7:15 P.M.," he said. "My eyes were blinded by a great luminous mass which seemed to touch the ground near the village of Tromborn. As it neared the earth, the color changed in what looked to me like Neon tubes. It was the shape of a small bus.
"It touched the ground for about 40 seconds ...
Finally it flew off, straight up in the air, lighted by an orange glow which changed to red. I heard nothing."

At Origny - en Tierache, Robert Chovet, his wife and brother-in-law were driving along Tuesday night when, he said, they practically ran down a flying saucer.

"It hovered several meters in front of us," he said. "An enormous orange disc at just about tree level. It was immobile for several seconds and then swooshed straight upward with dizzy speed."

Published in the regional newspaper "La Semaine dans le Boulonnais," France, October 1973.

UN OVNI DANS LE CIEL BOULONNAIS ?

Dans le viseur de son appareil, durant deux secondes, le spectacle d'un objet hors du temps, à la frontière des mondes

C'est une véritable bombe qu'a lancée Claude Plessis, samedi août, à la Brasserie Liégeoise, au cours de la réunion du Cercle d'Études des Phénomènes Spatiaux en présentant aux membres du C.E.P.S. la photo exclusive d'un engin volant non identifié, prise par un photographe amateur, au mois d'août 1969. Il y a quelque temps, sur le conseil d'un ami, le président du C.E.P.S. avait rendu visite à une personne qui, disait-on, avait en sa possession d'étranges documents. Claude Plessis a entendu cette personne et il a été rapidement bouleversé par les révélations qu'elle lui a faites ainsi que par le document qui lui a été remis.

Voici, l'histoire extraordinaire telle que l'auteur de la photographie l'a racontée à M. Plessis.

Le temps de tourner le compteur

« J'aime beaucoup la marche à pied, alors, souvent je me plais à faire des promenades à travers la région, muni de mon appareil photographique. Un bel après-midi du mois d'août, je me promenais dans la campagne boulonnaise, entre Prenecq et Étaples. A un certain endroit j'eus soudain le désir de prendre une photo, jugeant que le paysage en valait la peine. Je cadrai une portion du paysage dans mon viseur et JE VIS SOUDAIN APPARAITRE, DERRIERE LES COLLINES, UN NUAGE A L'ASPECT ÉTRANGE. J'appuyais sur le déclic et me décidai à prendre une seconde photo. Le temps de tourner la manette du compteur de mon appareil, le « nuage » avait disparu. J'ai oublié très vite cet étrange événement et ce n'est que lorsque le film fut développé que je m'aperçus que j'avais fixé ce curieux objet sur la pellicule ».

Claude Plessis, lui, ne s'en tint pas à cette explication un peu simpliste. Certes ce nuage, si nuage il y a, présente toutes les particularités d'un nuage lenticulaire, appelé par les spécialistes Alto-cumulus-lenticularis. La formation de ces nuages reste très mystérieuse et leur composition pose une énigme. C'est un phénomène assez rare mais qui s'est déjà produit suffisamment pour que l'on ne s'étonne pas, outre mesure, de son apparition. Ce qui est certain, en tout cas, c'est qu'ils ont la réputation d'être extrêmement dangereux sans que l'on puisse véritablement en expliquer la raison. En août 1915, par exemple, au sommet d'une colline, à Gallipoli, un nuage de ce genre s'était posé. 250 soldats y pénétrèrent et disparurent. Certains avions qui ont traversé ces nuages ont été désintégrés ou sont retombés mystérieusement.

Ce qui a intrigué Claude Plessis, c'est qu'un nuage lenticulaire ne disparaît pas aussi vite que celui qui s'est volatilisé devant l'auteur de la photo. De plus, ce genre de nuage se rencontre à 5.000 m. et il semble curieux de le remarquer à une hauteur de quelques centaines de mètres.

Claude Plessis a pu disposer du négatif et il l'a envoyé à Paris afin de le faire examiner par des spécialistes. Pour le président du C.E.P.S., il ne s'agit pas d'un nuage lenticulaire mais bel et bien d'un Objet Volant Non Identifié.

Attendre l'évolution de l'humanité

Cet extraordinaire document, ne fut pas le seul point de discussion des responsables du C.E.P.S. MM. Jacques Delescluse, Michel Steers, astro-physicien ; Paul Plessis, réunis autour du président, Claude Plessis et entouré des adhérents. On parla des faits récents qui se sont produits vers le 10 septembre à Équihen et qui ont été remarqués par de nombreux témoins. Il ne s'agissait pas de « soucoupes » mais de boules de 30 cm de diamètre, de couleurs bleues et rouges et comportant plusieurs branches. Selon le C.E.P.S., il s'agirait de sondes. Une thèse aurait été émise : nous entrons dans une nouvelle phase d'observation de la part de ceux qui nous étudient, il ne s'agit plus d'engins habités mais de sondes extra-terrestres qui auraient pour objet d'effectuer des études, de manière indirecte, les contacts directs ne pouvant être envisagés actuellement. On évoqua la thèse d'Aimé Michel : Depuis des siècles, les extra-terrestres étudieraient l'évolution de l'humanité en attendant qu'elle ait atteint un niveau suffisant pour chercher à établir un contact.

La prochaine réunion du C.E.P.S. portera certainement sur les résultats de l'expertise de la photo de l'O.V.N.I. prise en 1969.

Au mois de décembre, le C.E.P.S. étudiera, sans doute, de très près aussi, les premiers résultats de Pionnier 10 qui, lancé il y a deux ans, arrivera dans la banlieue de Jupiter, la plus grosse planète de notre système solaire qui possède douze satellites, à 778 millions de km du Soleil.

Marc DESOUTTER.

A UFO IN THE SKY OF THE BOULONNAIS?

**In the sight of his camera, during two seconds,
the display of an object out of time at the border of the worlds**

It is truly a bomb which was thrown by Clause Plessis, Saturday evening, at the Brasserie Liégoise [local pub], at the meeting of the Cercle d'Etude des Phénomènes Spatiaux [Circle of Space Phenomena Studies] when he presented the exclusive photograph of an unidentified flying machine taken by an amateur photographer in August 1969 to the members of C.E.P.S. A few times ago, on the tip by a friend, the president of C.E.P.S had paid a visit to a person who, it was said, had strange documents in his possession. Claude Plessis heard this person and he was quickly excited by the revelations that he made and by the document which was given to him.

Here is the extraordinary history such as the author of photograph told it to Mr. Plessis.

By the time to take a second shot

"I really like walking in the country, so, I frequently enjoy to make walks through the area, equipped with my camera. On a beautiful after midday of August, I walked in the Boulonnaise countryside, between Frencq and Etaples. At a certain place I had the sudden desire to take a photograph, judging that the landscape was worth it. I tallied a portion of the landscape in my sight and I SUDDENLY SAW APPEARING BEHIND THE HILLS, A CLOUD OF STRANGE ASPECT.

I took a shot and decided to take a second photograph. By the time I winded the film, the "cloud" had disappeared. That hardly lasted two seconds. I very quickly forgot this strange event and it is only when the film was developed that I saw that I had captured this curious object on the film."

Claude Plessis did not stick to this quite simplistic explanation. Admittedly this cloud, if it is a cloud, presents all the characteristics of a lenticular cloud, called by the specialists an Alto-cumulus-lenticularis.

The formation of these clouds remains very mysterious and their composition poses a enigma. It is a quite rare phenomenon but which already occurred sufficiently enough so that one is not astonished too much by its appearance. What is certain, in any case, is that they have the reputation to be extremely dangerous without anyone being able to truly explain the reason for that. In August 1915, for example, at the top of a hill, in Gallipoli [1], a cloud of this kind had landed. 250 soldiers penetrated in it and disappeared. Certain planes which crossed these clouds were disintegrated or fell down mysteriously.

What intrigued Claude Plessis is that a lenticular cloud does not disappear as quickly as the one which volatilized in front of the author of the photograph. Moreover, this type of cloud is found at 5000 meters and it seems curious to find one at a height of a few hundreds of meters.

Claude Plessis managed to get the negative and it sent it in Paris in order to have it examined by specialists. For the president of the C.E.P.S it is not a lenticular cloud but indeed of an Unidentified Flying Object.

Waiting for mankind's evolution

This extraordinary document was not the only point of discussion of the people in charge of the C.E.P.S., Mr. Jacques Delescluse, Mr. Michel Steers, astrophysicist, Paul Plessis and surrounded by the members. It was talked about the recent facts which occurred around September 10 in Equihen and which were noticed by many witnesses. They were not "saucers" but balls, 80 centimeters in diameter, blue and red colors and comprising several branches. According to the C.E.P.S., they may be probes. A thesis has been proposed: we enter a new phase observation on behalf of those who study us, there are no inhabited machines anymore but extraterrestrial probes which would have the mission to carry out studies in an indirect way, the direct contacts not being currently considered possible.

The thesis of Aime Michel was evoked: Since centuries, the extraterrestrials studied the evolution of humanity while waiting for us to reach a sufficient level to seek to establish a contact.

The next meeting of the C.E.P.S will certainly relate to the results of the expertise of the photograph of the U.F.O taken in 1969.
In the month of December, C.E.P.S. will study, undoubtedly, very closely too, the first results of Pioneer 10 which, launched two years ago, will arrive in the surroundings of Jupiter, the largest planet of our solar system, it has twelve satellites, at 778 million km of the Sun.
By Marc Desoutter.

STRANGE OBJECT ON PHOTOGRAPH, QUEBEC, CANADA, 2003:

This article was published in the daily newspaper: Le Journal de Québec, on October 16, 2003.

4 LE JOURNAL DE QUÉBEC / LE JEUDI 16 OCTOBRE 2003

Un ovni?

Photo Serge LAPOINTE

Est-ce un oiseau? Un missile Scud? Superman? Un avion? Le nouvel engin spatial chinois? Une soucoupe volante? Allez savoir. Toujours est-il que notre photographe Serge Lapointe a découvert cette intrigante chose en revoyant les clichés qu'il a croqués au moment du départ, mardi, du paquebot Queen Elizabeth 2. La photo a été prise à 14 h 23, du Vieux-Port de Québec, lorsque le vénérable paquebot contournait la pointe de l'île d'Orléans. Le photographe raconte n'avoir rien remarqué, ni vu ni entendu lorsqu'il se trouvait sur place et n'avoir découvert «la chose» qu'à son retour au Journal. La photo a été prise avec une lentille 300 mm montée sur un boîtier numérique Nikon D-1. Quelqu'un aurait-il vu la même chose?

A UFO?

Is this a bird? A Scud missile? Superman? A plane? The new Chinese spacecraft? A flying saucer? Who knows. anyways, our photographer Serge Lapointe discovered this intriguing thing when he re-examined the photographs he shot at the time of the departure of the steamer Queen Elizabeth 2 Tuesday.

The photograph was taken at 02:23 P.M., in the old harbor of Quebec, when the respectable steamer circumvented the point of the island of Orleans. The photographer says he did not notice anything, neither saw nor heard anything when he was on the premises, and that he discovered "the thing" only on his return to the Newspaper. The photograph was taken using a 300 mm lens mounted on a Nikon D-1 digital camera. Did anybody see the same thing?

Un étrange champignon a fait son apparition à Ronsenac où on aurait aperçu (aussi) une «soucoupe» volante !

Si une panne de courant ne s'était produite vendredi à la tombée de la nuit, à Ronsenac, M. Jean Deret, cultivateur au hameau de Latria, n'aurait pas eu l'occasion d'apercevoir, vers 9 h. du soir, alors qu'il allait fermer (le courant étant revenu) les commutateurs de ses écuries, un étrange phénomène.

A cent cinquante mètres environ de la ferme, qui est la propriété de M. Rouchaud, directeur de l'hôpital d'Angoulème, M. Deret aperçut en effet à l'orée du petit bois voisin, tandis que les chiens des alentours aboyaient à l'unisson, une lueur intense, de couleur orangée paraissant provenir d'un objet ayant la forme et la grosseur approximative d'une demi-barrique qui paraissait osciller de droite à gauche, à dix mètres environ du sol.

Pour être bien sûr qu'il n'était pas l'objet d'une hallucination, le cultivateur appela aussitôt son frère et sa belle-sœur.

Ceux-ci tardant à venir et les minutes s'écoulant, M. Deret revint en courant à la maison et se fit plus persuasif :

« Venez vite, on n'a jamais vu ça... »

Mme Deret ne se fit pas prier davantage et en même temps que son beau-frère, arriva à la grille de la propriété juste à temps pour voir l'étranger lueur descendre brusquement au sol tout retombe alors dans la nuit.

Les frères Deret, deux solides gaillards frisant la quarantaine, ne sont point peureux, mais, après avoir fait quelques mètres en direction de l'endroit où était apparue la mystérieuse lueur, ils rebroussèrent chemin, car, sait-on jamais !...

Samedi, aux premières heures de la matinée, M. Jourdain, maire de Ronsenac, qui chassait dans les parages, fut informé de la bizarre apparition et, en compagnie des frères Deret, se rendit sur place. Mais il ne vit que l'herbe foulée par les vaches qui paissent journellement dans ce champ.

Que peut-on en conclure ? M. Deret et sa belle-sœur sont d'une bonne foi absolue et leur témoignage est formel. Mais cette version supplémentaire au chapitre des soucoupes volantes a fait, on s'en doute, beaucoup parler à Ronsenac.

UN BIZARRE CHAMPIGNON

On ne peut évidemment faire un rapprochement entre l'apparition de ce « tonneau » orangé et la découverte faite la veille par M. Robert Deret, à quelque vingt mètres de l'endroit où disparut le mystérieuse lueur. En traversant le bois, le fermier de Latrie y avait trouvé en effet un champignon d'une forme absolument inconnue dans la région. Ce cryptogramme d'un blanc laiteux, a la forme et la grosseur d'une orange (encore) surmontée d'un cône spongieux de vingt centimètres de long environ dont l'extrémité ressemble à deux lèvres et comporte une sorte de membrane interne paraissant destinée à happer de petits insectes. L'intérieur de la boule est composée d'une matière visqueuse dégageant une odeur forte et désagréable.

Bien entendu, ce champignon a été montré à tous les habitants de Ronsenac et certains ne sont pas éloignés de penser qu'il s'agit là d'une expérience martienne ! ! !

Nous croyons plutôt qu'un botaniste donnerait une autre version de ce nouveau « mystère ».

M. Jean Deret montrant de la main l'endroit où il a aperçu l'étrange boule lumineuse.

A strange mushroom made its appearance in Ronsenac where a flying "saucer" was also seen!

If a power failure had not occurred Friday at the fall of night, in Ronsenac, Mr. Jean Deret, farmer with the hamlet of Latrie, would not have had the occasion to see, around 9 in the evening, whereas he was going to close (the power having come back) the switches of his stable, a strange phenomenon.

Within a hundred and fifty meters approximately of the farm, which is the property of Mr. Rouchaud, director of hospital of Angouleme, Mr. Deret saw indeed at the edge of the neighboring small wood, while the dogs of the neighborhoods were barking together, an intense gleam, of orange color, appearing to come from an object having the shape and the approximate size of a half-barrel who appeared to oscillate from the right to the left, at ten meters approximately of the ground.
To be sure that he was not the object of a hallucination, the farmer called at once his brother and his sister-in-law.

Those being long in coming and the minutes running out, Mr. Deret returned while running to the house and was more persuasive:
"Come quickly, this has never been seen..."
Mrs. Deret did not ask further invitation and at the same time as his brother-in-law, arrived at the fence of the property right in time to see the strange gleam going down suddenly on the ground, and then all is dark again.

The Deret brothers, two strong solids chaps in their early forties, are not timorous, but after having made a few meters in direction of the place where the mysterious gleam had appeared, they grained way, because, you never know!

Saturday, at the first hours of the morning, Mr. Jourdain, mayor of Ronsenac, who was hunting in the vicinity, was informed of the odd appearance and, accompanied by the Deret brothers, went to the site. But he saw only grass pressed by the cows, which feed daily in this field. What can we conclude from that?

Mr. Deret and his sister-in-law are of absolute good faith and their testimony is formal. But this additional version in the chapter of the flying saucers made - you can guess - the talk of Ronsenac.

One cannot obviously link together the appearance of this orange "barrel" and the discovery the day before by Mr. Robert Deret, at a few twenty meters of the place where the mysterious gleam disappeared. while crossing the wood, the farmer of Latrie had indeed found there a mushroom of a form absolutely unknown in the area. This cryptogamme of a milky white, with the form and the size of an orange (again) surmounted of a spongy cone of twenty centimeters length approximately which end resembles two lips and comprises a kind of internal membrane appearing intended to grab small insects. The interior of the ball is made up of a viscous matter releasing a strong and unpleasant odor.

Of course, this mushroom was shown to all the inhabitants of Ronsenac and some are not far to think that it is a Martian experiment!!!
We rather believe that a botanist would give another version of this "mystery"...

MM. REPELLINI ET OTTAVIANI INTERROGÉS HIER

"Oui, nous avons bien vu un engin inconnu

dont voici le croquis

posé entre Toulon et Hyères"

affirment les deux Toulonnais qui toutefois refusent de signer leur déposition pour "éviter les tracasseries"

LA S.N.E.C.M.A. REVELE L'EXISTENCE D'UN APPAREIL FRANÇAIS BAPTISE « COLEOPTERE » QUI DECOLLE A LA VERTICALE

M. Pierre REPELLINI

MM. PIERRE REPELLINI ET OTTAVIANI QUI ONT VU JEUDI SOIR A 18 h. 40 SUR LE CHEMIN LONG ENTRE HYÈRES ET TOULON UN ENGIN AÉRONAUTIQUE INCONNU ONT EU HIER UNE JOURNÉE CHARGÉE.

Policiers et journalistes les ont en effet harcelés, leur demandant croquis et précisions sur cette « soucoupe volante » et son occupant rencontrés par hasard.

Après avoir été interrogés le matin et l'après-midi par les services de la Sécurité de l'Air et les Renseignements Généraux, MM. Repellini et Ottaviani sont restés sur leurs positions et n'ont fait que répéter les déclarations qu'ils ont faites hier en exclusivité à notre journal.

« Oui, nous avons bien vu un engin mystérieux !

Oui, Repellini a parlé avec le passager de cet engin. C'était un homme comme nous et non pas un Martien. Il a parlé et nous avons même remarqué qu'il avait l'accent « pointu ».

Des croquis que l'on voudrait secrets ?

Pour vérifier leurs dires, les deux témoins ont fourni aux Renseignements Généraux un plan détaillé de l'engin. Ce plan a été dessiné par M. Ottaviani qui, officier mécanicien, affirme avoir pu remarquer les caractéristiques de l'appareil.

« C'était, nous ont dit MM. Repellini et Ottaviani, un engin circulaire posé sur deux béquilles. Il semble bien qu'il se soit soulevé de terre par une poussée de bas en haut. Arrivé à une cinquantaine de mètres de hauteur, la partie extrême de l'engin s'est mise à tourner, lâchant une vapeur orangée. En quelques instants, l'appareil avait disparu, filant à une allure vertigineuse en direction de Hyères.

* Suite en page 5 :
ENGIN INCONNU

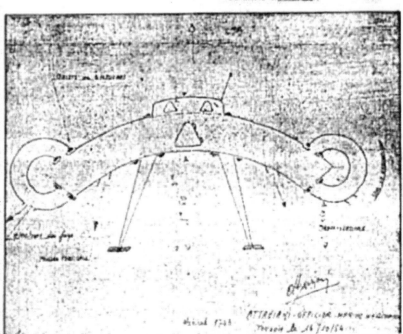

Voici le croquis de l'engin qu'a dessiné pour nos lecteurs M. Ottaviani, officier de la Marine Marchande. Indéniablement ses formes s'apparentent à celle d'une grosse araignée. Est-ce là le « coléoptère » qui décolle à la verticale dont l'existence vient d'être révélée officiellement.

"Yes, we really saw an unknown craft land between Toulon and Hyères"

claim the two residents of Toulon who however refused to sign their statements to "avoid problems."

Police officers and journalists indeed badgered them, asking for sketches and details on this "flying saucer" and its occupant met by chance.
After having been interrogated in the morning and after midday by the services of the Air Safety and the Renseignements Généraux [Intelligence], Misters Repellini and Ottaviani remained on their positions and only repeated the statements, which they made yesterday with exclusiveness to our newspaper.
"Yes, we really saw a mysterious machine!"
Yes, Repellini spoke with the passenger of this machine. It was a man like us and not a Martian. He spoke and we even noticed that it had a "pointed" accent.

Sketches, which would rather be kept secret?

To check their statements, the two witnesses provided to Renseignents Généraux a detailed plan of the machine. This plan was drawn by Mr. Ottaviani who, as engineer officer, claims he has been able to notice the characteristics of the apparatus.

"It was, told us MM Repellini and Ottaviani, a circular machine landed on two crutches. It really seems that it rose off the ground by a push upwards. Arrived at about fifty meters height, the extreme part of the machine started to rotate, releasing an orange vapor. In a few moments, the apparatus had disappeared, dazzling at a tremendous pace in direction of Hyères.

Enquête sur la soucoupe
découverte près d'Hyères
par deux Toulonnais

Ceux-ci, interrogés par la police de l'air refusent de signer leurs déclarations

M. OTTAVIANI en train de dessiner minutieusement le plan de la soucoupe.

LA RECONSTITUTION DE LA SCÈNE

Le « soucoupier » casqué et vêtu de verre s'avance vers MM. OTTAVIANI et RAPPELLINI : « Ça Français ».

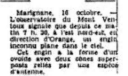

Marignane, 16 octobre. — L'observatoire du Mont Ventoux signale que depuis ce matin 7 h. 30, à l'est nord-est, en direction d'Orange, un engin inconnu plane dans le ciel.

Cet engin a la forme d'un ovoïde avec deux cônes superposés reliés par une espèce d'antenne.

Investigation on the saucer discovered near Hyères by two inhabitants of Toulon

The men, interrogated by the Air Police refused to sign their statements

M. OTTAVIANI in thoroughly drawing the plan of the saucer.
Marignane, October 16
The observatory of Mount Ventoux announces that since this morning at 07:30 A:M: in the north north-eastern sky, in the direction of Orange, an unknown machine hovers in the sky.
This machine with the form of ovoid with two superimposed cones connected by a kind of antenna.

Toulon

Soucoupe d'un style futuriste comportant une coupole avec bourrelets métalliques et des béquilles. Un Martien, ayant l'accent parisien, en sortit. Vue par un officier et par le patron du Bar des Pétanqueurs.

Toulon

Saucer of a futuristic style comprising a cupola with metallic pads and crutches. A Martian, having the Parisian accent, came out of it. Sighted by an officer and the owner of the Bar des Pétanqueurs.

UFOs Over Washington D.C.

Photograph – Rob Simone

AIR FORCE MATS INTELLIGENCE INVESTIGATING PILOTS SAUCER REPORTS, 1954:

Published in the daily newspaper: The Rocky Mountain News, of Denver, Colorado, USA, on Saturday, February 13, 1954.

5 to 10 'Saucers' Reported Nightly By Airline Pilots

By JIM G. LUCAS
Scripps-Howard Staff Writer

WASHINGTON, Feb. 12—Commercial airline pilots report between five and 10 flying saucer sightings each night.

Representatives of major airlines will meet Wednesday in Los Angeles with Military Air Transport Service (MATS) intelligence officers to discuss speeding up saucer-reporting procedures.

The idea will be to "get the reports in the quickest possible way" so that the Air Force can send fast jet fighters to investigate.

TRAIL IS COLD

Heretofore, commercial pilots have landed and then reported to MATS through their companies. By that time, the trail usually is cold. Now, pilots are instructed to flash reports direct from the air to MATS intelligence in Washington or to the nearest Air Force base.

However several "bugs" have been found in this plan. Some pilots, for example, don't know how to contact MATS intelligence. Others don't think it important enough. That's one angle to be discussed at the Los Angeles meeting.

Airline pilots are asked not to discuss their sightings publicly or give them to newspapers.

Navy Capt. Bernard Baruch Jr., MATS intelligence officer, is in charge of the project. Capt. Baruch's headquarters are in New York, but MATS intelligence also maintains a large staff at Andrews Air Force Base, Md., near Washington.

NUMEROUS SIGHTINGS

One well-informed source said that until recently the largest number of sightings were from the Southwest Pacific. Saucer sightings have been particularly numerous around Australia, where the British maintain a guided missile range.

Recently, however, there has been an increase in saucer sightings in the North Atlantic, this source said. Simultaneously, the number of oil slicks and submarine lightings in this area has increased.

The same source said flying saucer sightings are "fairly common" throughout the non-Communist world.

Washington, Feb. 12 -- Commercial airline pilots report between five and 10 flying saucers sightings each night.

Representatives of major airlines will meet Wednesday in Los Angeles with Military Air transport Services (MATS) intelligence officers to discuss speeding up saucer-reporting procedures.
The idea will be to "get the reports in the quickest possible way" so that the Air Force can send fast jet fighters to investigate.

TRAIL IS COLD

Heretofore, commercial pilots have landed and then reported to MATS through their companies. By that time, the trail usually is cold. Now pilots are instructed to flash reports direct from the air to MATS intelligence in Washington or to the nearest Air Force base.

However, several "bugs" have been found in this plan. Some pilots, for example, don't know how to contact MATS intelligence. Others don't think it is important enough. That's one angle to be discussed at the Los Angeles meeting.

Airline pilots are asked not to discuss their sightings publicly or give them to newspaper.

Navy Capt. Bernard Baruch Jr., MATS intelligence officer, is in charge of this project. Capt. Baruch's headquarters are in New York, but MATS intelligence alsomaintains a large staff at Andrews Air Force Base, Maryland, near Washington.

NUMEROUS SIGHTINGS

One well-informed source said that until recently the largest number of sightings were from the Southwest Pacific. Saucer sightings have been particularly numerous around Australia where the British maintain a guided missile range.

Recently, however, there has been an increase in saucer sightings in the North Atlantic, this source said. Simultaneously, the number of oil slicks and submarine lightings in this area has increased.

The same source said flying saucer sightings are "fairly common" throughout the non-Communist world.

This Time It's Hard To Brush Off Those Mystery "Saucers"

Radar control room of CAA at Washington airport tracked the strange objects on the large scope in center foreground. It shows position of aircraft within a radius of 70 miles.

Airlines pilot S. C. Pierman saw six "objects" at the same time the CAA radar did.

By DOUGLAS LARSEN
NEA Staff Correspondent

WASHINGTON (NEA) — The flying saucers are back.

And their return to the headlines has been the result of a startling new development:

For the first time, numerous and simultaneous visual sightings have been positively confirmed by official Civil Aeronautics Administration radar observations. This has happened twice under almost identical circumstances on two successive Saturday nights.

Up until now official and unofficial saucer debunkers have produced credible theories to explain away reports of visual sightings as natural phenomena. They have done the same for individual radar sighting reports.

But none of this reasoning satisfactorily explains away visual sightings absolutely confirmed by radar.

This remarkable new chapter of the weird flying saucer story was written in the skies over Washington for six hours before dawn on Sunday, July 20, and again one week later. The details and implications of what took place are now confirmed by CAA and the Air Force.

Since then the Air Force has quietly said it was closing to the press its special section at Wright Field in Dayton, O. which has been studying flying saucer reports. In addition, all information concerning that group's personnel, activities and budget is now strictly classified.

Full details of what happened the first night are being revealed for the first time by NEA Service.

These are the facts:

Beginning shortly after midnight, and continuing until dawn, eight experienced CAA radar operators and technicians, manning the air route traffic control center in hanger No. 6 at National Airport, tracked from seven to ten unidentified and mysterious objects performing strange gyrations in the skies in a 30-mile radius above Washington.

Harry G. Barnes, who has been with CAA for nine years, mostly in radar work, was in charge of the group. After making sure that the objects were not known aircraft and that the radar was operating perfectly, he checked his findings with the radar operators in the control tower. They instantly confirmed what he saw, and continued to do so. The two

SURVEILLANCE RADAR SCOPE, WASHINGTON NATIONAL AIRPORT

RADIO TOWER

AIRCRAFT PIP

AIRCRAFT PIPS

Large radar scope at Washington National Airport presents a picture like this to CAA traffic controllers. Mystery pips were tracked from midnight until dawn on the first night.

radars are completely separate units.

Later the radar at nearby Andrews Air Force base also confirmed the sightings.

When the center radar showed one of the unidentified objects in a low position in the northwest sky, the operators in the tower were able to see it. One of them, Howard Cocklin, who has been with CAA for five years, describes it:

"It was a good-sized light, yellow to orange in color. At first it looked like a great big star. Then it began to move in a manner which made you realize it couldn't be a star. There was no unusual high speed about its movements and at times it seemed to hover. We could see it moving around like that for about 15 minutes. It just disappeared into the northwest sky."

There are no windows in the center Barnes was operating. None of the eight men could leave to go outside to try to check their own radar sightings visually.

As is normal at that time air traffic was very light. But at the first opportunity an operator in Barnes' office contacted Capital Airlines pilot Capt. S. C. Pierman

shortly after he took off and asked him to look for the objects.

For about 14 minutes, Pierman was in direct, two-way communication with Barnes. While he was within radar range, Pierman was able to see six objects which showed up on the path indicated by the center's radar. Pierman's sightings reported to Barnes coincided exactly with the radar sightings, Barnes reports.

Pierman is a 17-year veteran of commercial flying and is described by Capital Airlines officials as very level-headed and "taciturn." After he landed in Detroit Pierman had this to say about the sightings:

"In my years of flying I've seen a lot of falling or shooting stars—whatever you call them—but these were much faster than anything like that I've ever seen. They were moving too fast for that. They were about the same size as the brighter stars. And they were much higher than our 6,000-foot altitude. I couldn't estimate the speed accurately. Please remember I didn't speak of them as flying saucers—only very fast moving lights."

Charles Wheaton, first officer on the flight with Pierman, a veteran of 12 years of flying confirms Pierman's sightings and adds:

"Before the other night, I always discounted alleged flying saucers as atmospheric phenomenon. But now I feel I have actually seen some active strange objects which defy explanation."

Another Capital Airlines pilot also reported seeing a light off his wing, which showed up in that position on the radar scope. Other pilots in the air that night, Barnes reveals, appeared to be reluctant to discuss the subject with him on the radio.

The mystery of the flying saucers had its start on June 24, 1947, when a Boise, Idaho, businessman, Kenneth Arnold, flew his private plane over the jagged peaks of Washington's Mt. Rainier. When he landed, he breathlessly reported having seen "a chain of nine saucer-like objects playing tag at fantastic speeds."

Since then there have been thousands of sightings all over the world, many obviously reported by crackpots. But a substantial number have been so strange and reliably described, even the Air Force has had to admit that they were unexplainable.

Many books have been written on the subject. Hundreds of magazine articles have treated all aspects of the question. However, a review of most of what has been written and officially reported on the subject points up several unique aspects to the recent Washington sightings:

It's the first time that three separate radar sets have reported identical sightings.

It's the first time they have remained under observation in one area for so long a time.

It's the first time so many completely responsible men, including radar operators and pilots, all observed and reported the same thing at the same time, with all reports checking so accurately.

Both nights there were scores of unofficial stories of persons in the area who claim to have seen one or more strange lights moving about in the sky.

Saul Pett, a news service reporter in River Edge, N. J., wrote a detailed story on one that he saw just before seven objects appeared on the CAA radar screen at National Airport. He said:

"It looked like a sphere, so deeply orange colored that it appeared almost the shade of rust. It was silent as death. It was moving too fast and evenly to be a balloon. I saw a flying saucer and you can't convince me that there is no such animal."

He said it disappeared in the direction of Washington.

The Air Force has the responsibility of finding out what there is to the saucer reports. After two years' study it finally reported in 1950:

"All evidence and analyses indicate that the reports of unidentified flying objects are the result of: (1) Misinterpretation of various conventional objects; (2) a mild form of mass hysteria; (3) or hoaxes."

Lt. Col. DeWitt R. Searles, an Air Force press officer, was giving the job of officially denying the existence of saucers from then on. His file on the subject was labeled "death of the saucers."

On June 17 of this year, however, Col. Searles was forced to reveal a slight alteration in the Air Force stand on saucers. He issued a statement which said:

"No concrete evidence has yet reached us to either prove or disprove the existence of the so-called flying saucers. However, there remain a number of sightings which have not been satisfactorily explained. As long as this is true the Air Force will continue to investigate flying saucers reports."

Air Force reaction to the recent Washington sightings has been curious, and its reports have been conflicting. A few minutes after CAA confirmed its sightings on the 20th it reported the fact to the Air Force in a normal but classified procedure.

For the next several days the Air Force claimed that its radar at nearby Andrews Air Force base did not confirm the findings of the CAA radar. Later, however, the Air Force reversed itself and admitted that the Andrews radar did pick up the objects, four hours after the first CAA report.

On July 26, then, the strange objects appeared on three separate radar sets for two hours. A week later the Air Force admitted that its Andrews radar had practically identical sightings to the other two all evening.

The first night no fighter planes went aloft to investigate the sightings. A week later, however, the Air Force sent up jets to try to get a closer look at the objects.

The only report from the fighter pilots was that they saw strange lights, moving too fast for the 600-mph jets to intercept.

Another conflicting Air Force report concerns a saucer expert from the new barricaded unit at Dayton, Capt. E. J. Ruppelt. He "happened" to be in town at the time. An AF spokesman said that he would interview all of the persons involved in the sightings.

A week later, however, Capt. Ruppelt had left town and had not contacted a single one of the CAA persons involved. Col. Searles reported that he had taken a copy of Barnes' brief summary report by long hand over the telephone next day. That constitutes the Air Force's only official recognition of the events of the 20th. The AF, however, now promises to make a thorough investigation of the events of both nights.

In the unofficial category of saucer study is the theory of Dr. Donald H. Menzel, a Harvard professor of astrophysics. It seems to have had most effect in debunking saucer reports among the experts.

He says visual sightings could be ordinary lights which are reflected from warm layers of air. And he says radar can produce a false pip in the same way.

According to several experts in Washington, who asked not to be quoted, Menzel's theory does not account for the simultaneous visual and radar sightings.

Further, it isn't likely that any warm layer of reflecting air would have remained constant for so long a period over Washington that night.

Coincidental with the recent Washington sightings and increased reports of saucer sightings all over the U. S. this summer, has been increased rumors around the Pentagon and from other government agencies attempting to explain saucers. And they appear to be coming from more reliable sources, although these sources continue to refuse to let themselves be identified.

Most persistent rumor is that Boeing Airplane Co. in Seattle, Wash., is either making flying saucers or has been in charge of the engineering of the project. The rumor goes that very small parts of the saucers are being made by widely scattered subcontractors and that the finished items are being assembled at some remote site.

A Boeing spokesman in Seattle flatly denies this rumor, as does the Air Force.

The descriptions of the saucers which have been sighted indicates that some radically new source of power would be needed to make the objects move as fast as they did.

If this were true it doesn't make sense that the Air Force would be expending such a tremendous effort to improve its present jet engines, which would be made completely obsolete by the new source of power. Nor would the Air Force be likely to have its saucers practice maneuvers early Sunday morning around Washington.

In the weirder category of rumors is the one that the saucers are either Russian-built or from

Towerman Howard Cocklin, after watching one of the objects, is sure it wasn't a star.

another planet and that several of them have crashed and have been picked up by the Air Force. It goes on to theorize that the Air Force has been able to repair some of them and make them operate and at the same time is trying to build some of its own just like them.

This would account for the Air Force being extremely interested in some sightings, and apparently very disinterested in others.

Col. Searles, who has had more experience in denying saucer rumors than anyone in the Pentagon, just laughs at this idea.

But nobody is really laughing at the strange objects tracked by radar over the nation's capital.

Published in the daily newspaper: The Sheboygan Press, of Sheboygan, Wisconsin, on August 4, 1952.

This time it's hard to brush off those mystery "saucers"

[Photo caption] Radar control room of CAA at Washington airport tracked the strange objects on the large scope in center foreground. It shows position of aircraft within a radius of 70 miles.

By DOUGLAS LARSEN NEA Staff Correspondent

WASHINGTON (NEA) -- The flying saucers are back.

And their return to the headlines has been the result of a startling new development:

For the first time, numerous and simultaneous visual sightings have been positively confirmed by official Civil Aeronautics Administration radar observations. This has happened twice under almost identical circumstances on two successive Saturday nights.

Up until now official and unofficial saucer debunkers have produced credible theories to explain away reports of visual sightings as natural phenomena.

They have done the same for individual radar sighting reports. But none of this reasoning satisfactorily explains away visual sightings absolutely confirmed by radar.

This remarkable new chapter in the weird flying saucer story was written in the skies over Washington for six hours before dawn on Sunday, July 20, and again one week later. The details and implications of what took place are now confirmed by the CAA and the Air Force.

Since the Air Force has quietly said it was closing to the press its special section at Wright Field in Dayton, Ohio, which has been studying flying saucer reports. In addition, all information concerning that group's personnel, activities and budget is now strictly classified.

Full details of what happened the first night are being revealed for the first time by NEA Service.

These are the facts:

Beginning shortly after midnight, and continuing until dawn, eight experienced CAA radar operators and technicians, manning the air route traffic control center in hanger No. 6 at National Airport, tracked down from seven to ten unidentifiable and mysterious objects performing strange gyrations in the skies in a 30-mile radius above Washington.

Harry G. Barnes, who has been with CAA for nine years, mostly in radar work, was in charge of the group. After making sure that the object were not known aircraft and that the radar was operating perfectly he checked his findings with the radar operators in the control tower. They instantly confirmed what he saw and continued to do so. The two radars are completely separated units.

Later the radar at nearby Andrews Air Force Base has also confirmed the sightings.

When the center radar showed one of the unidentified objects in a low position in the northwest sky, the operators in the tower were able to see it. One of them, Howard Cocklin, who has been with CAA for five years, described it:

"It was a good-sized light, yellow to orange in color. At first it looked like a great big star. Then it began to move in a manner which made you realize it couldn't be a star. There was no unusual speed about its movement and at times it seemed to hover. We could see it moving around like that for about 15 minutes. It just disappeared from the northwest sky."
There are no windows in the center Barnes was operating. None of the eight men could leave to go outside to try to check their own radar sightings visually.

As is normal at that time air traffic was very light. But at the first opportunity an operator in Barnes' office contacted Capital Airlines pilot Capt. S.C. Pierman.

"Before the other night I always discounted flying saucers as atmospheric phenomenon. But now I have actually seen some active strange objects which defy explanation."

Another Capital Airlines pilot also reported seeing a light off his wing, which showed up in that position on the radarscope. Other pilots in the air that night, Barnes reveals, appeared to be reluctant to discuss the subject with him on the radio.

The mystery of the flying saucers had its start on June 24, 1947, when a Boise, Idaho, businessman, Kenneth Arnold, flew his private plane over the jagged peaks of Washington's Mt. Rainier. When he landed, he breathlessly reported to having seen "a chain of nine saucer-like objects playing tag at fantastic speeds."

Since then there have been thousands of sightings all over the world, many obviously reported by crackpots. But a substantial number have been so strange and reliably described, even the Air Force has had to admit that they were unexplainable.

Many books have been written on the subject. Hundreds of magazine articles have treated all aspects of the question.
However, a review of most of what has been written and officially reported on the subject points up several unique aspects to the recent Washington sightings:
It's the first time that three separate radar sets have reported identical sightings.

It's the first time they have remained under observation in one area for so long a time.

It's the first time so many completely responsible men, including radar operators, and pilots, all observed and reported the same thing at the same time, with all reports checking so accurately.
Both nights there were scores of unofficial stories of persons in the area who claim to have seen one or more strange lights moving about in the sky.

Saul Pett, a news service reporter in River Edge, New Jersey, wrote a detailed story on one that he saw just before seven objects appeared on the CAA radar screen at National Airport.

He said:
"It looked like a sphere, so deeply orange colored that it appeared almost the shade of rust. It was moving too fast and evenly to be a balloon. I saw a flying saucer and you can't convince me that there is no such animal."

He said it disappeared in the direction of Washington.

The Air Force has the responsibility of finding out what there is to the saucer reports. After two years' study it finally reported in 1950.

"All evidence and analyses indicate that the reports of unidentified flying objects are the results of misinterpretation of various conventional objects; a mild form of mass hysteria; or hoaxes."

Lt. Col. DeWitt R. Scarles, an Air Force press officer, was given the job of officially denying the existence of saucers from then on. His file on the subject was labeled "death of the saucers."

On June 17 of this year, however, Col. Searles was forced to reveal a slight alteration in the Air Force stand on saucers. He issued a statement that said:

"No concrete evidence has yet reached us to either prove or disprove the existence of the so-called flying saucers. However, there remains a number of sightings which have not been satisfactorily explained. As long as this is true the Air Force will continue to investigate flying saucers reports."

Air Force reaction to the recent Washington sightings has been curious, and its reports have been conflicting. A few minutes after CAA confirmed its sightings on the 20th it reported the fact to the Air Force in a normal but classified procedure.

For the next several days the Air Force claimed that its radar at nearby Andrews Air Force base did not confirm the findings of the CAA radar. Later, however, the Air Force admitted that its Andrews radar had practically identical sightings to the other two all evening.

The first night no fighter planes went aloft to investigate the sightings. A week later, however, the Air Force sent up jets to try to get a closer look at the objects.

The only report from the fighter pilots was that they saw strange lights, moving too fast for the 600-mph jets to intercept.
Another conflicting Air Force report concerns a saucer expert from the now barricaded unit at Dayton, Capt. E. J. Ruppelt. He "happened" to be in town at the time. An AF spokesman said that he would interview all of the persons involved in the sightings.

A week later, however, Capt. Ruppelt had left town and had not contacted a single one of the CAA persons involved. Col. Searles reported that he had taken a copy of Barne's brief summary report in long hand over the telephone next day. That constitutes the Air Force's only official recognition of the events of the 20th. The AF, however, now promises to make a thorough investigation of the events of both nights.

In the unofficial category of saucer study is the theory of Dr. Donald H. Menzel, a Harvard professor of astrophysics. It seems to have had most effect in debunking saucer reports among the experts.

He says visual sightings could be ordinary lights when they are reflected from warm layers of air. And he says radar can produce a false pip in the same way.

According to several experts in Washington, who asked not to be quoted, Menzel's theory does not account for the simultaneous visual and radar sightings.

Further, it isn't likely that any warm layer of reflecting air would have remained constant for so long a period over Washington that night. Coincidental with the recent Washington sightings and increased reports of saucer sightings all over the U.S. this summer, has been increased rumours around the Pentagon and from other government agencies attempting to explain saucers. And they appear to be coming from more reliable sources, although these sources continue to let themselves be identified.

Most persistent rumor is that Boeing Airplane Co. in Seattle, Wash, is either making flying saucers or has been in charge of the engineering of the project.

The rumor goes that very small parts of the saucers are being made by widely scattered subcontractors and that the finished items have been assembled at some remote site.

A Boeing spokesman in Seattle flatly denies this rumor, as does the Air Force.
The descriptions of the saucers which have been sighted indicates that some radically new source of power would be needed to make the objects move as fast as they did.

If this were true it doesn't make sense that the Air Force would be expending such as tremendous effort to improve its present jet engines, which would be made completely obsolete by the new source of power. Nor would the Air Force be likely to have its saucer practice maneuvers early Sunday morning around Washington.

In the weirder category of rumors is the one that the saucers are either Russian or from another planet and that several of them crashed and have been picked up by the Air Force. It goes on to theorize that the Air Force has been able to repair some of them and make them operate and at the same time is trying to build some of his own just like them.

This would account for the Air Force being extremely interested in some sightings, and apparently very disinterested in others.
Col. Searles, who has had more experience in denying saucers than anyone in the Pentagon, just laughs at the idea.

But nobody is really laughing at the strange objects tracked by radar over the nation's capital.
[Photo caption:] Airline pilot S.C. Pierman saw six "objects" at the same time the CAA radar did.

[Photo caption:] Towerman Howard Cocklin after watching one of the objects, is sure it wasn't a star.

1952 ARTICLE FROM THE ALEXANDRIA GAZETTE:

William Daffron, reporter for Alexandria Gazette, July 29, 1952.

The Alexandria Gazette

AMERICA'S OLDEST DAILY NEWSPAPER—ESTABLISHED 1784

VOL. CLXIX—NO. 151   ALEXANDRIA, VIRGINIA, TUESDAY, JULY 29, 1952   FIVE CENTS

Weather, Tides and Sun

EYE-WITNESS STORY OF "FLYING SAUCERS" SEEN ALONG ALEXANDRIA-CLARENDON AXIS

Planes To Take Off Over River

Proposal Made As Remedy For Low Flying Craft

THE TRAIL of two "flying saucers," shown in the picture above, were taken by Photographer Al Blumthaugh of the Louisville Times. The time exposure was taken in July, 1947. (AP Photo)

Only Temporary Relief Seen For Area's Blistering Heat

Fairfax Men See Objects On Radar On Night Watch

By WILLIAM DAFFRON

Saucers Seen Again Early This Morning

SAUCERS SEEN AGAIN EARLY THIS MORNING:

Flying saucers circled the Northern Virginia area again this morning.

The CAA says its radar picked up the saucers about six straight hours early today as they circled between Herndon, and Andrews Field.
A CAA official estimated the objects were traveling between 100 and 200 hundred miles per hour in this morning's flight.
Simultaneously the Air Force stymied by the failure of its supersonic jets to intercept the flying saucers Saturday night, announced it was equipping its planes with special cameras to help solve the mystery.

Jet pilots from the 142nd Interceptor Squadron at Newcastle Del., for some time now have been on orders to shoot down any "unidentified" aircraft which ignores "orders" to land.

An Air Force spokesman from the Pentagon refused to say whether the saucers fall into the "aircraft" category.

He said the planes have been on 24-hour alert to defend the skies ever since the out-break of the Korean War and the pilots have been issued no specific orders to shoot down "saucers."

Saucer experts from Wright Field, Ohio have been called to Washington for a special conference on the phenomenon. The group was scheduled to arrive last night, but was delayed by plane trouble and will instead meet today.

Pentagon officials are expected to issue a statement on the results of the investigation to date.

A high-ranking Air Force official reiterated yesterday that the saucers are "not" some special experiment being conducted by "his" branch of the service. He stated, "that if the Army, Navy, Atomic Energy Commission, or any other government agency were conducting such experiments we would know about it."

"One thing I would like to do is dispel the belief by some that we are holding out something," he said. "We are not."

Scientists, military spokesman, and private citizens continue to offer a wide variety of explanations for the radar sightings at National Airport and Andrews Air Force Base.

An Air Force official said the spots on the screen might have been caused by tinfoil "windows" dropped by a B-36 bomber in recent Air Defense exercises up North. The tinfoil strips are used to "cloud" radar screens.

Scientists admitted little knowledge of sky phenomenon such as cosmic rays and electro-magnetic forces, but said they could cause radar reactions.

Still a third explanation traced to the "blips" registered on radar screens to the heavy use of television sets in the area during the convention.

In Alexandria, James H. Gillis, chief observer for The Air Defense volunteer observation post on Russell Rd., said his crew has not seen any flying saucers, nor have they received specific orders to watch for flying saucers.

"Our orders are to report any strange objects in the skies," he said. "We pass our reports on to the filter station in Baltimore which in turn alerts the interceptor planes."

Gillis said his crew, supposed to operate on a 24-hour basis, has had so few volunteer workers, he is struggling to maintain a 4 to 10 p.m. sky watch.

The Air Force said in the past few years they have received and evaluated more then 1000 sightings of "unidentified flying objects." Of these only a small portion remained inexplicable after investigation.
New reports are coming in to follow-up Saturday night's weird "sky chase" over Mt Vernon.

Sylvanus Jones, 25, a State Department clerk from Washington, said he saw " a small light" floating in space over the capital. He said he was sure it was not a star or an airplane light.
State Police in Indianapolis, Indiana, said they watched three flying saucers cavort in the skies overhead yesterday.

The new-type cameras being installed in the jet interceptors are specially designed to shoot "luminous phenomenon," the Air Force said. They operate on the same principle employed by astronomers in determining the composition of the stars.

Air Force scientists hope to determine the physical make-up of the strange lights and thereby identify their source.

The Washington Post — FINAL

The Weather

Seventy-fifth Year in the Nation's Capital

NO. 27,801   **MONDAY, JULY 28, 1952**   WTOP AM (1500) FM (96.3) TV (CH. 9)   FIVE CENTS

'Saucer' Outran Jet, Pilot Reveals

U.S. Protests Soviet 'Hate' In Aviation Day Posters

Air Chase Pictures Held Admission of 3 Attacks; Envoys Shun Big Red Show

Conquest by Terror
Russians Rule Satellites By Torture and Murder
By Leland Stowe

Stevenson And Truman Head 'Big 4' Campaign

Barkley, Sparkman Also Will Enter Stomping Campaign For Party Victory

Eisenhower, Nixon Plan Campaign

Will Invade South; Spirit of Unity Growing in GOP, Senator Declares

Dwight D. Eisenhower, Republican presidential nominee, shows his running mate, Sen. Richard M. Nixon of California, current angling technique at Ike's mountain retreat in Fraser, Colo.

Investigation On in Secret After Chase Over Capital

Radar Spots Blips Like Aircraft for Nearly Six Hours; Only 1700 Feet Up

By Paul Sampson
Post Reporter

Military secrecy veils an investigation of the mysterious, glowing aerial objects that showed up on radar screens in the Washington area Saturday night for the second consecutive week.

A jet pilot sent up by the Air Defense Command to investigate the objects reported he was unable to overtake the glowing lights...

"Saucer" outran jet, pilot reveals
Investigation on in secret after chase over capital
Radar spot blips like aircraft for nearly six hours - only 1,700 feet up

By Paul Sampson, Post Reporter

Military secrecy veils an investigation of the mysterious, glowing aerial objects that showed up on radar screens in the Washington area Saturday night for the second consecutive week.

A jet pilot sent up by the Air Defense Command to investigate the objects reported he was unable to overtake the glowing lights moving near Andrews Air Force Base.

The CAA reported the objects traveled at "predominantly lower levels"- about 1700 feet. July 19.

Air Force spokesmen said yesterday only that an investigation was being made into the sighting of the objects on the radar screen in the CAA Air Route Traffic Control Center at Washington National Airport, and on two other radar screens. Methods of the investigations were classified as secret, a spoken said.

"We have no evidence they are flying saucers; conversely we have no evidence they are not flying saucers. We don't know what they are," a spokesman added.

The same source reported an expert from the Air Technical Intelligence Center at Wright-Patterson Air Force Base, Dayton Ohio, was here last week investigating the objects sighted July 19.

The expert has been identified as Capt. E. J. Ruppelt. Reached by telephone at his home in Dayton yesterday, Ruppelt said he could make no comment on his activity in Washington.

Capt. Ruppelt confirmed he was in Washington last week but said he had not come here to investigate the mysterious objects. He recalled he did make an investigation after hearing of the objects, but could not say what he investigated.

Another Air Force spokesman said here yesterday the Air Force is taking all steps necessary to evaluate the sightings. "The intelligence people," this spokesman explained, "sent someone over to the control center at the time of the sightings and did whatever necessary to make the proper evaluation.

Asked whether the radar equipment might have been malfunctioning, the spokesman said, "radar, like the compass is not a perfect instrument and is subject to error." He thought, however, the investigation would be made by persons acquainted with the problems of radar.

Two other radar screens in the area picked up the objects. An employee of the National Airport control tower said the radar scope there picked up very weak "blips" of the objects. The tower radar's for "short range" and is not so powerful as that at the center.

Radar at Andrews Air Force Base also registered the objects from about seven miles south of the base.
A traffic control center spokesman said the nature of the signals on the radar screen ruled out any possibility they were from clouds or any other "weather" disturbance.

"The returns we received from the unidentified objects were similar and analogous to targets representing aircraft in flight," he said.
The objects, "flying saucer or what have you, appeared on the radar scope at the airport center at 9:08 PM."

Varying from 4 to 12 in number, the objects appeared on the screen until 3:00 AM., when they disappeared.
At 11:25 PM., twoF-94 jet fighters fro Air Defense Command squadron, at New Castle Delaware, capable of 600 hundred mph speeds, took off to investigate the objects.

Airline, civil and military pilots described the objects as looking like the lit end of a cigarette or a cluster of orange and red lights.
One jet pilot observed 4 lights in the vicinity of Andrews Air Force Base, but was not able to over-take them, and they disappeared in about two minutes.

The same pilot observed a steady white light in the vicinity of Mt Vernon at 11:49 PM. The light, about 5 miles from him, faded in a minute. The lights were also observed in the Beltsville, MD., vicinity. At 1:40 AM two-other F-94 jet fighters took off and scanned the area until 2:20 AM., but did not make any sightings.

Visible two days

Although "unidentified objects" have been picked up on radar before, the incidents of the last two Saturdays are believed to be the first time the objects have been picked up on radar-while visible to the human eye. Besides the pilots, who last Saturday saw the lights, a woman living on Mississippi Ave., told the Post she saw a very "bright light streaking across the sky towards Andrews Air Force Base about 11:45 PM. Then a second object with a tail like a comet whizzed by, and a few seconds later, a third passed in a different direction toward Suntland, she said.

The radar operators plotted the speed of "Saturday night's visitors" at from 38 to 90 mph, but one jet pilot reported faster speeds for the light he saw. The jet pilot reported he had no apparent "closing speed" when he attempted to reach the lights he saw near Andrews Air Force Base. That means the lights were moving at least as fast as his top speed-a maximum of 600 mph.

One person who saw the lights when they first appeared in this area did not see them last night. He is E.W. Chambers, an engineer at Radio Station WRC, who spotted the lights while working early the morning of July 20 at station's Hyattsville tower.

Chamber's said he was sorry he had seen the lights because he had been skeptical about "flying saucers" before. Now he said, he sort of "wonders" and worries about the whole thing.

Leon Davidson, 804 South Irving St. Arlington, a chemical engineer who made an exhaustive study of "flying saucers" as a hobby, said yesterday reports of saucers in the East, have been relatively rare.
Davidson has studied the official report on the saucers, including some of the secret portions never made public, and analyzed all the data in the report.

Davidson, whose study of saucers is impressively detailed and scientific, said he believes the lights are American "aviation products"-probably "circular flying wings," using new type jet engines that permit rapid acceleration and relatively low speeds. He believes, they are either "new fighter," guided missiles, or piloted guided missiles.

He cited some of the recent jet fighters, including the Navy's new " F-4-D, which has a radical "bat-wing," as examples of what the objects might resemble.

Davidson thinks the fact that the lights have been seen in this area indicates the authorities may be ready to disclose the "new aircraft" in the near future. Previously, most of the "verified saucers" have been seen over sparsely inhabited areas, Davidson explained, and now, when they appear here, it may indicate that "secrecy" is not so important any more.

Published in the daily newspaper: The Bridgeport Post, Connecticut, USA, on July 28, 1952.

Jet Interceptors Fail to Contact Ghostly 'Saucers' Over Capital

WASHINGTON, July 28—(AP) Radar—which normally doesn't show something that isn't there—has picked up "flying saucers" near the nation's capital for the second time within a week.

Jet fighter pilots searched the skies without directly contacting anything during the six hours that four to 12 unidentified objects intermittently appeared on radar screens at Washington National airport and nearby Andrews Air Force base.

Described As 'Lights'

One pilot said he saw four lights approximately 10 miles away and slightly above him, but they disappeared before he could overtake them. Later, the same pilot said, he saw "a steady white light" five miles away that vanished in about a minute.

So far as could be determined, this was the first time jets have been sent on the trail of such sky ghosts.

Officials carefully avoided mentioning "flying saucers," just as they did when radar picked up seven or eight unidentified objects near Washington last Monday. But the Air Force was expected to add the report to its long list of saucer sightings, which officials say are coming in faster than at any time since the initial flurry in 1947.

An Air Force spokesman said all necessary steps were being taken to evaluate the newest phenomenon.

Later an Air Force spokesman said:

"We have no evidence they are flying saucers; conversely we have no evidence they are not flying saucers. We don't know what they are."

There was no agreement whether the recent reports are the first of such mystery objects appearing on radar. At least, officials agreed they are unusual.

Radar normally does not register anything without substance—such as light. But it can pick up such things as a bird in flight or a cloud formation. And one expert said radar is not infallible.

The Air Force reported that between four and 12 unidentified objects appeared Saturday night on the radar screen at the Air Route Traffic Control center operated by the Civil Aeronautics Administration. Their position was estimated at 10 miles east of Mount Vernon, Va., which is near Washington National airport.

Jet 'Contact' Fails

Word went to the Air Force, which sent up two jet fighter interceptor planes from a base at Newcastle, Del., some 90 miles from Washington.

When the planes appeared on the radarscope, the CAA tried without success to guide the planes into contact with the mystery objects. It was during this search that the pilot made his two sightings of lights.

The planes left for their base at an early hour today and the two other jets took over and stayed in the area an hour without making contacts.

The pilot who saw the lights said they "were really moving"—faster than 600 miles an hour. But radar operators at Andrews Air Force base said they moved at a "slow rate of speed"—38 to 90 miles per hour. This could mean the same pattern as last week's sightings—slow moving objects with bursts of speed.

One woman in Washington reported she saw "a very bright light" streak across the sky toward Andrews Base. Later, she said, she saw an object with a tail like a comet whiz by and a few seconds later a third in another direction.

Jet Interceptors Fail to Contact Ghostly 'Saucers' Over Capital

WASHINGTON, July 28 -- (AP) Radar normally doesn't show something which is not there - has picked up "flying saucers" near the nation's capital for the second time within a week.

Jet fighter pilots searched the skies without directly contacting anything during the six hours that four to 12 unidentified objects intermittently appeared on radar screen at Washington National airport and nearby Andrews Air Force Base.

Described as 'lights'

One pilot said he saw four lights approximately 10 miles away and slightly above him, but they disappeared before he could overtake them. Later, the same pilot said, he saw a "steady white light" five miles away that vanished in about a minute.

Officials carefully avoided mentioning "flying saucers" just as they did when radar picked up seven or eight unidentified objects near Washington last Monday. But the Air Force was expected to add the report to its long list of saucer sightings, which officials say are coming in faster than at any time since the initial flurry in 1947.

An Air Force spokesman said all necessary steps were being taken to evaluate the newest phenomenon.

Later an Air Force spokesman said:
"We have no evidence that they are flying saucers; conversely we have no evidence they are not flying saucers. We don't know what they are."

There was no agreement whether the recent reports are the first of such mystery objects appearing on radar. At least officials agreed they were unusual.
Radar normally does not register anything without substance - such as light. But it can pick up such things as a bird in flight or a cloud formation. And one expert said radar is not infallible.

The Air Force reported that between four and 12 unidentified objects appeared at 9:08 p.m. Saturday on the radar screen at the air route traffic center operated by the Civil Aeronautics Administration. Their position was estimated at 10 miles east of Mount Vernon, Va., which is near Washington National Airport.

Jet 'Contact' Fails

Word went to the Air Force, which sent up two jet fighters interceptor planes from a base in Newcastle, Del., some 90 miles from Washington. The pilot who sighted the lights said they "were really moving" - faster than 600 miles per hour. But radar operators at Andrews Air Force Base said they [...] at a "slow rate of speed" - - [...] miles per hour. This was much the same pattern as last week's sightings - slow moving objects with bursts of speed.

One woman in Washington reported she saw "a very bright light" streak across the sky towards Andrews Base at about 12:15 p.m. Later she said she saw an object with a tail like a comet whiz by and a few seconds later a third in another direction.

From the Alexandria Gazette, USA, July 28th, 1952

**Jet Fighters Outdistanced By
"Flying Saucers"
Over Mt. Vernon And Potomac**

Jet fighters of the Eastern Interceptor Command today were maintaining a
24-hour alert for "flying saucers" over the Alexandria vicinity.
The order was issued after radar operators at the CAA Air Route Traffic
Control Center at National Airport sighted the mysterious objects Saturday
night- the second time in eight days.

The Air Force said two jets pursued "between four and twelve" of the
elusive objects Saturday night, but the pilots reported they were unable to
get any closer than seven miles before the saucers disappeared.
One pilot said he saw "a steady white light" about ten miles east of Mt.
Vernon. His supersonic jet, traveling at a speed of more then 600 miles per
hour, was outdistanced when he sought to overtake the object.

Initial appearance of the objects was reported at 8:08 p.m. EDT Saturday.
Two jets from the 142nd Fighter Interceptor Squadron, at Newcastle, Del.,
zoomed into action and scouted the area in relays until 2:20 a.m.
Radar operators at Andrews Air Force Base just across the Potomac River
from Alexandria reported a "long series of sightings on and off until
midnight."

Between seven and twelve of the fiery discs had been picked up by the
radar equipment at National Airport last week. Radar experts said the
instruments are not infallible but normally don't show something that isn't
there.

Radar will not usually register something without substance such as light
but will pick up birds and dense cloud formations. A CAA spokesman said,
however, that the mysterious objects recorded definite "blips" on the radar
screen similar to those given off by aircraft.

Meanwhile, the Air force clamped a tight lid of secrecy on investigations
being made by the military. Information gathered on the local sightings is

being sent to a special saucer center at Wright Field, Dayton Ohio, where all such reports are evaluated.

Capt. E.J. Ruppelt, who heads the special saucer investigation crew, said at Dayton last night that most of the saucer information is highly classified and added that many of the reports he received are spurious.
This was believed to be the first time that the Air force, in the past skeptical of the saucers' existence, has acknowledged them to the point of giving Interceptor pursuit.

Col. Jack C. West, commander of the 142nd Squadron, said his jets are ready now to go in the action again "at a moment's notice."
CHICAGO - Several scientists, still stumped for an explanation of "Flying Saucers," are convinced that the mysterious objects really exist.
One expert said they may be space ships from another planet.

Reports of fast traveling extremely light objects over Washington during the weekend gave weight to the theory that the "saucers" are real, according to some experts.

"I definitely believe the objects sighted over Washington were not someone's imagination," said R. L. Farnsworth, president of the U.S. Rocket Society, a reputable organization devoted to the study of rocket travel.
Farnsworth said, "There is a possibility" they are interplanetary space ships. He added there is no way for him to know, with certainty what the objects were.
"Interplanetary space travel is definitely possible," he said. We know there is vegetation on the planet of Mars, and this could be an indication that there is life on that planet.

Dr. J. Allen Hynek, an astronomer at Ohio State University, said he thinks the persons who reported seeing the "saucers" were not just letting their imaginations get the best of them.

He said he was convinced these persons saw something- "some type of object or phenomena."

But Hynek said it "highly improbable" that the "saucers" come from another planet.

"There would be too vast a distance and to much of an engineering problem involved," he said.

One scientist, who asked that his name be withheld, speculated that the "saucers" might be experimental aircraft developed by the U.S.

If this is the case, he said, it's time the government quit playing jokes on the people."

The same scientist said he thought it was "slightly fishy" that many of the reports came from the general area of Washington and the atomic proving grounds in New Mexico.

UFO News From Turkey

Hürriyet   GUNDEM

Türk pilotun UFO

UFO nedir?

UFO, İngilizce 'Undefined Flying Object'in (Tanımlanamayan Uçan Cisim) kısaltılmışı. Uzaydan geldiği öne sürülen hava araçlarını tanımlamak için kullanılıyor. Ve UFO tartışmaları, yüzyıllardan bu yana insanları meşgul ediyor. Türkiye dahil dünyanın birçok yerinde, zaman zaman UFO gördüğünü iddia edenler, uzaydan gelen başka canlıların dünyamızda olduğuna inanıyor. Ancak, bugüne kadar hiçbir ciddi bilim adamı ve bilimsel kuruluş, yeryüzünde UFO'ya kesin olarak rastlandığını kanıtlayabilmiş değil.

Eğitim uçuşu için Hava Kuvvetlieri'nde kullanılan T-37

A special report from the author:

August 2001, Turkey's National Newspaper reports on a UFO encounter near the Turkish town of Izmir with a Turkish Air Force Pilot during a routine training mission. Over the course of a few days, the Turkish Air Force offers different explanations to dismiss the UFO story. The flock of birds and weather balloon theories are offered to public.

I was in Istanbul Turkey as this event unfolded and I quickly contacted the Turkish Air Force spokesperson for clarification of the UFO encounter.

Each time I was told a different cover story, the next day it would appear in the headlines. I personally collected and saved all of these newspaper clippings.

at sonra Bornova'da kameraya yakalandı!

UFO'lar Ege'ye aşık

Türkiye gündemini
son günlerde sürekli meşgul
eden UFO'ların özellikle Ege Bölgesi
civarında sıkça görülmesi dikkat çekiyor. Önceki
gün Uşak'tan yine UFO ihbarları geldi. Halk panik içinde
UFO'nun gökyüzündeki salınışını izledi. Ardından Yalova'lılar
telefona sarıldı: "Gökte parlak beyaz ışıklar saçan bir cisim var" diye.
Yalova'nın Altınova ve Çiftlikköy ilçelerinde yaşayanlar UFO gördüklerini iddia ettiler.
Ve son olarak UFO iddiası, Hava Kuvvetleri Komutanlığı'nın raporlarına girdi.

A graph showing the recent UFO sightings in Western Turkey.

Radarla tespit edin

Dinçer, durumu telsizle İzmir'deki İkinci Ana Jet Üssü'ne bildirerek, UFO'nun radarla tespit edilmesini istedi. Üsten, "Sizin uçağınızda yüksek hareketlilik tespit ediyoruz. Ancak etrafta ikinci bir cisim saptanamıyor" yanıtı geldi.

NASA'ya bildirilecek

Konuyla ilgili incelemenin halen devam ettiği ve önümüzdeki günlerde olayın, NASA başta olmak üzere uluslararası kuruluşlara intikal ettirileceği bildirildi.

çizmeye başladı.

kırıyoruz.

Harekât Merkezi: Sizin dışınızda ikinci bir cisim tespit edemiyoruz.

T-37 uçağı: Cisim üzerimize doğru geliyor.

Harekât Merkezi: Radar tespiti negatif.

T-37 uçağı: Cisim kanatlara yaklaşıyor. Arkamıza geçti. Ben de tono ile onu önüme alacağım.

Harekât Merkezi: Tekrar ediyorum, ekranda tespit negatif.

T-37 uçağı: Cisim şimdi önümüzde, bu resmen bizimle hava muharebesi yapıyor.

Harekât Merkezi: Devam edin.

T-37: Cisim aniden kayboldu.

CANDARLI KORFEZI

İZMİR KÖRFEZİ

Çiğli

İZMİR

Metehan Demir

■ 17. sayfada

The transcript of the radio communications between the pilot and tower reveal the UFO was not visible on radar.

The close encounter is told here in greater detail. According to the pilot, the UFO came within 50 feet of his fighter jet. The UFO demonstrated astonishing flight maneuvers that were far more advanced than any known military aircraft. The UFO accelerated beyond the speed reachable by the pilot's T-37 fighter jet.

Pilot Üsteğmen İlker Dinçer'in UFO gördüğünü rapor etmesi, Türkiye'de dikkatleri yine bu konuya çekti. Türk Hava Kuvvetleri'nde bundan 14 yıl önce de ciddi bir UFO vakasının daha yaşandığı ortaya çıktı. İki F-16'nın ne olduğu belirlenemeyen bir uçan cismi, atmosferin en üst katlarına kadar kovaladığı bildirildi.

F-16'lar 1987'de UFO kovaladı

14 YILIK SIR

Hürriyet'e bilgi veren güvenilir kaynaklar, 1987 yılında iki F-16 savaş uçağının dakikalarca takibine rağmen, bir UFO'nun atmosferi terk ederek ortadan kaybolduğunu belirtirler. Aynı kaynakların anlattığına göre tam 14 yıl önce yaşanan nefes kesen olay şöyle gelişti:

F-16 uçaklarının Hava Kuvvetleri envanterine girmeye başladığı 1987 yılında iki

HKK'DA UZAY DAİRESİ KURULDU

İlk Türk astronotu

This article refers to a similar UFO event involving the Turkish Air Force from 14 years ago.

Uçuşta hayal çok oluyor

TÜRK Hava Yolları'nın İstanbul-Tokyo arasındaki ilk uçuşuydu. A310 tipi uçağın Tokyo/Narita Havalimanı için bir saatlik uçuş kalmıştı. İlk uçuşun Mesul Kaptan Pilotu, şimdiki Türk Hava Yolları Uçuş İşletme Başkanı Mustafa Kolko idi. Beni kokpite çağırdı.

Gece uçuşuydu ve gökyüzünde müthiş bir ışık vardı. İzlediğimizde dönüyor gibiydi. Koskoca bir ateş topu halindeydi. Kaptan bana, "İşte çoğu zaman bu tip görüntüler pilotları yanıltır. Bunu uçan daire sanırlar. Bu başıboş kalmış bir uydunun güneş enerjisi panellerinden yansıyor. Bir ışık yansıması. Atmosferden böyle görünüyor." dedi.

Bu sırada altımızda bir başka uçak vardı. Sanırım biz 12-13 bin metre yüksekteydik. Altımızda seyreden uçağın pilotu ile irtibat kuruldu. Kaptan Kolko gördüğü ışık kitlesi ile ilgili olarak Tayland Hava Yolları'nın kaptan pilotu ile konuştu. İkisi de bu görünen ışığın bir uydunun panellerinden meydana gelen bir yansıma olduğu konusunda mutabakata vardılar.

Tayland Hava Yolları uçağının pilotu bölgede bunun sıkça görüldüğünü, ışık kırılmalarının sık sık rapor edildiğini ve aşağı ile yapılan görüşmelerin sonucunun hep aynı olduğunu söyledi.

İnişten sonra bir araya geldiğimiz pilotlar, gökyüzündeki yanılmaların ne kadar çok olduğundan söz ettiler. Gece uçuşunda Venüs yıldızının peşine komutanın uçağı sanarak takılan genç pilotlardan söz edildi. Bu yüzden yakıtı bitip düşen Amerikalı pilotların hikayeleri anlatıldı. Ama her seferinde gökyüzünde karşılaşılan farklı görüntüler aşağıya rapor ediliyor. Radarda aynı görüntülerin olup olmadığı araştırılıyor. Bir sürü soru işaretleri de ortaya çıkıyor.

Uğur CEBECİ

Çandarlı'da öğrencisiyle eğitim uçuşu yapan bir pilotun, 3 gün önce UFO gördüğünü, cismin uçakla bir tür "hava muharebesi" yaptığını rapor etmesi, tartışmaya neden oldu. Havacılık uzmanları, uçuş sırasında pilotların halüsinasyon görebildiğini ya da ışık yansımalarını UFO sandıklarını söylüyorlar. Psikiyatristler ise, halüsinasyonun psikolojik bir rahatsızlık olduğu, hem pilotun hem öğrencisinin aynı anda aynı halüsinasyonu görmesinin mümkün olmadığı görüşündeler.

İki pilot da uçan lokomotif gördü

1970'li yıllarda iki F-104 uçağı kolda yani birlikte uçarken, pilotlardan biri havada binlerce metre yükseklikte lokomotif gördüğünü iddia eder. Önce hayal gördüğünü zanneden pilot, bu gördüğünü diğer F-104'te uçan pilota da söyler. İkinci uçaktaki pilotun cevabı çok ilginçtir. O da iki uçağa doğru uçan bir lokomotif görmektedir. 1986 yılında ise Ankara'da garip ışıklar görülünce şimdiki Akıncı Üssü'nde hazır bekleyen iki alarm uçağı havalanır. Pilotlar tarafından da rapor edilen bu ışıklar yarım saat kadar görülür ve kaybolur. Cisimler radarda tespit edilemez ve olay karanlıkta kalır.

Komutanlık: Meteoroloji balonu

The Turkish Air Force claims the UFO was actually a weather balloon, however it was later determined by the Metrological Dept. of Turkey that no balloons were in the area at that time.

MiT'te UFO masası var mı

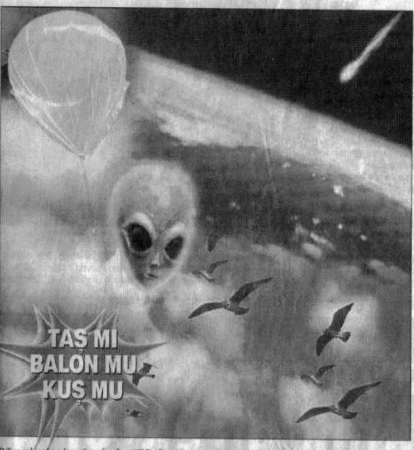

TAŞ MI BALON MU KUŞ MU

ÜSTEGMEN İlker Dinçer'in İzmir Çandarlı Körfezi açıklarında eğitim uçuşu sırasında gördüğünü söylediği UFO bilmecesi dün de çözüme kavuşamadı. Hava Kuvvetleri Komutanlığı söz konusu cismin meteoroloji balonu olduğunu belirtirken, 'UFO Masası' kurduğu iddia edilen MİT'ten bu iddiayı doğrulayan ya da yalanlayan bir açıklama gelmedi. Sirius UFO Uzay Bilimleri Araştırma Merkezi Başkanı Haktan Akdoğan ise Hava Kuvvetleri Harekat Daire Başkanlığı'nca konunun incelendiğini belirterek şöyle konuştu: "Harekat Daire Başkanlığı'ndan bir yetkiliyle görüştüm. Açıklama yapmıyorlar. Aşırı temkinliler. Raporları ve radar çıktılarını göreceklerini, inceleyeceklerini söylediler."

Bu arada Zaman Gazetesi'nin haberinde Milli İstihbarat Teşkilatı'nın konuyla ilgilendiği iddia edildi. Haberde "Doğrulanmamakla birlikte MİT bünyesinde bir UFO masası kurulduğu belirtiliyor" denildi.

Bilimadamları bugüne kadar UFO diye öne sürülen kanıtların hiçbirinin doğru olmadığını, değişik atmosfer olayları ya da meteoroloji balonu olduğunu belirttiler. Bilimadamları, göktaşlarının ve kuş sürülerinin de gökyüzünde yanılsamaya neden olduğunu söylediler.

BİLİM ADAMLARI, GÖKTAŞI OLDUĞU GÖRÜŞÜNDE

EGE Üniversitesi Gözlemevi Müdürü ve Fen Fakültesi Astronomi ve Uzay Bilimleri Bölümü Başkanı Yardımcısı Prof. ... canlı olduğu zannediliyor. Eğer içinde yaratık olsa bugünlere kadar bilinirdi. Çünkü uzayda binlerce ... ışık saçan bir göktaşı olabileceğini belirten Evren, şöyle devam etti: ... Taş parçaları gökyüzünde yanarak hareket ediyorlar. Yanma bittikten sonra atmosferde toz halinde ...

All of the excuses offered by the Turkish Air Force, a meteor, a weather balloon or a flock of birds are strongly questioned by the writer and definitively disputed by the pilot himself.

TÜRK Hava Kuvvetleri'nin iki pilotu, eşine az rastlanan bir olayın tanığı oldu. 122'nci filoya bağlı bir T-37 tipi jet eğitim uçağı, İzmir Çandarlı Körfezi açıklarında yaklaşık yarım saat boyunca bir UFO ile it dalaşı denilen taktik savaş oyunları yaptı. Pilot Üsteğmen İlker Dinçer, harekat merkeziyle yaptığı konuşmada uçan cismi şöyle tanımladı:

"**Sıradışı bir durumla karşı karşıyayız. Huni ile disk arası aşırı parlak, ayaklı ve yüksek süratte uçan bir cisim var.**"

Türk havacılık tarihinde ilk kez karşılaşılan ve resmi kayıtlara bu şekilde geçen olay, önceki gün öğle saatlerinde Çandarlı semalarında meydana geldi. Türk Hava Kuvvetleri'ne savaş pilotu yetiştiren İzmir 2'nci Ana Jet Üssü Komutanlığı'na bağlı bir T-37, Öğretmen Pilot Üsteğmen **İlker Dinçer** ve deniz pilot teğmen öğrencisinin yönetiminde saat 12.30 sıralarında eğitim uçuşu yapmak için havalandı.

RADARDA GÖRÜLEMEDİ

Uçak, Çandarlı açıklarına geldiğinde, havada perdövites (motor durdurma) ve intibak hareketleri yapmaya başladı. Bu sırada Üsteğmen **Dinçer** ve öğrencisi 'tanımlayamadıkları', disk şeklinde parlak bir hava cismi' ile karşılaştılar. Dinçer ilk şoku atlattıktan sonra durumu yer kontrole ve Kütahya yakınlarında bulunan 'Bölge Savaş Harekât Merkezi'ne bildirdi.

Savaş Harekât Merkezi'nden, bu cismin radarda belirlenmesini isteyen Üsteğmen Dinçer, bir süre esrarengiz cismin çevresinde dolaşmaya başladı. Birkaç saniye sonra Savaş Harekât Merkezi'nden yanıt geldi:

"**Sizin uçağınızda yüksek hareketlilik belirledik. Ancak etrafta ikinci bir cisim saptanamıyor.**"

UÇAĞI UFO'YA YÖNELTTİ

Bunun üzerine Üsteğmen Dinçer, uçağı esrarengiz cismin üzerine yöneltti. Dinçer'in ifadesine göre, tanımlanamayan hava aracı da uçağa doğru yöneldi.

YAN YANA UÇTULAR

Esrarengiz araç, T-37'nin kanadına yaklaşıp, birlikte uçmaya başladı. Dinçer'in, "Cisim kanatlara yaklaşıyor. Arkamıza doğru geçti. Ben de tono ile onu önüme alacağım... Şimdi önümüzde, bu resmen bizimle hava muharebesi yapıyor" sözleri telsizden duyuldu.

UFO, yaklaşık yarım saat uçağın çevresinde manevralar yaptı.

HIZLA KAYBOLDU

Deneyimli bir pilot olan Üsteğmen Dinçer de esrarengiz hava aracının hareketlerine karşılık verdi. Havada yarım saat boyunca süren ve zaman zaman da tehlikeli manevraları içeren it dalaşı, UFO'nun birdenbire müthiş bir hızla gözden kaybolmasıyla son buldu.

HAVA KUVVETLERİ İNCELİYOR

Çiğli'deki üslerine dönen pilotlar, olayı raporla da amirlerine bildirdiler. İncelenmenin sürdüğü, Hava Kuvvetleri'nde büyük şaşkınlık yaşandığı belirtildi.

Önümüzdeki günlerde olayın, NASA başta olmak üzere uluslararası kuruluşlara intikal ettireceği bildirildi.

■ **Metehan DEMİR / ANKARA**

Kapadokya'da da UFO heyecanı

TURİSTİK ve doğal güzellikleriyle dünyanın ilgi odağı Kapadokya'da da UFO heyecanı yaşandı. Nevşehir'in Ürgüp İlçesi 370 Evler'de yaşayan **Hasan Topatan** ve **Nebi Kolay** aileleri, gece yarısı balkonda otururken, Aktepe mevkii üzerinde geniş ışıklar saçan ve ortasında büyük parlaklık olan cisim gördüklerini iddia ettiler. 5 saniye kadar görülen cismin sonra hızla kaybolduğunu belirten **Nebi Kolay**, şunları söyledi: "Balkonda oturuyorduk. Birden uzakta parlak bir cisim gördük. Yaklaşık 5 saniye görülen cisim sonra ortadan kayboldu. UFO olduğunu tahmin ediyoruz"

■ **Noci İŞLER / ÜRGÜP, DHA**

T.C.
HAVA KUVVETLERİ KOMUTANLI
GENEL SEKRETERLİK
BASIN BÜLTENİ

TARİH   : 08 AĞUSTOS 2001
BÜLTEN NO : 29

1. METEOROLOJİ GENEL MÜDÜRLÜĞÜ'NÜN ÇEŞİTLİ ZAMANLARDA RUTİN OLARAK KULLANDIĞI GÖZLEM BALONLARI GENEL OLARAK BÖLGEDE BULUNAN HAVA KUVVETLERİ BİRLİKLERİ İÇERİSİNDE VEYA YAKININDA KONUŞLU METEOROLOJİ BİRİMLERİ TARAFINDAN KULLANILMAKTA OLUP, BÖLGEDE UÇAN HAVA KUVVETLERİ KOMUTANLIĞI'NA AİT UÇAKLAR UÇUŞ ESNASINDA BU BALONLARI UÇUŞ EMNİYET MÜLAHAZASI NEDENİYLE BÖLGE RADARLARINA VEYA UÇUŞ KULELERİNE RAPOR ETMEKTEDİRLER.

2. GEÇMİŞ DÖNEMLERDE BASINIMIZ BU KONULARDA BİLGİLENDİRİLMİŞ OLUP HAVA KUVVETLERİ KOMUTANLIĞI İLE KOORDİNE EDİLMEYEN HABERLER KAMUOYUNU YANILTICI BİR MAHİYET KAZANABİLMEKTEDİR.

3. 08 AĞUSTOS 2001 TARİHLİ BASINIMIZDA ÇIKAN HABERLER BU KONUDAKİ EN SON ÇARPICI ÖRNEKLERDENDİR. BASINIMIZDA BU TİP KONULARDA GENELKURMAY BAŞKANLIĞI'NDAN TEYİD ALINMADAN HABER YAPILMASININ KAMUOYUNU YANILTACAĞI DEĞERLENDİRİLMEKTEDİR.

KAMUOYUNA SAYGIYLA DUYURULUR

İRTİBAT :
ORHAN TAMER
HV.PER.BNB.
BAŞHALK.Ş.MD.
TEL.:0.312.4143542

In the fax I received from officer Tamer, the Turkish Air Force spokesperson, he said the UFO was in fact a weather balloon regardless of the Metrological Dept. of Turkey stating otherwise, and further stated weather balloons should not be released near Air Force training grounds.

UFOs in Asia

Newspaper headline reporting a UFO sighting in Malaysia.

Newspaper from Thailand describes UFO activity near the capitol.
A description of pilot sightings and cars being "levitated" are
described by eye-witnesses.

จานผี U.F.O. เปิดตัว
ลักพาคน-รถ จู่ๆอาจ
ลำแสงดูดกลางไฮเวย์

อากาศขนาดใหญ่มากมีเส้นผ่าศูนย์
กลางราว 200 ฟุตได้"

"ขณะมันลอยอยู่เหนือไฮเวย์นั้น
มันลอยนิ่งสนิทและไม่มีเสียงเครื่อง
ยนต์หรือเสียงใดๆหลุดลอดออกมาเลย"

"ทันใดนั้นผมคิดอะไรได้จึงรีบ
ไปที่รถสายตรวจ ผมมีกล้องติดรถเป็น
ประจำไว้ใช้ถ่ายอุบัติเหตุที่เกิดขึ้น ครั้งนี้
ผมจึงใช้กล้องถ่ายรูปยานยูเอฟโอ ได้
อย่างจะๆ"

ผู้อยู่ในเหตุการณ์อีกผู้หนึ่งทราบ

เหตุสยองขวัญกลางวันแสกๆ ยาน ยูเอฟโอ
มนุษย์ต่างดาว ใช้แสงดูดรถจากถนนซูเปอร์ไฮเวย์ต่อ
หน้าต่อตาคนนับร้อยเกิดขึ้นที่ชานกรุงบัวโนสไอเรส
เมืองหลวงประเทศอาร์เจนตินา ในอเมริกาใต้

ดวงตานับร้อยคู่จับจ้องรถเก๋งที่ซเฟโรเอ็ท
คาวาเลีย ถูกลำแสงประหลาดจากย่านพระกลมดูดลอย
ขึ้นไปอย่างช้าๆ เหตุการณ์ทั้งหมดนี้อยู่ในสายตาของ
ตำรวจทางหลวง ซึ่งเป็นผู้รักษาการณ์อยู่บนยอดเนินและได้
ถ่ายรูปเป็นหลักฐานเอาไว้

"นับเป็นเหตุการณ์ประหลาดที่สุดในชีวิตผมไม่เคย
เจออย่างนี้มาก่อนเลย" จ่าตำรวจพาเรซิลโก เปเรซ กล่าว
อย่างไม่หายงง "ยานอากาศลำนั้นลอยอยู่เหนือซูเปอร์
ไฮเวย์ สูงเหนือระดับพื้นดินราว 300 ฟุต จากนั้นปล่อย
ลำแสงสีน้ำเงินเจิดจ้าออกมาจากท้องยาน ลำแสงจับตรง
ไปยังรถเก๋งซเฟโรเอ็ทคันนั้นเป็นวัตถุวงกลม"

"ผมยังเป็นคนขับรถเก๋งเป็นผู้ชายวัยกลางคนกับเมีย
นั่งอยู่ช่วงหน้า ด้านหลังมีเด็กหญิงวัยรุ่นรวม 3 คน นั่งอยู่
ทุกคนอยู่ในสภาพหวาดกลัวสุดขีด เพราะกำลังถูกดูดเข้า
หายานมีรูปทรงกลมลอยอยู่ด้านบน"

เหตุการณ์ลักพาคนกับรถแปลกกลางถนนครั้งที่เกิด
ขึ้นเมื่อวันที่ 6 สิงหาคมที่ผ่านมาในขณะเป็นชั่วโมงเร่งด่วน
มีรถใช้ซูเปอร์ไฮเวย์สายนี้อย่างคับคั่ง

ขณะนั้นเองจ่าพาเรซิลโกผู้เป็นตำรวจมานานกว่า
19 ปี ได้หยุดรถสายตรวจดูความสงบเรียบร้อยของยวด
ยาน เขาเป็นเราลูกคนนี้จึงสามารถเห็นทางจราจรด้านล่าง
ได้อย่างชัดเจน

"เวลานั้นราว 10.30 น. มีเสียงคล้ายเสียงฟ้าร้อง
ดังขึ้น ผมมองไปบนท้องฟ้า ก็ไม่เห็นมืดมิดเลย จึงคิดว่า
น่าจะเป็นการทำไซเก็บกู้ของเครื่องบินรบกองทัพอากาศ
แต่แล้วทันใดนั้นได้มียานทรงกลมอย่างหนึ่งลอยออกมา
จากหมู่เมฆด้านถนนอย่างรวดเร็ว ความเร็วนั้นสูงมาก
จนผมคาดคะเนไม่ถูก" จ่าพาเรซิลโก กล่าว

ทีแรกนึกว่าคนใจดูตาฝาด ผมจึง
ตามองไปอีกทีมันยังคงเป็นยานทรงกลม
มีสีเทาๆ รูปร่างคล้ายจานคว่ำ เป็นยาน

行旨在建立私交
關係影響不大

方，明居正認爲，中共對美
敵意少一點。美國的立足點
和平、民主和現代化的政
反面中共把美國看成死對頭
不大槪不會變」。明居正表
說明美中關係互動的極限，
真的會處得很好」。
的影響，明居正指出，台灣
並非是台獨，卻是成功的民
民主與不民主的對抗，變
胡錦濤的美國行，就是希望
美國相信它是一個統獨的紛
渋。有可能造或程度上的俊
洛杉磯支堅理事長周清樑
平案，他們現時發起「一
安南和總統美國，促請他
藉此維持台海永久的和平

圖明居正指出，胡錦濤來美除
了藉此鞏固他在國內的地位
外，更要以「見面之後三分
情」來與美國建立私人關係，
令雙方以後可以「比較容易說
話」。　　　（記者馬爾婷攝）

聖蓋博傳教中心 234 歲

聖蓋博傳教中心(San Gabriel Mission)年度的連續3天慶
生園遊會，2日傍晚正式登場，不少民眾在下班或晚餐後，與
家人來到現場走走看看，享受各種文娛及康樂節目。大會除
了設有吃喝玩樂的攤位、遊戲、抽獎外，還安排各式各樣的
民族表演節目。作為洛杉磯發源地的聖蓋博傳教中心，今年
已邁是234歲了，而爲了紀念這個大日子，主辦單位除了在
這個週末推出寵物及服裝比賽、動物祝福典禮、切蛋糕等慶
祝儀式，更於星期天早上舉行大型的「走到洛杉磯」活動，
讓民眾可以親身體驗200多年前 Los Pobladores 貧苦居民徒
步奔遷的情況，見證珍貴的歷史時刻。圖與文：記者馬爾婷

破解UFO之謎尚難揭盅

本報記者宋俊杰特里活報道

不明飛行物（UFO）到底是不是子虛烏有，還是有真
切實據？UFO研究專家西蒙（Rob Simone）2日在第42屆美
國UFO論壇上表示，他收集了從古至今大量的證據證明
UFO絕對不是杜撰的，當然這並不是說現在就能夠解開
UFO之謎。他表示，這些證據來自各個國家和不同的時
代，甚至早在20世紀初就有人在中國天津拍下UFO照片爲
證。

西蒙表示，很多西方古代繪畫中都描述了 UFO 存在的
現象，在1350年代科索沃地區的一幅圖畫中，展示了兩個
不明飛行物體，每一個不明飛行物體中還有一個人在裡
面，左邊的
一個人是坐
著，而右邊
的一個人則
是回頭看。
還有一幅講
述耶穌降臨
的圖畫當
中，描述了
一個人乘坐
一種不明飛
行物體來到
人間，這個
景象是「聖
經」中任何
地方沒有提
到過的。

圖西蒙的身後的屏幕上顯示著中國古書
中對 UFO 的圖畫和記載。
（記者宋俊杰攝）

在東方同樣有很多關於這些不明飛行物體的記載，西
蒙向大家展示了一幅來自中國古書中的圖畫，描繪兩個人
坐在一個輪車上，車上還插著兩個紅色的旗子，圖片上還
用中文寫著簡單的解釋文字。到近代以後中國也繼續有關
於UFO的記載，特別是在20世紀初的天津，民眾突然發
現天空中出現一個不明飛行物體爭相觀看，有一個人把這
個情景拍成照片，在這個照片中還有一個人把指頭指向天
空中的不明飛行物。西蒙表示，因爲他的女朋友是台灣
人，所以有機會學習一些國語，並且幫助他接觸到一些中
國文獻和記載中中國人關於UFO的見證。

西蒙表示，在近代西方也是有大量的證據證明 UFO 的
出現，其中廣爲流傳的一張照片就是，在俄國的一個森林
之內一些軍人在觀看一個墜落的 UFO 殘骸，很多人對這個
照片的真實性表示懷疑，但是他從照片上人們的服裝和槍
支以及人們的動作表情判斷，這個照片可能反映的是真實
情況。他說，在墨西哥，人們也多次目擊 UFO 的出現，因
爲現代科技的發展，很多目擊者可以把當時的情況拍攝成
爲錄影。在播放一些不同的錄影之後，他表示，UFO 的形
狀可以是多種多樣的，甚至可以變化組合的。西蒙強調，
儘管有這麼多的證據，但是人們還是沒有辦法破解 UFO 之
謎。

Note from the author:

From China's Sing Toa News

I gave a lecture on International Ufology at a conference in Hollywood,
CA., which was featured in the Chinese Sing Toa daily newspaper.

Pictured, middle right, I'm standing before a 1400 A.D. Chinese illustration
of craft able to "fly on the wind" used during my lecture. (see page 271)

Crop Circles – The U.K.

UFOs IN THE
HEADLINES
Real Reporting
on a Real
Phenomenon

Rob Simone

Biography

After more than 10 years as an independent researcher and research analyst into many areas of unexplained phenomenon, Rob Simone earned a legal degree, moved to Sedona Arizona in the late 1990's and began working for the civil activist organization, C.A.U.S. Citizens Against UFO Secrecy.

Rob worked directly with the director, Peter Gersten, Esq. C.A.U.S. was featured regularly on Art Bell and countless other radio and TV programs for the organization's use of the legal system to expose the government's secrecy and cover up of "black budget programs" and instillations.

Rob became the world's first "para-normal para-legal" collecting affidavits, eyewitness testimony and photographic evidence for FOIA (Freedom of Information Act) requests for various lawsuits brought against the D.O.D. (Dept of Defense) and the Federal Government.

This involved liaisons with many other research groups, coordination of media, and direct contact with witnesses, government insiders and high-level military officials whose stories can now be told.

One of these lawsuits was appealed all the way to the Supreme Court, and is still used today as a legal precedent.

Then, in 2000, Rob set off on a three-year trip around the world to the most mystical, sacred and powerful places on earth, investigating cultural and historical links to the metaphysical components of many ancient civilizations and belief systems.

This included gathering first-hand accounts from indigenous peoples and tribal elders of the unexplained aspects of their social and religious constructs, both past and present.

Rob Simone is an award-winning media personality and accomplished TV and radio producer. In addition, Rob has authored 2 books and is a featured writer for national magazines.

Rob has hosted radio shows in Australia, Katmandu Nepal on HBC FM, and currently in London England on 104.4 FM, and was recently included in FATE Magazine's "Top 100 Ufologists" list along with Zecharia Sitchin, Dan Aykroyd and Steven Spielberg.

Rob is Executive Director of Universal Sound and Light Productions and founder of A.I.R., The Association of Independent Researchers. Rob now lives in Los Angeles where he continues to produce radio and television projects related to the field. Rob has been featured in FATE Magazine, Japan's Nippon TV, Fox News, China's CCTV, Channel 4 U.K., and recently on the 2-hour History Channel program "Decoding The Past."

Beyond All Borders

By Rob Simone

Rob has just completed his manuscript "**Beyond All Borders**" which is the continuation of this book and contains all of Rob's research and the full account of his global adventures.

This is the true story of Rob's experiences of moving to Sedona, working with the civil activist organization C.A.U.S. Citizens Against UFO Secrecy. C.A.U.S. was the first organization to bring lawsuits against the U.S. Government in an attempt to release classified documents relating to the UFO cover-up.

Then an around the world adventure that would go through the Outback of Australia, the Himalayas in Nepal, through Asia, into the Middle East, to the Great Pyramids at Giza, rediscovering the Ark of the Covenant, exploring mystical dimensions and meeting the Dalai Lama.

Rob traveled through 25 countries interviewing indigenous peoples and tribal elders about the unexplained and paranormal components of ancient civilizations and their historical links to major religions and belief systems. There is a special focus on the folk legends and supernatural aspects of Islam and the Holy Koran.

This included surviving dangerous battles in the Israeli/Palestinian conflict and the warring factions in Yemen. There is also a compilation of interviews from the past six years of Rob's broadcasting career in Australia, Nepal and London, which highlights some of the most amazing moments in talk radio.

This new book is over 350 pages and is the product of over 10 years of research and travels to the most mysterious and sacred places on earth.

Publisher inquires welcomed.

ROBSIMONE.COM

UFOs In The Headlines

Real Reporting on a Real Phenomenon

By

Rob Simone

www.RobSimone.com

UFOs In The Headlines

Real Reporting on a Real Phenomenon

By
Rob Simone

Headroom Publishing

www.RobSimone.com

UFOs
In The
Headlines

Real Reporting
on a Real Phenomenon

By
Rob Simone

Headroom Publishing

www.RobSimone.com